THE DIARIES OF CYNTHIA GLADWYN

THE DIARIES OF
CYNTHIA GLADWYN

EDITED BY
MILES JEBB

CONSTABLE · LONDON

First published in Great Britain 1995
by Constable and Company Ltd
3 The Lanchesters, 162 Fulham Palace Road
London W6 9ER
Copyright © 1995 Miles Jebb
ISBN 0 09 473130 6
Reprinted 1996
The right of Miles Jebb to be identified as
the editor of this book has been asserted
by him in accordance with the
Copyright, Designs and Patents Act 1988
Set in Monophoto Garamond 12pt by
Servis Filmsetting Ltd, Manchester
Printed in Great Britain by
St Edmundsbury Press Ltd
Bury St Edmunds, Suffolk

A CIP catalogue record for this book
is available from the British Library

CONTENTS

ILLUSTRATIONS

INTRODUCTION

My mother began her diary at the age of forty-seven, and so I shall begin this introduction with a brief sketch of her life up to that age.

Cynthia Noble was born on 20 November 1898 at Jesmond Dene House, Newcastle-upon-Tyne, the home of her grandfather Sir Andrew Noble, around whose authoritative personality much of her early life revolved.

Andrew Noble had for many years been the chief adviser and close collaborator of William Armstrong in the development and manufacture of rifled artillery. He now presided over the formidable armament and shipbuilding firm of Armstrong Whitworth as Deputy Chairman, while his brilliant chief, now elevated to the peerage, had retreated to the seclusion of his Northumbrian country house, Cragside. Noble succeeded to the chairmanship after Armstrong's death in 1900, and the international reputation of the company was never higher than in 1905, when the Japanese fleet, largely built by Armstrongs, decisively defeated the Russian at the Battle of Tsushima. Further expansion followed, accelerated by the outbreak of the First World War, shortly after which Sir Andrew Noble died.

Presiding over domestic life at Jesmond Dene House was Andrew's wife Margery, whom he had married when he had been a young artillery officer stationed in Quebec. Her Scottish-Canadian forthrightness and frugality provided a perfect match for her husband's industrious and commanding nature, and Henry Newbolt has written that it was hard to tell which was the stronger character. With their six children around them they rented houses in Northumberland such as Lorbottle and Chillingham for holidays and sport, and then in 1905 acquired the Ardkinglas estate in Argyll, on which they commissioned Robert

Lorimer to build a great house, in part emulation of Cragside. Here Sir Andrew, by now a baronet, could feel comfortably close to his ancestral roots on Clydeside.

Saxton, Cynthia's father, was the second son of Andrew and Margery Noble. He was now living in London as the director primarily responsible for liaison with the Admiralty and the War Office, the two principal clients. This involved the provision of much sumptuous entertainment in which, though it was not really to his own taste, he was admirably assisted by his wife Celia.

Celia Brunel James was already related to Saxton when she became engaged to him at Jesmond Dene House at the age of nineteen. Her father Arthur James was a housemaster at Eton and her late mother Florence had been the daughter of Isambard Kingdom Brunel, the celebrated engineer. Celia was his only grandchild, and hence became the custodian of a great tradition. She inherited Brunel's furniture and moderate fortune, and subsequently wrote a biography, *The Brunels, Father and Son* (Cobden Sanderson, 1938). From the half-French Isambard she inherited a deep affection for France and all things French, and from his wife Mary she derived the highly cultivated sense of art and music that permeated the Calcott and Horsley families. Taught by Clara Schumann, she was a more than competent pianist and an assiduous concert-goer; and a central theme of her entertainment was the provision of music parties, with leading performers such as Casals, Suggia, Myra Hess and the d'Aranyi sisters. Throughout her life Celia maintained a certain aloofness, half enjoying the social world, half despising it: she said she would have liked to have been an ambassadress or a nun, but could not be sure which.

In order to increase the scope and grandeur of her parties, Celia persuaded Saxton to sell their already large house at 69 Eaton Place and buy a larger one in Knightsbridge – Kent House. A magnificent music-room was created, decorated with murals by the Spanish artist Sert, who also painted a set of panels for their country house; and there was plenty of space for family portraits by Jacques-Emile Blanche, vast Chinese screens, and Japanese gongs acquired during semi-ambassadorial visits to Japan on behalf of Armstrongs. Meanwhile Saxton had also purchased the large Wretham estate in Norfolk, solely for its pheasant and partridge shooting, and had commissioned Reginald Blomfield to build a spacious neo-Georgian mansion on it.

Into this opulent and cultivated world Cynthia was born, and grew up during the years of supreme national self-confidence that preceded the First World War. From an early age she observed those close to her with an intuitive perception, and recalled them vividly in later years. Of her uncles and aunts her paragon was Lilias, a beautiful and talented woman who never married – but was not above conducting an amorous friendship with Admiral Lord Fisher. Cynthia's oldest sibling Humphrey was six years her senior, but her constant companions were her sister, brother and first cousin, Marjorie, Marc and Veronica. A visiting child found herself obliged to join them in high-minded pencil-and-paper games, starting with 'Great Men beginning with B'; and there were constant writings of short stories (with ghosts as an habitual theme) and composing of poems and acting of charades. In all these they were much encouraged by the Cochrane brothers – Alfred, an Armstrongs director who had married her aunt Ethel, and Arthur, a herald who became Clarenceux King of Arms.

In 1912 Cynthia followed her sister to Northlands, a small girls' school at Englefield Green, conveniently close to Eton. This was run by Miss Weisse, who imparted knowledge to her flock more by the influence of her personality than by more formal methods, telling her girls 'I don't care if you leave here unable to add two and two together so long as you *want* to know'. Miss Weisse was German, and music figured large, and her protégé Donald Tovey, a noted interpreter of Bach, was usually in residence at Northlands. However, it can be said of my mother, as Sir Osbert Sitwell said of himself, that she was educated during the holidays, fortified by her excellent memory. She was introduced to opera at an early age, Saxton regularly subscribing to four seats at Covent Garden for the opera and ballet seasons. In the summer of 1913 her uncle George Noble hired a yacht and took several of the family on a private cruise around the coasts of Italy, with visits to the principal antiquities. Cynthia assiduously recorded her impressions, and her future talent as a diarist is perhaps best seen in this description of a woman who shared their carriage in the train from Paris on their return journey:

. . . a frightful, loud, talkative, common (etc) lady. I couldn't make out whether she was French or German, for she talked both to the man she was with, and also very bad English which she was very proud of. As a matter of fact she had quite pretty clothes on – a black and white chequered skirt with a blue coat. She had a small hat, with a long flowing blue veil attached to it, and a large muff. She annoyed me and Marjorie with her horrid loud voice, and made remarks about the people in the carriage in German – I suppose she thought we didn't understand. After a while I sat down to read *The Last Days of Pompeii*.

But the Great War changed many things for Cynthia and her family. Marc, as a captain in the Royal Artillery, was killed in action at Ypres; and the achievements of the Nobles, whose wealth was built on armaments, were seen to have tragic undertones, of the sort that Wagnerians might recognize from scenes in *Das Rheingold*. Armstrongs was unable to cope with the slump that succeeded the war, and was not well led by the man whom Saxton and John chose to succeed their father as chairman – John Meade Falkner, by nature an antiquary and best known for his Hardyesque novels. After a few years the Bank of England stepped in (the first time it ever came to the rescue of an industrial 'lame duck') and forced a shotgun marriage with the more powerful Vickers. The family shareholdings were now virtually worthless, and henceforth the Nobles lived on their savings. In addition to this, Saxton and Celia came to live rather separate lives, other than at Kent House. During the winters he retreated to a flat in Monte Carlo (where he kept a mistress), she to a flat in Rome. Wretham seemed superfluous and very expensive, and was eventually sold; and Celia then bought Fleet House, which faced the Chesil Beach near Weymouth, set among scenes familiar to her from Falkner's novel *Moonfleet*.

During the 1920s Cynthia continued to live with her parents, and galvanized them into keeping up their round of entertainment, organizing and enlivening weekends at Wretham and dinner parties at Kent House. She also developed her own wide circle of friends. Among them was Walter Turner, the Australian musicologist and music critic of the *New Statesman*, who fascinated her with his powerful and passionate personality. She would often spend weekends with interesting families, and I like to think of her staying as the guest of that Edwardian beauty, Mrs Willie James, at Moncton House in Sussex in the years before her hostess's son Edward converted it into a surrealist fantasy; or with Elizabeth Russell (author of *Elizabeth and her German Garden*) in her

Swiss chalet; or among the Jewish intelligentsia gathered around Sir George Lewis at his house in Rottingdean.

In 1929 Cynthia married Gladwyn Jebb, a year or so younger than herself, but already a high-flyer in the Diplomatic Service who had recently returned to the Foreign Office after a posting in Teheran. The son of a Yorkshire landowner who had abandoned his estate and was about to sell it at the bottom of the market, Gladwyn had acquired at Eton and Magdalen College, Oxford, a reputation for intellectual strength and independence of mind, and his handsome good looks complemented Cynthia's exquisite miniature beauty. Each stimulated the other in a conversational and social round that was not merely enjoyable, but had a sense of purpose. At a time when Britain was still a Great Power, the British Diplomatic Service enjoyed immense authority and prestige. There being, as yet, no female diplomats, it fell to the diplomatic wives to provide, albeit in a minor key, a feminine participation in overseas representation. This was a function for which Cynthia was eminently suited. She was not at all interested in the intricacies of policies and politics, and her whole approach was entirely personal and intuitive. Indeed, part of her skill was to avoid entering into profound discussions on the issues of the moment, but rather to set the scene for discussions by others, and the mood for confidences and revelations.

After a year in London, living in a small house in Royal Avenue, Chelsea, Gladwyn was posted as a Secretary at the Embassy in Rome, where he remained till 1935, and where Cynthia already had friends, acquired during visits to Celia's flat. During the period before the Abyssinian Crisis the Fascist government was not yet hostile towards Britain, and there were many opportunities for influencing opinion, particularly against alliance with Nazi Germany. By now Cynthia was the mother of three, myself and my sisters Vanessa and Stella (named after Jonathan Swift's pseudonyms for his two literary ladies). Marjorie, Gladwyn's sister, married Enrico Scaretti, a Roman investment banker. Her story of how she survived through the war, and of her life at the Castello di Trebbio, is told in her memoir *Tuscan Heritage* (Victor Gollancz, 1976).

Most unusually for a diplomat, my father was then stationed for fifteen years in London. This was partly because of the closure of so many missions during the war, and partly because of his successive promotions within the inner circle of policy-makers. On their return from

Rome my parents decided not to acquire a house but to live with Saxton and Celia at Kent House and to go to Fleet for weekends and holidays; and it was from these houses that Cynthia endured the foreboding which hung over those with an understanding of foreign affairs during the three years that preceded the outbreak of war. During the winter of 1939 Fleet, by now in a military area, was vacated. After the bombardment of London in September 1940, Saxton and Celia abandoned Kent House also, and moved to Royal Crescent, Bath – a dangerous move, as it transpired, because within a few months the Luftwaffe attacked Bath, destroying two houses in the Crescent. Ardkinglas House, now occupied by Cynthia's first cousin Johneen Noble and his wife Elizabeth, then provided a safe haven for Cynthia's daughters and for herself and her son during school holidays; though, strangely enough, it too was in the firing line, its windows being shattered by a German bomb. But for most of the war years Cynthia suffered the dangers and tensions of London with Gladwyn in a rented attic flat at 119a Mount Street, which is where we find them at the commencement of her diary. Or rather, there and at Bramfield Hall in Suffolk, found by Cynthia and purchased by Gladwyn at the end of 1945.

The period of her life recorded in her diary (1946–71) covers the crowning years of Gladwyn's career as a diplomat, and a further decade during which he played an active part as a parliamentarian. It suffices to say in this introduction that in 1950 he was appointed Ambassador to the United Nations in New York; in 1954 he became Ambassador to France; in 1960 he left the Diplomatic Service at the compulsory retirement age, and was granted a peerage; and in 1965 he joined the Liberal Party, to become its spokesman on foreign affairs in the House of Lords, and a tireless advocate for the promotion of Britain's entry into the European Community. In *The Memoirs of Lord Gladwyn* (Weidenfeld and Nicolson, 1972) he has given an eloquent description of his career in the realms of foreign policy. *The Diaries of Cynthia Gladwyn*, with their accentuation on personal matters and relative unconcern for political affairs, now provide a volume complementary to his.

Gladwyn and Cynthia moved in social circles that were mainly Conservative. Most of their friends were upper-class people who endured the penal taxes of the postwar Labour government with resentment. But Gladwyn's career as a leading civil servant brought him and his wife into constant touch with the prominent politicians of the

Left. This, together with an inherently Liberal attitude which they both shared, enabled them to traverse the political divide without incongruity. With many friends acquired during their postings in Rome, New York and Paris, as well as from among the Jewish émigrés to England, their outlook was altogether broader and more international than that of many of their contemporaries, especially before the advent of television and jet travel. Well before the concept of the European Community, they were more attuned to Western European values than to concepts of British imperial destiny. But their patriotism was fervent and unswerving, and Cynthia constantly demonstrates her convictions as to the unassailable superiority of English character and tradition, second only to the Scots (or the Scotch, as she called them). As one who had endured the terror bombing of London, she could hardly have been expected to feel charitable towards the Germans in their total defeat, or sympathetic to those Parisians or New Yorkers who had got through the war without physical danger.

The diary that Cynthia kept during these years was inscribed in her clear though florid handwriting into a series of hardback manuscript books with unlined pages of thick white paper. She wrote when she felt like it, and never for more than a few days consecutively. And her enthusiasm for her diary waxed and waned, so that its coverage is uneven. In a first flush of enthusiasm in 1947 she wrote extensively and also included several references to previous years. During her time in New York she largely neglected it, though she did write several diary-letters to her mother and me, which I have treated as substitutes. During the decade after my father's retirement from diplomacy, she kept it going as a regular exercise. The inspiration to keep a diary arose from her visit to Paris in 1946 – appropriately so, since Paris was her indubitable spiritual home, to which she returned whenever she could.

The diary ceased in 1972 for two reasons. Social life was less intense, and *The Paris Embassy* was nearing completion. This was published by Collins, with Philip Ziegler as editor, in 1975 to critical acclaim (and republished by Constable in 1986). The jacket, illustrated by Osbert Lancaster, depicts a coach and horses at the foot of the steps of the Hôtel de Charost, a prelude to Cynthia's elegant text and scholarly research into this historic building, acquired as the British Embassy by the Duke of Wellington in 1814. Her book also comprises acute character sketches of each ambassador, from the Great Duke to Sir Ronald

Campbell, who had to flee before the German advance in 1940. Thereafter she was reticent, not wishing to write about her contemporaries, though she could undoubtedly have produced very amusing chapters about the three decades from the Coopers to the Soames.

For these same reasons she wanted her diary to be kept entirely private during her lifetime, even though she hoped that one day it would be published. Its tardy appearance is due to her great longevity, for, like her mother and sister, she lived to over ninety. Nor were these last two decades of her life in any way enfeebled or pathetic. Conserving her energy with plentiful sleep and resting long in bed, and with a close attention to diet, she maintained a formidable round of entertainment, of attendance at operas, concerts, galleries, even of travel. She amazed her fellow passengers on a cruise around the Eastern Mediterranean in 1982, clambering all over the classical sites and joining in all the fun and the dancing. Until at any rate her last two years her vivacity and her conversation were quite remarkable. Only a month before her death, by now utterly exhausted by an undiagnosed internal disease, did she consent to have a hospital check-up. She was taken back to die in her bed at Bramfield on 21 September 1990. Her ashes are buried in the Brunel tomb in Kensal Green.

During these concluding years she was wonderfully sustained by Gladwyn's equally remarkable energy. In particular, he regularly prepared her meals, having taken up cooking in his seventies when they no longer employed a cook at Bramfield, Cynthia playing her part by meticulous manual dishwashing. He also drove her everywhere – for she never learnt to drive a car – always waiting patiently for her to get ready as her habitual unpunctuality became more extreme. For nearly thirty years they would drive down to Bramfield every weekend, returning to London laden with flowers and the food supply for the week. In 1989 they celebrated, with a dinner in the Garrick Club, sixty years of a united and rewarding marriage. At the time of writing Gladwyn is still in good health and with his memory unimpaired, having attended the House of Lords almost daily for thirty-four years since his retirement from the Foreign Office.

What people most remember about Cynthia – as expressed in letters received after her death – is her sparkle and vivacity, and her sense of intimate enjoyment and affectionate friendship. Her conversation was composed of a delicate blend of intelligence and mischief, and she exuded charm and gaiety, enriched by her enchanting laughter. She always made the most of things, and the most trivial matters, such as mundane shopping, or the placing of an ornament, or a chance remark about some historical subject, were often transformed into sources of interest and fun. She was good with bores and fools, leaving them with the impression that she had enjoyed their conversation, and smoothing feathers ruffled by Gladwyn's habitual dismissiveness towards them. Her judgements of people were usually extremely discerning, though she certainly had a tendency to be over-censorious, and sometimes revised her initially adverse judgements, as will be seen.

From her youth she always wanted to shine and to turn the eyes of a company when she made her entry. And this she continued to do until her last years, most notably in her appearance in the House of Lords at the State Openings of Parliament, glittering in her tiara, ruby necklace and diamond earrings, her skin unwrinkled and looking half her age. This stunning effect was achieved by a rigorous maintenance of personal standards. She never slouched, but always sat upright. She never permitted the sun to reach her face, but wore a hat or even raised a parasol. Though short-sighted, she only wore her spectacles when absolutely necessary, and never at parties, at which her principal contrivance for recognizing people was the every-ready cheek proffered for a kiss. She never slurred or hurried her speech, but spoke with a bell-like clarity, always pronouncing the 'h' in words such as which and why and what, as she had been taught to do as a child. Every meal, even alone with Gladwyn at the kitchen table, was a ceremony, where everything had to be correctly presented, to the accompaniment of enlivening converse.

Together with these attributes there also went a rigid determination. She was quite unabashed in securing invitations to stay with acquaintances, or in insisting on being driven to the door of some country house she thought she would like to see over, even though she had never met its owner. She would oblige Gladwyn to take her to every lighted candle. She could be maddeningly meticulous. She was adept in getting other people to do things for her, and employed to good effect a personal and persuasive approach to which servants and tradespeople usually responded with evident admiration. She was socially and personally competitive. I recall once travelling with her to Paris on a BEA flight on which she had managed to secure VIP treatment, which meant being escorted across the tarmac to the aircraft before the other passengers. We had hardly begun our progression when a female passenger, deeply resentful at the attention being given to Lady Jebb, broke ranks and proceeded to overtake us. To the astonishment of myself and the BEA official, my mother responded to the challenge, and the two women quickened their pace to a race-walk, shot up the steps side by side, and disappeared through the aircraft door in what was in effect a dead heat.

The last words I ever heard my mother utter were spoken in the hospital when I asked her to recite the sonnet 'Shall I compare thee to a summer's day?', which she did faultlessly. I am confident that death forbears to brag that she wanders in his shade, and to me her eternal summer shall never fade.

EDITOR'S NOTE

I have selected for publication approximately a quarter of the total manuscript text of Cynthia Gladwyn's diary. The unpublished text generally follows the same themes, but is of less general interest. It includes a great deal of domestic trivia, social references confined to 'who was there', and sheer repetitiveness. I have also pruned down many of my selected passages by means of omissions of intermediate sentences or phrases, and sometimes superfluous adjectives (especially 'beautiful' and 'pretty'). I have also corrected spelling mistakes, and have reduced the frequent use of French words to instances where the point would be weakened by translation.

A few of the entries were written after a lapse of time, but I have throughout placed them chronologically to the events they describe.

The great majority of all the persons mentioned are now dead. If any of their living relatives feel hurt at Cynthia's comments, I can only apologize. But I do feel that her judgements must stand as part of her observation of the fascinating social world in which she moved.

I have confined my comments to footnotes which provide the essential explanations of persons and events. Because this is the diary of a diplomat's wife, I have given particular attention to the careers of other diplomats. Because it is the diary of an intelligent woman, I have throughout provided the maiden names of all wives – several of whom would doubtless have had careers of their own if they had lived a generation or two later.

I am grateful to my father and sisters for their approval of my edited version of the diaries, and to Kenneth Rose and Philip Ziegler for reading it and providing helpful suggestions.

For ease of reference I list below the first-name references that appear most often in the diary:

Anthony:	Anthony Eden, later 1st Earl of Avon
Ava:	Viscountess Waverley
Diana:	Lady Diana Cooper
Gerry:	Gerald Wellesley, 7th Duke of Wellington
Gladwyn:	Gladwyn Jebb, later 1st Lord Gladwyn (Cynthia's husband)
Harold:	– in early years, Sir Harold Nicolson
	– in later years, Harold Macmillan, later 1st Earl of Stockton
Humbo:	Sir Humphrey Noble (Cynthia's brother)
Mar:	Marjory Madan (Cynthia's sister)
Miles:	Miles Jebb (Cynthia's son)
Mother:	Celia, Lady Noble (Cynthia's mother)
Nancy:	Nancy Mitford
Osbert:	Sir Osbert Lancaster
Rab:	R.A. Butler, later Lord Butler of Saffron Waldon
Raymond:	Raymond Mortimer
Selwyn:	Selwyn Lloyd, later Lord Selwyn-Lloyd
Sam:	Samuel Courtauld
Stella:	Stella Jebb (Cynthia's younger daughter), later married to Joel de Rosnay
Sybil:	Sybil Colefax
Vanessa:	Vanessa Jebb (Cynthia's elder daughter), later married to Hugh Thomas, later Lord Thomas of Swynnerton

1946

❧

Bramfield, Suffolk, November

I must be the worst wife of a diplomat since I don't really like 'abroad'.
But I have been extraordinarily lucky in only having to spend four
years in official life outside this country, and that was in Rome, which I
knew well already. It seems to me that to be sent to some foreign
capital for two or three years is one of the snags of a diplomatic life.
However, going abroad for a visit is in a different category, and when it
is to Paris, the call is not to be denied. So when I had the chance of
going there this autumn, in spite of being twice already this summer, I
hastily made plans for departure. The Conference[1] was to end definitely on 15 October, so if I were going there at all, I had to be quick
about it.

   The first thing was to get a seat on the Golden Arrow, as I don't
hold with flying. I hoped to join Oliver and Maudie Harvey,[2] and
travel in luxury with porters and stewards and cabins. But alas, Mr
Porter (so rightly named) of the Communications Department, far
from accommodating me, a mere idle wife, in the Golden Arrow,
couldn't even find a seat for the great Sir Oliver. This important person
had been forbidden to fly by his doctors, and all that the Foreign Office
could procure for him and his wife and secretary were stools in the

[1] The Conference of the Allied Powers to determine the peace treaties to be signed
with the Axis Powers, excluding Germany and Austria. Gladwyn was the British
Assistant Under-Secretary of State responsible for the peace treaties.
[2] Sir Oliver Harvey, later 1st Lord Harvey of Tasburgh (1893–1968), married to Maud
Williams-Wynn. Deputy Under-Secretary of State, subsequently preceding Gladwyn
as Ambassador to France.

Trianon Bar, an appalling example of modern decoration where one drinks synthetic cocktails hoping to become oblivious to a bad Channel crossing.

So my only alternative was to get a proper seat several days later, or else to throw caution to the winds and take to the air. But I wasn't going to risk going in an ordinary machine; oh no, there had been too many crashes lately. Nothing would satisfy me except a seat in the Secretary of State's private plane.[3] True, it was a Dakota, but specially solidly built to carry the special and solid Cabinet Minister whose safety was of the utmost importance. I felt I could risk that.

I therefore rang up the Private Secretaries' Office, and an enchanting man named Kinna was most solicitous, and finally it was arranged that I should go in the first plane-load to Paris on the morning of 2 October, the rest of the party, including Mr Bevin, following in the afternoon. Mr Kinna was extremely comforting, and said he always carried a St Christopher on him, and would hold my hand if necessary, and pray. I discovered later that he was an ardent Papist, for which the Secretary of State used to tease him, saying he wouldn't be happy till he had married Kinna to a Presbyterian.

I was already nervous when I got to Croydon, and then came the alarming moment when I stepped up into the plane, took my seat, and the door was shut. We taxied to a remote corner of the airfield and waited so long with the engine running that I was convinced that something must be radically wrong. But finally we moved off again and suddenly I observed that the ground was slipping away beneath, and lo and behold we were in the air, at the mercy of the gods, the elements, the laws of gravity and Mr Kinna's St Christopher. Once we were properly up it really wasn't at all bad. In fact it became interesting and even beautiful, and I became composed enough to appreciate the extreme luxury of it all. There were only eight seats, and I was in the front left-hand one. There was a desk at which no doubt the S of S would write important dispatches, but at which I tackled *The Times* crossword. There were earphones in which I could hear the Light Programme. An obliging steward brought a selection of magazines, and later refreshments;

[3] Ernest Bevin (1881–1951), Secretary of State for Foreign Affairs 1945–51. Gladwyn was among his most trusted advisers, referred to by him as 'Mr Minority' because of his independent views, and of whom he said, 'Whatever you may say about Gladwyn, he ain't never dull.'

and the pilot came along from time to time with a map pointing out our exact position.

When we approached Paris our pilot had the brilliant idea of giving us a little tour around it. We saw buildings, so clean and light in colour, and the Seine shining brightly, and the Eiffel Tower looking curiously low. Then we began to come down, and I was seized with a moment of dread. But all went well, St Christopher didn't forget us, and there we were on *terra firma* once more. I was greeted by Shirley Morgan,[4] Gladwyn's secretary, looking very summery in a pink linen dress.

At the Georges V we had a comfortable suite, sharing a sitting-room with the Harveys, though not quite so 'slap up' as the suite we occupied in May when Gladwyn was representing the Secretary of State. That had been Von Rundstedt's abode during the war, and it was something like one sees in the cinema. But I am sure Von R's spirit must have been thoroughly stamped out by the subsequent presence of Ernie and Flo.[5]

Having changed into evening dress, Gladwyn and I went down to the S of S's suite. Here we received an affectionate greeting from Mr and Mrs Bevin. The others present were just his personal staff – Bob and Esmene Dixon,[6] Henniker, and Kinna. This is what the S of S enjoys most – a friendly party where he can hold forth, sometimes indulging in badinage, sometimes saying most interesting things, and sometimes showing great shrewdness. 'Mother' opposite tries occasionally to carry on a conversation with her nearest neighbours, thinking no doubt she should keep up the conventions of an English meal. But he doesn't approve of this, and before telling a story he looks round the table, pausing, till he has caught everyone's attention. He has a dynamic presence, and looked well after his recent illness.

He and I carry on a merry argument about the Scotch. It never fails to amuse him that I, being half Scottish, uphold them, whereas he, being purely English, derides them. I, 'Now, Mr Bevin, you must admit that the Scotch made the Empire': Mr B, 'I've 'eard they made the

---

[4] Shirley Morgan, later Marchioness of Anglesey (1924–   ): daughter of the author Charles Morgan, and Gladwyn's personal assistant.

[5] Florence Townley (1882–1968), wife of Ernest Bevin.

[6] Pierson Dixon, later Sir Pierson (1904–65), married to Esmene Atchley. Principal Private Secretary to Ernest Bevin, subsequently succeeding Gladwyn as Ambassador respectively to the United Nations and France.

'ippodrome, and that's about all.' Mr B, ' 'Ave you ever 'eard of the
Scotchman who lent a Jew a five pound note?': I, innocently, 'No?': Mr
B, 'There never was one'. He is very funny about Mrs Bevin's remarks
when he returns home in the evenings, for which he has two stock
answers. Either she says 'Is that you, Ernest?', to which he replies 'oo
else were you expecting?'; or she says 'So you've come 'ome', and he
answers 'I 'aven't anywhere else to go'.

Sometimes he can be serious, and this particular evening I was interested to hear him hold forth on how monstrously the USA had behaved
towards Courtaulds.[7] Then suddenly he makes one laugh heartily, as
when we were talking about not knowing French words, and I said that
Gladwyn had got into the Foreign Office entirely because he had
known the French for seaweed: 'So that's 'ow they get in? I wondered
'ow they get in!'

Mrs Bevin must have been pretty once. Indeed, she has a good skin
still, and a gay eye which is lost behind spectacles – the greatest deter-
rent to charm, as Eddy Sackville-West once wisely said. We had sat
around the table for about three hours, for he hates a move, when suddenly he pushed his chair back saying he must go to bed, and thus the
evening ended.

One Sunday we made an unforgettable expedition to Vaux le
Vicomte, the famous château built by Fouchet who, after giving a fête
there for Louis XIV, caused such jealousy in the heart of the Roi Soleil
that he was sent to prison where he languished for the rest of his life.
Gladwyn and Bob Dixon marched off briskly down the vista, as though
they were starting on a long Sunday afternoon walk, their goal being a
distant statue, while Oliver and I wandered around more leisurely,
admiring the formal planning and the enchanting gardens, and sniffing
the delicious smell of the box hedges warmed by the sun. We also tried
to avoid the diplomatic bores who abounded.

The château is moated, and approached from the garden side by a
significant flight of stone steps. One could visualize Louis XIV
emerging from the house and being overcome with envy at this superb
invention; and Monsieur, with his rouge and high heels, stepping

---

[7] During the War British private investments in the United States had been used to
pay for American support for the war effort. After the War the compensation offered
was far less than expected.

carefully down to the garden; and Madame, all grace and charm – '*On dirait qu'elle demande le coeur, voilà le secret de Madame*';[8] and Cardinal Mazarin's red robes sweeping the steps; and perhaps Madame de Sevigné, enchanting and warm-hearted, thinking she would write a long letter describing the scene – indeed all her letters about the Fouchet trial are intensely moving. But I awoke from my reverie to see the stocky, homely but vigorous figure of the Secretary of State, alone but for his detective whom he had just told to go indoors and get some refreshment before our return to Paris, and not to miss the champagne.

One evening he gave a huge dinner at the embassy for the Dominions. The big dining room was used for the first time since the war, and the splendid gold plate which had belonged to Pauline Borghese adorned the table. It was a stroke of genius on the part of the Duke of Wellington to have acquired the house and its contents for England after Waterloo.[9] We were all assembled – all the ladies in day dresses – and I was chatting to some friends when I felt a sharp tap on my neck and turned round to find it was Mr Bevin who had flicked me with his finger by way of greeting.

Diana Cooper's[10] bedroom is Pauline Borghese's, with her lovely bed and furniture, and decorated in crimson and gold. I thought of that beauty of long ago gazing at herself in the mirrors, and moving languorously around the room. Now another beauty occupies it, and if slightly faded she still has glamour and brilliance and intelligence. Diana has most cleverly converted a very ordinary bathroom into an Empire tented room by draping a striped material from the centre of the ceiling and down the walls.

After the dinner some men staggered in with a piano, for Mr Alexander[11] had an urge to play while the company sang and danced, and soon there was a mighty roar of 'You are my honey-honey-suckle',

[8] 'Monsieur' and 'Madame' had been Prince Philippe, Duc d'Orléans, brother of Louis XIV, and his wife Princess Henrietta of England, daughter of Charles I.
[9] The British Embassy, formerly the Hôtel de Charost, had been owned by Pauline Borghese, sister of Napoleon, and purchased, together with its contents, by the British Government in 1814, the year before Waterloo (Cynthia had not yet researched her subject).
[10] Lady Diana Manners (1892–1986), wife of Sir Alfred Duff Cooper.
[11] Albert Victor Alexander, later 1st Viscount Alexander of Hillsborough (1885–1965): First Lord of the Admiralty.

and other time-honoured songs. I retired with Duff Cooper[12] to a
marble corridor, and we sat, I sipping champers and he whisky, a little
removed from the community singing. He said 'One day I hope I shall
see you and Gladwyn here. You would do it beautifully'. I said hastily
(feeling embarrassed because there had been so much talk of our taking
their place), 'Oh but that was only a rumour; there's no truth in it'. And
he replied 'I don't mean just yet, because Gladwyn's too young to be
ambassador here, but in a few years. You would like it, wouldn't you?'.
And I said 'Who wouldn't?'. He then went on to talk about other things,
of his brilliant young friends who had been killed in the last war, and
what a loss they were now, and of politics. We somehow began talking
of memoirs, and he said it was a lamentable thought that the only
person who was seriously keeping a diary, and had already deposited a
number of volumes in the British Museum, was that American pip-
squeak (alas naturalized British), Chips Channon. However it seems all
is well, for Duff is also writing his memoirs, so our present age will be
recorded for posterity by his highly intelligent pen.[13] There are some
things very nice about him: he reads Diana to sleep every night.

A great deal of our time in Paris as wives was spent waiting for our
menfolk who disappeared into the unventilated and smoke-laden
atmosphere of the Luxembourg for hours, I might almost say for days,
since sometimes they do not emerge till the early hours of the morning.
One hot evening in July I remember waiting with Maudie till eleven
before we began a succulent feast of cold ham and strawberries, prepared for Oliver and Gladwyn, and then they came in at about one
o'clock having eaten and drunk already with Mr Bevin.

Sometimes I'd have to spend ages giving drinks to unknown foreigners who were waiting to see Gladwyn, and the conversation was often
difficult to maintain. The most curious guest Maudie and I entertained
was Father Philip Langdon, a great jolly abbot with a huge paunch and
an inexhaustible supply of improper stories: he should never have
entered the Church. On another occasion Antoine Bibesco lunched.
Gladwyn had taken an immense dislike to him, and didn't put in an

[12] Sir Alfred Duff Cooper, later 1st Viscount Norwich (1890–1954); Ambassador to
France. As a former Conservative minister his tenure was precarious under the
Labour Government, but he was retained till the end of 1947.
[13] Sir Henry Channon's diaries, edited by Robert Rhodes James, were published in
1967; Duff Cooper's diaries have not yet been published.

appearance, so Cadett of the BBC filled the gap, though he and Antoine didn't hit it off either, both wishing to be the lion of the party, if one can call an elderly Parisianized Romanian a lion.[14]

There were always interesting people connected with the Conference itself – Masaryk, Spaak, the Americans and the Russians.[15] I never really met Molotov, but Vyshinsky several times. He had a most amiable smile and manner, but the coldest, flintiest eyes. I tried to get out of him across the luncheon table whether conditions in Russian villages were like those in our Suffolk village, where there is no running water in any house. Mr Bevin had once said to me that the Labour Government would see to it that every house in the country had a tap, and I am sure he meant it. But here was Mr Vyshinsky telling me in the cold light of day that everywhere in Russia there was plumbing. I fear he must have misunderstood, or wilfully misled me. He drank not a thing and made off back to his work as soon as he could.

Of French friends it is very difficult to write – several we used to know well have behaved badly, especially society people. Maudie and I went to an unforgettable cocktail party in the summer at Aymone de Brantes'.[16] She is a charming pathetic figure, whom I knew well in London, and her husband, very much the *fine fleur* of France, disappeared into a concentration camp and was never heard of again, leaving her disconsolate and with five children. She lives in a lovely ground-floor apartment in the Avenue Montaigne, typically Parisian in its decoration with grey walls, and with an old Coromandel screen, lamps in large Chinese vases, and some exquisite pieces of French furniture.

There in a solemn circle, which soon became intensely animated, were gathered in that sweltering summer heat a group of people to meet us – but alas they were all 'yellow', they were positively gamboge. They had certainly not helped to win the war. Jean de Gaigneron was

[14] Prince Antoine Bibesco (1878–1951) had been in the Romanian Legation in London before the War, and had married Lady Elizabeth Asquith. Thomas Cadett was the veteran Paris correspondent for *The Times* before the War, and now for the BBC.
[15] Paul-Henri Spaak (1899–1972) and Jan Masaryk (1886–1948), the Foreign Ministers of respectively Belgium and Czechoslovakia, who had both been in exile in London during the war.
[16] Aymone de Faucigny-Lucinge (1905–93), widow of François, Comte de Brantes, who had been Military Attaché at the French Embassy in London.

there. I knew him well in the old days when I used to stay with Jacques Blanche, and in Blanche's studio he was an intelligent and delightful talker, and quite a good painter. But here he was, rather desiccated and deteriorated, disliking the war years merely because they had interfered with his comfort, and disliking even more the brave new world we now live in. But the last straw at the de Brantes party was the entrance of Jenny de Margerie, wife of Roland, who had been at the French Embassy before the War and had always been considered to be the friend of England, the loyal man who understood us: but with a difference, for when France fell he went to Shanghai and was actively anti-British, so much so that he was not even taken back into the Quai d'Orsay but put on leave of absence. So we were rather dismayed when his boring wife greeted us as long lost friends – which was just about what we were and meant to remain![17]

But I mustn't belittle the fine people of France. I remember meeting at tea at Madame Langweil's old Madame Parodi,[18] the mother of the patriot and a wonderful old lady, who said with tears in her eyes, '*Merci pour l'Angleterre*'. Madame Langweil, herself an Alsatian Jewess, had to hide from the Germans. Her old house, 61 Rue de Varennes, had frequently been the hiding-place of the Resistance. It had once belonged to Talleyrand, and she told me how when Clemenceau came to see her there, he had said, 'What, did that old rogue live here?'. There were fine rooms with old boiseries, in which Madame Langweil had placed her famous collection of Chinese works of art. One felt awed at being in the presence of so many beautiful and ancient things. Her two Coromandel screens were magnificent, particularly the white and gold, though it seemed to be crumbling away owing to the damp of the house, and Gladwyn said it ought to be in a museum. I believe Lady Ripon, an Edwardian beauty, said 'Give me a chair in front of the screen, and leave me alone: I want to look at it'. Madame Langweil had cloisonné vases set in ormolu which had belonged to Colbert, and a set of Empire furniture of the Duc de Montesquieu (Madame de

[17] Jenny Fabre-Luce, wife of Roland de Margerie (1899–1990). He had been Counsellor in the French Embassy in London 1933–40, and was subsequently French Ambassador to the Vatican, to Spain and to Federal Germany.
[18] Hélène Vavin, wife of Professor Dominique Parodi. One son had been killed by the Gestapo, and the other was about to become French Ambassador to the United Nations.

Montesquieu had been 'Qieu Qieu', the governess of the Roi de Rome). Nearly all these famous things had been taken by the Germans, but practically all had since been recovered.[19]

Another remarkable old lady I met, and with whom I sought an acquaintance, was Madame St René Taillandier, the writer. She is lame now and sat, like so many French hostesses, with her back to the empty fireplace. On each side was a table piled with books, and her guests ranged in a semi-circle on excessively uncomfortable chairs. I brought her an offering of tea, and told her how I had read her enchanting book *La Princesse des Ursins* during some of those bad blitzes in London, there in bed in our top-floor flat, and how I was completely oblivious to the terrific bombardment and transported by her delightful writing into the time of Louis XIV, and could only think of Madame des Ursins being given '*le pour*',[20] and the grimness of the Spanish court, and the little Queen with her crazy heart. Madame Taillandier had spent some time in England, in 'le Surbiton', and like all French people admired the works of Charles Morgan. As always in a French salon, the conversation was excellent.

We had several lovely meals in restaurants, but the prices were staggering. It was grim to think that the poor people who couldn't afford the black market prices practically starved. Masaryk described the old chauffeur who used to drive for the Czechoslovak Embassy, now reduced from a fine big man to a thin tragic man living on 300 francs a month. 'I emptied my pockets and pressed all my money on him', said Masaryk. There must surely be something wrong with the whole system when this sort of thing happens. We grumble at our queues and regulations in England, but it is a fairer state of things, and that is something to be proud of.

The time had now come for me to return to our monastic austerity. The delegates were about to leave on the *Queen Elizabeth* for New York, where the Peace Conference was at last to be brought to a conclusion. I thought it would be fitting and friendly to give a cocktail party on our last evening in Paris. Gladwyn was decidedly damping over this happy

[19] Saxton Noble had purchased extensively from Madame Langweil, who acted as a dealer, acquiring in particular Coromandel screens and jade.
[20] When the French Royal Court travelled, only the most important people had rooms reserved for themselves alone, a distinction designated by the prefix '*Pour…*' in front of their names on the doors.

idea, though he thoroughly enjoyed it when it took place. He said it would cause offence if we didn't ask everyone, and when I suggested the sort of people I thought we should invite, he wanted to know 'on what system the victims were to be selected?'. Actually it was a roaring success, and a good time was had by all. The scene of merriment was a pretty awful room done up in somebody's notion of the English Baronial Hall – a great overhanging chimney-piece, Knole sofas, tapestries on the walls.

The private plane had been ordered at ten the next morning, too early for my liking, and there was the usual rush habitual to an unpunctual person. However, accounts were settled, clothes rammed down in suitcases, tips given, good-byes said, and at last we bundled into the cars and set off for Le Bourget. Despite a foggy morning the journey was good, and at the other end the Customs kind. How pleasant to see kind English faces, and to join the stream of slow-moving orderly traffic that didn't hoot all the time, even if we knew our lunch was going to be dull and not swilled down with wine. So back to the Pont Street Dutch architecture of Mount Street, with Mrs Cunnington to welcome us up to the top floor; and there I was home again happily ensconced among the prettiest Regency furniture that can be found, but all the happier for a visit to Paris *en princesse*.

1947

Mount Street, London, 16 February

We are in the midst of the Coal Crisis,[1] and the public has to endure
great discomfort and deprivation, but 'we can take it'. Mrs Cunnington
called us at 8.30 this morning, and turned on the electric fires so as to
give us half-an-hour's warmth until nine o'clock when all heating and
lighting is cut off. I had my bath, turned on the electric kettle, filled my
hot-water bottle, and then went into the sitting-room where, wrapped
in two rugs and with the hot-water bottle at my feet, I settled down to
breakfast in an icy atmosphere. Indeed, Gladwyn remarked (with an
eiderdown round him) that it was a particularly cold day. We bore it until
about five minutes later he gave a shout of horror, for he had observed
that the window was open all the time. We had endured the icy blast
with the same stiff upper lip that had accepted bombs and rockets and
black-out and queues and all the things that just couldn't be helped.

Mount Street, London, 18 February

Another arctic day, colder than ever. I went to shop in Harrods,
knowing that they generate their own electricity. At the centre of
Harrods is a large hall with rows of armchairs, in which a posse of
weary elderly people had come to roost, to spend the hours in compar-
ative warmth by a glimmering light. What were they thinking of in this

---

[1] The winter of 1946–7 was the most severe in England since 1880–1, and blizzards
exacerbated the crisis caused by miners' stoppages.

twilight? I suppose of past comforts, of houses with servants who answered bells and put coals on the fire and drew the blinds and curtains when dusk fell, and brought tea, and polished silver. But now they were grateful for this refuge, where it was too dark even to read.

I returned home, put on my best hat, and armed with a bicycle lamp against the black-out, set out for Westminster to see Sybil Colefax.[2] Sybil's charming house in Lord North Street is done up and furnished in the prettiest but safest and most unobtrusive of styles. Just a good background for the illustrious. Rose Macaulay was there today. She has an exquisite sensitive face. She said it was monstrous that the BBC had cut the Third Programme because of the fuel crisis, as it is the one good thing we get, and only broadcasts from six to eleven in the evenings. We all urged her to take the matter up. Pritchett was there, at a loose end because the *New Statesman*, like other periodicals, has been suspended.

Mount Street, London, 20 February

It is still cold, and snowing into the bargain. Gladwyn and I are spending a quiet evening at home, enjoying a delicious meal fit for a prince. Pea soup out of a tin; a small lobster each (price 2/2d each); lettuce with a proper salad-dressing from almond-oil as a substitute for olive-oil (very expensive at 21/- for a large bottle); a Camembert cheese (2/6d); and a glass of Austrian hock, two bottles of which had been given us by Dr Gruber, the Austrian Foreign Secretary. Then some dates. We then turned on the wireless, and are now listening to Harold Nicolson[3] giving a talk on France. Gladwyn and I agree that his manner of speaking on the radio is most unconvincing. He tries to give the impression that he is not reading his script. He over-emphasizes too many words, hesitates, repeats himself, talks slowly and then suddenly with rapidity, and altogether speaks in a way that no one does in ordinary conversation. Nonetheless I believe he is one of the most popular of broadcasters.

[2] Sybil Halsey (1874–1950), widow of Sir Arthur Colefax: *salonnière*, and founder of the decorating firm of Colefax and Fowler.
[3] Harold Nicolson, later Sir Harold (1894–1962), married to Vita Sackville-West. Diplomat, politician and author, he had been Counsellor at the Legation at Teheran at the time when Gladwyn was Third Secretary.

Mount Street, London, 21 February

I trekked to Westminster this afternoon to see Ava Anderson[4] who was
ill in bed – everything pink and white, herself, the bed and the decoration of her room. She talked of old days, Wigs' death, the birth of her
child, and Lady Grey, and was very amiable and pleasant. I owe my
introduction to the Glenconner family to Ava, and am always grateful as
Lady Grey[5] was a great influence in my life when I was young. Ava and I
were remembering what a wonderful atmosphere of comfort and
charm and intellect she gave to her home.

Sir John Anderson came in after tea; a kind sensible man with a
paunch. They seemed devoted to each other, but I think he is shrewd
enough to see through her. By the way, the only time that Sir John
Anderson ever met Stephen Tennant, the latter was 'made up' with a
curious shade of orange, and mistakenly took such a violent fancy to Sir
John that he wrote next day inviting him to lunch *tête à tête* at the Ritz. I
need hardly say that the invitation was refused.

Mount Street, London, 23 February

At five I went to see Violet Woodhouse.[6] She has a form of jaundice
which goes on for ages. I was admitted to her presence as to the holy of
holies. Gordon Woodhouse begged me to stay only a short time, but
she was in such good form that I stayed an hour. She lay on a couch in
front of the fireplace in which burned two electric fires full on. She was
in black and red, with an enormous paste cross, and looked very
wonderful, though she said she was dying. She is a great artist, and
therefore I suppose that her prejudices, lack of patriotism, and malice,
must to an extent be forgiven her. She lives in a world of her own,

[4] Ava Bodley, widow of Ralph Wigram and wife of Sir John Anderson, later 1st
Viscount Waverley (1882–1958). He was formerly Home Secretary and then
Chancellor of the Exchequer in the wartime government, and was now Chairman of
the Port of London Authority and of the Royal Opera House.
[5] Pamela Wyndham, widow of Edward Tennant, 1st Lord Glenconner, had then
married Edward Grey, 1st Viscount Grey of Fallodon (1862–1933), Foreign Secretary
1905–16. Her youngest son was the effeminate Stephen Tennant.
[6] Violet Gwynne (1871–1948), married to Gordon Woodhouse. She was a
harpsichordist, clavichordist and pianist.

surrounded by adulation, but when one hears her play her clavichords, one is moved by her mastery and passion.

Bridget[7] says that Nancy Rodd[8] is returning from Paris. Fancy that. Apparently the Communists have been making nasty quips about Palewski having an intimacy with the sister of Hitler's friend, meaning that barmy Unity.[9] I say that Nancy has just returned to have a bath, and that she's not aware of the austerity that the fuel crisis had landed us in.

Mount Street, London, 25 February

Tonight we dined with Tom Goff, and have just returned almost frozen by the chill of 46 Pont Street. But it was a delicious meal, cooked by Lady Cecily, and it was lovely to be back again in the same old house, with the same old butler to wait on us. Tom was in excellent form; he is the best company in the world when in the right mood. It is strange to think how he started life as a promising barrister and now has become a professional maker of clavichords and harpsichords. Violet Woodhouse prefers his to Dolmetch and all the others. He showed us his harpsichord, and it really is magnificent, a great achievement.

Mount Street, London, 26 February

Sydney Butler[10] came to tea. She asked me, confidentially, to find out from Sam whether his Renoir picture *La Loge* had been cleaned at Lord Lee's house during the War. A most unpleasant story is going round, she said, emanating from Graham Sutherland, that when being cleaned by Ruhemann, and in the presence of Kenneth Clark, the cheek of the

---

[7] Lady Bridget Parsons (1907–72), who occupied the flat below Cynthia and Gladwyn in 119a Mount Street.

[8] Nancy Mitford (1904–73), wife of Peter Rodd. She was now living in Paris, and in love with Gaston Palewski, formerly wartime Principal Private Secretary to General de Gaulle in London.

[9] Unity Mitford (1914–48), infatuated with Hitler, had gained his friendship and access to his private entourage. She was assumed to be a British spy, until she attempted suicide at the outbreak of war.

[10] Sydney Courtauld (1902–54), daughter of Samuel Courtauld and first wife of R.A. Butler. She was by way of being Cynthia's closest woman friend.

woman fell off and had to be put on again. This same man was entrusted with cleaning of the National Gallery pictures, about which there has been a great deal of controversy. If he really did something so drastic to *La Loge* he should not have been given this job, or be defended by Kay Clark.[11]

Mount Street, London, 27 February

Went to Heywood Hill's bookshop after lunch hoping to see Nancy, and I found her there, in a wonderful Paris hat, such as might have been worn about 1905. She gave most disquieting news about the fashions that are being shown there, for I can't think how we can ever achieve such a complete change of silhouette on our coupons – long skirts for day wear, either hobble or crinolines, sloping shoulders, hair parted in the middle and looped over the ears.

Mount Street, London, 28 February

I dined with Sam[12] in his lovely house; an excellent dinner, and we drank Chianti. We talked about Communism, rather guardedly in front of William the footman; and Christ, and women, and all sorts of deep subjects about which Sam argued with Courtauld vehemence. He is amazingly vigorous and wise. Quite the nicest person in the world, who brings out the best in everybody. I deplore his devotion to Christabel,[13] who is to my mind affected, insincere and calculating. But it is in keeping with Sam's nobility of character that he should see good in her.

No. 12, North Audley Street is a rare gem, and full of lovely objects and pictures. I tried to find out when *La Loge* had been cleaned, leading the subject round to this most tactfully and circuitously, via Kenneth Clark and the National Gallery pictures. Sam says he is very bad about

[11] Kenneth Clark, later Lord Clark (1903–83), married (firstly) to Jane Martin. He had been Director of the National Gallery 1934–45.
[12] Samuel Courtauld (1876–1947): Chairman of Courtaulds, and founder of the Courtauld Collection and the Courtauld Institute.
[13] Christabel MacNaghton (1890–1974), wife of Henry McLaren, 2nd Lord Aberconway.

dates, but he thinks it was probably cleaned by Ruhemann a year or two before the War, but I must admit he was vague on the subject.

Mount Street, London, 2 March

Today we went down to Eton. This time we went by Waterloo, and travelled with Sebastian Earl – an old Etonian King's Scholar who is now Managing Director of John Lewis – an important job but perhaps hardly worthy of his record.

Gladwyn came across a letter the other day from Edward Marjoribanks, a brilliant scholar and President of the Oxford Union, whose life was cut short tragically. In this letter, written in the twenties, he predicts who will be the successful people of his generation. It was curious to read that he thought Seb Earl would be at the top of the tree. Also Bob Boothby – a hard drinker, who has hardly fulfilled his promise as a politician, though he is probably the most brilliant debater in Parliament. Incidentally, Bob was our best man, but rather *faute de mieux* since Gladwyn's more intimate friends were unavailable. I think the other man mentioned by poor Edward was Clive Birt. Anyhow, Seb Earl was supposed to 'dream of being a dictator over us all'.

We lunched at the Bridge Hotel, and then returned to Miles' house, where I had a chat with Dr Prescot. He is a delightful yet enigmatic character; sometimes he is completely silent. Once a parent went to have an interview with him, and having sat for some time with a stranger who never uttered a word, she finally asked whether he too was waiting to see Dr Prescot. 'I *am* Dr Prescot', the man replied.

Mount Street, London, 6 March

This evening we dined with the Hore-Belishas.[14] He has married a most charming and remarkable woman, and they seem very happy. She was an ambulance driver in France in 1940, and was taken prisoner. The maid who looks after her is a children's nurse who was interned with

[14] Leslie Hore-Belisha, later 1st Lord Hore-Belisha (1893–1957), married to Cynthia Elliot. He had been Secretary of State for War 1937–40.

her. The butler and the chef are disabled service-men. Cynthia Hore-Belisha devotes a great deal of her time to looking after the badly wounded who have been disfigured and are waiting for their final operations. She tries to cheer them up and given them confidence. Leslie Hore-Belisha is lucky to be married to such a rare person. He is monstrously ugly, but very likable and kind-hearted, and an intelligent man in many ways. He is supposed to see himself as another Dizzy, but he isn't a chip off that block by any means, though he has a certain drive and flourish.

Clare Beck[15] was there. She must be a good deal over fifty, has had three husbands, five children, quantities of lovers, and looks like an angel, and a young angel too. She has all the exquisite charm and lovely manners that her mother, Lady Grey, possessed. I expect she is pretty hard-boiled, and believe she only cares for bridge, but she is a most attractive person.

Our host kept calling for general conversation, which of course is essential for amusing talk. But I must say that I notice that whenever people clamour for this form of conversation, it generally means that they want to hold forth to the company themselves.

Maudie Harvey must now be hurtling across White Russia, and it is to be hoped that Mrs Bevin doesn't know. It seems strange that beloved Maudie should be the cause of such jealousy on the part of Flo – not for Uncle Ernie's affections, but because Mrs Bevin had been induced to stay at home by being told that no wives were allowed on the expedition. Mrs Bevin is supposed to have a bad effect on her spouse in that she nags him and worries him (albeit being very devoted to him) and forgets to remind him about his pills. So it was strongly recommended by his medical adviser that she should not accompany him to Moscow. Maudie, however, was considered essential to Oliver's welfare by both him and her, and Elsie Strang thought she would enjoy the trip; and therefore these two started weeks ago making preparations of the most elaborate nature, including a series of injections against all the awful diseases that might attack them. Then, if you please, someone lets the cat out of the bag, and Flo goes off the deep end and announces that if 'Lady Oliver' is going, she will go too. So Mr Bevin said no wives will be

[15] Clarissa (Clare) Tennant (1896–1960): married successively to Adrian Bethell, Lionel Tennyson and James Beck.

allowed at all; and Maudie, with her Welsh temperament, thoroughly and violently reacting to the monstrous injustice of the situation, angrily and tearfully unpacked and had unpleasant words with the Private Secretaries.

At the last moment, the Secretary of State relented and said Maudie might go provided nobody saw her. It being too late for her to buy a false nose, she had to travel Third Class with the typists, and not be seen at the signing of the Treaty of Dunkirk. I am sure it will leak out sooner or later.

Mount Street, London, 14 March

Not very eventful week, but two meals in Embassies kept us well fed – one certainly gets nicely satiated in Corps Circles. Our lunch at the Greeks was on Wednesday, and given in honour of the McNeils.[16] I had the Duke of Palmella on one side, which was quite pleasant; the other side of me had to put up with Sir John Monck, that curious desiccated retired official.[17] There were rows of diplomats there, and the conversation at table kept on getting wrong – as it often does at those formal occasions, leaving some person cold-shouldered and silent, while the neighbours jabber away at their *tête à têtes*. There ought to be a Master of Ceremonies to direct the guests and tell them when to turn about. If you're going in for formality you might as well do it properly. We came home in the McNeils' car. Hector is a bright star in the Labour Party, and I am sure he will be helped by his wife, who is charming, intelligent and sensible. Both are Scotch which, of course, always has enormous appeal. Irish charm and Welsh wizardry pale before the great qualities of the Scottish.

Last night we dined with the Italians, which was a more intimate affair, about twelve of us, and very pleasant. As usual, when dining with the Carandinis,[18] Gladwyn and I have a heated argument as to how to

[16] Hector McNeil (1907–55), married to Sheila Craig. Minister of State for Foreign Affairs.
[17] The Duke of Palmella was the Portuguese Ambassador, and Sir John Monck (1883–1964) was Marshal of the Diplomatic Corps.
[18] Count Nicolo Carandini (1895–1972), married to Elena Albertini. Italian Representative in London pending the ratification of the peace treaty in September.

get there. Being about five 'stone throws' distant, it is obviously an extravagance to hire a car. But if I am in evening dress I do demand a taxi, even if it means having to bowl all the way round Grosvenor Square. However, last night it was damp and no taxi was forthcoming, so to Gladwyn's delight we had to foot it.

The Carandinis are particularly nice – if only the bulk of Italians were as nice as they are, how much more we would respect their country. They mind very much, and naturally, not yet being recognized, for he is merely a Representative, not an Ambassador, and I suppose this rankles all the more since they were so anti-Fascist.

Sibyl was at the dinner, and Harold Nicolson. He has just joined the Labour Party, and I really wonder whether he is an asset to them. He has changed sides a good many times and, delightful though he is, I am inclined to think he is a bit woolly. Can Harold be after a peerage now? I shouldn't be surprised.[19] Though he is a friend, I must honestly say that I never feel really at ease in his company. He is too complicated and tied up, but of course he is not at his best with women. Also he has a habit of being tactless or offensive or inaccurate on some given point, and then appears to enjoy apologizing and admitting he was in the wrong, particularly if it can be done in public. All very strange. Vita, his wife, is, on the other hand, a noble creature and a great poetess – but she has her peculiarities.

Today I saw in the gossip column of the *Telegraph* that Oliver has been very ill in Moscow, but is better. What luck that Maudie was with him; but I fear that Mrs Bevin may now know that he has his wife to look after him.

I had Emerald[20] on the telephone tonight for close on an hour. She wanted my permission for Gladwyn to dine with her tonight, but he wouldn't go in the end. She was full of gossip – Archie Inverchapel is not a success in Washington, Duff is to get a peerage and the Garter, is Sachy[21] in love with Bridget?, can Bridget be in love ever?, and a thousand other trivialities, and then she ended by wanting me to go to two concerts with her. She must be close on eighty, dresses like eighteen, and is quite absurd and futile, but well read, and with a terrific enjoy-

[19] Cynthia's surmise is correct, as is revealed in his published diaries.
[20] Maud Burke (1877–1948), widow of Sir Bache Cunard, whose death she celebrated by changing her name from Maud to Emerald.
[21] Sacheverell Sitwell, later Sir Sacheverell (1897–1988), married to Georgia Doble.

ment of life which one can't help admiring, and sometimes a very amusing conversationalist. Her face has been lifted out of all recognition, but her figure and movements are extraordinarily young. She has a fantastic passion for Gladwyn, to which he is quite indifferent.

I feel quite an affinity with other diarists, now that I keep one myself, and it is amusing to glean their respective methods and objects. I think we must all be frank and admit that we have posterity at the back of our minds – no, Ruth Lee is the one exception. She has kept a diary for years, short and succinct, with the unselfish purpose that when Lord Lee writes his memoirs he will get the facts correct. Elena Carandini keeps one. Hers is written on loose sheets, so if in after years she should become embarrassed or incriminated, the offending page can be removed. I believe that during the War her diary had to be hidden. Harold also uses loose sheets, on which he types the morning after. Sir Ronald Storrs has quite a different method. As he lies in bed at night, after turning out the light, he speaks his thoughts into a dictaphone, which is afterwards typed out by a secretary. Duff Cooper's diary is detailed, and of course beautifully written. As for the reactions to life of that twerp Chips Channon, I am sorry to say they are mounting up in the British Museum.[22]

Mount Street, London, 15 March

Quite a typical Saturday. I was called at eight by Mrs Cunnington, and then had a blissful hour of semi-consciousness till nine, when Vera came and rapped on the door saying in broken English that breakfast was ready and it was eggs. I generally at this point ask Vera what the weather is like, and whatever she says I dress as though she had said the opposite. Vera is a Swede who cleans here in the mornings; or rather, doesn't clean. But at any rate she appears, and is absolutely honest, and we all like her.

After breakfast I read the papers, and telephone, and go to my bath. One good thing about these flats is that we are most fortunate in getting

[22] Duff Cooper's diaries are apparently of a sort that Cynthia would have found profoundly shocking, and contain no fine writing. Chips Channon's are acclaimed as being a brilliant account of London high society in the 1930s and 1940s.

hot water. And another thing is that we have the service of Mrs Cunnington, who is the nicest woman in the world. She is the real old-fashioned type of servant, fast disappearing from our midst; calm, philosophic, and an excellent cook. She takes a personal interest in our welfare, as though we were all part of a large family. She is the making of this place, which has many glaring disadvantages. But I have a great affection for it. I have spent many happy times here, and also anxious times during the war and when I had pneumonia all alone on the top floor.

It is curious to look back on those nights when Bridget Parsons and I used to sit on the staircase, wrapped in rugs, trying to talk about trivialities while the great thunder of the Blitzes raged and the whole building shook and the lights dipped. One didn't know for sure which crashes were our guns and which were bombs. Then at last the All Clear would sound and we'd go back to our beds. I always remember the first of the flying bombs, and the sinister realization that it was something quite new we were having to contend with, and being puzzled at not getting the All Clear.

Lord Newborough lives on the first floor. He is an eccentric and irascible old peer with beautiful manners, and is alleged to be descended from Philippe Egalité, and I really think he might be a Bourbon from his appearance. He was in the Navy in the last war, together with his devoted manservant, Tilson, who was a petty officer. His nautical past has made him run everything on a system of bells, and in the basement Mrs Cunnington and Tilson have to be on the alert lest they get the number wrong. For instance, one bell means he wants Tilson; two, breakfast; three, he is going out; four, he has come in; and so on. He has a rather common mistress called Gertrude (said to have been a telephonist at the Langham) who occupies his back flat.

Anyhow, to return to this morning, I dressed and went out to the bank to cash a cheque, and then took up my position in the butcher's queue, where I suddenly was accosted by Peter Rodd, who had been to see Bridget. He said 'he must sometime have a talk with Gladders and would only keep him five minutes', but of course I knew that means five hours. I then did the round of the shops, Dixon the grocer, and Mr Montagu for vegetables, and dumped all my goods in the basement; and then I went round to 39 Hill Street where there is a restaurant we often patronize when alone, and get a solid well-cooked meal for four shillings. I generally find friends, and just as I was finishing today, Bridget came in. After lunch I returned home and wrote letters, and at about half past four I started off to join Gladwyn at the cinema in Coventry Street to see *Les Enfants du Paradis*; after which a cosy supper by the fire – cutlets, leeks and potatoes, and then a nice jam omelette.

Mount Street, London, 19 March

On Monday we had Nancy Rodd and Osbert Lancaster[23] to dine. We had smoked salmon, and a nice fat chicken from Bramfield, salad and a Camembert cheese. Nancy and Osbert were at their best – I forgot to mention that his wife came, and she is rather a bore and wears spectacles the whole time. Osbert much enjoys talking and can be brilliantly amusing, but sometimes the sentences are almost too carefully constructed and would be better read than spoken. His is bringing out a book on Greece, illustrated by himself. After we had eaten we moved from that part of our sitting room which we call the dining room to the part we refer to as the drawing room; that is to say, we sat round the fire.

Anyhow, we were all happy talking when the bell rang and in came old Prod, sozzled and in a talkative mood. He is like the Ancient Mariner and goes drivelling on incoherently for hours. We treated him with firmness, but he tried a typical Rodd gambit, some nonsense about being horrified at Howe's appointment as Governor of the Sudan; and when we asked who he would have preferred he replied 'Gladders', and off he was, mumbling away about Africa. Having been metaphorically sat on by us all, he relapsed into sleepy silence and concentrated on the whisky. Eventually he remarked that he had a large car waiting outside, so he took Nancy away. But Osbert said he didn't for a moment believe there was a car, and as they went downstairs we looked out of the window and of course the street was quite empty. Strange to say, Nancy is devoted to him, but she must find him a crashing bore.

I think all the Rodds suffer from a strong inferiority complex, which

[23] Osbert Lancaster, later Sir Osbert (1908–86), married (firstly) to Karen Harris. Writer and artist, whose 'pocket cartoons' in the *Daily Express* had delighted Cynthia and her circle during the War years.

makes them want to hold forth at great length, to hint at mysterious sources of information, to imagine that only they can deal with a given situation. They look upon Italy as their particular perquisite merely because over thirty years ago their father was Ambassador there.[24] Francis left the Diplomatic Service when he was still a Third Secretary, because he thought he ought to have been given more rapid promotion. I should say that his business career has been something of a disappointment to him. But fortunately he has the House of Lords, which provides a wonderful opportunity for talking, airing views, starting up new hares, and being in the public eye, and I believe he is considered one of their best speakers. At this very moment he has moved an important debate on the grave economic situation of this country.

Yesterday I lunched with Peter Derwent at Boulestins. Opposite me was Lady Vansittart. She is a strange woman, exquisite but affected, and with a curious melancholy about her, a sort of helplessness, and very indiscreet. I don't think she has been a great asset to Van, except that she is decorative and colossally rich. He seems to have fizzled out. He was such a brilliant dynamic personality, and now he just reiterates the same old thing without cutting much ice. As Gladwyn says, 'he is right in the wrong way'.[25]

Last night we went to a most extraordinary dinner given by a fantastic couple called Hulton.[26] I can't think why we were there, or why Gladwyn accepted, and I suspect the whole thing was organized by Emerald. Hulton is the illegitimate son of a baronet, and some say he would like a peerage and is wondering which side will give it to him. He was supposed to be extremely Left, but his Russian wife is fed up with Labour people, and the object of last night's gathering was to show Hulton how preferable the right wing is. For this purpose they had,

[24] The three brothers were Francis, 2nd Lord Rennell (1895–1978), Peter (1904–68), and Gustaf (Taffy) (1905–70). All three were involved in Italy in the Allied Military Government of Occupied Territories (AMGOT), known in Cynthia's circle as 'Amgotterdammerung, or the Twilight of the Rodds'.
[25] Robert Vansittart, Lord Vansittart (1881–1957), married to Sarita Ward. As Permanent Under-Secretary of State for Foreign Affairs 1930–38, his anti-Nazi views had been so vehement that he had been 'pushed upstairs' as Chief Diplomatic Adviser.
[26] Edward Hulton, later Sir Edward (1906–88), married (secondly) to Nika Yourievitch. Founder and proprietor of *Picture Post*, the leading weekly illustrated magazine.

oddly enough, invited Gladwyn and me. Less oddly, Rab[27] and Sydney, Thorneycroft, Alastair Forbes, Loelia Westminster, the Gages, Massigli, a perfectly dreadful Hungarian man, and one or two others, and of course Emerald.

The scene of the orgy was the Hultons' suite at the Dorchester. I was next to Rab at dinner, and I enjoyed this very much. I thought how much he must mind that he can never now attain the position of Viceroy – it was always his greatest ambition. Attlee sent for him the other day to discuss the appointment of Mountbatten, and Rab told me that for a moment he was tempted to believe that he was going to offer it to him. Rab said that Winston had never forgiven him for opposing the Cripps plan – otherwise he might have become Viceroy instead of Wavell.[28]

To turn to lighter matters, Mrs Hulton was late appearing for her own dinner because she was having difficulty in getting into her new Paris dress – a tremendous creation the effectiveness of which depended on her wearing a real old-fashioned corset to tighten her waist. Most amusing and attractive, I thought. I wore my last Paris dress, which I think won't date much; at any rate, it was much admired by Loelia. It is a romantic dress.

Mount Street, London, 21 March

Charles Morgan has come into our life fairly recently through Sam, who met him through Osbert Sitwell. Sam has the greatest admiration and veneration for Charles, who he thinks has some message full of mystic meaning to give to the world through the medium of novels. Some people, including Osbert, can't stand them, though he struck up a friendship with Charles when the latter wrote a letter of sympathy at a time when Osbert was bringing a libel action against someone who said that the Sitwells weren't artists.

---

[27] R.A. Butler, later Lord Butler of Saffron Walden (1902–82), married (firstly) to Sydney Courtauld. He had been Minister of Education in the wartime government, and was subsequently Chancellor of the Exchequer, Home Secretary, Deputy Prime Minister, and Secretary of State for Foreign Affairs.
[28] In *The Art of the Possible*, R.A. Butler records that in 1942 he was approached on Churchill's behalf as to whether he would accept the viceroyalty, but declined.

When we first met Charles, his wife and family were still in America. Sam was more absorbed in the meeting of his friends and family with this sensitive and attractive writer, than he was in the course of the War, or the fate of Courtaulds. We and the Butlers were asked to dine at the Connaught, and we had to come at different times, very precisely, so that we shouldn't burst on Charles' horizon in a single mass. We were on tenterhooks lest we should do or say the wrong thing, but in the end the evening went off extraordinarily well, and Charles talked easily and with animation (which we were told he wouldn't), and everyone liked him (with the exception of Gladwyn, who thought he was bogus, but likes him now), and good Sydney fell practically in love with him.

When Charles' wife returned to England we never met her, but Sam asked me to take an interest in his daughter, so I got her an invitation to Queen Charlotte's Ball, and she became a great friend and eventually Gladwyn's secretary. She accompanied him on all his conferences last year, and did extraordinarily well.

Charles has wonderful blind adorations for certain people, for instance Churchill, and he avers that if Churchill told him to do some-thing, no matter what it was, or to go to the ends of the earth, he would gladly do so. I wonder whether men should desire to be ordered about by some leader merely because they are under his spell and not because of his wisdom, or commonsense, or other obvious qualities. It savours of an emotional schoolboy, or even more, a schoolgirl. However, it is fre-quently met with. I remember Francis Rennell, many years ago when he was a coming bright star in the City, saying that so great was the charm of Montagu Norman, that if he were to order Francis to go and work in a small bank in the outposts of the Empire (it is dramatic the way the Leader is supposed to bid one to go to the remotest parts) on £300 a year, he would do so without a murmur. You bet he'd have murmured!

Bramfield, Suffolk, 22 March

The rooks are busy making their nests, and are a great feature of the place, I often think. 'The birds in the high hall garden' might be a descrip-tion of Bramfield, for we stand high above the village. The house looked fresh and clean, the Maloneys were beaming and now want to stay on, there was a lovely log fire in the Elizabethan fireplace in the drawing-room, an ample tea, and the late afternoon sun slanted in from the garden window. After tea we went for a walk. Aeneas Reay[29] does not appear to have brought proper country clothes, and his exquisitely pressed grey pinstripe suit and unsolid shoes are evidently what he proposes to wear 'thorough bush, thorough briar'. So the sight of him made us modify our walk, taking him round the village, showing him the church, and then, sticking to the road always, to gaze at a clean distance at Broad Oak farm, which I prefer to call Bramfield Old Hall, as it once was. We then came home, got through a good deal of sherry, and dined at about eight. Gladwyn cheated by changing, and for some reason elected to wear a silly spotted red bow tie to make him appear not changed.

Bramfield, Suffolk, 23 March

My bedroom here is very pretty, and gets a great deal of sun through its three windows. The walls are pink,[30] and the curtains lovely old chintz ones from Wretham, with a great splashing floral pattern of pink and blue and green in a white ground. My bed is a Venetian four-poster with very thin posts and iron plumes on the four tops. On the walls are Bartolozzis, and the dressing-table is a real Victorian affair of white ersatz muslin, rigged up by Mrs Foster, the carpenter's wife, according to my instructions. The house has very good proportions, and nearly everything about it is well-constructed and pleasing to the eye. Sometimes I wish that it had not been altered in the eighteenth century; I feel it would have been more compact and less imposing, and wonder what it then looked like. I also wish I could find out more about the history of the house. It was occupied by the same family, the Rabetts, for four hundred years.

Mount Street, London, 26 March

Tonight we went to an 'Ordinary' again; it was, as always, in a private room at the Dorchester. It was the first that Sybil had given since her

---

[29] Aeneas MacKay, 13th Lord Reay (1905–63): a Dutchman who had inherited a Scottish peerage.
[30] In her piece on Bramfield in *The Englishwoman's House*, Cynthia admitted to a 'predilection for pink, pale pink, with a speck of black in it to relieve the crudity'.

accident, and it was like old times. We were about thirty, and most of us were those who had dined like this together ever since the first days of the War. It had been a wonderful idea on her part, for everyone (except very important persons) paid their own meal, and yet she organized it, so had all the fun of giving a party. And we all enjoyed it enormously as a good way of meeting friends at a time when everyone was so scattered and everything uncertain.

I remember those early Ordinaries at Lord North Street in the first winter of the War when nothing seemed ever to happen. Then in the summer, I remember the Ordinaries when too much had happened – Dunkirk and the fall of France. At this time there was a great influx of refugees: Mlle Curie; Somerset Maugham (busy describing how badly everybody else had behaved getting away in the boat, but I am told he was not too brave himself); Maurois (an ignoble character, he proved to be); Maurer (a Jewish-American journalist who behaved magnificently at Bordeaux); and many others.[31] I remember Ben Nicolson,[32] newly in uniform, an artistic and most unwarlike figure, but he said, with such staunchness and enthusiasm, 'I think there's something rather wonderful about our being alone against the enemy'.

Then after the bad blitzes started Sybil's dining-room had tree-trunks in it, and Sybil herself used to go every night to sleep in the shelter in Smith Square. We lost only one great friend through enemy action, and that was Maurice Ingram. Dear kind Maurice. He was always at the Ordinaries, wearing tweeds, which he did in London as soon as the War started as some sort of outward and visible sign of the change which had come to the world.

When the blitzes became too bad and rations smaller and transport difficult and the number of guests increased, the parties took place at the Dorch. But we got a less good meal at a higher price, and some appalling stuff to drink which was said to be Algerian wine but was probably methylated spirits. Then later the sherry was knocked off, then the wine, and now we just have watery beer or cider. But the price

[31] Cynthia's slur on Somerset Maugham's behaviour appears to be unjustified. But her criticism of André Maurois reflects the general annoyance in Britain that he refused to stay with de Gaulle in 1940 and went on to America where he spoke disparagingly about Britain's 'finest hour'.

[32] Benedict Nicolson (1914–78), son of Harold Nicolson. Deputy Director of the King's Pictures, and later editor of the *Burlington Magazine*.

remains the same – 15/- a head, and one often wonders whether one's neighbour, if a bore, was worth the 7/6d.

Tonight we were at three tables, and I as usual had one to arrange. Sybil's writing is almost indecipherable, and she gets very annoyed if one puts anyone wrong. And still more annoyed if people ask to be changed round because of some fancy or dislike, though I always considered they had the right to this since they were paying their own. I had on my left Bill Bentinck (straight from the divorce courts),[33] and on my right Bill Whitney (a nice American but a bit of a bore).

Mount Street, London, 29 March

Today was muggy and wet, and not propitious for the Boat Race, which we were to see at the invitation of Ava and Sir John Anderson from the launch of the Port of London Authority. A great many diplomats were there, all in most unsuitable clothes and obviously intending to spend all the time they could below where an excellent tea was provided. But not so the new American Ambassador, Mr Douglas. He stood it out in the rain, though it cascaded off his hat, anxious to give the impression that he was thoroughly enjoying it. Alas, poor Oxford seemed to lag further and further behind, and lost by ten lengths. Harold, who is very sentimental, moved to the opposite side of the boat, and Vita said it was because he couldn't bear to see Oxford lose. I thought he was moved to tears, but perhaps it was the rain, for by now we were all drenched.

Mount Street, London, 31 March

Lunched today with the Birkenheads to meet the American Ambassador. Anthony Eden was there, very amiable, and asserting that he was delighted to be out of office and having a rest, and not to be in Moscow.[34]

---

[33] William Cavendish-Bentinck, later 9th Duke of Portland (1897–1990). His divorce, when Ambassador to Poland, occasioned Bevin to force him out of the Foreign Service.
[34] Anthony Eden, later 1st Earl of Avon (1897–1977): Foreign Secretary 1935–8, 1940–5, and 1951–5, and Prime Minister 1955–7. Gladwyn had briefly worked directly for him in 1931, and had admired him during the War years as a first-class negotiator, though never falling for his charm.

He is extraordinarily nice, but not impressive, or brilliant, or sound, or shrewd, or a great orator (he never wrote his own speeches), or indeed anything much. But he certainly must have something to him to have achieved all he has. For one thing, he inspires hero-worship. All sorts of people such as Oliver Harvey, Jim Thomas and Bob Dixon, to mention only three, have waxed eloquent about him to me, put him on a pedestal, so dazzled by his altitude that they aren't aware of his weaknesses. He has tremendous personal charm, of an almost feminine nature; and one may admire his persistence and energy, till it becomes obstinacy. But I wonder if he will go down in history as one of our great politicians.

Mount Sreet, London, 1 April

I went with Gladwyn to the Soviet Embassy where we had vodka and caviare, saw Churchill and Anthony Eden, talked to the Russians (some of them through an interpreter), and quite enjoyed ourselves. We talked to John Strachey, who has a different and nicer wife from the one we used to know. Harold Macmillan lifted us home, and told us some amusing stories about Winston not hearing or pretending not to hear in the House.

Bramfield, Suffolk, 5 April

This evening we went to dine with the Vannecks, driven there by old Borrit, an extraordinary character who keeps bees, mends clocks, sells antiques and is the village barber. Heveningham is a beautiful house, decorated by Wyatt. Andrew Vanneck[35] bought it from his brother, Lord Huntingfield, and is most appreciative of its loveliness. He was married first to that tiresome Louise Campbell (known as Wee-Wee) and, strange to say, he once lived in our flat. His present wife is a Swede, and extremely nice. We like him enormously, and he has been kind and friendly. But he is a curious man, nervy, pernickety, and I am told has a violent temper. Rumour has it that he was once struck by lightning. He is a very good host, and lives in a few rooms in his colossal house.

[35] Andrew Vanneck (1890–1965), married (secondly) to Britta Bonde.

The small room he uses as a dining-room is very pretty and intimate and has prints pasted symmetrically all over the walls, such as I have only seen at Stratfield Saye. We had a delicious meal, soup made from young nettles gathered by our hostess and treated as spinach; goose; blackcurrants canned at home and as succulent as though they came from a summer garden – they were home-canned, so we are now going to invest in a canning-machine – and excellent wines. The *bonne bouche* of the evening, however, the almost unobtainable and expensive pâté de foie gras, had been ruined by being cooked on hot toast, and Vanneck showed his annoyance. Apart from this unfortunate incident we had a delightful evening, and came home after eleven. A howling gale tonight.

Bramfield, Suffolk, 11 April

We are going to have hare tomorrow night for dinner, and this entails a lot of talk, excitement, speculation and advice, because Kitty has never cooked one before. However, Mrs Clarke, the butcher's wife, is giving us the recipe, and preparing the victim, and lending us the stew-pot, so I hope it will be a masterpiece, not a failure. The village is very pretty, and there generally are a good many acquaintances to be greeted as one goes down the street. The Post Office, which is also the grocery, is a well-stocked little shop, and much less of a muddle than Dixon Gibbs in Mount Street.

Mount Street, London, 22 April

Yesterday I went to the opera with Ava Anderson. I had an egg for tea, when the dressmaker came and altered the jacket of my very ancient coat and skirt, nipping it in at the waist in the approved new fashion, and thereby, I hope, enabling me to wear it this season. I then dressed, wearing my black nylon full skirted Paris dress, with pale blue velvet ribbons, and my diamonds. I then rushed off, rather late, in my hired car and to the Royal Box where, strange to say, I arrived much too early.

The Royal Box is a perfect example of Edwardian luxury and comfort: gilt chairs covered in red, red carpet, and a truly wonderful ladies' lavatory of great discretion, with a good solid old-fashioned seat such as is rarely seen these days. Ava and Sir John arrived, and her nephew, and Henry Anglesey, Hugh Fraser and Lady Caroline Scott. How lucky Ava is to have someone as efficient as Sir John to look after her, planning everything with the greatest care. Having seen us comfortably arranged in a row in the box, he retired to go to the Pilgrims' Dinner for the new American Ambassador. Gladwyn was to go there too, and we were all to meet again at the Andersons' house afterwards. The opera was *Rosenkavalier*. It was well done, considering it was an English company, but possessing nothing of the élan of a real Austrian performance. At Lord North Street the party from the Pilgrims' Dinner were already upstairs, so we had to eat hurriedly and then join them. The Ambassador was accompanied by his shadow, an exceedingly common man called Piggy Warburg, who has gone around with several ambassadors, and I think does no good to Mr Douglas.

Bramfield, Suffolk, 23 April

Sydney Jebb and Bernice arrived by hired car, rather late for tea.[36] They had been motoring all day, having left Haslemere at a quarter to ten. Sydney emerged from their car while a terrific gale was blowing and torrential rain falling. He looked amazingly dapper and erect despite his seventy-six years, with a scarf round his neck, huge black fur gloves, a rose in his buttonhole, and a beautiful tie-pin. He accused us of living in the back of beyond. They couldn't find a pub, so had at last stopped for lunch at a restaurant called the Valentine, and Sydney was annoyed to find there was no wine list. He had then asked for a bottle of sherry, and the waiter would only bring him a glass, so he hadn't thought much of the Valentine. Moreover, he had embarrassed Bernice by looking around the room and remarking in a loud voice, 'What a very middle-class lot of people everywhere! I don't see a single honest working man'.

---

[36] Sydney Jebb (1871–1949), Gladwyn's father, married (firstly) to Rose Chichester (Gladwyn's mother), and (secondly) to Bernice Richards. A supreme eccentric, who wrote addresses on envelopes in reverse, and refused to recognize 'daylight saving' summertime.

Bramfield, Suffolk, 29 April

We made an expedition to Wretham in Reeve's car. I always like seeing my old home again, but this time it was rather a shock to find that it had become a granary. One thought of all the beautiful oak floors, the mahogany doors from the old War Office, all the chimney-pieces and fittings wasted. When Blomfield built it for Father before the First War, little did they think that this huge costly house would sink so low in just over thirty years.

Mount Street, London, 1 May

I went with Miles to see him off at Paddington. We were early, and walking up and down Platform Number 1 with Miles made me think of journeys I had made from there. Just before war was declared, but when we knew it was inevitable, Father had seen me off to Fleet. We came about two hours too early, imagining there would be a state of confusion at the station, but there was none. As far as I remember, the journey to Weymouth took me eight hours, and I had to change at remote places. The previous night, or rather at about two in the morning, the telephone had rung in our bedroom at Kent House, and Gladwyn (who was then Private Secretary to Cadogan) heard the Poles had given us the signal arranged if the Germans crossed the frontier. Many people believed that London would be badly bombed, so I was made to go to the country without delay.

I remember also being on Number 1 Platform when Gladwyn insisted on my hastily going to Bath when the flying bombs had started, and what a dreadful pandemonium there was; queues and confusion everywhere, trains not starting – I think I had to wait three hours. My porter abandoned me, rather naturally, fairly early on, but I persuaded him to carry my cases, containing my most valuable possessions, to a seat; and as there can be no queues on Number 1 itself, and the train was to start from there, I sat patiently, too alarmed to be hungry. It was a relief to arrive in Bath and not hear those horrible explosions at frequent intervals.

Bramfield, Suffolk, 3 May

In the morning I went to the Private View at the Royal Academy. An uninteresting show, and all the people one always sees there turned up. Same old bores like Edgar Dugdale and Clifford Smith, same old wags like Oliver Esher, same old snobs such as Courtauld-Thomson, same bright old things such as Lady Willingdon, same enthusiasts like Charlotte Bonham Carter, same nice dim persons like Winnie Graburn. Then of course the usual eccentric types, bearded Chelsea, bearded country, or Pre-Raphaelite beards; we saw one old man who obviously had, since his youth, modelled his appearance on Walter Crane. And 'arty' women, moth-eaten women, smart women and lesbian women. Everyone talked about Winston's two pictures, which were extraordinarily vigorous, especially the one with the reflection in the water.

Bramfield, Suffolk, 11 May

On Saturday we got up at crack of dawn to come here. Mrs Lovett had come in to help, the village was agog, for the Chancellor of the Exchequer was invited.[37] He and Ruth Dalton, and the McNeils, arrived for lunch, and the whole visit went off beautifully. Fortunately the weather was perfect, so a great deal of time could be spent sunning ourselves on the lawn. Dalton was most genial. He and Hector and Gladwyn sloped off to the pub on Saturday, which must have caused a sensation at the bar.

Mount Street, London, 12 May

I returned to London, laden with good things from the country. As Hugh Dalton said, when enjoying one of our good meals, 'In the country one is often surprised, and sometimes gratified'. Well, I returned gratified. I arrived towards tea time at the flat, and had a lovely

---

[37] Hugh Dalton, later Lord Dalton (1887–1962), married to Ruth Fox. Chancellor of the Exchequer. In 1940, when he became Minister of Economic Warfare, Gladwyn had been transferred from the Foreign Office to become his Foreign Policy Adviser and chief lieutenant in the task of 'setting Europe ablaze'.

time arranging flowers – lilac, laurel, tulips, primulas, blossom – had a refreshing bath, dressed in my ancient dinner dress, with a spray of Bramfield lilies to rejuvenate it, and then Gladwyn and I set off for the Iti Embassy. The Carandinis and we chatted and passed the time till we sallied forth to the Savoy Grill, where we were to meet Sybil and Gerry.[38] Gerry was at his best. He is an enchanting and intelligent companion. He is accused of pomposity, and one cannot deny the charge, but at times he is simple, positively humble, and always alert, educated and knowledgeable, and intensely affectionate.

He had received the Royal Family that morning at Waterloo on their return from South Africa. He had been attired in his best suit – moth-eaten, green with age, his top hat battered and furry. Mr Attlee was similarly in a shabby tailcoat, and Mr Chuter Ede had his tie about two inches below his collar. But Monsieur Moriny de Aragoa, the Brazilian Ambassador and doyen of the Diplomatic Corps, was in an immaculate suit, his top hat new and shining, and, to crown all, mauve gloves.

Mount Street, London, 13 May

Today was a perfect day, 'a day stolen from time'. Mar and Nicola[39] and I went forth in a car that Mar had hired, into the past, into happiness, into the country. Our goal was Chicksands Priory, the home of Dorothy Osborne, which in 1910 my parents rented from Sir Algernon Osborne. As Logan Pearsall Smith said, 'One is always happy if one enjoys pilgrimages; there is always somewhere to go'. Shefford Church looked very much restored, but must have appeared so when we knew it. We remembered it well inside – the porch where Mother took me when I felt faint, the cushioned pew we sat in. I could still see Mr Osborne (the younger son who had become the clergyman) reading the litany in his beautiful voice; I could still remember my own discovery that by screwing up my eyes I could see more clearly the hymn numbers. Mr Osborne used to tell

[38] Gerald Wellesley, 7th Duke of Wellington (1885–1972), married to (though separated from) Dorothy Ashton (d. 1956). As Lord Gerald Wellesley he had been known as an architect, and he had succeeded unexpectedly to the dukedom on the death of his nephew in action in 1943.
[39] Cynthia's sister Marjorie Noble (1896–1987), married to Geoffrey Madan; and her daughter Nicola, later married to Gordon Campbell.

such amusing stories, of how when he was marrying an illiterate couple, and the man had to repeat 'I plight thee my troth', he had said 'I plight thee my tooth'. We found the graves of George Osborne and his family, and, as Mar said, their goodness seemed to live on.

I just remember long hot August days, grown ups rather solemn, the women wearing lovely voluminous summer dresses. I remember a treasure hunt, and the very spot in the library where Marc told me not to read it to him as it would strain my eyes (for the light was fading). Whenever we think of our childhood, thoughts of Marc loom very big. He was the promise of the family, the charming, intelligent, affectionate companion of our own age (Humbo being older, grander and more remote) who might have achieved so much.

Mount Street, London, 15 May

Here I am, sitting in my armchair by the telephone ready to go to bed (it being after 10.30), and for the last hour Gladwyn has been lying opposite me on the sofa sound asleep. We had a delicious meal at home; sole (Mrs Cunnington has got the first soles from our fishmonger along the road since 1939, and so I got some too) and asparagus, salad, and rhubarb from Bramfield. Lilies of the valley from Bramfield arrived this morning and scent the room. Yet there is Gladwyn, sleeping happily and heavily ever since the nine o'clock news. At about eleven he will no doubt wake up, yawn, stretch, open his Foreign Office pouch, and settle down to work till well past midnight.

He did vouchsafe one joke, I will admit. When we had finished eating he said, 'Shall I ring for them to clear?' – a remark which carries one back to a lovely comfortable existence when bells worked, and when rung they were answered by 'they', that wonderful race who lived to give us comfort, who knew how things ought to be done, who made life so easy.

Mount Street, London, 28 May

At five I was to go to tea at Sybil's, and arrived there about ten past. Fortunately I had changed, as there seemed to be quite a few people in the room. I greeted her, and Harold who was next to her, and didn't realize that the *pièce de résistance*, with his back to the light, proved to be the Duke of Windsor.[40] The rest of the company was Bogie Harris, Osbert Lancaster, Mrs Kahn and Ben Nicolson. I sat next to the Duke. At first glance he appears extraordinarily youthful, a boyish figure and his small retroussé nose giving him a very juvenile look. But as one examines him more carefully one is almost unpleasantly shocked to see how old, wrinkled and worried his face is, and how pathetic his expression. His hair is golden and I fancy must be dyed, for he must be over fifty. All this was noticed by my short-sighted eyes, which are usually kind to lines and blemishes. He was amiable and alert, but one was terribly aware of his instability. He talked a great deal, not interestingly, but keenly – in fact, he hardly drew breath. We discussed conferences, the Russians, servant difficulties, the French, places he'd been to, and so on. I envy his remarkable memory; he appeared to remember dates and names with ease and accuracy. He spoke with a profound American accent, and used American expressions which rather jarred on me. He kept looking at his watch and wondering why the Duchess didn't arrive, and finally dashed into the next room to telephone to find out what had detained her. Finally Wally came.

Impeccably dressed, in a beautifully simply suit – a yellow skirt and black jacket, small black hat of taffetas on the back of her very neat hair, lovely shoes, the whole appearance one of good grooming and good taste. Her face pleasant, smiling, not plain and not good-looking. Of course nobody curtsied to her.[41] I had only met her once before, years ago, at Diana Fitzherbert's, and reminded her of this, and we spoke of Diana. She was then Mrs Simpson, and I remember Diana telling me how Wally had found a wonderful new fortune-teller who had told her, 'You can't have your cake and eat it'. And when I asked what this referred to, Diana said, 'Oh, don't you know, she is devoted to her husband, but has got off with the Prince of Wales, and wants to keep them both'.[42]

Osbert seemed to think, from gossip he has heard, that Palewski has

[40] Formerly Edward VIII.

[41] To the great chagrin of the Duke of Windsor, his brother George VI had refused to accord the style and rank of Royal Highness to the Duchess.

[42] Cynthia also alleged that at the time of the abdication Wallis Simpson said, 'You can't abdicate and eat it'.

behaved very badly to Nancy Rodd, and that she is remaining in Paris more in a spirit of defiance than because she is enjoying it.

Mount Street, London, 3 June

Two big dinners, two nights in succession, in this heat-wave, have proved exhausting. Last night the party was at the Belgian Embassy, tonight at the Chilean. Both were in Mr Bevin's honour, and enjoyable, had there been but a breath of air. The Secretary of State was in grand form both nights; optimistic, genial, joking. Tonight he came out of the dining-room before the other men and sat sprawling in an easy-chair while all us women were sitting round the room talking in a stiff circle. No one seemed to move, and Mr Bevin had to shout across at us. So to relieve the situation I boldly went over and sat on his right, and Elena Carandini on his left, and thus we had some simple amusing chat, of the nature the S of S enjoys when relaxing. The Polish Ambassador joined us.

Bramfield, Suffolk, 8 June

The Carandinis came for the weekend; they motored us down late on Friday night. We had no one to meet them in the end, but they seemed delighted to be quiet and enjoy the country, and there was a great deal of praise of rustic life, and peasants, and shooting, and pure air. In spite of all this it turned out that Nicolo had never pulled a trigger, and he wore the kind of clothes that foreigners do wear in the country – a well-pressed immaculate grey suit, and long narrow pointed shoes. Elena spent a good deal of time in the kitchen showing Kitty how to make a risotto and gnocchi; the results were perfection.

Mount Street, London, 11 June

Gladwyn tonight went to Eton to address the Eton Political Society, of which Miles is a member. Meanwhile I entertained three charming male friends before going to Sam's party. Sam came, very shy and agitated, and feeling the responsibilities of the evening ahead. Gerry Wellington and David Crawford[43] were the other guests. David is a rare visitor to London, and a very rare person, quite one of the most charming and sympathetic of people.

Afterwards we walked round to Sam's exquisite house in North Audley Street, where we heard the Griller Quartet play Purcell, Mozart and Beethoven. A really lovely evening, and I kept on thinking how wonderful it was that we should all be assembled there again after eight years; that we had all survived the War, and Sam a severe illness last year; and that the house hadn't suffered in any way from the blitzes. Christabel and I were asked to shepherd the guests, since Sydney was in America. The drawing-room is extraordinarily pretty: it has a coffered dome, modelled on the Pantheon.

Mount Street, London, 16 June

As we returned this morning in the train from Suffolk, one old lady said to her companion, 'I'm afraid that we gave the Dean rather a jolt'. I pine to know the context. The same old body later angrily rattled *The Times* I had lent her, and told her obviously paid humble obsequious lesser lady companion that since Mr Bevin couldn't even speak English properly, how could he possibly make himself understood in French, let alone Russian? No wonder he was such a failure, 'Not like Mr Eden', she said. (Was Mr Eden such a success in Russia?)

Mount Street, London, 17 June

This evening we dined at Kew with Nancy who is staying in an old house on Kew Green, belonging to a pansy called Mark Ogilvie Grant. Nancy insisted on it being a gala evening, so we all had to change, and Ogilvie Grant wore a very pretty dinner suit. Nancy wore her two-hundred pounder from Gres which she got last year: very lovely but not

---

[43] David Lindsay, 28th Earl of Crawford (1900–75), married to Mary Cavendish. He was Chairman of the National Gallery and subsequently Chairman of the National Trust, and had been a close friend of Gladwyn when at Magdalen College, Oxford.

worth more than £50 at the most. It had a black velvet bodice, transparent chiffon on the midriff and (so she says) fifty yards of chiffon in the skirt, bordered deeply with black velvet. No dress is worth what she gave for it, and it was all coming to pieces.

Mount Street, London, 18 June

I had a letter this week from Sybil who is staying in Florence with Berenson. Instead of giving me her news she asked me to organize an Ordinary to console her for returning to Hades – not very complimentary to the old country. She then gave a long list of names, addresses and telephone numbers, so I have been busy and think I have now rounded up most of the invited. I have asked a large number of them to come to drinks with me first, as we never get a thimbleful at the Dorch. I hope Sybil won't think I am trying to steal the thunder from her, and that I am like Julie de Lespinasse, starting up a rival salon.

Mount Street, London, 23 June

Tonight to the Clarks' box at Covent Garden for *Trovatore*. We then went to supper with them at Hampstead. They live in an exquisite house, and have lovely taste and unending money with which to indulge their taste. But perhaps this is the flaw in their lives. Everything is too rich and easy for them. They are a strange pair, and there is something curiously inhuman and unreal about them. They had brought bales of furnishing materials back from Italy, which they duly declared, and hadn't had to pay duty on a single inch of it. This good luck would happen to the Clarks.

Mount Street, London, 26 June

We lunched with the Daltons in their flat in 11 Downing Street; they use the two top floors. The rooms are beautifully proportioned and large, and they have a lovely view over Horse Guards' Parade. The dining-room was in the attic and rather hot in this weather, but we had an excellent meal. The party consisted of Ruth and Hugh, Gladwyn and me, Aidan Crawley and John Freeman, both interesting able young Labour politicians. John Freeman is Under-Secretary at the War Office. He was very amusing about Monty and analysed his character very well.

Gatcombe Park, Gloucestershire, 30 June

After an early tea Sam and I went out for a drive in the car, our objective being Berkeley Castle. It looked magnificent, but we couldn't see over it and only penetrated through the first gate. Gladwyn and I used to stay there when old Lord Berkeley was alive, and I remember huge house-parties there. On one occasion there was a discussion about Edward II's murder, Lord Berkeley maintaining that no one in the village could possibly have heard him scream. So Gladwyn and Simon Elwes went into the place where the awful scene was supposed to take place, and though it was late at night Lord Berkeley knocked up the night-watchman (who appeared after a few minutes dressed in a green overcoat and a top hat), and the rest of the guests went outside both gates which were then shut. I must admit we didn't hear a sound, though Gladwyn and Simon were shouting for all they were worth through the open window.

Mount Street, London, 9 July

We dined at the Duke Restaurant and entertained Lord Pakenham,[44] the Kirkpatricks[45] and the Robin Brooks. Pakenham lets his sentiments run away with his very brilliant brain in a most distressing manner. His whole conversation was an apologia for the Germans. We let Ivone deal with him, which he did in the most subtle way, worthy of Jesuitical training. It was like Marc Antony's oration, for he began by praising the Germans and enumerating their merits, and then carefully slipped in

[44] Frank Pakenham, Lord Pakenham, later 7th Earl of Longford (1905–), married to Elizabeth Harman. Chancellor of the Duchy of Lancaster, with responsibility for German affairs.
[45] Sir Ivone Kirkpatrick (1897–1964), married to Violet Cottell. Deputy Under-Secretary of State for Foreign Affairs, later High Commissioner for Germany, and subsequently Permanent Under-Secretary of State for Foreign Affairs 1953–7.

some grim facts about them. But I doubt whether Lord P chose to believe him. His whole attitude was one of religious sentimentality; 'before I was converted', 'after my conversion', he kept on saying. I hope he is soon relieved of his present office, for he must be a menace. He is a very nice man, but shockingly mistaken in his judgement.

Mount Street, London, 16 July

Today I went with Mar and Nicola by car to Eton to take Geoffrey's ashes[46] and place them in Mr Luxmoore's Garden, as arranged with the Claude Elliotts. There was just the old gardener clipping, and in the distance a group of people sitting. The ashes were put just below the summer-house, among the flowers. It was a most perfect day, and Eton looked particularly beautiful. One could understand the great romance of the place, which puts it into a different category to rival schools. One thought of Geoffrey, brilliant, handsome and full of promise, a promise, alas, which never was fulfilled, for he never could get on with people in life, and became strange and estranged, except to a very few friends. Geoffrey's ashes could not have lain in a more peaceful spot, there in that lovely garden, watched over by the chapel and college buildings he loved so well.

Mount Street, London, 17 July

I went to the House of Lords to have tea with Lord Cherwell.[47] The House of Lords is, to my mind, perfection. How I enjoy its pomp and ceremony, its mustiness and dustiness, the Gothic architecture, and the respect shown to their lordships. I hope it lasts a long time. The Prof was very caustic and entertaining at tea, and told me some funny

---

[46] Geoffrey Madan (1894–1947) had been a notable scholar and classicist at Eton and Balliol. After serving in the First World War he attempted unsuccessfully to make money in the City, and was then stricken by meningitis. He is best remembered for his collection of literary ephemera in *Geoffrey Madan's Notebooks*.

[47] Frederick Lindemann, Viscount Cherwell (1886–1957). He had been Scientific Adviser to Churchill during the War, and a forceful advocate of terror bombing of German cities.

anecdotes about Winston. Apparently the latter was annoyed that his doctors didn't wish to make public the nature of his recent operation. 'Why not?', said Winston; 'I'm told some most respectable people have had a hernia'. The Prof is scared stiff of Communism, like some others I know, and is almost pro-German consequently, and of course very pro-American.

Rob and Hannah Hudson are wild in their accusations against the Government.[48] They seem to believe that it consists entirely of crooks and lunatics. Rob says the food situation is so serious that next year we shall have people dying of starvation in the street. I took this statement fairly calmly for I remember in the first year of the War hearing from the same lips that we would all be reduced to living in workmen's cottages and that there wouldn't be enough leather in the country to honour the coupons for shoes. It was amusing to hear him declare that he had no wish to be Prime Minister, for he and Hannah are the most ambitious creatures in the world. But the reason he gave was that he doesn't want to have to sit around and be polite to people! I felt inclined to comment 'You couldn't if you tried'.

Royal Crescent, Bath, 19 July

Muriel [Gore] and I set forth into the town at about eleven, and hastily combed the shops. At Angel's there is a lovely music stand which I am most tempted to buy for Miles; at Jolly's a shaving stand suitable for Gladwyn. As we hope to get our War Damages money soon, I feel opulent.[49] At noon we landed up at Colonel Jenner's where Mr Nelson-Ward joined us. I had warned Muriel that our beaux would be rather old, indeed both are well over eighty, but spry and gallant, and they look upon us as quite young, which is pleasing.

In the Jenners' house there is not an object which is not lovely and priceless. Mrs Jenner does wonderful embroidery, caskets and mirror-frames covered with satin and elaborately worked as in Charles II's time. She is a genius, but was ill and we could not see her. We sat in the garden,

---

[48] Robert Hudson, later 1st Viscount Hudson (1886–1957), married to Hannah Randolph. Had been Minister of Agriculture and Fisheries in the wartime government.
[49] Virtually all Gladwyn and Cynthia's furniture had been destroyed by an incendiary bomb which fell on the Harrods Depository in Barnes.

Muriel and I on one of those swinging garden-seats. But the Colonel and Nelson-Ward, on more steady chairs, trembled even more than us as with their palsied hands they tried to offer us coffee and biscuits. Colonel Jenner seized the magnificent Queen Anne coffee pot and poured it all over the place instead of into the exquisite coffee cup. So I took over.

Mr Nelson-Ward was immaculate in his summer clothes – short black coat, pale grey trousers, correspondent shoes, a cane, and altogether the picture of an aged English aristocrat. One might take him for a retired colonel, not the retired clergyman he is. But his chief claim to fame is to be Nelson's great-grandson, and to remember well his grandmother Horatia. There is quite a case for the theory that she was the daughter of Nelson and the Queen of Naples, not Lady Hamilton, so we like to see a likeness to the Hapsburgs in Mr Nelson-Ward. He doesn't mind much who his great-grandmother was, so long as he is descended from 'The Admiral'.

Muriel and I lunched with Leslie Hartley[50] at Bathford, and we found there David Cecil. He is just finishing a book called *Two Quiet Lives*, being on Dorothy Osborne and Gray, the poet. He is most charming, but obviously delicate, and has all the best of the Cecils in him.

We returned to the Crescent, and at six a cocktail party took place there – quite an event in Bath, but everyone turned up, the more aged aided by one stick, the even more aged by two.[51] Mr Nelson-Ward arrived first and stayed almost last. He took up a good position in the front of the drawing-room where he could view all the guests as they arrived. 'Who is that lounge-lizard?' he asked, as the youngish intellectual entered; and when he heard it was Lord David Cecil, he hastily saw a likeness to other members of that illustrious family and covered up his mistake. I fear the 'King of Bath' is a snob.

Royal Crescent, Bath, 20 July

We called in on Mr Nelson-Ward in his bed-sitting room in the pseudo-nursing home where he lives. He is surrounded by such Nelson relics as

---

[50] L.P. Hartley (1895–1972): author and critic.
[51] Bath in the 1940s was known as 'the place where the young can't live and the old can't die'.

he has not given to Greenwich. On the mantelpiece is a bust of Nelson, and below it hangs a laurel wreath presented annually by Violet Woodhouse. Above is a copy of a large picture of Horatia; above his bed, Lady Hamilton by Romney; above his washhand stand, another drawing of Lady Hamilton; and all around numerous prints, drawings, busts, deathmasks and other representations and possessions of the great ancestor.

Royal Crescent, Bath, 21 July

I find that Colonel Jenner always lays his table, cleans his silver and washes his precious glass, and indeed I am not surprised as it is priceless. But how much better to use the lovely things and get pleasure from them, instead of putting them away. It was a wonderful dazzling display of silver and crystal, but as Colonel Jenner said sadly, it was a case of 'Lucullus dines with Lucullus', as Mrs Jenner is ill upstairs.

Mount Street, London, 24 July

Earlier in the day I had a *rencontre* that I would have liked to have dealt with differently. The scene was Heywood Hill's bookshop, the person Oswald Mosley. He had that look in his eye (they both had) that people no doubt acquire when they are accustomed to being shunned – a kind of studied indifference. Then he began at once talking excitedly about his son Nicky's engagement. Both Oswald and Diana Mosley are evil characters, Lucifer fallen from heaven, and he in particular has a sinister and almost hypnotic power.

Bramfield, Suffolk, 4 August

A gloriously peaceful Bank Holiday weekend, just ourselves and the children. Gladwyn and Miles worked hard in the garden, and today on getting stakes and wire netting put up for the chicken run. We shall have quite a farmyard soon, directly we get the chickens and the ducks, and we already have a pig. He is called Roger, and is so pretty that I doubt we shall have the courage to kill him. The papers are full of the crisis. The situation is bad, but everyone who knows anything expected it would be bad after the War, though the public was kept in ignorance. It will mean hard times for us all. I guess that matters would have been even worse had the Conservatives got in two years ago. But I must confess that I have enjoyed the escapism of these lovely sunny days, in the quiet garden flanked by fine old trees, and the red house, mellow and wise in its age, seemed comforting and to be saying that England had weathered just as bad storms in the past.

Bramfield, Suffolk, 21 August

I spent a good deal of time talking to the Prof. [Lord Cherwell] in the garden. We gossiped about many subjects. He is violently anti-Russian, and absurdly suspicious of the motives of the present government. Considering he is the person who gave Winston advice, and worked out important statistics, it is strange that he should be very inaccurate when by way of stating facts. He says that Dalton ordered fifteen new suits before clothes rationing came in. When I queried this, saying that I had known Hugh all these years, he admitted that he didn't know it for a fact, but that some friend had been told so by a tailor. I said that Dalton had never been well dressed, and just didn't believe it. Then he stated that John Strachey had accepted to dine with a rich business-man at the Hungaria Restaurant, and that dinner for twelve had come to £300. I asked how it could possibly have come to this, even allowing for all the brandies and cigars; and the Prof admitted that it may have been £150, thus reducing the shocking sum by half. It gives one a poor impression of statisticians – Sam always said that you can easily make them prove a point either way – and of a Conservative peer who produces such distortion of the truth.

All the same I adore the Prof. He took a great fancy to Vanessa and Stella, writing in Stella's autograph book his family motto, '*In Stella Tutus*', and asking her to sing for him; and in the evening we persuaded him to play the piano himself, which he did with great energy and emotion, showing quite a different side to the cynical scientific brain that is usually to the fore.

Bramfield, Suffolk, 8 September

Moly[52] was privileged to see my Paris diary, which I think amused him.
He noted that I was scathing about French society, and agreed it was a
justifiable criticism. We talked of those who had been at the Embassy,
and how they had all preferred to go over to Vichy when France fell,
though some of them changed over in due course. Even René Massigli,
the present Ambassador, didn't behave all that well at first. He too was
Vichy, but his archives in Paris, when examined by the Germans, were
thought to be not sufficiently loyal to the cause, and he was dismissed
from his post (I think as Ambassador to Constantinople). We tried to get
him away via Syria, but he wasn't prepared to take such a drastic step, and
he retired to Switzerland, where he remained till the situation clarified.
Then, and only then, did he take the great jump – literally so, as it meant
being whisked over from France by night by our secret agents.

Royal Crescent, Bath, 14 September

Vanessa, Stella and I came here on Thursday and found the house well
staffed with old retainers. It is strange that Mother – who likes to sit in a
howling draught; hardly to eat; never to heat a room, or soak herself in a
hot bath; to have little yapping dachshunds all over the sofas and chairs
and altogether make things as austere as possible – yet manages to have a
staff. Last night she gave a most successful evening party, which was the
main reason for our visit. Evening dress was worn at my suggestion, as I
wished to see Mr Nelson-Ward all got up before he died. And very beautiful he looked too, in an immaculate dinner-jacket, an exquisitely pleated
soft shirt, his pince-nez dangling from a black silk ribbon, and a red carnation in his button-hole. Vanessa made a lovely picture in a Poiret frock of
Mother's of before the First War, in the Empire style; and she wore a gold
Mellilo necklace, and cameos which Mother is leaving her. Stella had to be
in fancy dress as she is too young to wear evening dress, so she put on a
pretty eighteenth-century costume, in which her great-grandmother had

[52] Sir Orme Sargent (1884–1962): Permanent Under-Secretary of State for Foreign
Affairs 1946–9. He had worked in the Foreign Office in London for most of his
career, having been a Foreign Office official in the days when the Diplomatic Service
was a separate career – a 'grub' rather than a 'butterfly'.

got engaged to her great-grandfather (Florence Brunel to Arthur James) when acting Lady Teazle some eighty years ago.

Mount Street, London, 5 October

Today I was in the company of the most beautiful, tasteful, kind, sensitive woman I know – Lady D'Abernon.[53] She is nearly eighty, and is still so lovely that one is reluctant to take one's eyes off her.

She lives in the Barn at Stoke D'Abernon, since the Manor House is still rented by the government for the psychological testing of candidates for the Civil Service. I always say that half an hour with Lady D'Ab would be a much better way of assessing a young entrant's merit. The Barn has been converted by her magic hand. Everything is pretty, beautifully arranged, and with the individual touch which she has given to all the other houses I have known her in. She has always had some magnificent things, but it isn't these that strike one most. It is the gracefulness with which they have been placed, the right touches of colour.

I first saw her when I was a child. We had just gone to live in Kent House and used to go skating at the Prince's Club, just round the corner, where frescoes on the walls, being in the Egyptian style, were incongruous to the ice. I remember among a whirl of grand talented grown-ups who could waltz and do all manner of complicated figures, seeing a tall proud-looking woman who was Lady Helen Vincent. I don't think I consciously came across her until the winter of 1925 when I went to Berlin, and Princess Helena Victoria gave me an introduction. I thought her beautiful, but remote and rather frightening. Queen Alexandra had just died, and I remember thinking her mourning dress was a work of art in itself – she disliked pure black, and at one evening party wore a black tulle dress relieved by a scarf of pale grey tulle, and she had one black pearl ear-ring and one grey one.

Lord D'Abernon was then still in magnificent health, and I must say that even at that age was one of the most fascinating men I have known. They were an astoundingly handsome couple. And they were still so

[53] Lady Helen Duncombe (1868–1954), widow of Edgar Vincent, 1st Viscount D'Abernon (1857–1941). He had been Governor of the Imperial Ottoman Bank 1889–97, and Ambassador to Germany 1920–6.

when, in 1932, I got to know them very intimately in Rome. Lord D'Ab
had by then started the long illness which gradually got worse and
worse, and he was no longer the alert figure he had been. But he still
retained his brilliant quick mind, his good looks, and his charm of
manner. As Mrs Strong said, 'He used to be a young Jove, and now he is
a magnificent Jupiter'. Lady D'Ab was as beautiful as ever, even more so
because she seemed to have softened in her manner and was almost
tender to him. As time went on and he became worse, this touching
devotion was more and more apparent; and his by then speechless gratitude and admiration of her was very moving to see, particularly when
one heard stories of their early days of married life. He had been a great
coureur des femmes and was dubbed 'the Piccadilly Stallion'. And he had a
rather shady episode long ago with the Ottoman Bank in
Constantinople, and she had at one time left him, not able to stand it any
more, and gone to Cairo, where Lady Cromer advised her to return to
him. I fancy they lived rather apart until Berlin, when she greatly
admired his brilliance and made a superb hostess for him.

How well they looked, that old couple, coming forward to greet us in
their apartment in Rome when we first went to dine, she in a wonderful
dark red velvet dress, her short grey hair in lovely loose curls, her skin
very made up but exquisitely smooth – only people with such a fine
texture of skin can afford to use so much make-up with success. Lady
D'Ab's skin is dazzlingly white, she is like a white light, her cheeks
slightly coloured, her eyes bright as a young girl's, her neck smooth; but
she always (since I knew her) seemed to hold her chin forward, I
suppose to conceal a tendency towards a double chin; and now this has
become quite a stoop. Her voice is rather husky and not very strong; her
hands and feet bad – large, and curiously unfeminine. And then when
one talks to her one is delighted at her kindheartedness, good advice
and amusing retorts.

John Leslie was there and our conversation was animated.
Afterwards we wandered in the garden, looking so pretty on this perfect
autumn day, and then she took us into the Manor House, sadly altered
since I had last seen it. I thought of the happy weekends I had spent
there, and saw the bedroom I used to have. I remember Winston being
there in about 1937. He came late, and we were at dinner by the time he
had changed. I was next to Lord D'Ab who was by then hardly able to
move, and he would be fed beforehand and then wheeled into the

dining-room and placed at the head of the table, as he liked to see us all though he could only with difficulty join in the conversation. I remember Winston's delicacy of feeling, waiting standing by his chair to introduce himself, till the opportune moment occurred, not wishing to surprise him or take him unawares. The next night I was placed between them at dinner and acted as a sort of interpreter, being one of the few people who could understand Lord D'Ab's faint whisper, and pass the still amusing phrases on to Winston. He was charming the way he desired to bring out his host; he kept on reminding him of his old days of brilliance – 'Do you remember, Edgar, that time in the House when . . .', and so forth. Then there was some wonderful occasion in South Africa when they had been playing poker (who with? I can't remember) and Lord D'Ab (in his almost inaudible voice) hissed out, 'A thousand pounds to see the hand'. Having difficulty in speaking, he made his sentences as concentrated as possible. For instance, I once asked him what had been the great charm of Laura Lyttelton (the sister of Margot Asquith, who had died young), and he whispered back, 'Gin-and-water voice'.

Then I remember one summer evening when Antoine Bibesco came from London and found Lady Desborough and Evan Charteris (who had long ago been lovers) and others, and he said, 'What ghosts from the past'. And another time when old Count Metternich came, and there was deep emotion in his shaky voice as, on the steps to the terrace, he came forward saying, 'Oh, Lady Helen'. How lovely to be Lady D'Abernon, and to see always on people's faces an expression of pleasure because they are gazing on someone so rarely beautiful. I have often noticed this involuntary appreciation, and she accepted it with natural grace, for she has such good sense, and no coquetry or vanity, and I am told she never had, even in youth.

> *Pourquoi plaignez vous des ans, belle marquise?*
> *Une rose d'automne est plus qu'une autre exquise*[54]

[54] These lines had been inscribed into Helen D'Abernon's album by George Moore. Cynthia quoted them in her tribute in *The Times* in June 1954, a tribute which concluded with Shakespeare's lines:

> . . . hear this, thou age unbred
> Ere you were born was beauty's summer dead

Mount Street, London, 8 October

Today I went to lunch with Victor and Peggy Mallet who are just off to Rome. I should imagine that they would do very well. Victor has good qualities and abilities and is jovial, but it can't be denied that he also has a tendency to bore and can at times be tactless. As we were today *en famille*, a son and daughter present, I could judge how exasperated they some-times got with him, in spite of great devotion. Peggy is very still and quiet, matter-of-fact and sensible, but hard reverting to type. With her fair smooth hair brought back softly into a bun, very little make-up, clothes good but lacking in chic, she is distinctly Germanic, and put me in mind of a prettier Frau Von Hassell – and, this being so, it is strange that the new Embassy she will occupy is the old German Embassy where the Hassells lived.

Mount Street, London, 20 October

'Maudie Dear' rang up just before dinner tonight to tell me the exciting news that she and Oliver are to go to Paris, as the Duff Coopers are leaving in January. Oliver had rung her up minutes before – she wanted me to know at once. I am glad for them, and think they will be a com-pletely natural and suitably correct pair.

Mount Street, London, 24 October

On Wednesday I dined with Ruth Dalton and went to a French film. Ruth blossoms out in the most delightful way in the presence of any-thing French. She has a real love for the French and their quick-witted-ness and art of living. She is altogether a most sincere woman, and I like her more and more. I don't think the average person realizes how genuine and good a great many of these Labour people are. Ruth deplores Shinwell, and the way he put the blame on his experts and the muddle he made of the coal situation. I wonder how much influence she has on Hugh. He is unpopular, with his bullying and hectoring manner, which is a pity as this side of his character is not present when he is at his ease with friends.

Everyone seems to predict (I fancy from politeness) that Gladwyn should get an embassy soon, and I can never succeed in convincing them that we don't wish to go abroad – unless it was Paris, which would be a plum too delicious to refuse. To Italians I include Rome in our choice, though I would prefer not to go there. Niccolo even had the temerity to ask me whether I had a lover here, that I was so reluctant to leave! I said, 'What a question!', which indeed it was.

Mount Street, London, 26 October

Last night I went to Francis' birthday party, given by old Lady Rennell who is about eighty-three and extraordinarily handsome and erect in spite of a slight stroke and having recently broken her leg. It was great fun and a lot of friends were there, both ancient and youthful. Nozzy[55] and Ernest Emmott walked me home – fortunately it was dry – and Ernest (commonly known as 'Withering Heights', being about six foot four inches tall, disproportionately thin, and a kind but crashing bore) never drew breath once, but gave us, all the way, a lecture on charm, blissfully unaware it is a quality he lacks. Lady Rennell's house, 1 Spanish Place, used to belong to the Bowens, and it was there, in the drawing-room some twenty years ago, that I first met Gladwyn.

Mount Street, London, 13 November

There was an enormous dinner and reception at the Italian Embassy. Practically all the Cabinet were there, and a good dollop of Foreign Office headed by Moly whose birthday it was, and various Italians, the *pièce de résistance* being Count Sforza,[56] in honour of whom we were all gathered. The Carandinis' successors, the Gallarati-Scotti, are a charming, cultured, very respectable couple, he rather aged and very much of a stage diplomat. After we had waited fully half an hour we went in to dinner where there was an enormously long table, beautifully decorated

[55] Sir Richard Nosworthy (1885–1966): had been Commercial Counsellor in Rome when Gladwyn and Cynthia had been stationed there.
[56] Count Carlo Svorza, Italian Foreign Minister.

and lit by red candles in the lovely candelabras. I was very pleasantly placed, being between Sir Stafford Cripps and Oliver Harvey. I had never met Sir Stafford before, but had heard a great deal about him from Sam. It was he whom Courtaulds briefed for their case against Celanese, and Sam was impressed by his integrity, honesty and ability.

Mount Street, London, 14 November

Last night I heard the news that Hugh has resigned from being Chancellor of the Exchequer and his place is being taken by Sir Stafford Cripps. What an extraordinary surprise. This morning I rang up Ruth Dalton to tell her how sorry I was about it all. She said the journalist (the political correspondent of the *Star*, a man named Carvel) had pestered Hugh for some information about the Budget just as he was about to enter the House, and in a momentary aberration Hugh had told him a few things, which appeared a quarter of an hour later in one small edition at 3.45. At 4.15 the full Budget was recorded in all the editions. Directly Hugh was told of this earlier edition he went to the Prime Minister and offered to resign, but Mr Attlee wouldn't hear of it; and Ruth herself attached little importance to the incident. Then, after Churchill's tribute to Hugh in the House, he (Churchill) wrote to Mr Attlee saying he had received further information and felt it necessary that there should be an enquiry by a select committee. After this, the PM had to accept the resignation. It seems a tragic end to his efficient tenure of office.

I spoke to Francis Rennell on the telephone. He hates Hugh because Hugh found him very pro-Italian just before Italy came into the War against us, and Francis was convinced that they would not side with Germany, and wished Hugh (the Minister of Economic Warfare) to give them all the oil they wanted. So did Phil Nichols and Maurice Ingram, and none of them have ever quite forgiven Hugh for finding them wrong.

Mount Street, London, 19 November

I returned last night from Gatcombe, where I went on Saturday. Sam had asked me and Christabel together, and also Andrew Butler, who had ratted at the last moment. So it was just us three, and the two nights Christabel was there gave me ample opportunity of studying her. She is the most egotistical person I have ever met. She sees herself, the whole time, playing different parts – the perfect wife, the devoted mother, the charming mistress, the brilliant woman of the world, and the whole while she is selfish, heartless, scheming, hard. I am really not going to enumerate the extraordinary way she carried on, always trying to be the centre of everything, the elaboration of her deceitfulness, the trouble she takes to score a point, to attract attention, or be praised for ingenuity. Though he still loves her dearly, she exhausts him. He is a weary sick man, and she tires him with her absurd affected talk. One absurdity I can't refrain from mentioning. She claimed as her spiritual parents 'Jesus Christ and Cleopatra'!

What a relief it was when she went. We settled down to a happy peaceful restful domestication with quiet interesting talks; Sam knowing, I hope, that nothing was required of him, and he could just be silent or talk when he wished, and drop off to sleep if he felt inclined. He is so good that he should be made as comfortable and happy as possible in his declining years.

Mount Street, London, 3 December

Sam died swiftly and peacefully on Monday afternoon. Dr Shirley rang up to tell me the news; he said (and I thought it was very nice of him) that Sam had been alone in the room with the nurse and Lil.[57] One misses him so terribly. He was so good, so just, loyal to his friends with a loyalty I have never met with before. Dear Sam. Whoever knew him loved him; he believed the best of people, and they were at their best with him. As *The Times* said, he was a great citizen.

---

[57] Meaning the spirit of his late wife Elizabeth Kelsey. She had been a patron of music, establishing the London Opera Syndicate and the Courtauld-Sargent concerts.

1948

❧

Bramfield, Suffolk, New Year's Day

The house looks very pretty with green decorations, and the Christmas tree fills up the entire hall and is best viewed from the gallery. It is decorated with silver and has red candles. The crèche we had from Rome is on a table in the hall, and lit with nightlights. The dining-room is entirely lit by candles; the red-velvet drawing-room curtains look gloriously warm and luxurious.

We saw the New Year in with all the rites which I remember being solemnly performed all the New Years of my life. As Grandpapa was Scottish, it was a matter of great importance to speed and welcome the respective years with ceremony, sentimentality, hope and joy. A little before the appointed hour, we sing a song which Grandmama used to play:

> There's a sound of joy and singing
> In the halls of mirth and light,
> Thy passing bell is ringing,
> Old year, goodnight, goodnight!

Then we put on cloaks and go outside to welcome the New Year, and kiss each other in the cold damp dark in confused rotation. Then back to the fire, where the mulled claret is awaiting us by the hearth, and we pour it into Miles' enormous silver tankard (given him by Sam), and pass round the loving cup, everyone making a toast each time they drink.

Mount Street, London, 14 January

I see that Violet Woodhouse has died. She was an extraordinary woman, exquisite, gifted, almost witchlike, with something of an angel and something of a devil in her. She inspired an almost godlike adoration – she was fastidious, compelling, sometimes wonderfully generous and sometimes very malicious.

It is said that as a young girl her parents wanted her to marry Lord Gage (Rainald and Vera's father), who was a widower, and very musical. To escape from this, she rushed to Gordon Woodhouse and begged him to save her. He had three friends living with him: Bill Barrington, Denis Tollemache, and a man called Labouchere. When she married Gordon, they all continued to have a ménage together, and thus came about this happy arrangement of Violet and her four husbands.

I never knew Labouchere; I believe he was killed in the First World War. Denis was charming, and died some years ago. Gordon, always devoted, and seemingly a dull man, was really a great authority on furniture and old things, and a wonderful cook, it being his role to see to the practical organization of the household. Bill was very attractive, and it was said that he was Violet's love and that she was at one time made unhappy and jealous by him. Personally I have the impression that her relationship with these four men was platonic, and that is why it was possible for them all to live together. Certainly, in the years between the wars it all seemed harmonious, the three adorers sharing one study when they were at Nether Lypiatt, which was furnished with three desks. And now those two old men, Gordon and Bill, having nursed and cherished Violet through her long illness, are left to mourn her. They must be lost without her.[1]

It was Ava Anderson (then Bodley, and Becky Sharpe personified) who first took me to Violet's house at the end of the First War. Violet lived in Ovington Square, and every Sunday afternoon she was at home and used to play and give tea. I was thrilled at entering this milieu where I first met the Sitwells and all sorts of people I longed to know.

---

[1] Violet Woodhouse's 'court' of four husbands was subsequently described in Osbert Sitwell's *Noble Essences*.

Mount Street, London, 11 February

On Thursday Alan came to dine with me.[2] Since Gladwyn was away, I gave him the chance of selecting the company, thinking perhaps that after such a long passage of time he would prefer not to be *tête à tête*. He has been out of my life for nine years. I told Helen he had got behind an iron curtain, and she said she often wondered whether there was anybody behind the curtain. In order to make the dinner a success, I went round to Mr Polly at Jacksons who advised a carefully selected Burgundy. In due course the fire was lit, the table laid, the candles lit, the wine *chambré*, and Alan arrived. Directly he came upstairs I knew all would be well. How we laughed and talked, and remembered old times. What is more pleasant than an evening with an old friend!

Last night I had drinks with Oliver and Maudie, who had come over for the investiture. Maudie looked tired, and so far she has done nothing but boring diplomatic calls, left cards, had difficulty with the servants, and altogether had no private life of her own. The private attaché is kept busy seeing that bills are kept low. Anybody coming to the Embassy in the previous regime ordered drinks as though he or she were at the Dorchester – Jean Cocteau, for instance, would arrange to meet some friend there; and when there was a conference all the secretaries and typists and hangers-on were to be found shaking cocktails at all hours: Diana Cooper once surprised them at this in the middle of the morning. I suppose she and Duff hadn't the strength of mind to put a stop to it. Anyhow, Maudie tells me they left £7,000 worth of debts in Paris!

Bramfield, Suffolk, 22 February

Here we are in Suffolk again. The landscape is as wintry as though it were Christmas – wild, dark, snowy and piercingly cold. And all this in contrast to last weekend when I came down with Deirdre [McLaren] and Alan [Lubbock]. Then it was warm, with a promise of spring in the air; snowdrops out, catkins dangling against blue skies, birds singing 'New, new, new, new',[3] and altogether an exquisite moment to visit the

[2] Alan Lubbock (1897–1990), married to Helen Bonham Carter.
[3] As in Tennyson's 'The Throstle'.

country. We went for long walks, and walked again after tea, it was so beautiful.

Deirdre found peace and happiness in this atmosphere, so much in contrast to the country life and way of living of her in-laws. Alan was at his best – gay, kind and a wonderful companion. He sang favourite songs and read poetry in the evening. To please me he read Tennyson; I liked very much 'The Day Dream', which I did not know. He liked Bramfield enormously, and wants to come again when the children are here. He appreciated all the little signs of their love of the place, and said that homes never really come alive unless there are children loving them.

Mount Street, London, 26 February

Today was one of the happiest days of my life. We saw Miles win the mile at Eton. It was a perfectly glorious day, sunny and cold, the snow had melted considerably and the course was dry, the sky blue, and the trees the delicate colour that comes just before the shoots are about to come out. Off went the gun, and off the runners. By the time I dared look, I observed that Miles was about third or fourth and one boy was well ahead. Dr Prescot said shrewdly, 'We aren't taken in by that'. Round they went the first time and the second time, by now Miles gradually creeping up and running easily, always looking round from time to time to see where he was in relation to the others. In the third round he had got the corner, and in the last round and a half he was leading, and there he was on the last lap (Gladwyn standing near the tape saying, 'Sprint, sprint') and then he reached home. It was just like the Newbolt lines:

> He saw the School Close, sunny and green,
> The runner beside him, the stand by the parapet wall,
> The distant tape, and the crowd roaring between,
> His own name over all.

Later we went to tea in a private room at Rowlands, where we were invited to meet some of Miles' friends. I sat at the head of the table with Lloyd, the President of Pop,[4] exquisite in his purple velvet waistcoat

---

[4] Anthony Lloyd, later Lord Lloyd of Berwick (1929–): President of Pop was equivalent to Head Prefect.

with three shields dangling from his watch-chain, on my right. Miles, by
the way, wears a red waistcoat that can be seen a mile off.

Mount Street, London, 12 March

I spent last weekend in bed with a sore throat, but on Monday night I
couldn't resist getting up and going to the opera, as Ava had asked me to
hear the *Walküre*, and I had not heard any Wagner since the War and was
curious to know how I would react to it. When I listened again to that
sensuous music I felt the old magic once more; it was like somebody
stroking me again with a velvety touch and I was entranced and gave in
to the seduction. But all the same the spell didn't quite work, the wine
didn't entirely go to my head, for part of me remained sober enough to
remember Hitlerism, SS men, concentration camps, cruelty, fanaticism,
blond heroes. Nazism was very much identified with a cult for Wagner.
I'm not sure Wagner wasn't inspired by the devil, for the devil sees that
things are jolly well done. Flagstad sang divinely; she is a superb
Brunhilde, beautiful in her massive way, and with great nobility. Hotter
was also first rate. They sang in English, but one did not mind it.

On Wednesday there was sad news in the papers. Jan Masaryk has
committed suicide. Possibly he felt it the only way out, having decided
to remain Foreign Minister under the Communist regime. When
Gladwyn first heard about Masaryk remaining he said he had sold his
soul. He was much criticized abroad, and was the recipient of many
cruel gibes, which he must have minded intensely. Underneath his
buoyant exterior, always cracking absurd jokes, telling vulgar stories,
talking slang, making light of tragedy, there was a sad depressed spirit,
serious and heavy-hearted.

Once I got very close to him. It was during an air raid and we were all
dining with Sybil at the Dorchester, a whole crowd of us, and some of
them just the last people one would wish to be with at a serious moment
– such as Loelia Westminster and Ann Rothermere and their pretty
awful boy friends. It became so very noisy that we all thought it better to
move to the staircase that leads to the lounge, for the private room in
which we had dined had no protection whatever above. So we all sat on
the stairs, listening to the rockets and bombs and feeling considerably
shaken. I was next to Masaryk, and I remember feeling suddenly that I

knew him intimately because we were together facing something that might be the end of us. Poor Masaryk. He should have been spared this very sad end.

Mount Street, London, 15 March

We stayed the night at Stanstead,[5] where everything was enchantingly unchanged. The Dick Caseys were also there, and my! aren't they dull![6] I knew her long ago as Mae Ryan; she really is very nice, and so is he – but a crashing bore. He bombarded me with a series of dull questions as to diplomatic life in London. At the end of dinner Rab started on India, naturally a sore subject with him, and he criticized the appalling loss of life there and openly blamed the Mountbattens for being a party to this tragedy and for minimizing the figures. This didn't go down well with the Caseys, who think highly of the Mountbattens, so there was quite a heated discussion, which was fortunately brought to an end by them having to catch the late train to London.

Mount Street, London, 22 March

Gladwyn has had to do one of his disappearing tricks, this time to USA.[7] I often say that if I can't produce him more often, and am always explaining away his absences rather lamely (for sometimes a certain amount of secrecy is attached to them), people will begin to suppose that he has been purged. However, in this particular case the cat was badly let out of the bag. I had said goodbye to him about 5.30 and saw him leave in one of the Foreign Office green cars for Northolt. At about ten that evening he rang up to announce that he was still in England, for after they had been half an hour in the air a radio message was received saying that a foreign voice had informed them that there was a bomb on board. So, much alarmed, they retraced their steps, got out, and everybody had to be searched and all their luggage unpacked.

[5] Rab and Sydney Butler's house in Essex.
[6] Richard Casey, later Lord Casey (1890–1976), married to Marian Ryan. He had been a member of the War Cabinet, and was subsequently Governor-General of Australia.
[7] To sound out the Americans on the possibility of a North Atlantic Treaty.

No bomb was found, so it was obviously a hoax. The result of all this being that the *Daily Telegraph* came out with 'Bomb hoax on envoy's plane'.

Mount Street, London, 23 March

Dined with Enid Bagnold in Hyde Park Gate.[8] We sat at a round table in the large drawing-room; there were twelve of us, and I was happily near the fire. The meal was superb – cream all the way through, starting with bortsch. The explanation being that Enid keeps a cow in the stables at the back of the house, which she and her daughter milk.

Bramfield, Suffolk, 7 April

Yesterday Sir Stafford Cripps announced his Budget, and I must say it was pretty staggering. Though not a capital levy, it is as near as makes no difference. I imagine we are ruined, but as I have nobody with whom to discuss the matter, I don't really understand it all.[9] Walking in the garden this morning in the lovely mild spring air, everything made so gay with the bright yellow of the daffodils and primroses, the blossom on the large pear tree coming out, the birds singing, the leaves about to open, it all seemed so happy and full of hope, as April always is. So it was difficult to be depressed. I thought to myself 'The best things in life are free', but wondered how long we shall be allowed to enjoy it here.

Mount Street, London, 15 April

I came up from Bramfield on Sunday to attend the Pilgrims' Dinner the next night, in honour of Mrs Roosevelt. I wore my best, and the Jebb

---

[8] Enid Bagnold (1889–1981), married to Sir Roderick Jones. She was an author and playwright (notably, of *National Velvet*), and he was Chairman of Reuters.
[9] The Budget included an additional 'once and for all' tax on investment income, rising to 50%. Since the standard rate of income tax was 45%, rising on higher incomes, some people had to pay more than their total income, and so it was a capital levy in all but name.

diamonds, and Gladwyn wore his white tie and tail-coat for the first time since 1939. When I used to look at all those boiled shirts and white waistcoats put away all these years and yellowing rapidly, I often wondered whether we should ever see them worn again; and, lo and behold, here they were resuscitated, a bit tight, but nevertheless the genuine article. Gladwyn also wore his CB and CMG for the first time.

We were at Table 7 and could see old Winston remarkably well and Mrs Roosevelt quite well. I had Gladwyn on one side and Simon Rodney on the other. He is a nice mutt, very simple, with a positive worship for his cousin, Winston, and the Conservative Party, and a gentlemanly distrust of anything he suspects of being 'pink'. 'Isn't Sir Oliver Harvey rather inclined to be pink?'. I answered, with a certain amount of asperity, 'Not at all. Sir Oliver gets on with the present government just as well as he got on with Anthony Eden, who was a great friend of his. He is the perfect civil servant, he has no apparent politics, but works for the good of his country, as all civil servants should.' This was a new one on Simon Rodney's simple soul.

Mrs Roosevelt speaks with a charming, soft, very English voice, quite unlike her outsize appearance. Her speech was read, but made to sound impromptu. It was a little high faluting, but I love that. Winston was not on his best form, and was somewhat facetious, which I thought was out of keeping with the occasion. It was Sir Campbell Stuart's Big Night, and didn't he let us know it![10] He was announced with every title and decoration he had managed to scrounge, and he said his say, but I really don't remember what it was.

Mount Street, London, 26 April

A new embassy has been inaugurated in Mount Street, not to be confused with the Brazilians at the other end of the road. The embassy I speak of consists of modest premises; two rooms and a half, and a bathroom, all on the top floor, though of course the situation is very central and a good address. It has the merit of costing the tax-payers

[10] Sir Campbell Stuart (1885–1972): Treasurer of the Franklin Roosevelt Committee, which erected, by means of public subscription, the statue of the President in Grosvenor Square.

nothing, since there is no extravagance involved, no series of vast reception rooms, no large staff of liveried men-servants, no *bella figura* to impress foreigners, no officious female secretaries such as are the bane of Maudie Harvey's life. Indeed, there is not even the expense of a chancery – merely a few unpaid attachés and a faithful counsellor or two.

All this because Gladwyn has somehow contrived to get himself made an ambassador to the Western European Union.[11] I am perfectly happy to be an ambassadress, as long as it does not involve going abroad, and at any rate this new appointment means a reprieve for at least a year. Gladwyn doubtless will enjoy it, and travel around with Uncle Ernie a certain amount; and if this new status may sound a little phoney, what of it?

Mount Street, London, 4 May

By the way, I forgot to mention, when writing a few days ago, about one extraordinary feature of Maudie's life in Paris. She is called at 8.30, but may find herself greatly delayed and sitting about in her bedroom guarding a Foreign Office red box. This contains Oliver's papers which he has taken up to read the night before. During the War a spy, disguised as a valet, cleverly managed to photograph such a box in one of our embassies,[12] so Oliver dare not let the precious object out of his sight. But if he were to take it with him to his bathroom it might get splashed. So the long-suffering Maudie must sit over it and wait till Oliver emerges.

I wish to assure whoever reads this that the Mount Street Embassy knows no such restrictions; that we get up when we like, which is generally as late as we possibly can; and that as Mrs Cunnington is, like Caesar's wife, 'above suspicion', there could be twenty red boxes littering up our modest sitting-room without there being any fear of some foreign-paid varlet pointing a camera at them.

---

[11] He was the British Representative on the Permanent Commission of the Brussels Treaty, the precursor of the North Atlantic Treaty Organization, with the personal status of ambassador.
[12] Cicero, in the Embassy at Ankara.

Mount Street, London, 9 June

I was invited by the Andersons to go for a trip down the river to see the docks. We sailed down past Greenwich and then went into the docks through the locks, and had lunch on the way home to Tower Bridge. I had an amusing conversation with Violet Bonham Carter about relationships with one's children, for (as I told her) it seems Shirley [Morgan] was perfectly happy living with her and would sooner have gone on doing so permanently than return to her own parents. Lady Violet said that the golden rule, of never asking one's children what they have been doing or where they have been, applied to everyone in a household. Everybody has the right to be as secretive as they wish about their doings. I am sure this is true and wise.

Mount Street, London, 2 July

The Youngers invited us to a fork supper at their house in South Kensington. We found ourselves in the bosom of the Labour Party. Already in the room when we arrived were that remarkable couple, Jenny Lee and Aneurin Bevan.[13] She has great personality and strength of character, and I should say, common sense. Quite pleasant-looking in a homely way, and sincere; but, like some orators, she was inclined to gesticulate and hold forth even in ordinary conversation. Aneurin Bevan, with his charm of manner, vitality and Welsh accent, seemed positively delightful. Also present was a distinctly tiresome woman called Miss Fell, who was something in the Central Office of Information. She evidently was out to try and charm Bevan, for she draped herself in attitudes at his feet, pretending to caress the dachshund the while, which she previously had been criticizing.

[13] Aneurin Bevan (1897–1960), Minister of Health, married to Jenny Lee, later Baroness Lee of Ashridge (1904–88).

Bramfield, Suffolk, 12 July

I see in the papers that Emerald Cunard died on Saturday. I can't
imagine what many people will do without her. For though she didn't
entertain on a large scale, she was always entertaining a few friends.
Some of the people one met there lately were pretty dull, but in the
old days it was most amusing. Emerald herself was never dull. She was
almost brilliant in her audacity and surprising conversation: glittering;
sweeping in her statements; amusing; full of gossip but not actually
malicious; devoted to her friends, but could be unkind if she had
something against anybody; very much alive, so much that it is difficult to think of her being dead. On the occasions I have been alone
with her I have found her really delightful to talk to, chiefly because
she was so well-read and interested in life. She could be extremely bad-
tempered, especially with waiters, who obviously loathed her. She was
never called till eleven o'clock and could hardly get anywhere for
lunch till about 1.30. Her best hours were late at night when she loved
to talk and retain her guests till the early hours of the morning. Her
face was highly made-up and she had once had a lovely white skin, but
it had been so much lifted and treated that it was something fantastic
to look at, and I never could make out what was wrong with her
eyelids, for her very bright eyes looked out from such a curious wrinkled made-up mask. Her figure was excellent and upright, and she
dressed neatly but much too young for her age. Her jewellery was
lovely – I remember particularly a large eighteenth-century diamond
rose. Her hair golden. Once one got accustomed to the whole effect it
no longer seemed ridiculous, for she was so youthfully alert in mind;
but I was quite surprised to learn that she was only about seventy
when she died.

She returned to England in about 1943 to live at the Dorchester,
where she had a suite furnished with her own things. She was always
in after five, so it might be said she had a salon. She gave tea to her
guests at that hour, and was always reluctant to offer them drink. In
fact, she hated people drinking. She had a curious horror of any
excess in drinking, smoking, emotion, even in amorousness; though,
as to the latter, she seemed to enjoy getting her impressions at second
hand.

Mount Street, London, 19 July

I spent this weekend staying at the Provost's Lodge at Eton with the Martens.[14] Everywhere are books – on shelves, heaped on tables. Objects everywhere. In each room, a rug lest one felt cold. We were a very clerical party. The Dean of Westminster, Dr Don (one feels he should have been the Dean of St Paul's); Canon and Mrs Crawley from Windsor, who brought with them an American bishop and his wife. The bishop was very handsome and unspiritual, but he was nicely balanced by the canon, who wore a small skull-cap and had a magnificent medieval face and a great asceticism, and might have stepped down from a stained-glass window.

After sherry we moved into the election hall where we were to dine, in great style. The Provost is a delightful host, pleasant, easy-going and amusing. He showed his American guests round the Lodge, explaining in a charming way anything of interest: for instance, slapping the bishop on the back, 'There's George III for you, my lord; don't throw a stone at him', when we came to that monarch's portrait. On Sunday Miles brought two friends for dinner at the Lodge. Simon Barrington-Ward (the son of the editor of *The Times* who died so suddenly in the spring) was brilliant, attractive and extremely nice, but excessively talkative.[15] 'How that boy does jaw', commented the Provost good-humouredly afterwards.

Mount Street, London, 30 July

Passing St Martin-in-the-Fields I went in and sat in the beautiful Wren church where Gladwyn and I had been married on a foggy cold January morning nineteen-and-a-half years ago. Pat McCormick, the Bishop of Norwich, and Percy Maryon-Wilson, had performed the ceremony.[16] They met me and Father in the porch and preceded us up the aisle to the strains of Blake's 'Jerusalem'. I was followed by a retinue

---

[14] Sir Henry Marten (1872–1948), and his sister. He had been Gladwyn's history tutor at Eton.
[15] Simon Barrington-Ward (1930–   ): later Bishop of Coventry.
[16] Pat McCormick (1877–1940) was the Vicar of St Martin's; and the Bishop of Norwich was Bertram Pollock (1863–1943), known to Cynthia at Wretham.

of small children. Bob Boothby was best man, and said afterwards it has been a pleasure to be best man to a sober bridegroom, as the last time he had to perform this duty had been to Gavin Henderson who had to be walked round St Margaret's before he was presentable in the church.

Bramfield, Suffolk, 19 November

The reason I have not written for so long in my diary is that I have had a tiresome accident which caused me a good deal of pain. Back in June, as I was getting my suitcase down from the rack as the train approached Liverpool Street, I contrived to tear some muscle fibres in my right shoulder. I thought little of it at the time, but as time went on it became increasingly painful, and eventually I had to have it manipulated under an anaesthetic and even now it is not absolutely right.

At the end of October I went to Paris with Gladwyn who is there with the United Nations. The first thing that struck me in Paris as we drove from the station was that the women were wearing their skirts much shorter than in London. This is disturbing and confusing, for we have only just managed, with great thought, expense and ingenuity, to lengthen our hems and alter our silhouette to the long full-skirted effect that Paris was wearing a year ago and which was dubbed the 'new look'. The fashions were beautifully but fantastically expensive, even with the franc devalued to about 1,100 to the pound. An evening dress could be 300,000; a day dress 100,000; a mere *copieuse* charged 30,000. Many in society borrow for some special occasion, if they are considered smart or well-known enough to advertise the firm. Personally I much dislike this idea of borrowed clothes, though I find that most of the Embassy wives follow this custom. My own clothes, bought in honest English fashion, were perfectly adequate, if a trifle too long. At any rate they were 'a small thing, but mine own'.[17]

On this particular visit to Paris I saw more old friends than I had done two years ago, and with the passage of time the sense of guilt about the War had faded into the background. Thus it was easier to be

[17] But when she was Ambassadress Cynthia constantly borrowed clothes, principally from Jacques Fath till 1957 and then Jeanne Lanvin.

with them, and to enjoy their good qualities and be less conscious of their faults.

Gladwyn and I and Sammy Hood[18] gave what I think could be described as a brilliant cocktail party in Sammy's house, 66 Rue Pergolese. On the staircase Sammy had hung a large oil of his celebrated ancestor, and there were prints of admirals all round the rooms, which much impressed the French as being very English. Soon the guests streamed in, a large number of whom were unknown to me: Palewski, who is on the water wagon, complains that he has lost his incentive.

We lunched with Nancy one day at her charming house, 7 Rue Monsieur. The large living-room on the ground floor has Nancy's bedroom leading out of it, a small room in which a great deal of space is taken up by an enormous bed above which is an oil painting of Gaston Palewski by Madame Auric. There are two schools of thought about this altogether curious affair. One of these believes, as Osbert Lancaster says, that 'when it comes down to brass tacks, so to speak, the friendship is platonic.' I am rather inclined to agree with this faction, and fancy that Nancy's chief interest in Palewski lies in the extraordinary passion she and all her sisters have in dabbling in politics, or rather, being connected with somebody in a big political way – for instance, Unity and Hitler, Diana and Oswald Mosley. Palewski is an eminent follower of de Gaulle. A Pole by descent, if not by birth, he is undoubtedly a bounder, and if Nancy is seriously devoted to him she must suffer greatly from his notoriety with other women. However at the moment she has 'Prod' with her, and seemingly for a long time. Having come into some legacy he gives up his existing job (if there is one) until the sum is blown. Therefore he is with his wife in Paris, spending most of his waking hours in the Travellers' Club or in the bars. Nancy was dressed in full Highland costume. A kilted skirt of Royal Stuart tartan and a plaid worn diagonally across her shoulders. Apparently she met the Duke of Windsor at a party in this get-up, and he didn't approve at all, and said to the Duchess, 'We'd better be going 'ome now'.

Home again in London, Nigel [Nicolson] told me an amusing story about Ben. Ben looks after the King's pictures, and Princess Elizabeth said to him, 'I'm thinking of having my portrait painted by Oswald

[18] Samuel Hood, 6th Viscount Hood (1910–81): Counsellor at the Paris Embassy.

Birley. Do you think that would be a good idea?' Ben was unable to make any answer; he merely gazed back at her dumbly, and thus they remained, staring at each other for what seemed to him an eternity. The Duke then remarked; 'That evidently was not a good suggestion': so the Princess said, 'But who would you choose for a portrait then, Mr Nicolson?'; and Ben stated dramatically and decisively: 'Ma'am, the art of portraiture is dead in Europe'.

Bramfield, Suffolk, New Year's Eve

This evening Vanessa went to the Henham Harriers Hunt Ball at Flixton with Mrs Pollock, the late Bishop of Norwich's widow (a gay, feckless good-humoured woman who he had made his secretary and then married – she being then about twenty-five or so, and he well over sixty) and her daughter Rosalind. Vanessa, with a courage which I was delighted to observe, went to the dinner accompanied by a young man who she had not seen since she was about two years old, one young man having failed us already. He was due to arrive at Darsham Station at 7.20 and make a lightning change. She was dressed in her best taffeta and, with a narrow black velvet ribbon round her throat, and a Mellilo brooch Aunt Lily had given me, she really looked beautiful. I only hoped that the young man would prove worthy of such an exquisite *jeune fille en fleur*. But meanwhile time passed and he did not arrive. The rest of us sat down to dinner, and finally he came, a little young man with spectacles, rather sure of himself in manner but perhaps unsure underneath. Anyhow, there he was, pitchforked into a family of strangers, told to change as quickly as possible, and whirled off to some more strangers. Vanessa could not see him properly because, being all dressed up for the party she had not got on her spectacles and she anxiously asked what he really looked like, while he was upstairs. The whole thing was rather like a scene in a play.

1949

Mount Street, London, 4 February

Last night we went to *The School for Scandal*. Sybil, who is an intimate friend of 'Viv' and 'Larry'[1] procured the Royal Box, the party consisting of Sybil, Gladwyn, me, Fred Warner and Nigel Nicolson. It was quite delightful – beautiful scenery, and dresses designed by Cecil Beaton. Sir L O was an old sad charming Sir Peter, absolutely shattered when the screen fell and revealed Vivien Leigh who had been the perfect minx and now showed real shame and grief. If one were to criticize, it would be to say that such an excellent play should not be disturbed by cheap little affectations. Such things completely spoilt the glorious scene when the gossips are spreading rumours of Sir Peter having fought a duel. Instead of being able to concentrate on the delightful development of the rumour, one could hardly take in the words because the actors were made to prance around in circles almost as though they were dancing.

Afterwards we went round to see the Oliviers in her dressing-room – a large room just off the stage, filled with masses of flowers. Vivien Leigh is small and slight, but she has lovely eyes, a very pretty retroussé nose, a heart-shaped face, and she was very animated and alert and intelligent to talk to. He was a great deal taller than I had imagined, exceedingly good-looking , and he was modest and charmingly shy. I told him about Stella's admiration for him; he pressed my hand, saying; 'Tell her to go on loving me always'.

[1] Sir Laurence Olivier, later Lord Olivier (1907–89), married to Vivien Leigh (1913–67).

Bramfield, Suffolk, 19 February

Gladwyn was to have received the accolade at an investiture fixed for 1
March. But it seemed possible that he would not be in England on that
date, and therefore not allowed to use the title for sometime to come.
But suddenly Miss Marchmont rang me up very excitedly to say that we
were bidden to Sandringham the next day, to dine and sleep.

We reached Wolferton Station a little after six, from where we were
ushered into a large car and were soon bowling along the broad impeccably kept drive towards a large sprawling mid-Victorian building. We
swept round under a porch, and there were several servants awaiting us
dressed in what is now the Royal Household livery, and really nothing
more than navy-blue battledress with the royal monogram on it, an
economical and sensible uniform devised in the War by Sir Piers Legh.
We got out of the car, and then shook hands with Tommy Lascelles
who was in the hall. Lady Hyde came forward, and a figure was slowly
approaching from the other end of the big hall; 'The Queen', murmured Lady Hyde, so I went to meet her and curtsied.

The Queen is about my height. She has very dark hair which I should
imagine must be dyed; blue eyes; a pretty skin, with very little make-up
on it; a very charming smile which, even in repose, remains in her
expression, giving an expression of serenity and agreeableness. This,
enforced by a soft voice and considerate, sympathetic and tactful words,
produce an effect of great charm.

After a little talk she suggested that I might like to take off my hat and
see my room, and then perhaps come down for a game of Oklahoma.
This I had never played but was told it was a form of rummy. I remembered that in royal circles one plays a great many games of all sorts – *toujours les petits jeux* – and I heard from Ben of 'Murder' frequently being
played at Windsor, and from friends who had stayed at Glamis how they
sang and danced Nuts in May after dinner.

There was a lovely fire burning in the grate in my bedroom and the
housemaid was unpacking. The walls were thickly plastered with small
watercolours of the Edwardian period. There was a large mahogany
double bed, flanked by a pair of po cupboards, all this discreetly
screened off by a screen with pictures hanging on it. An armchair by
the fire, a sofa at the foot of the bed, a marble-topped wash-hand stand
with a good old-fashioned set of crockery on it – a large basin and a

smaller basin, a good selection of glasses (tooth, wine and medicine) and carafes. Then a large wardrobe for hanging clothes, and a 'gentleman's wardrobe' for lying clothes; a coat-stand with hooks on it such as one might have in a hall; a writing-table, on which lay every conceivable accessory to writing – a variety of pens, bottles and brushes for wetting stamps, rulers, elastic bands, clips, paper-knives, and a magnifying-glass, all with large 'A's for Queen Alexandra affixed to them; a pretty china clock with *'Qu'elles soient toutes heureuses'* written on it – in fact chiming clocks abounded everywhere in the house, and there was another on my mantelpiece. By the dressing-table stood an object that puzzled me for a while. It was a tall small table, and on it a brocade cover over a sunk cushion of red velvet. I guessed it must be for maids to lay out their mistresses' jewels: a wonderful touch, this! Between me and Gladwyn was a bathroom, red-carpeted, beautifully solid in fixtures, also hung with pictures; the bath towels were vast solid ones, unobtainable these days.

Having tidied myself, I went down to the hall. All the entourage get on very well together, and this obviously is of great importance, since they are thrown so much on each other. There is a good deal of time when they have to hang around waiting, always ready to spring to their feet the moment royalty appears. The time is passed in light badinage, which to my taste would soon pall. This game was chiefly carried on by Townsend and Legh,[2] and the intellectual level was not high but certainly good-humoured. Lady Hyde and I laughed obligingly at the sallies.

Suddenly we all leapt up, for the Queen had returned and suggested a game of Oklahoma. In the midst of our game there was a movement heard off, and the King walked briskly into the room followed by Gladwyn and Lascelles. The King was in tremendous form, alert, cracking jokes, moving about easily, and obviously his state of health had greatly improved. While we were talking, waiting to resume our card game, Princess Elizabeth and Prince Philip also appeared, and the Queen introduced me as Mrs Jebb, whereupon the King at once corrected her, 'Lady Jebb', he said; and he said to me, 'Didn't you feel a little something happen round about seven?'. He then came and helped me

[2] Group Captain Peter Townsend (1914–95), Equerry; and Sir Piers Legh (1890–1955), Master of the Household.

with my cards. All very homely and informal, calling the Queen 'Ducks', and shouting for 'Buttons and Bows' to be put on the radiogram which the Edinburghs had turned on.

At eight o'clock we went to change for dinner, which was at 8.30. There was a considerable wait until the King and Queen appeared. She wore a very beautiful dress, unmistakably Hartnell, of black net richly embroidered with coloured paillettes, very much crinolined, and with little puff sleeves and a black net scarf: her usual three rows of pearls and some diamonds. She really looked magnificent as she came from the passage round the archway, walking slowly and with grace, and carrying the bulk of her figure encased in its swinging panniers with an unforgettable dignity. The King wore a smoking jacket of what I took to be Royal Hunting Stuart.

Princess Elizabeth has pretty light-brown curly hair, worn short; a fair skin with soft English colouring; pleasant features, and a most charming mixture in her expression of eagerness to please and yet a serious awareness of her rank and responsibility. Her charming diffidence was very appealing, for a touch of genuine gravity was always the traditional barrier which separated royalty from the common herd, warning them that no liberty should be taken. But all this with a sweet smile, a very pretty soft voice, and a certain gaucherie in her walk, showing her to be still just a young girl. Two of the most delightful sidelights that I noticed on our visit were the real devotion and affection between the Princess and her husband and the Princess and the King. The father and daughter seemed happy in each other's company, and talked together eagerly and animatedly. She and Prince Philip spent a great deal of time talking and discussing their plans, all most naturally and affectionately. Gladwyn, who had quite a talk with Prince P, had a most favourable impression of him.

We went in to dinner, first the King and Queen, followed by Princess Elizabeth and her husband, then me and Lady Hyde, and then the men. At table, in front of the King, was an array of objects containing his favourite delicacies or necessities – such as medicines, biscuits, iced water and other things. The dinner was excellent without being ostentatious. The conversation slid along easily, if neither profoundly or intellectually. The King is naturally alert, highly strung, simple and downright. I never once heard that impediment in his speech we are so accustomed to hear in his broadcasts. Like all royalty he likes a good

straightforward joke, and if it borders on improprieties such as lavatories, all the better. While we were having coffee the doors were
opened and there appeared a piper who walked twice round the table
playing; I revelled in this Scottish rite, but Gladwyn thought it an unnec-
essary touch.

After this the Queen rose and the ladies left the room, I curtseying to
the King before we went out. All this ceremony, this curtseying and
standing about, was, I suppose, the usual polite behaviour in good
society in the eighteenth century. We live so unceremoniously these
days, and manners have so deteriorated, that it was a constant effort to
remember it all. I do honestly feel that curtseying is a gesture that has
now become obsolete, and its absence would in no way detract from the
dignity of the Crown.

At about half past eleven the King said it must be time to go to bed.
Our original plan had been to leave next morning. But when Gladwyn
joined me upstairs he said that the King had sent a message asking us to
stay for lunch.

I came downstairs a little before eleven, at which hour the
Edinburghs were departing. Princess Elizabeth was in a fur coat
without a hat; the baby, very sweet and looking fine, in the arms of his
nurse. At a discreet distance stood a personage in black whom I took to
be the housekeeper, Mrs Butcher. The Duke kissed the Queen
goodbye, and then with a quick gymnastic movement kissed her hand,
which I believe is the correct procedure. It was a drizzling day, and
Gladwyn and I felt some alarm at seeing the Duke, who has the reputation of being rather a wild driver, starting off on a long journey driving
the two immediate heirs to the throne.

Before lunch we were asked to sign our names in the visitors' book,
and to write only the date on which we left – this last a custom I had
not met with before. Tommy Lascelles then showed us the old
Edwardian book containing the weights of the guests. People were
expected to write down what they were wearing at the time of being
weighed, and this naturally led to facetious remarks such as 'In hunting
boots after a heavy meal', 'In a négligé' and 'In a peignoir'. He pointed
out the name of the Duke of Clarence, the elder brother of George V
who was to have married Queen Mary but died very suddenly (of
drink, Lascelles told Gladwyn). When the Duke of Clarence stayed at
Sandringham his valet was asked what time his master would want

breakfast, to which the servant replied, 'His Royal Highness is always sick at eleven'.

My impression of the royal family, particularly of the King and Queen, is that in some ways they are extremely human, agreeable and sensible. And yet as individuals they are completely apart from the ordinary person, and this is because their existence is so unnatural. The King, who represents a typical Englishman, is not in fact in the least like one. He is that race apart, royalty, and his Germanic blood is noticeable in the guttural tone in his voice. In ordinary life he would have remained an ordinary man, but always a very good one. The Queen too is quite unlike any other woman. The conventional but elaborate appearance, the slow dignity and agreeable charm, all belong to a person who is not leading an ordinary life. And one is tempted to wonder how she might have developed if she had made a non-royal marriage. On the other hand one must remember that the comfort and ease and smoothly-running itineraries are only one side of the picture. There must always be a sense of anxiety and strain in their responsibilities, and their concern for the state of the country; in the fear of decreasing popularity and creeping socialism; in taxation; in changing ways. In spite of all this they continue to live the life they have always led, to keep up as much ceremony as modern times permit, and to set a magnificent example to their people of real goodness, correct behaviour, and integrity.

Mount Street, London, 2 March

We dined tonight at the Swedish Embassy. Mme Haeggloff is a most extraordinary woman. She is Italian, and has apparently offended many Swedes by being very rude to them, which cannot be a wise move. Sometimes she has violent excesses of temper and throws the furniture out of the window. And on one occasion, in Moscow, when the Ambassador was in uniform and about to present his credentials, she locked him in the lavatory and left him there for several hours. Then she annoyed people when giving a fancy-dress party the other day. A lot of trouble and expense was taken about the costumes, but Mme Haeggloff herself appeared in ordinary clothes.

Old Quarries, Gloucestershire, 20 March

Sydney and I are spending the weekend with Ruth Lee in Gloucestershire.[3] Ruth is a charming, gentle, sweet feminine woman, with a helplessness which comes from her rich American upbringing followed by a life perfectly organized for her by her husband. She left all decisions to him, and because of him latterly saw few friends. Thus she is now completely alone with beautiful possessions, adequate money, but no particular interests. She is not a weak character, but a pale pastel character, delicate and not strongly marked. I observed that she and Sydney suited each other perfectly – Sydney brisk, practical, dominating, not wasting words, making sensible decisions quickly. I feel they might become good friends, so that the Butlers, coming frequently to Gatcombe to see after the farm, may help to solve Ruth's lonely problem of how to go on living at Old Quarries.[4]

On Saturday we made an expedition to a most interesting place – Highnam Court, near Gloucester. This is a large house, built in about 1660 on the site of an older house burnt down in the Civil Wars. Inside, living entirely alone, was a most eccentric elderly man called Mark Gambier-Parry. He looked unhealthy and *mal soigné*, and was suffering from gout and also from some affliction to his eye, for round his head was a gauze bandage which held in place a rather insanitary pad of cotton wool which he was constantly adjusting. Being cold, he wore a greatcoat and carried a stick to support himself. He inherited the place from his grandfather who, as a handsome young man of seventeen, did the Grand Tour and began collecting Italian primitives, which was unusual at that time. Apparently he and Prince Albert were almost the only people doing so. Highnam Court is thus full of exquisite pictures; and, having no relation who appreciates them, Mr G-P has said he will leave them to the Courtauld Institute, though he has never put this in writing. He turned to

---

[3] Ruth Moore, widow of Arthur Lee, 1st Viscount Lee of Fareham (1868–1947). She was the American heiress on whose money he was able to pursue his political career, and to purchase the Chequers estate, which he gave to the nation in 1917 as a country residence for British Prime Ministers.

[4] The Gatcombe estate was adjacent to Old Quarries, and Samuel Courtauld had purchased it as a favour to his great friend Arthur Lee, who had been sunk in gloom at the thought of it being acquired for a (sic) lunatic asylum. It was subsequently sold to the Queen, who gave it to Princess Anne.

Ruth with, 'It is interesting to think that one day our pictures will be cheek by jowl', a statement which she and Sydney did their best to amplify.[5]

The bedrooms had not been touched since 1850, and were just like those I remember so well in my childhood: wallpapers, chintzes, no electric light, iron bedsteads, large suites of furniture. I thought of the maids bustling around with clothes, bringing cans of hot water, placing the tin bath in front of the fire, dressing one, undressing one, brushing one's hair. The house would have been full of relations and guests, and now it was echoing and empty save for this lonely cranky old man. Mother remembers the house in the days of its grandeur, being taken there when she was about sixteen by her father, Arthur James.

Mount Street, London, 21 March

Tonight we dined with the Terence Maxwells, and afterwards went on to a party at the Italian Embassy for prizes to be given to Laurence Olivier and other film stars who were chosen by judges at Venice.

We arrived about an hour after the party had started and were greeted by Jane and K. Clark on the pavement, who told us in loud voices that it was a most dreadful party and they were leaving and wished their car would turn up, and we should on no account pay off our taxi as we should certainly need it again in a moment. All this could be overheard by the servants of the Embassy and the chauffeurs and the bystanders who were waiting outside to catch a glimpse of the film stars. I thought it showed very bad manners on the Clarks' part and very typical of them. They had a long wait for their car and so were able to repeat their remarks to those who arrived after us, such as Nigel Nicolson, Oliver Esher and Sybil. In fact, they were picketing the party!

Mount Street, London, 26 March

David and Sybil Eccles[6] were lunching with us on Thursday, and David told us how the previous day he had been in the House of Commons

[5] Anthony Blunt eventually succeeded in securing this collection for the Courtauld Institute, despite the prevarications of Mark Gambier-Parry.
[6] David Eccles, later 1st Viscount Eccles (1904–   ), married to Sybil Dawson. He was subsequently Minister of Education.

Andrew Noble, Cynthia's formidable grandfather

Celia Noble with her daughters Marjorie and Cynthia

Diana Cooper reclining on the bed of Napoleon's sister Pauline
at the British Embassy, Paris

Ernest Bevin signing the Peace Treaties in February 1947: standing, from left, Christopher Mayhew, Orme Sargent, Oliver Harvey, Hector McNeil and Gladwyn Jebb

Harold Nicolson giving one of his radio talks

John Anderson, with his wife Ava, about to present his budget in April 1944

Samuel Courtauld, the sensitive
and discerning patron of the arts

Sydney, daughter of
Samuel Courtauld and wife
of R A Butler

R A Butler as a young politician in the 1930s

when Hector McNeil was making a speech which was so excessively boring that, for want of something better to do, he suggested to his neighbour that they should ogle the pretty girl who had come to hear the debate from the Speaker's Gallery. They made signs to her, to which she quickly responded. Imagine his consternation on learning today that this had been Princess Margaret. He was annoyed with himself for making such a mistake, but also surprised that she responded so readily.

Bramfield, Suffolk, 10 April

Nigel Nicolson is here for the weekend. He is such a nice kind person, but a little too much absorbed in himself, and too conscious of all sorts of little mistakes he may have made, and which he exaggerates, I fancy, to make a story. In fact, his whole conversation was about various gaffes of which he had been guilty. This is very like Harold, his father.

Bramfield, Suffolk, 8 May

I called on dear old Lady Thompson, who lives at the Priest's House at Blythburgh. She has a friend with her as a companion and leads a delightful happy life in her pretty house and lovely garden, above the strange desolate land of the Blyth. She spends her evenings reading, and said she wouldn't part with her evenings for fifty thousand pounds. That indeed is the way to live; that is civilization. She is also a glorious pillar of British honesty. Recently on a journey she told the railway ticket office that as she had made a detour by Oxford she owed British Railways 2/6d, to which the man replied, 'Well, who is to know about it?' To which she said indignantly, 'But *I* know!'

Bramfield, Suffolk, 19 May

Tomorrow I go to Evan Tredegar's memorial service at the Oratory.[7] He was a very old beau of mine. Mad, hectic, a curious mixture of being

---

[7] Evan Morgan, 2nd Viscount Tredegar (1893–1949). Contributed essays to the Royal Society of Literature on Donne and on Mysticism in Verse.

highly religious and not a little vicious; yet he was a good friend always, amusing, a generous host, and above all, he had *beaucoup de race*. I remember a party at Claridges. We were about a hundred, and the Infanta Beatrice was on one side of him, and I on the other. This led to a lot of gossip, but it was quite untrue that we were ever engaged, though I think old Lord Tredegar would have liked it, for he got on with me very well. But I think I was one of the few respectable people Evan had brought into the family circle, and his father was pleased that I took trouble with him. I expect he could not understand Evan's oddness, and religious mania, and curious way of living. Indeed, who could?

Mount Street, London, 13 July

Last night we were up very late as we went to a ball given by the Allied Circle. The Duchess of Kent, escorted by Sheila Birkenhead, was there, and we sat at her table. She is very amiable, and a very handsome woman. Rab once told me that the Duke of Kent talked to him most maliciously and scathingly about the King and Queen, saying they were middle-class. The most delightful part of the evening's entertainment was a performance by the Marx Brothers; there is something really endearing about them. Sir John Maud,[8] having engaged Harpo in conversation, discovered him to be a good family man with four children.

Mount Street, London, 14 July

This evening D'Arcy Osborne came to see me and we spent about an hour having a most charming talk.[9] He is a delightful and sympathetic person, very tied up in many ways. He is a great friend of the Queen. He now lives in Rome in the flat which used to belong to Lady D'Abernon.

---

[8] Sir John Redcliffe-Maud, later Lord Redcliffe-Maud (1906–82): Permanent Under-Secretary at the Ministry of Education, and subsequently Ambassador to South Africa.

[9] D'Arcy Osborne, later 12th Duke of Leeds (1884–1964). He had been Minister to the Holy See, and was incarcerated in the Vatican during the German occupation of Rome 1943–4.

He said he thought there was much more cause for Communism in Italy than here, because there were certain people still hugely rich there, and some really starving. Peggy Mallet, it seems, does not like being in Rome and does not conceal the fact, which is a pity; but Victor is very happy. So we gossiped away and then D'Arcy had to go and dress to go to a party at Buckingham Palace.

Mount Street, London, 20 July

Today Vanessa and I went to the Cavan wedding.[10] It was at St Peter's Eaton Square, which I had not been in since my early childhood when we lived in Eaton Place. I was able to point out to Vanessa the gallery where we sat. We then went on to the reception at Lord Strafford's house in St James's Square, and how nice it was to have a party in a fine old large dignified house.[11] There was a tremendous crowd, and when the Queen wished to leave, Jack Ward had to show her out by the back stairs.

From the wedding, where we enjoyed champagne, we went to Humbo's cocktail party,[12] or rather, champagne party, for Gordon and Nicola.[13] It was a most merry affair, but I doubt how much Gordon enjoyed meeting such a rowdy affectionate lot of people, who were chiefly preoccupied with being together and a little oblivious of the happy occasion. Such a kissification, such reminiscences, such elementary family jokes.

I then moved on to the Makins' party.[14] This is an annual late July function in the Makins' parents' house in Queen's Gate. It is strange to

[10] Mark Longman (1916–72), a second cousin of Gladwyn, was marrying Lady Elizabeth Lambart, daughter of the late Earl of Cavan.

[11] Destined in time to become the Libyan Embassy, besieged after the murder of WPC Yvonne Fletcher in 1984.

[12] Sir Humphrey Noble (1892–1968), Cynthia's brother, married to Celia Weigall. He had inherited the baronetcy of his grandfather Sir Andrew Noble, that of Noble of Ardmore and Ardarden.

[13] Gordon Campbell, later Lord Campbell of Croy (1921–), was about to marry Cynthia's niece Nicola. A diplomat, he was subsequently a Member of Parliament and became Secretary of State for Scotland.

[14] Sir Roger Makins, later 1st Lord Sherfield (1904–), married to Alice Davis. A Deputy Under-Secretary of State and subsequently Ambassador to the United States 1953–6, his diplomatic career moved in parallel with Gladwyn's.

think that the Makins' is now the only private house in this road. It was built in about the sixties and is a perfect example of a rich man's home of that date, and fortunately it has never been changed. The William Morris wallpapers are still on the walls, and he also designed the fireplace and the curtain material. There are many Pre-Raphaelite paintings; and several old retainers complete the picture.

Bramfield, Suffolk, 23 July

The Pakenhams came for a brief weekend. He has a brilliant brain – I believe he is considered about the best speaker in the House of Lords – but his emotions sway his brain to such an extent that one could describe him as unbalanced. Elizabeth is very pretty, with an almost beautiful expression in her countenance, gentle, serene, and understanding. She must be well under forty and looks young in spite of having produced eight children. In addition she is extremely intelligent. It was she who became a Roman Catholic; it is said that she then converted him, and he converted her to Socialism. Frank Pakenham told me that when he first had an audience with the King, the King stammered out straight away, 'Wh-wh-wh-what m-m-made you join them?'; and Frank didn't really know whether he was referring to the Roman Catholic Church or the Labour Party. He assumed it was the latter and gave a rather lame answer, for he thought his real reason, that every individual had an equal right, sounded disloyal to the monarch.

Frank, sitting on the lawn after lunch, was very outspoken about his party, and I thought Elizabeth might wonder at the wisdom of these confidences, though I tried to give an impression of discretion. He said what a menace Aneurin Bevan was, how unpopular Hugh Dalton was, how jealous Bevin was of Morrison, etc., etc. Nothing very new, but perhaps he should not say these things about his colleagues.

Strasbourg, 10 August

My summer holidays have suddenly been diverted into a quite new and unexpected channel. Instead of spending them quietly and uneventfully at Bramfield, picking roses and lavender in the garden, going for long walks through the fields and woods, having strong cocktails and simple conversation with the neighbours, I find myself, *à l'imprévu*, translated to Strasbourg. The reason for this is the Council of Europe, which Gladwyn has to attend.[15]

Today I dressed smartly in black in honour of the opening of the Council. At lunch beforehand I was introduced to Strasbourg food, and it is indeed stupendous and delicious. It was staggering to see how much was put on our plates, how succulent it was. At a little after three, Mrs Bevin and I went off in our car to the opening. Everything in the street was gaily decked out – crowds watching us, girls in Alsatian dress, troops and police. We entered and sat in the front row of the tribune, from where I saw many friends and celebrities. The opening was brief. Herriot[16] made an eloquent speech, and then M Reynaud[17] proposed that everything should be adjourned till the next day, this being to allow M Spaak to become President when the Belgian election results were out.

We returned to our hotel, the Maison Rouge, and, it being very hot, we were glad of tea offered to us in the Bevins' sitting-room. Here two electric fans cooled the air as the S of S cannot stand too much heat. A pair of socks, hung up on a string at the bedroom window, presented a homely touch. The tea seemed strong to me, but the Bevins referred to it as coloured water and Mrs B adjured us to stir the pot with a teaspoon. Later we dined with the Bevins, a superb meal chosen by Eddie Tomkins who has French blood and so knows what's what.[18] Uncle Ernie sank his large genial weight down in his chair and began the conversation with the pleasant informality and friendliness which is his great charm. He asked Mme Lange whether she knew English, and on hearing that she did he grinned, 'Good, we'll now know not to say anything against you'. He seemed in cracking form, except for a brief interlude when he had to take a pill for his angina, and retire for a few minutes to the bedroom. But he soon returned, all smiles and jokes.

[15] It was on Gladwyn's suggestion to Bevin that the Council of Europe was based at Strasbourg, as a gesture towards eventual Franco-German reconciliation.
[16] Edouard Herriot (1872–1957): President of the French National Assembly and a former French Prime Minister.
[17] Paul Reynaud (1878–1966): French Prime Minister.
[18] Edward Tomkins, later Sir Edward (1915–), and later married to Gill Benson. He was subsequently Ambassador to France 1972–5, and she had been Cynthia's social secretary at the Paris Embassy.

Strasbourg, 11 August

Winston is behaving in a most difficult way, which is depressing to all
who sincerely wish this Council to be a success. As a Frenchman said to
us, 'We understand, for we too suffered from a great statesman who
would not retire': he was thinking of Clemenceau. I must not omit to
mention what Bevin calls 'the Churchill circus' – Randolph, Duncan
Sandys, and all his hangers-on. All intriguing hard.

We went to a Mozart, Bach and Rameau concert in the cathedral. The
music was so inspiring in that beautiful setting that it seemed a good
omen, and one felt that perhaps the Council of Europe would resolve
itself successfully after all. We were received at the door of the cathedral by the archpriest, a tall, thin, distinguished figure, with a pale gaunt
face, an aquiline nose, and great dark eyes. He looked like Richelieu. He
spoke perfect English and had the most courtly manners. The cathedral
was beautifully lit, and between the piers in the nave hung splendid
tapestries which belong there and are brought out on special occasions.
It all made an unforgettable impression; and in addition I had the
honour of being presented to that fine old statesman, M Herriot, whose
writings I have always admired. He is aged, large, cumbersome, but a
splendid old man of great eloquence.

Strasbourg, 12 August

This morning I was to go with the Consul's wife to see the famous clock
in the cathedral strike twelve, and I asked Mrs Bevin if she would care to
come, as it is a great sight to see. All manner of complicated things
happen in close succession, including the passing of the twelve apostles
and the cock crowing three times. The crowd was dense, but we
managed to get Mrs Bevin a chair by explaining to the verger who she
was. He was a strange figure, bursting out of his dark blue coat, his red
face adorned by the most striking large red beard, beautifully kempt and
ill-according with a revolting halitosis that emanated from him; alas, he
insisted on speaking to us at the closest range. His admiration for the
British was great, and there was a long yarn about Trafalgar Square and
Lord Nelson – at whose name he solemnly popped on his little grubby
velvet cap which he had dropped on the floor, in order to remove it

again with a reverend flourish. He then said that if Mr and Mrs Bevin would care to visit him and his family he would give them a good cup of Lyons tea. At these magic words Mrs B's eyes brightened, her homely face showed eagerness; 'Oh, I would like that', she said; 'Mr Bevin and I would enjoy that. The one thing we have been longing for is a good strong cup of tea'. But I fear this delightful expedition could not be fitted in.

In the afternoon I went to tea at the Préfeture. A stately staircase led up to a large landing where Mme Peira received us (me and the Consul's wife). We were ushered into a large room where sat a huge circle of thirty or forty women. They looked as though they had been arranged in order to play some game, but it was merely for the convenience of polite conversation. The party then herded into the dining-room where a tremendous spread was offered: choice of tea, coffee, champagne, orangeade, sandwiches, cakes, patisseries, sweets, chocolates, ices, fruits, savouries. And all beautifully arranged, flowers everywhere, tapestries on the walls, liveried footmen.

Back at our hotel we gathered to hear the speeches in the Place Kleber from our balcony. Winston, of course, stole all the thunder, and his opening was enchanting: *'Prenez garde, je vais parler français'*. The crowd, despite accounts in the papers, was not immense, and not wildly enthusiastic.[19] But this is characteristic of Strasbourgers – steady people, slow to show emotion, with natural dignity. After Winston had spoken the crowd began to thin, but Spaak, who followed, spoke with such great confidence and good sense that he held his own after the star turn.

Strasbourg, 13 August

After a huge lunch we went on a boat on the Rhine. This was rather a wasted afternoon, and was only of interest to me because it was the first time that I noticed that I was having prophetic dreams. Last night I woke with a vivid dream that over my head was a large orange-coloured canopy, the corners squared, and for some reason I felt alarm. I

[19] According to Martin Gilbert's account (in his *Winston Spencer Churchill*) the only window in the square with no spectators was that of Ernest Bevin's sitting-room.

wondered, half dreaming, what it could be, and had it not been for the
clear-cut corners I would have guessed that this orange pall was a dark
London fog. On the boat the Consul-General told me about the tragic
death of the Information Officer the other day, crushed by a crane at
Calais while watching his car being unloaded. I looked upward and saw
the orange awning of the boat over my head just as I had seen it in my
dream. A trivial incident, but all such of my dreams are previews of little
unimportant things that happen in passing during the following day.

Strasbourg, 14 August

Today we went with David and Sybil Eccles to a wine feast at Colmar.
Gladwyn and I were unexpectedly treated *en prince*. For no sooner had
we sat down at a nicely selected table in the huge marquee and formed a
cosy little circle of friends, than there rushed up Roland de Margerie's
young son (not, of course, the one who has become a Jesuit), to say that
the Mayor was searching for us.[20] So Gladwyn and I were whisked off
to the high table, and there I found myself in a place of honour, on the
left of the Mayor and opposite the Préfet, and surrounded by deputies,
ministers, businessmen, and not a woman for several yards. As we ate,
dancers wearing Alsatian costume sang, among other songs, '*Vous
n'aurez pas l'Alsace et La Lorraine*', which used to irritate the Germans
after they had annexed the two provinces in 1871. After lunch we
watched the decorated carts process around the square, and then
walked to the museum. Gladwyn had by now discovered that the
Eccleses were waiting for us in their car, so we rather hastily made our
excuses.

There followed a beautiful drive home, going up by way of
Kayserberg and dining at the Duc d'Alsace at D'Aubernin. Here we had
a moment of horror when the maître d'hotel told us that a large table
next to ours was reserved for the Préfet and his party – we having only
an hour before parted from him with a fine-sounding lie invented by
Gladwyn that Eccles had to dash straight back to Strasbourg to dine
with Churchill. But our guardian angel arranged for the Préfet to have a
puncture. Thus home to our hotel having had a glorious day.

[20] Emmanuel de Margerie (1924–92): subsequently French Ambassador to Britain.

Strasbourg, 17 August

I went to the Assembly this afternoon and heard Churchill speak. Tonight we dined with the Eccleses and they talked freely about him, as they had been with him the previous night. He lives at a villa put at his disposal by the City of Strasbourg, where everything is provided for him, though he refused to accept the wine, saying, 'I have my own resources'. His private plane, a Dove, awaits him in its hangar. He sent a wire for Mrs Churchill to come: 'It's no good, Clemmy, you must come'. She had been bathing in France and thus arrived with two bathing-dresses, a bathing wrap, and rope sandals, ill equipped for entertainments in Strasbourg. David has the impression that Churchill is by no means dependent on his family, but likes them to be around. Sybil said that Winston held forth for a long time on Napoleon, and gave a moving description of the Hundred Days: wonderful language flowed from him and there were tears in his eyes. Churchill was also very funny about whether Attlee would go to America about the financial crisis: he thought not, because 'when the mouse is away the cats might play'.

Gladwyn has been playing an important role as a go-between, since the Conservative and Labour Parties seem unable to work together at this Council. As the whole object is to form a united Europe, it is a pity we can't produce even a semblance of British unity. Feelings run high, people become petty, objections are made to certain wordings, and there is obviously a lack of desire to pull together. So I hope Gladwyn has unobtrusively been able to do some good.

Brussels, 18 August

I arrived here by train to stay with the Pollocks, the Rendels being away. Bill is now an attractive and kind eccentric.[21] He goes to the office in a loud tweed suit, with hat, shirt, tie and waistcoat, all green. Time, and a charming wife, have sobered him down into an original, endearing figure – a far cry from the days when he wore black suede shoes as a

---

[21] William Montagu-Pollock, later Sir William (1906–93), married (secondly) to Barbara Jowett. Counsellor in the Brussels Embassy.

young Third Secretary at the Rome Embassy evening parties, and shocked Sir Ronald Graham; and walked down the wrong side of the Corso, and was arrested and could speak no word of Italian. Or when he arrived at Fleet for a house-party in his Baby Austin wearing a mask he had bought at the Weymouth Woolworth's, and had nothing with him but his camping clothes that he had already worn for a considerable length of time.

Brussels, 19 August

I went this evening to see Simone Dear. She is an old friend of mine, for we worked together in the War at Seaford House. Now she has established herself very quietly and discreetly in a suburb of Brussels (she is half Belgian) to be near M Spaak, of whom she is the *grande amie*. Simone goes to Strasbourg tomorrow and was busy packing. She showed me everything, including the ping-pong table where S takes his exercise; and then we sat while she talked of him and his career and all she hopes he will do. She looks upon him as a god, and he is indeed one of the great men of our time. I gather, from what she tells me, that he is very humble, and that her effusive praise, which makes some people suppose he likes flattery, is really a necessary antidote to his over-modest opinion of himself. Their friendship began early in the War, when he was a refugee in England and his wife remained in Belgium. Thus it sprang up naturally, and I suppose became too big a thing to be abandoned, though to the outsider he gives the impression of being a happy family man.

Mount Street, London, 10 September

The New Zealanders who took Flat 2 for the summer have a television set, and as they are away for a few days, Mrs Cunnington let Stella and me look at it for a treat. I think we did not get it working absolutely right, for I was unable to recognize Mary Bartlett who was announcing; but the Somerset Maugham play was good, and we were entranced at the novelty of it all.

Royal Cresent, Bath, 15 September

We went to see Fleet, where we had not been for nine years, and where the children spent so much of their childhood. Alas! it was horribly changed. We knew it had become a hotel, but had not bargained for it being a third-rate one. Awful furniture, awful colours, awful alterations, awful people, awful food. The Grove and the Pleasure Garden were so overgrown one could not walk in them: the hill was ploughed up and the beauty of the landscape was gone. Fleet was such a romantic place. It was the setting for *Moonfleet,* and I really think Mother bought it largely on that account, for Mr Falkner was such a great friend of the family. She saw it first on a November day. She had left London in a thick fog and arrived at this wonderful lonely spot by the Chesil Beach when it was bathed in bright sunshine. But it was equally impressive in storms, when great winds shook the house, and the spray rose high, and the undertow could be heard even from Dorchester.

Hôtel de la Poste, Rouen, 25 September

A curious band of pilgrims has arrived in France with the object of unveiling a plaque in the little village of Hacqueville in memory of Sir Marc Brunel. They comprise Mother (his great-granddaughter); myself, Humphrey and Celia; and Miles, Vanessa, and Peter Noble. Hacqueville is a small village about the size of Bramfield, but it was built on the principle of ribbon-development and so consists of one long wide street. There are some four hundred inhabitants, of whom about sixty are Communists.

Bunting was hung across the road, and the villagers were already beginning to muster as we arrived. We drove straight to the Mairie, where we were welcomed by the Mayor, the Sous-Préfet and others. More and more people crowded in, many of whom said they were descendants of the Brunels, so we introduced ourselves as cousins. We were then marshalled into the old church, where everything was draped in black as for a memorial service. A long mass followed, incense was swung about, three collections were made, and then we trooped out to go to Brunel's birthplace. A modest room, charmingly arranged as a little museum, was all that was to be seen. A spacious yard, with large picturesque farm-buildings, completed the scene. It all looked very pretty on this warm September day.

We then marched down the village street again to where a large marquee had been erected, laid out for lunch. We were much amused by one item on the long menu – '*Souvenir de la Tamise*', which was a liqueur between the meat courses; this witticism being the inspiration of one of the Mayor's sons, both of whom were *pompiers* in the village.[22] After the unveiling of the plaque on the Brunel house came the speeches, and Mother made hers with astounding success. What could appeal more to the French mind than a great-granddaughter of Brunel, and a grand-mother into the bargain, and, above all, a widow? Besides these obvious advantages she made a really excellent speech without any notes; some-times, it is true, she wandered away from the microphone, but as she has a clear voice, this was of minor significance. The applause was loud and long; a gendarme, standing well forward in front of the dais, joined in heartily; and then all pressed round Mother to shake hands and assure her it had been *magnifique* and *formidable*. After which the band played, slowly and painfully, an almost unrecognizable rendering of the National Anthem, repeating everywhere they possibly could. Thus the afternoon wore on, and after a third visit to the Brunel home we repaired to the tent for a *vin d'honneur*, and then we were all released.[23]

Dieppe Ferry, 26 September

As we drove through the Normandy landscape I was so much reminded of the old days with the Blanches, when on lovely blue-skied autumn days, such as this, they used to take me with them on delightful expedi-tions to see the neighbours in old châteaux, or some pretty church or view.[24] We went through Offranville and stopped outside the little

[22] The principal engineering achievement of Sir Marc Brunel (father of Isambard Kingdom Brunel) had been the construction of the original Thames Tunnel.

[23] In 1993 a similar *jour de fête* was held at Hacqueville, at which the main streeet was renamed Rue Marc Isambard Brunel by Cynthia's son.

[24] Jacques-Emile Blanche (1861–1942) painted several portraits for Celia Noble and became a great friend of the family. But he later grew embittered as his finances wilted, and died at Offranville during the German occupation, which he condoned. His memoirs, *La Peche aux Souvenirs*, contain ungenerous remarks about the Nobles.

château. It seemed so welcoming and familiar that I almost expected to
see Blanchie emerge, perhaps wearing a straw boater and an old-fashioned cloak with a cape on it, walking with his toes well pointed out-
wards as he had always been made to do, his feet encased in
tight-looking narrow pointed shoes, and an agonized expression on his
face, which came not from pinching boots but a pessimistic
apprehensiveness about life in general.

On arrival at Dieppe we went to the Giffards' house. M Giffard is a
solicitor; a round, red-faced robin-like man in a check coat. He at once
questioned us about England over a glass of port. He was anxious as to
the fate of the 'gentleman' under the Labour Government: did he still
exist, with his hunting and shooting, his butler, his honesty and his club?
At dinner, with two bottles of champagne on the table, the subject was
still being thrashed out, and various amusing stories were told to illustrate the honesty, or, alas, the dishonesty, of the British. For M Giffard
had had a most unfortunate experience with a military policeman on
sentry duty, immensely impressive and tall. This pillar of integrity from
his great height had seen little M Giffard pass close by him, and had
said, out of the corner of his mouth, 'Want to buy any cigarettes?'
Monsieur G was so profoundly shocked that he replied he didn't smoke,
which was not true. I had to counter this with my story of Lady
Thompson's superb honesty.

The sanitary arrangements here, as in other French houses, were
primitive, and there was only one lavatory available for all, something '*le
gentleman*' would have boggled at straight away. It was horribly in need of
ventilation, and I doubt whether the window had ever been opened.

Bramfield, Suffolk, 5 October

Mr Foster is behaving very temperamentally over the paintwork in
Gladwyn's study, for he maintains it will be impossible to match it to the
distemper on the walls, and I insist on his going on mixing till it is right.
He speaks the most beautiful old English, such as saying that a particular screw is not 'mighty enough' for the sconce he is 'offering up', and I
was charmed to hear him say of the walls this morning, 'When you
come in at the door that'll smile at you'. He sometimes produces quite
poetic sentences. I have been wondering whether he is not some mute

inglorious Milton, which might account for his moodiness, which is well-known in the village.

Mount Street, London, Trafalgar Day

Amongst those present at lunch at Sybil's were John Maud and Chris Mayhew.[25] John Maud helped to hand round the dishes in a most professional way, the daily help having failed to turn up. He is renowned for his excellent manners and consideration for others – almost too good to be true in an Englishman. Chris Mayhew recently met Lord Beaverbrook,[26] who charmed him to such an extent that when Chris was asked whether he would get in at the next election, he quite frankly answered that he thought not, for last time he had two opponents who split the votes, and also the constituency boundaries had been changed. He noticed that the Beaver took a little pencil and pad from his pocket and scribbled something down, but the innocent fellow thought no more of it. Until he read his confidential remarks word for word in the Crossbencher column of the *Sunday Express*, under the heading 'A Doomed Man'.

Mount Street, London, 28 October

At lunch at Ruth Lee's today I met, for the first time in at least twenty years, Mrs Stirling, previously Lady Elgin, and previous to that Mrs Ogilvy. As a middle-aged widow, Lady Elgin was produced in our family by Humbo, then a young man, who greatly admired her. She used to figure large in Wretham house-parties, and Muriel and I were very critical of how she ingratiated herself with the men and ignored the women. When the men were out shooting all day she was thoroughly bored. But when they returned as dusk approached she rushed to get out their slippers and warm them by the fire, to strip off wet clothes and ask anxiously how the day had gone. Then, after dinner, when the ladies

---

[25] Christopher Mayhew, later Lord Mayhew (1915–); Parliamentary Under-Secretary of State for Foreign Affairs.
[26] Max Aitken, 1st Lord Beaverbrook (1879–1964); proprietor of the *Daily* and *Sunday Express*, and the *Evening Standard*.

would be talking together, a noise heard off would indicate that the men were leaving the dining-room. At once Lady Elgin would seat herself on a prominent stool in the middle of the drawing-room, her skirt spread in voluminous folds, her embroidery taken up and her head bent forward intently upon her work. Her daughter Anne Ogilvy (timid, red-haired, frightened) was summoned in a hurried whisper and made to sit on the floor at her mother's feet, her dress also artistically arranged. So the vulnerable male, as soon as he had left his port and coarse talk, entered this feminine atmosphere and beheld a touchingly sweet grouping of mother and daughter.

Her method of greeting me was typical, and I feel can only properly be appreciated by Muriel. I went to meet her saying, 'How are you, Mrs Stirling, do you remember me?'. To which she replied: 'I know; wait a minute; it's Cecilia – little Cecilia Judd'; and she turned to Ruth with a gesture, and said, 'You can't think how pretty she was twenty years ago!' I must admit she chose to be quite amusing at lunch, chattering away, quoting Mme de Sevigné, up to all her old tricks.

Stratfield Saye, Hampshire, 30 October

We are spending the weekend with Gerry and I fear that in this extremely cold house I have been unable to live down a cold which came on yesterday. I am in a wonderful great pompous bedroom, with a half-tester over the bed, the whole draped, festooned, pleated, quilted, braided, ribboned, in fact with everything that could possibly be thought of if one were decorating a bed. The bathroom is carpeted with thick crimson felt. The bath is edged with mahogany and the lavatory pan, dating from the Great Duke's time, is of a charming blue and white pattern, with a good solid mahogany seat and a plug you lift up, not pull down. In the bathroom also is a foot-bath (which I am sure no young person would recognize); and tooth-glasses of such a size and quality that I am sure the like could not be bought in England today; and a silver spoon.

When one emerges from one's bedroom at Stratfield Saye one has a long way to go. The yellow drawing-room where Gerry sits when there is company is a lovely room, beautifully arranged. Everywhere there are writing-tables, all equipped with splendid solid inkpots, good leather blotters, and leather boxes for writing paper – all the leatherwork stamped with the gilt W and ducal coronet. A good lengthy well-written letter should, one feels, be composed at these tables, no hurried scribbled note.

Mount Street, London, 12 November

Rumour has it that Chris Mayhew has been seen lunching with Buchman and subsequently closeted with a Communist. Perhaps Chris has really joined the Oxford Group and has the wild ambition of converting the Soviet Union. What enchanting speculations this evokes – Stalin 'come clean', flint-eyed Vyshinsky 'god-controlled', all the thugs having 'quiet times'.

Bramfield, Suffolk, 10 January

On 28 November we dined with the John Russells.[27] Mrs Russell is a lively handsome woman who was once Miss Greece. At one time she was married to Paul Louis Weiller, a not very reputable French character. During the War he wished to get some of his large fortune safely to America, which he contrived to do by settling it on his wife and sending her over there. She then decided to leave him and marry John Russell of the Foreign Office. She and John Russell live in the grandest way. She is invariably dressed by Dior or Balenciaga, and their pretty old house has been done up regardless of expense. So we all sat down to a tremendous feast on silver plates, and in the midst of our carousing John Russell suddenly clinked his fork against his glass and announced a Monsieur Carra. A modest looking man came in and sat down at a small table on which he started playing a zither. 'That's the famous tune', everybody said; and it wasn't till a month later that I saw *The Third Man* and recognized the haunting Harry Lime Theme.

On 8 December Tony Gandarillas gave a farewell party for the Rochés which I recall merely because I witnessed the correct form of

---

[27] John Russell, later Sir John (1914–84), married to Aliki Diplarakos. Subsequently Ambassador to Spain.

diplomatic handshake suitable for such an occasion, though I can't see Gladwyn adopting it. The donor of the salute was Leon Subercaseaux and the recipient Louis Roché.[28] At a suitable moment, when the floor is not too crowded, the donor with perfect timing approaches the departing diplomat with a gallant stride, head erect, shoulders back, and an air of friendly reassurance. There is a smile on his face and yet a tearful look in his eye – the dago's notion of a 'stiff upper lip'. As he nears his quarry he intones richly, *'Eh bien, mon cher'*, at the same time raising his right arm stiffly to shoulder level. By this time it is to be hoped that the mournful figure in front of him has had the wit to put out his hand, for this is to be no ordinary handshake. For Leon, after a splendid pause, brought down his arm as stiffly as he had raised it, and landed it unerringly in Louis' palm, at the same time cementing the clasp with a grip of the left hand. This position was held for a considerable time, during which protestations of affection, of regret, of the hope of meeting again one day in some other post, of the smallness of the world, of courage, flowed from Leon's mouth. Both parties were quite exhausted when it was at last over.

On 14 December Gladwyn and I gave a dinner at the Allies Club. Miles and Vanessa were fortunately here for it, and except that the champagne was uncorked with the loudest of reports, like birthday guns going off, the dinner was a good one. It had originally started with Kenneth Clark telling Gladwyn at his club that his son Alan was interested in Yugoslavia, so we had Fitzroy MacLean to meet him. I thought Alan Clark was an ambitious opinionated young man. K and Jane are both hard nuts who could do with a crack, though Sydney, with whom I lunched next day, says that when K is without Jane he becomes at once a much nicer person.

On New Year's Eve we spent the day at Flixton. The Adairs[29] are kind charming people with a curious affection of laugh, indescribable in pen and ink – a sort of gentle echoing braying, nervously reiterated after every sentence. This strange mannerism is not surprising in Enid Adair; but 'General Allan' was magnificent in the War, an enthusiastic leader and hero to his men and officers.

[28] Tony Gandarillas was Attaché and Leon Subercaseaux Counsellor at the Chilean Embassy, and Louis Roché was Counsellor at the French Embassy.
[29] Major-General Sir Allan Adair (1897–1988), married to Enid Dudley-Ward. Flixton Hall was subsequently pulled down.

The early Victorian Adairs had built a vast sprawling house in the Jacobean style, regardless of expense. We wandered from room to room, from wing to wing, from conservatory to conservatory (yes, there are two), through the long hall where the hunt ball will take place, up the large staircase, Enid pulling up blinds so that I could see the pictures. Above the gallery was an equally long saloon, which never had electric light. It had two fireplaces and two of everything, and at the centre was an enchanting roundabout settee. And every piece of furniture had its own dust-cover, fitting snugly, waiting in vain for an army of well-trained housemaids to come and remove it and display the lovely yellow silk underneath. In one wing somewhere lay old and dying Lady Adair, a senile widow, tended by a faithful old servant, seldom visited by Enid. One of the best touches in the house was a large stuffed bear, a tray clasped in one paw, the other upraised and holding an oil lamp.

1950

❖

Mount Street, London, 4 February

It was a nice mild afternoon, so I walked across St James's Park to Sybil's. Through Berkeley Square, which is being tidied up, and where the old plane trees look in better setting than when ATS used to drill under them, trampling down the grass and crocuses, on down St James's Street; over the bridge from where Buckingham Palace on the right and the Foreign Office on the left looked quite exquisite in the misty February sun. I passed the Glenconners' house on the corner of Queen Anne's Gate, which I remember so well in the old days, such pretty large rooms giving the feeling of a country house. Big Ben was just chiming four o'clock as I turned into Dean's Yard and passed Number 17 where I used to go so often when the Carnegies lived there. Then along Great College Street, where we went to classes at Mrs Alfred Lyttelton's house;[1] then down Barton Street and Cowley Street, whose little old panelled houses are now the abodes of comfortably-off Conservative MPs who like to live within easy reach of the House.

And so I reached Lord North Street. The familiar smell of burnt rosemary greeted me as Mrs Dacre's comfortable form opened the door. The doctor had been that morning and said she was no better and no worse. Olga Lynn was upstairs, I was told. I went up to Sybil's room. She lay in her pink curtained bed with pink quilt and wrap and a soft pink light, surrounded by flowers. It was like a conservatory, and the

---

[1] Edith Balfour, second wife of Alfred Lyttelton (1857–1913), who had been Colonial Secretary.

biggest and best bouquet, being a present from Edwina Mountbatten, was placed on a coffer at the foot of the bed. I'm glad I don't have to dust that room, with all the intimate photographs of celebrities, and the small furniture that has been ingeniously crammed in, and the wireless, medicines, orange juices and telephones. When the tea tray came I wondered where it could possibly be placed. By this time Olga Lynn had been replaced by Rose Macaulay, and then I left after Desmond Shawe-Taylor and another man arrived, as I felt four was too much. But this stream goes on for most of the day, and Mrs Dacre told me that Ivor Novello comes every morning.

Mount Street, London, 6 February

Tonight we dined with Charlotte Bonham Carter.[2] She had intended it to be a fork dinner at 7.45, but then decided to have the meal sitting down as the Gallarati-Scottis were coming. This began in great confusion, for two people invited later in the evening thought they were invited to dinner, and Mrs Andreae, who was to sit on the Ambassador's right, arrived three quarters of an hour late with the curious excuse that she had overslept. To meet the Italians Charlotte had collected a strange assortment of peers, only one of whom was reputable – Lord Talbot de Malahide, who acted as a sort of butler dispensing drinks beforehand; in fact, it wasn't till we sat down that I realized he was a fellow guest, for I had not been introduced to him. The other two were Gavin Faringdon and Patrick Kinross. Then there was Steven Runciman, a most peculiar type, though now that his hair is reasonably short he looks better than he used to. We were told not to change, but Charlotte enlivened a short wool red dress with red flowers in her hair. She is very kind but slightly dotty. There was a moment towards the end of the dinner when she vanished from the table and we wondered whether she had gone to another party.

---

[2] Charlotte Ogilvy (1893–1989), widow of Sir Edgar Bonham Carter: a *salonnière* renowned for her energy into extreme old age in assembling a wide mix of guests for a very simple buffet supper.

Mount Street, London, 17 February

Today we lunched at the Bevins' to say goodbye to the retiring Argentine Ambassador. These lunches given by the government lack the personal touch. Gladwyn was shocked that they should serve 'champagne or burgundy' as soon as we sat down. I was next to Lord Alexander. Uncle Ernie looked tired, but revived slightly at the end. I remember so well that same house in Carlton Gardens when the Northcliffes had it, particularly a lovely music party at which Melba sang, and when Lord Lee saw me come upstairs. Nearly thirty years ago, alas!

Mount Street, London, 21 February

I entered Sybil's drawing-room and found her sitting on the centre of her sofa, her feet up on a low stool and concealed by her bright jade-green silk shawl. She confessed that when the moment had arrived for her to dress and descend to the drawing-room, she hesitated and was on the point of renouncing this first attempt at her salon. But her fine strong spirit had evidently got the better of her frail ageing body. With her usual courage she was planning to go with Vivien Leigh to a matinée of *Venus Observed*. VL said, would it not be wiser to wait a little 'until the weather was a tidgey bit warmer'; but Sybil didn't like this procrastination at all and was determined to fix a date soon.

Then the guests began to pour in – Ava, the Eshers, Gielgud, Terry Rattigan, Beverly Nichols, Robert Lutyens and his new ménage, the Kenneth Clarks, Pauline Rickett, and many more, though no politicians, it being Election Week. Osbert [Lancaster] said that many people at Oxford would vote for Elizabeth Pakenham rather than Quintin Hogg because, when undergraduates, she had been so popular and he unpopular.[3] Pointing to Eddie Sackville-West, now closeted with Sybil on the sofa, Osbert remarked how well one's hypochondriacal friends always looked; and indeed Eddie told me that he was about to have a holiday for the first time for eleven years – I had imagined he was always on

---

[3] Nevertheless, Quintin Hogg managed to retain his seat as Member of Parliament for the City of Oxford.

holiday. By now the crowd was beginning to thin, so we all slipped away leaving Sybil tired but happy.

Mount Street, London, 23 February

This evening I went to the *Daily Telegraph* election party. I believe at least two thousand guests were invited, and some said there were another thousand gate-crashers. Gladwyn felt he should not go, as most civil servants thought they should not be seen at such a Conservative gathering. I plunked myself down at a table with the Gallarati-Scottis, the Belgians and the Swedes, feeling that in this diplomatic company I could not be accused of favouring Right or Left. By now the results were beginning to come in, and as they were largely Labour there were boos and hisses. As time went on and Labour greatly predominated, faces became downcast and, in spite of the champagne, spirits low.[4] Finally, at about one o'clock the party was a feast at which there were only skeletons. As we left that seething room at the Savoy, I was told that there were three others just as crowded. It was like hearing one of those strange facts about the heavens, that there are masses more Milky Ways than the one we can see, and masses more suns and earths.

Magdalen College, Oxford, 5 March

We have been spending a delightful and comfortable weekend here with the President, Tom Boase, who lives in style in his lodgings, with an impressive butler and an excellent cook, and is himself the kindest person in the world. He gave a dinner for us to which came, among others, the D'Entrèves and a history don called Taylor, who is said to be a 'fellow traveller'.[5] He is most intelligent and amusing, but I dare say

---

[4] Labour got in with an overall majority of five seats.
[5] Professor Alessandro D'Entrèves (1902–85), Serena Professor of Italian Studies, and Alan (A.J.P.) Taylor (1906–90), both Fellows of Magdalen. D'Entrèves was a gentle humanist. Taylor (no longer a political 'fellow traveller') was the maverick historian who tilted at the Oxford establishment and deeply despised President Boase, and who was about to be divorced by his (first) wife, Margaret Adams.

difficult. His wife, we were told, was only interested in high-brow modern poets, but actually she was quite easy to talk to. We sat after dinner in the lovely tapestried drawing-room.

On Sunday morning we visited Miles' rooms in the New Buildings, with their high proportions and lovely view. We then walked around Oxford landing up first for drinks with Billa Harrod, where we found John Foster and Mr Hulton, and then on for a gossip with Prof Cherwell. After lunch we went sightseeing, not neglecting the mid-Victorian buildings which are now greatly admired. And I must say I genuinely like Balliol Chapel, Keble Chapel, and the Italianate museum inspired by Ruskin. At Keble Tom made the unfortunate slip of asking whether we could see 'The Light that Failed'; but it was even odder to be told in reply that 'The Light of the World' could not be seen on Sundays![6]

Mount Street, London, 8 March

We went to the reception for President Auriol at the French Embassy. I wore my best clothes, my lovely wildly expensive new blue-grey satin picture dress from Worth, very pretty and undating, I hope, with its pink flowers on the skirt. Then the family necklace round my neck and the tiara on my head, and the sable cape, which Mother gave me, dyed a rich brown most successfully, and long white gloves which I had not worn since the War. Thus arrayed, with Gladwyn with his decorations, we went forth in a taxi. I was introduced to Auriol and asked him whether he remembered that night when he had escaped to England and dined with Viennot. He said he did, and Mme Auriol laughed and remarked that he must have looked *très joli* with his beard. Mme Massigli was in a tremendous Dior dress, Mme Auriol in one from Fath which I preferred; I have no doubt that neither paid for their dresses but wore them as advertisement.

---

[6] Holman Hunt's representation of Christ as 'The Light of the World' was housed in an annex to Keble Chapel. *The Light that Failed* is the title of a novel by Kipling.

Mount Street, London, 22 March

The news is out, announced this morning. Mrs Cunnington called me
with, 'Well, you must count your blessings: it might have been
Moscow'[7].

After having my hair done I collided with Freddie Birkenhead also
emerging from Mr Everest's – evidently he fears baldness. I said, 'What
do you think of our new appointment?', and he replied, 'Oh God, New
York: you *can't* go there: you can't go to *America*. They're not civilized.
You can't imagine how appalling it is there. You go out to dinner at
about eight and are plied with endless stiff drinks, and then at about a
quarter past ten you'll go to dinner and eat some terrible cold food, with
no wine, just iced water'. And as for the teenagers, he said, they are the
most awful spoilt and whiney creatures. I told him I was proposing to
take Stella: 'Well, that'll be the end of her', he said.

Mount Street, London, 18 May

I found myself at a most curious lunch today. Mrs Neville Chamberlain
was our hostess. She is a good-looking, agreeable, and pleasant white-
haired woman, the epitome of conventionality. It is unbelievable that
she should be the sister of that mad amusing Irish character, Horace
Cole, whose daring practical jokes have become classics. The lunch
party was to receive Eva Reading into the Conservative fold, so I wondered why I had been asked.[8] That same evening, at the Italian Embassy,
it was amusing to see, in a bottleneck between the drawing-rooms, Lady
Violet Bonham Carter, and Bongie,[9] and Megan Lloyd-George all cheek
by jowl with the renegades – the Readings and the Rennells. I thought
that fur would fly, but all passed off quietly.

[7] Gladwyn had been appointed Representative to the Security Council of the United
Nations in New York, with the rank of a 'Grade One' ambassador.
[8] Eva Mond, married to Gerald Isaacs, 2nd Marquess of Reading. He had just joined
the Conservative Party, and she was active in campaigns for women's rights, child
welfare, and support for Israel.
[9] Sir Maurice Bonham Carter (1880–1960), married to Lady Violet Asquith, later
Baroness Asquith of Yarnbury (1887–1969). He had been Private Secretary to
Asquith when Prime Minister, and she was now the matriarch of the much-dimin-
ished Liberal Party.

Bramfield, Suffolk, 19 May

One of the great joys has been the arrival of Gladwyn's car, a Hillman Snipe, which he will take to America.[10] Today we set off in it and motored to Wretham, my old home, or rather, what remains of it, for it has now been pulled down. We picnicked by the ruined church, once kept so well mown, but now wild and uneven and more like the grave-yard it originally was. We sat just where, as Titania, I had lain on a damp bank in which a hot-water bottle was concealed. In the audience, equally damp, were Ma'am[11] and the Bishop of Norwich. Inside the church was an amateur orchestra with Mother playing the piano and Aunt Ethel and others fiddling away at the Mendelssohn music of the *Midsummer Night's Dream*. There were all the usual quarrels and flirtations which go with private theatricals.

Balblair House, Invernesshire, 15 September 1951[12]

It is just a year and a day since Stella and I set sail for America on the *Queen Elizabeth*, feeling very melancholy as the great ship slowly moved away from the dock at Southampton.

The decoration of the QE is appallingly vulgar. Osbert Sitwell (who, with Edith, and David Horner, was on board) thinks that great luxury has always been vulgar. We were disgusted by the commonness of our companions at the Doctor's table, and in fact there was nobody very agreeable on board. Our other fellow-travellers included Vyshinksy and other representatives to the UN General Assembly.

The skyscrapers tower up from the small rocky island to provide a beautiful skyline by day and night, like a city in fairyland. But below, the streets are dark, dirty, dusty and noisy. The population lives in a vortex, rushing round and round in an excited nervous youthful whirl. The

[10] From 1939 till 1950 Gladwyn did not run a car.
[11] Princess Marie-Louise (1870–1956) was the younger daughter of Princess Helena, third daughter of Queen Victoria. She lived in straitened circumstances and for two years stayed at Kent House as the guest of Celia and Saxton.
[12] From June 1950 to May 1956 Cynthia ceased to write a regular diary. This reflective passage was written when on holiday in Scotland the following year, at a rented house on the estate of Lord Lovat.

accentuation is on youth. Nobody must look old or be old: the wisdom of age is not respected, and nearly all the elderly men dye their hair and do their best to marry young wives.

Coming from England one is aware of the appalling waste – just too much food, drink and comfort – making people soft. They seldom walk, and apologize for the shortest flight of stairs. At the first touch of cold the houses, hotels, shops, clubs, and trains are overheated: at the first touch of heat, they are air-conditioned. Food is generally bought ready to eat, the bread already cut. Clothes are ready-made, and many wives don't know how to hold a needle. People don't know how to do things for themselves any more, and their lives have become completely artificial and unnatural.[13]

They boast that they wear their hearts on their sleeves, whereas in England, I tell them, we keep it in its proper place, where it beats with fidelity. Although in casual encounters (such as addressing someone in a queue) the Americans would be more cautious than the English, at a social gathering they break the ice at once with one hearty plunge, greeting everyone by their Christian name and feeling completely at home, whilst the Englishman remains reserved and formal. But when it comes to really intimate friendship, after a long period of initiation, the latter is often more sincere.

The Englishman is reputed to drawl his 'a's, to clip his words, and to effect superiority over the honest simple American, who keeps his trousers up with a belt and despises 'pinstriped pants'. So it is amazing to find how the whole country has taken Gladwyn to their hearts.[14] His popularity is nationwide. This is very touching and very pleasant. He is recognized in the streets and welcomed by strangers, asked for his autograph, and altogether treated like a film star. They are curiously emotional in their reactions in a way that strikes us as slightly

[13] The contrast between London and New York, the first war-weary and the second futuristic, was infinitely greater than today.

[14] Gladwyn had flown out to his new post immediately after the outbreak of the Korean War at the end of June, the greatest crisis yet faced by the United Nations. By the time of Cynthia's arrival he had established himself in the Security Council as the champion of the West against the Communist East, in verbal sparring with the smooth and resourceful Soviet Representative, Yakov Alexandrovitch Malik. This coincided with the first nationwide TV 'hook-ups', and millions watched the debates which served to strengthen the American public's resolve to fight back at the aggressors in Korea.

silly. For instance, one evening, while I was waiting in the hall at Essex House while Gladwyn fetched the car to go out to dinner, a highly respectable and quite important-looking elderly man came up to me and said with sincerity, 'You've got just the darlingest husband in the world and we all love him'. One could not imagine these words falling from the lips of an educated Englishman. But of course, they are grateful for the way they feel Gladwyn has rescued them from a dilemma, and naturally this gratitude has made it very easy for me to arrive here, in an aura of reflected glory. Normally I am sure it is more difficult for the English, than it is for other nationalities, to get on in America.

When Stella and I were transplanted from our floating hotel to Essex House we were completely bewildered and couldn't take roots. From the windows of our suite on the eighteenth floor I looked down on Central Park wonderingly, having been warned by my maid that the most dreadful things happen there. The little toy cars, rushing along or coming to a standstill at the traffic lights, exhibited an air of futility. Our suite was decorated in pale grey and green in the latest Regency style, and the telephone rang incessantly.

It was worse for Stella, who was at a loose end, whereas I found all my engagements filled up for about three weeks ahead. However we very soon went round to interview Dr de Marco, a handsome flashy young businessman sitting in a smart room with all the latest types of lamps and furnishings, the strangest sanctum I have yet been in, having pre-conceived ideas of what such a place should be like from Eton, Blunt House and other seats of learning. He was surprised, on asking Stella questions about her previous education, to find that at East Haddon Hall she had done eight different subjects. 'Eight subjects! That's a big load! Did you ever hear of such a heavy load, Mrs Romanov?', he asked of a neat elderly woman in black who had just come into the room – no doubt a relative of the late Tsar. She was equally amazed, and promptly removed Stella for a psychological test at which, I was relieved to hear, she proved to be very intelligent. Soon it was happily arranged that Stella could become an honorary scholar and a weekly boarder, conve-nient for our pocket and much better for Stella, who became her old self at the prospect of being with contemporaries again, though actually all the girls turned out to be older than she, worldly, and most of them engaged. The sad tale that she had failed in her School Certificate was fortunately offset by the impressive fact that she had been head girl, and 'therefore a leader', Dr de Marco said.

On weekends we went to the palatial residence at Oyster Bay we had inherited from the Cadogans. Our first dinner here was for the Security Council. By strict protocol I sat between Mr Austin and Malik. The former is a kind blustery woolly old buffer from Vermont, quick tempered, but loyal to England. Malik is a sinister figure with a sneering mouth, yet he can laugh heartily.

In town I invariably go to a woman's lunch. Men are not seen at this meal; they are down-town hard at work making money for the women. The women are brought up to be 'bright', which means a great many wisecracks. They are lively and interested and sometimes intelligent. They are spoilt by their menfolk from the cradle upwards, and with all the material advantages which they take for granted, and the tremendously important position they hold in the country, they have lost the usual feminine attributes – they have no grace, softness or charm. This is indeed a matriarchy.

The men appear in the evening in time for drinks. Because they are so busy making money all day they have no leisure for any intellectual pursuits, and consequently are not so agreeable to talk to as the women. It is said they die young of heart attacks and duodenal ulcers; but before this fate comes to them they have divorced and remarried several times and eventually been landed with a younger woman, which accounts for the fact that most of the wealth is in the hands of the women.

I belong to two women's clubs, the Colony and the Cosmopolitan. Both provide excellent service and many amenities. Certain parts are marked 'Silence', but everywhere one hears the sound of female tongues working at full speed. In my mind's eye I see the well-fed ladies of New York, with many rows of pearls around their necks, and wearing the silliest of hats. Their ready-made clothes are certainly of wonderful value, ranging from the extremely expensive to the delightfully pretty. They all wear beautiful shoes, nylon stockings, very well done hair, and altogether are infinitely better groomed than Europeans. Their faces have a hard look, and in spite of beauty culture their skins are leathery. In the winter one notices more the high standard of dressing from the wonderful fur coats every woman wears. One really is shocked to see such costly furs in such quantity when part of the world is not sufficiently clad, as one is to see so much food (and so much wasted) when part of the world is starving. I agree with Lady Astor who said she never wanted to see a mink coat again, and was saying she was going to wear only a fig-leaf in future. I met a woman at lunch in an Alaskan seal coat, who said that she had just bought a beautiful dark mink; and then she had seen a Negress wearing an identical coat, so she had gone straight home and told her maid to 'hang it in the closet, where it still hangs'.

When I think of an American I conjure up a vision of a man or woman standing before me holding a tumbler containing 'whisky on the rocks', which means neat with ice. This is excused by saying it is so much better for one than a cocktail, which may be true in moderation. But, as Tommy Davies said to me, 'American life is to be more or less drunk every evening between 6.30 and 8.30.' The prelude to a dinner-party consists of a good hour in drinking and eating titbits – and this is often after having been earlier to a cocktail party, come home, changed, and sallied forth in evening dress. This habit dates, I am told, from Prohibition times, when people met privately before their non-alcoholic meal. Now, as then, one goes into dinner a bit intoxicated, and sits in a room entirely lit by candles, to a feast of lavish food which is curiously tasteless. Vegetables are uninteresting, and the meal invariably ends with an ice. And there is no wine, except on very rare occasions. I am told Californian wine is excellent, so there is no need to import it.

This habit of heavy drinking is practically universal. It is disillusioning to find it in even the most respected families. The wife of Junius Morgan had most certainly had too much the night we met them at dinner at General Crittenburger's on Governor's Island. And young Mrs Adams, daughter-in-law of Charles Francis Adams (head of the 'First Family of Boston') had likewise when we went to lunch there.

We moved to our new home on the Hudson at the end of November. It is only half an hour from New York, in a place called Riverdale – once a fashionable country locality, where a few respectable old families had property, but now practically unknown to people who think only in terms of Long Island.

Our house has the merit of being quite old for America. It was built by a Mr Morris before 1840. He and his wife landed by here by boat, and, climbing to this site the young wife remarked that the hill went up as it were in waves, so it was named Wave Hill. After the Morrises the house was owned by the publisher Appleton, and here he entertained, it is said, Thackeray and Faraday and other eminent English people. It then became the property of Mr Perkins, the father of our landlady; and at one time Theodore Roosevelt's parents rented it when the future President was a rather delicate little boy, as the air here was considered beneficial for him. He ran about the garden and its then entirely rustic surroundings, and had happy memories of Wave Hill. Later, Mark Twain lived here. And, to complete our list of celebrities, Toscanini spent the War years in this house, using my bedroom for music. As I lie in bed, gazing through my bow window at the lovely old fir tree just below the terrace, and the Palisades in the distance, I like to think of the beautiful sounds that have filled this room. Attached to one end of the house is a large Gothic hall about a hundred feet long, with nine windows, a fire-place and a beamed roof. This is for us a most fortunate addition, as it is perfect for cocktail parties, dances, or our big Security Council dinners. We duly weeded some of the less suitable furniture from the house and put in some of our own, including things which Gladwyn has inherited from his father, and some pretty objects that Mother has most kindly sent over, including her lovely Louis XVI harp.

Our first guest of renown was Mr Attlee, who chose to come and stay in December, when we had hardly had time to settle in.[15] He brought with him Roger Makins and Denis Rickett, and a couple of detectives, and we had a cocktail party, followed by a dinner party at which I was the only woman. All would have gone well had there not been an unfortunate hitch over the luggage, which somehow took about three hours to be sorted out and arrive here. No Conservative Prime Minister could have been more anxious to appear for dinner in evening clothes than Mr Attlee. Eventually he went at least to have his bath, and appeared a little later at the top of the stairs wrapped in a fortunately voluminous bath towel, anxiously asking for news. Just about eight o'clock the baggage turned up, so all was well.

[15] The Prime Minister was stopping off on his way to Washington to confer with President Truman following the Chinese military intervention in Korea.

1951

Balblair House, Invernesshire, 15 September[1]

Everybody who comes to Wave Hill admires the house and its English atmosphere, the peace of the surroundings, good air, lovely garden and really spectacular view. We look straight down to the 'lordly Hudson' (true, the railway runs along the margin of the river, but in summer we don't see it) and across to the Palisades, preserved thanks to Mr Rockefeller. As Washington Irving prophesied, exactly a hundred years ago, 'Some day the trains will come screaming through this valley, but those old rocks will remain; improvement cannot improve them; and they will be the same hundreds of years hence'. Our view is so beautiful that it is difficult to decide at which season it is most impressive. I like it in the fall, when all the trees are incredibly brilliant; the woods look almost as if they were on fire, so vivid are the reds and yellows. The sky is bright blue, and there is a clarity and a briskness in the atmosphere that makes a startling contrast to our European autumns, with their 'mists and mellow fruitfulness', their pleasant melancholy and smell of bonfires and damp leaves.

Wave Hill enables us at weekends to live the sort of life we like. We can put on country clothes, go for walks, see nobody if we wish, and feel as far removed from the hectic vortex of New York as if we were on the other side of the Atlantic. Very different was the weekend we spent with the Du Ponts at that amazing house near

[1] During the decade when Gladwyn was stationed abroad (1950–60) Bramfield Hall was let, first to Neville and Christabel Berry, and then to Thelma de Chair. Gladwyn and Cynthia therefore rented houses for their summer holidays.

Wilmington, Winterthur, which has now been given to the nation as a museum. Already only a small part of it was used by the Du Ponts,[2] but even this allowed them to have a house-party of about sixteen. They were all the rich Long Island set, well-fed, uninteresting, bejewelled. All the time which was not engaged at cocktails or meals was spent at the canasta and bridge tables. They never walked or enjoyed the country.

The first afternoon, directly we arrived, we all went off in huge cars to see the colossal conservatory which belongs to a Du Pont relative, and we wandered slowly from plant to plant in the hot damp atmosphere, admiring rarities. We then returned for tea. Games were resumed, but I was delightfully occupied in being shown his famous collection by Mr Du Pont. In fact, it took the whole of the weekend to see it in its entirety. I have never seen such a wonderful display of beautiful stuffs – curtains and covers – as were kept there in a huge air-conditioned room. So what with sightseeing, and walking with Mr Du Pont, and seeing his farm and gardens, I really had a most pleasant visit, and only encountered my fellow guests at meal-times.

On the Sunday morning we all went to church in a fleet of cars. The church was packed, and the elaborate Episcopalian service was heralded by a large choir, part female, the latter being highly made-up and their hair styled in impeccable waves and curls. At the end of the service, as soon as we rose from our seats, I was amazed to hear a loud chattering from all sides, and the chit-chat continued quite undaunted by the presence of the clergyman who stood at the door to shake us by the hand as though we were leaving a party. Back at Winterthur I made some comment on the excellence of the sermon, to which one of the rich ladies replied, 'I know, he's a lovely preacher. He somehow makes one want to do something, I don't quite know what'; and then she was off about how she nearly made Little Slam the previous evening. People say that the Americans are religious, but I think they are the most materialistic people in the world, and so little aware of spiritual values that their services and churches make very little difference to them.

[2] Henry Francis Du Pont (b. 1880); director of the Wilmington Trust and founder of the Winterthur Museum.

Wave Hill, New York, 20 May (letter to MJ)[3]

We met Cardinal Spellman, who looked like Mr Pickwick and was the most convivial and unceremonious Cardinal I have ever struck. He indulged in some badinage which I could not properly hear as there was such a noise from the crowd that surrounded us, but it ended with his making the parting shot, 'I won't try to pull that one on you!' (Shades of Richelieu, Manning and Newman).

Wave Hill, New York, 1 June (letter to MJ)

I must tell you about my adventures in Kentucky, for really it was an extraordinary experience, and I have been in another world, at the back of beyond.

On Monday the Binghams' luxurious car whisked me about two hundred miles south east from Louisville.[4] This took about five hours and the latter part of the journey was over a twisty road through the mountains, full of coal lorries and called Hell's Highway. We eventually reached a small place called Hyden, where the Frontier Nursing Service has a hospital on a nearby hill. Later I got into the car again and was taken to a point about three miles away where a jeep was waiting, with two nurses in breeches. I got in and clung to whatever I could in terror as we plunged off the road down a track in a small creek, and then into a river. We meandered about, trying to keep to the more shallow parts, and, once on the further side, went hurtling along a surface like the face of the moon, full of craters. We then climbed a hill and came to a stop at a group of longish log houses and stables which comprise Wendover, the centre of the Frontier Nursing Service, and home of Mrs Breckenridge, who started it.[5] I had no sooner clambered out of the jeep than she appeared – a charming, elderly woman, very practical and energetic. She took me into the building which was her house, and it was extraordinarily like Hunding's house in the *Walküre*, except that there

[3] From New York Cynthia wrote several 'diary letters' to her mother (CN) and to her son (MJ): trans-Atlantic telephone calls were expensive rarities.
[4] Barry Bingham (b. 1906): President and Editor of the *Louisville Courier Journal*. He had arranged this expedition for Cynthia on learning of her interest in the Hill Billies.
[5] Mary Breckenridge (b. 1881): dedicated herself to a lifetime of service to nursing.

was no tree or sword. We then had a sort of communal meal with the nurses and secretaries at a long table.

Next morning breakfast was brought to me by a nurse at about eight o'clock, and at nine I sallied forth in a jeep with a nurse and a picnic. We visited two outposts, which involved motoring about sixty miles, most of it over wild tracks. For anyone who likes nursing and riding it must be a wonderful life, and I must say they were all remarkable women and seemed to get on perfectly together. It was like a monastic settlement, with Mrs Breckenridge as the Prioress. The area covered by the Service is some seven hundred square miles, and they look after 10,000 people.

The mountain people were tall, aquiline, handsome and distinguished, with courtly manners, graceful ease, nobility of look, and altogether a remarkably fine race. Their long thin bones and refined hands might have belonged to aristocrats. They are of pure English, Scottish or Welsh descent, their ancestors being those who, in the great push west at the end of the eighteenth century, chose to remain in the Appalachian mountains. And there they still are, with their blood unadulterated by the mongrel population of America today.

They are a friendly and hospitable people, whose faces broke into smiles as we approached. And the language they spoke was music to the ears. With soft voices they used such expressions as 'begone' instead of 'go away' to the dog; 'the edge of the dark' instead of twilight; and 'they never see a stranger', meaning they see friends in all. An old woman told me she 'never saw a well day'; and an old man, accused by the nurse of chewing tobacco, replied, 'I own to true'. 'Nesties' is the plural for nest, 'beasties' for beast. Their 'yeah' was much softer than the ordinary American form.

It is wrong to say that these charming people are backward. Intelligence tests have shown them to be on a high level, but they have lacked education. Their wooden cabins are pretty ramshackle. All have verandahs, on which the family seems to spend a great deal of time sitting and contemplating. I returned to Wendover at about six o'clock, glad to be back after a long day in the open bumping about in the jeep. The next day the nurses motored me into Lexington from where I caught the train to New York. To arrive in this city after those days in the remote mountains was such a contrast that I have hardly got accustomed to it yet.

Wave Hill, New York, 11 June (letter to CN)

We have been much concerned about the 'missing diplomats', particularly because Alan Maclean is the younger brother of Donald.[6] Donald is extremely tall and good-looking, quite spectacular in fact, and had a breakdown last year, and got into the hands of the brilliant and dissolute Philip Toynbee, who seems to have influenced various other people, such as Ben Nicolson. It is possible that Burgess is only on some great debauch, but it is all very unpleasant, whatever the outcome is.

Platon, Leclercville, Lotbiniere County, Quebec, 6 July (letter to CN)

Don't tell Aunt Ethel but, no later than my first night with the de Lotbinieres I learned of a juicy bit of old scandal, hitherto unknown to me. It appears that Grandmama's father, Archibald Campbell, had a Spanish mistress who lived above the office which was in the lower part of Quebec, and thus conveniently removed from his home which was near the Citadel. By this charmer he had children who married into some eminent old Canadian families; and when the lady died her lover put on her tomb 'Blessed are the pure in heart'! No doubt this accounts for Aunt Ethel, when we were looking at some old photographs, mumbling that her grandmother had a very sad time.

It has been most interesting being in Canada. Directly I crossed the border it was like being in France. Beautiful agricultural and timber country, the people fine-looking, quiet and solid and talking the French of Louis XIV and having the most exquisite courtly manners (they bow from the waist when introduced), and they had built large churches and splendid barns in the old Normandy style. George [Tamboni], who had driven me up, was horrified at the primitive life in Canada – he had never before seen cows on the road, and was scornful that not one house had a television aerial, which goes to show what happens to

[6] Alan Maclean (1924–   ) was Private Secretary to Gladwyn. On 25 May Donald Maclean and Guy Burgess defected to the Soviet Union. Herbert Morrison, who had briefly succeeded as Foreign Secretary on the death of Ernest Bevin, insisted that Alan should resign from the Service. He subsequently became a director of Macmillan.

Italians when they become spoilt by town life, for I feel sure his own parents lived in the most poverty-stricken way south of Naples before they emigrated.

(an account of an extra-sensory perception, sent to Veronica Gainford[7])

In August 1951 Judy Montagu lent me Breccles for about ten days. She knew that I had known and loved the place since childhood, as it practically marched with Wretham. Breccles is a beautiful Tudor house of mellow brick, which originally belonged to a well-known Catholic family, the Wodehouses. It has a priest's hiding hole, and the reputation of being haunted. The servants were in a wing built out on the left of the house.

A few nights later I heard somebody moving about in the room above mine. Distinct footsteps on the floorboards, and at one moment as if something like a piece of furniture was being dragged along. I turned on the light, sat up in bed, felt very frightened and wondered whether I had the courage to open my door, fumble for the light switch and cross over to the other side of the house where Miles and Vanessa slept. The movements seemed confined to the room above mine, and I resolved to stay unless I heard them move out towards the stairs. After about half an hour they ceased. Eventually I turned off the light and tried to sleep.

The next day I found the explanation. It was the butler's room. He, Clements, an aged and trusted servant, slept at the lodge which was quite close to the house. But here was his room, with his evening clothes neatly laid out on one of the beds, and I at once deduced that since we had been alarmed about a prowler a few nights before, Clements was sleeping in the house.

However, on the Saturday night it was pouring with rain, and when he came in to bring the drinks, I remarked that it was a good thing that he did not have to return to his lodge in such a rainstorm. He looked surprised and murmured something about going there despite the awful weather. At which I said in genuine astonishment, 'But you are

[7] Veronica Noble (1900–1995), a first cousin of Cynthia, and widow of Joseph Pease, 2nd Lord Gainford. In the family she was known as Bon, and Cynthia as Bin.

sleeping here, Clements'. He replied, 'I only sleep in the house when there is a very late night here, and you have been going to bed early'. I, beginning to be alarmed, expostulated, 'But you were here a few nights ago! I heard you moving about just above me'. He then looked at me very closely saying, 'Surely you haven't been hearing things in that room, my lady?' By now, struggling for an explanation, I murmured, 'Perhaps it was a cat or a bat or something', which he echoed reassuringly. I was quite relieved to think that there were only two more nights in Breccles.

When I went to see Judy later I rather lightly told her of my experience. She at once said that the haunted part of the house was at the opposite end, and that her parents had had the whole place exorcized. As far as she knew there were no ghosts now. We talked of other things and I said goodbye. Just as we reached the door she suddenly said, 'I've just remembered. Something did happen in that room at Breccles'.

Four men (including Duff Cooper and Freddie Cripps) had been playing golf and, on returning to the house, rang for drinks to be brought. The footman said that the butler had the key of the cellar, and he was out. After about half an hour they rang again, but the butler had not come back. A little later the footman was told he must find the butler, and he returned to say that he could not find him and that his bedroom was locked. The men thought they had better see for themselves, and as there was no sound from within they broke open the door and found that the butler had shot himself.

21 Square du Bois de Boulogne, Paris, 26 November (letter to CN)[8]

My birthday party was held at the Elysée,[9] it being the night of the President's dinner party. I wore the little Empire headdress you gave me, and it was much admired and is so light and pleasant to wear. The dinner was a magnificent affair with about 200 guests and masses more for the reception afterwards. It was beautifully done, as only the French know how, and altogether very brilliant. My neighbour, who knew what he was in for, had most wisely lunched only on carrots, the more to be able

[8] The sixth General Assembly of the United Nations was held in Paris whilst the UN building in New York was under construction.
[9] The Elysée Palace, residence of the President of France.

to appreciate the celebrated wines and food, as the President's chef is world-famous.

We contrived to do a little sight-seeing during the evening, and penetrated into some lovely rooms where we were shown the Empire furniture, and the carpet of the Légion d'Honneur. The furniture in the room which had been Josephine's salon was upholstered in pale blue and silver silk, very pretty but a little cold. The walls were pale grey with some rather earlier little Cupids painted on them. In this room Napoleon signed his first abdication, and Napoleon III and the Duc de Mornay planned the Coup d'Etat.

1952

21 Square du Bois de Boulogne, Paris, 20 January (letter to CN)

Today Gladwyn and I went to Chantilly to lunch with the Coopers.[1] They have a charming house, all the furniture and decor so pretty, and with a touch of Bohemianism and untidiness. Diana C herself lovely, but wearing extraordinary clothes for Sunday lunch in the country – a tan-coloured felt skirt ornamented with black braid and tassels, a black wool jumper, sandal shoes, and a huge black hat covered with feathers and tied under her chin. There was a large assortment of odd and amusing people and a noisy informal atmosphere, with a pug puppy running around.

I was taken over the house afterwards. There are many pictures, drawings, busts and wax heads of Diana, and some drawings by her mother in lovely frail pencil-work. One of Harry Cust;[2] and one of Queen Victoria old and in profile, which made her look ethereal, which she surely cannot have been. And a pretty water-colour of the Duchess done by Queen Victoria herself.

---

[1] Although it contravened normal British diplomatic practice, Duff Cooper had stayed on in France after his retirement as Ambassador, a grateful French Government offering him retention of full diplomatic status and the lease of the Château de St Firmin at Chantilly.
[2] Harry Cust is assumed to have been Diana's natural father. Her mother was Violet Lindsay, wife of Henry Manners, 8th Duke of Rutland.

Wave Hill, New York, 3 March

We dined with Cecil Beaton and Freddie Ashton[3] before the performance of their new English ballet, *Picnic at Tintagel*. They were a little
apprehensive about its reception, but Cecil was in such high spirits that,
when I told him the extraordinary news that Leigh Ashton was engaged
to a strange character called Mrs Garland, he said his night was made
and it didn't matter whether the ballet was a success or not.[4] In point of
fact the audience didn't dare show what they felt because they were
uncertain what line to take until they had read the criticisms in the next
day's *New York Times* and *Herald Tribune*. Cecil says this irritates him
immensely.

Wave Hill, New York, 9 March

We have had an orgy of the Oliviers this week – *Caesar and Cleopatra* one
night and *Antony and Cleopatra* the next. The Shaw was by far the best,
since to my mind Vivien Leigh is just the right pretty fascinating minx to
play his Cleopatra. Laurence O made himself into an aged, stooping,
sad, smiling Julius Caesar, which is surely a travesty. The next night he
was most handsome, wearing his own nose again, and bearded; but,
again, not my idea of Antony, who surely was a great coarse man, with a
vulgar sense of humour. Vivien Leigh was the same pert charmer of the
previous play, in no way able to convey the passion and dignity of
Cleopatra.

Wave Hill, New York, 18 March

It is impossible to get people here to understand our being in Court
Mourning.[5] I go about as black as a crow, even with dark stockings, and

---

[3] Cecil Beaton, later Sir Cecil (1904–80), photographer and designer; and Freddie
Ashton, later Sir Frederick (1904–88), choreographer.
[4] Sir Leigh Ashton (1897–1983), Director of the Victoria and Albert Museum, and no
relation to Freddie Ashton, was marrying Madge Garland (marriage dissolved in
1962).
[5] George VI had died on 6 February.

we are not allowed to go to cocktail parties or large dinner parties, with the one exception of the Security Council dinners. At first they imagine we refer to some personal bereavement, and when we explain it is for the King, they just look very surprised and incredulous. Pressing us to attend a dinner for twenty-four, a hostess said that one of her guests was in mourning for a brother, so surely it was all right for us to accept.

Wave Hill, New York, 20 March

We dined with Nin [Ryan].[6] Her house overlooking the East River is very intimate and pretty, and has an altogether personal atmosphere, unusual in this city. Just as we were about to leave, at 11.30, the newest Duchess of Argyll arrived. This is Margaret Whigham that was, a much advertised *Tatler* beauty, but doll-like. She and Ian, who is pretty dissolute now, go very little to Inverary and I believe are not liked at all in that lovely part of Scotland from which they take their title. New York at the moment seems to abound in rather second-rate duchesses, as Loelia Westminster is also here. At a recent party she went very silent when she heard of the Rothermeres' divorce. 'That's upset all my plans', she said; 'I always had a free bedroom at the Rothermeres'.

Wave Hill, New York, 23 March

M et Mme Moch came to lunch. He was at one time Prime Minister of France, and was splendid in the Resistance.[7] Discussing the question of royalty in France, he said that the Comte de Paris didn't have a chance as nobody in France wants a king. When the then Princess Elizabeth was on her visit to Paris, as they went up the steps to the Opéra she turned round to wave to the crowd, who cheered with such enthusiasm that the Duke of Edinburgh was moved to say to Moch, 'But why did they guillotine them?'; to which he replied, 'Because they were French'.

[6] Margaret ('Nin') Kahn (1902–95), wife of John Barry Ryan. She was a leading figure in New York Society.
[7] Jules Moch (b. 1893) was never Prime Minister of France, but as Minister of the Interior quelled the Communist Party's attempt to bring down the government by strikes and riots in 1947–8.

Wave Hill, New York, 29 March

The Toscanini concert took place this afternoon: we heard it from Nin Ryan's box. Toscanini was eighty-five the other day, but so vigorous and young in spirit that one can hardly believe it. Afterwards we dined with the Cowles.[8] They must be immensely rich, and have spent an incredible amount on making their house truly hideous. It was all very modern, and the worst touch of all, to my mind, was to dine off a black table cloth – at the head of which Mrs C sat in a very high-necked black jumper, with thick spectacles and her hair tied back with a black bow.

Wave Hill, New York, 3 April

An old lady, Mrs Murray Crane, gave a most delightful musical evening in her apartment in Fifth Avenue tonight – a performance of an opera by Jean Jacques Rousseau called *Le Devin du Village*, it being two hundred years since it was first given. I had no idea that Rousseau had ever written an opera. It was altogether charming, with only three characters, and the room was arranged at one end with a curtain and a rustic scene. It was the first music party I had been to in this country. Afterwards there was a delicious supper. Mrs Crane has, I believe, a salon; certainly she is a most enterprising woman.

Wave Hill, New York, 4 April

The Oliviers came to lunch today. Their success here has not been as great as they expected. The theatre they are in is for musicals, and has bad acoustics for them. And the abominable New York habit, of touts buying up all the seats and then selling them for a profit, has caused many complaints. This is no fault of the Oliviers, but they get some unpleasant letters which he minds, and he remarked that he was like a clay pigeon being sent off in order to be shot down. He also resented

[8] Mike Cowles (b. 1903), married to Fleur Fenton. He was President of Cowles Magazines (*Look, Quick,* etc.), and she was a newspaper columnist who in 1953 was sent as a special representative of President Eisenhower to the coronation of Queen Elizabeth II. She married, secondly, Thomas Meyer.

remarks by some American diplomats, travelling on the *Queen Elizabeth*, to the effect that they would see the Oliviers didn't come to America again because they were Communists. This stems from the fact that LO's name appeared on some Committee for Cultural Relations with the Soviets during the war.

Wave Hill, New York, 6 April

Cecil Beaton came to lunch today *en famille*. He was most amusing and we had a fine gossip. After lunch he took photographs for *Vogue*, which was really the purpose of his visit. An assistant arrived with two lamps, two small cameras, and an instrument for testing light; and the system was that Cecil took a whole mass of photographs very rapidly, telling us to move or look this or that way, or himself moving around and getting different angles of us. When he had finished one film, he quickly seized the second camera while the assistant changed the film. No more tripods or velvet tablecloths or holding a position. I asked him what makes a person photogenic, and he said a flat expansion of face, high cheekbones, small features and a nose giving no shadows. Small eyes didn't matter, or a large mouth. He could see at once that I would not photograph at all.

Wave Hill, New York, 8 April

Our engagements today were centred around the Queen of the Netherlands. She is a most excellent example of what post-war democratic royalty should be. For one thing, all curtseying has been abolished: Queen Juliana certainly loses no dignity by only receiving handshakes. She was far better looking than I expected. Her figure and clothing were as they should be, not in the height of fashion, but pleasing to the eye. Had she been slim and chic she would not have given such a happy impression of regality and integrity. She appeared as the sensible virtuous head of a sensible virtuous people. Her face, without any pretensions to beauty, was beautiful in its earnestness; and her naturalness, in expression and manner, was really delightful. She has a charming voice, and the speech she made was excellent, advocating patience and spiritual awareness. At the Security Council dinner in her honour I walked in on the arm of Mr Malik, all gotten up in a white tie, and we sat opposite Mrs Malik who wore three rows of pearls which I surmise came from the neck of some Grand Duchess killed in the revolution. The table was decorated with roses and freesias flown from Holland, and much of the menu was Dutch.

Wave Hill, New York, 9 April

We dined with Mrs Lewisohn who has moved to a flat overlooking the East River, with a magnificent view through her plate-glass windows, though one enjoyed by many other well-to-do New Yorkers, and not as romantic as ours over the Hudson.[9] Her Cezannes were at the Metropolitan for an exhibition, but she didn't seem to lack for pictures. After dinner we were treated to a deplorable form of entertainment of which Americans are very fond. When the men had joined us, she clapped her hands, made us sit in a circle, and announced that we were to ask questions of Admiral Kirk, just returned from being Ambassador in Moscow, and Gladwyn. The unfortunate victims had to answer as best they could without being indiscreet or being led to take a line which they could not defend. I wonder why it does not occur to these hosts and hostesses to cultivate the art of conversation and of listening with interest, thus drawing forth from the lion they have just fed much more interesting confidences than they can ever hope for in these forums.

Wave Hill, New York, 10 April

Tonight we dined with the Henry Luces in their marvellous apartment, with the correct East River view from the correct uncurtained windows.[10] The drawing-room was twice as high as the rest of the

[9] Margaret Seligman (b. 1896), married to Sam Lewisohn. She was a prominent educationalist.
[10] Henry Luce (b. 1898) married (secondly) Clare Boothe. He was the founder of *Time*, *Fortune* and *Life* magazines; she was a playwright, Congresswoman, and subsequently US Ambassador to Italy.

rooms, giving it a grandiose European character. I had never before met Clare Luce. She must be a brilliant woman, but very neurotic and full of conflict. She is beautiful, but looked extremely ill. It was her birthday, and all sorts of strange silly presents were brought to her, such as a colossal balloon, and a set of 'I like Ike' apparel consisting of a jaunty little hat and stockings thus inscribed. We sat at three tables in two rooms. I was seated on Harry Luce's right. He promised to launch a campaign against the habit, prevalent in England as well as America, of using Christian names at first acquaintance.

Wave Hill, New York, 18 May

We have just returned from a visit to the Mid West. We entered the vast polished marble hall of the Grand Central Station – so different from our old draughty dirty London stations – and went through the processes of finding our platform. Sitting in our compartment we had the pleasure of travelling up the Harlem River and then the Hudson, passing just below Wave Hill and other familiar landmarks. We had supper brought to us and then went to bed in our most comfortable sleepers, complete with lavatory (shades of night journeys in the War, sitting up in Third Class carriages). We were thus able to arrive in Chicago next morning looking impeccable, to be greeted by the Consul General, Berkeley Gage, and various other officials, not forgetting a photographer from the *Chicago Tribune*.

Berkeley Gage is half American, very kind, hearty, but with good sense. His open friendly manner has made him most popular and able to crack the hard nut of Chicago. At his cocktail party, given for us, we met a good cross-section of Chicago society. The salient point of the party was the presence of the infamous Colonel McCormick. This strange character, an egotistical megalomaniac, has a profoundly unhappy face which breaks curiously into a shy and almost charming smile. I have seldom seen such a miserable tortured expression. He is violently anti-British, some say because he was bullied at his English private school, others because he didn't receive some decoration after the First World War, but at all events because of his inherited Irish hatred of our country. British visitors find him disarming to meet, but then are disillusioned to read some montrously venomous article about

them in the *Tribune*. I was forced to greet this sinister man, tall, dressed
like an English country squire, by linking little fingers, because he was at
that moment drinking a whisky and his hand had got wet. That over, we
talked pleasantly enough on trivial matters – American cities, skyscrapers, helicopters. His (second) wife was a rather vulgar, but not bad,
woman.

Another curious person at the party was Mrs Adlai Stevenson, whom
I remembered a few years ago in London. She insisted on divorcing her
husband because he became Governor of Illinois and she gave out that
she wasn't interested in politics. The truth is that she resented no longer
being the important one in the ménage. Now that he may be standing
for the Presidency, she blackens his character. Altogether I had an
impression of an unhappy, selfish, neurotic woman, on top of which
she was distinctly tight and went on shouting after everybody else had
gone. She and the Colonel were certainly strange types, but the rest of
the company were more normal and pleasant.

Next morning Berkeley motored us to the environs of Chicago
where most people live, in charming 'homes', as they are always called
over here. We went to see a rich old couple, Mr and Mrs Max Epstein,
who have a wonderful collection of pictures and furniture, chiefly
English. But our dear old host was just as anxious that we should see his
modern bathrooms as his 'El Gereco', as he called it. We also called on
the McCormick Blairs, the *crème de la crème* of Chicago life, who just
could not have been nicer or more interesting, or more pro-British.
They and the Chauncey McCormicks are both ashamed to bear the
same name as that of the Colonel. We also visited the University of
Chicago, where we saw the betatron and cyclotron in a mysterious labo-
ratory underground. We had to remove our watches, but I still had my
umbrella, which suddenly began to behave in a most extraordinary way,
like a poltergeist. It was like being in a hall of surprises at an amusement
arcade – a cold blast shot at one from a fan, passages suddenly closed,
and various mild explosions made one jump.

After this we dined with Clifton Utley, the television commentator,
and then went to see Gladwyn being televised, which was most entertaining. While waiting we watched various advertisements being televised – a silly smiling young man with a winning manner recommending
cornflakes; and then a sympathetic older man with greying hair, grey
suit, black tie, altogether dressed impeccably like a banker, posed

himself in an informal attitude against a table and advised us with irresistible charm to insure our lives for our wives and daughters.

The next morning we rose early and caught the train to Springfield, about three hours journey, where we lunched with Adlai Stevenson.[11] The governmental mansion was a roomy Early Victorian house with a lot of white paint and nice unfashionable furniture. After an excellent lunch we went sightseeing and visited Lincoln's tomb and home and the reconstructed village of New Salem, where he lived. All very well done, except that they had omitted to put a bedside table in the bedroom.

We dined on the train, changed at Chicago, and then caught the midnight train to Buffalo. Here we lunched with a most charming and brilliant young man of twenty-three called Cary Welch, who had been asked to entertain us as his father was away. He had the manner and assurance of a man far older and yet was not conceited. He took us to the Art Gallery and the Niagara Falls in his grandmother's ancient Rolls, and altogether was most helpful and amiable. At lunch with him we met a clergyman who invited us to dine and attend an impromptu meeting of the English Speaking Union, before catching our night train. About forty people came, amongst them a remarkable old clergyman who resembled some eighteenth-century divine and had been at Oxford and followed the course of the Scholar Gipsy on his bicycle: he asked many questions about England and deplored the ignorance of America, which he attributed to lack of classical education.

Wave Hill, New York, 11 June

The great event of the week was the Garden Party. We had been instructed to ask no British people, which caused much resentment. On the morning of the great day Carmen, Henrietta and I did the flowers, supplementing the garden produce with sweet peas from the florist. At the last moment Gravett,[12] who had suddenly become good-humoured and co-operative, had the brilliant suggestion that we must have a flag;

---

[11] Adlai Stevenson (1900–65), previously married to Ellen Borden. Governor of Illinois and Democratic presidential candidate in 1952.
[12] Thomas Gravett was the dependable but irritable butler inherited by Cynthia and Gladwyn from the household of their predecessors the Cadogans at Oyster Bay, and who subsequently accompanied them to Paris.

so one was dug out of the Consulate and affixed above the porch just before the guests arrived. At four thirty the guests began to dribble in. Gladwyn and I stood trying to decipher the garbled names the announcer shouted at us – one man was announced as 'Mr Urine'. Six hundred and seventy persons filed before us, and my pale silk gloves gradually became black, and my hand almost bruised, since early in the proceedings a man gave me a violent crushing squeeze. The party had all the usual appurtenances – strawberries and cream, and a band. I truly think it was a success, and so it was all the more annoying to read in the *Evening Standard* that the wicked old Beaverbrook was criticizing us for wasting money. I forgot to mention that we managed to prevent any reporters from coming.[13]

Wave Hill, New York, 12 June

Tonight Mr Rorimer organized a delightful escapade in the form of a picnic party in the Cloisters.[14] It was small and informal, and medieval, for Mr R would allow no knives or forks, so we ate chicken with our fingers. We went into the cloister, or rather, the garden where all the herbs are grown, and that itself was an amusing diversion for it was fun trying to identify them all as we sat around eating our delicious food. When it became too dark we went inside and saw the treasures in perfect solitude and leisure. Mr Rorimer was in high spirits because Mr Rockefeller had just donated ten million dollars to the Cloisters.

Wave Hill, New York, 22 June

We have just returned from staying with the Eugene Meyers. He runs the *Washington Post* and is a man of great influence. Their house, built just before the First War up on Mount Kisko, is large, with long wide pas-

---

[13] Cynthia remained blissfully impervious to the resentment felt by the lesser correspondents towards diplomatic *hauteur*.

[14] James Rorimer was Director of the Metropolitan Museum's Department of Medieval Art. This was based at the Cloisters, a pseudo-Gothic edifice overlooking the Hudson in northern Manhattan, incorporating a medieval cloister, removed from Spain, embellished with glazing and heating.

sages and very good workmanship, and filled with a great many Chinese and French things. Mr Meyer is elderly: his family was originally French, which accounts for his civilized animation and vigour. Mrs Meyer was German, and looks it, and is a great authority on Chinese art. There was a dinner party last night and a lunch party today. Staying in the house was the exceedingly handsome Danish ambassador, and the Gallups of 'Gallup Poll' fame. It never ceased raining, but we went for a wet walk this morning round the lake. Mr Meyer was amusing and shrewd. He said that FDR was 'amoral' and did certain things that were dishonest, rather as one might say that Lloyd George did. He was very pungent about MacArthur and his self-conceit, and how he could make a speech in the style of Napoleon, Caesar or anybody, as the situation required. Gladwyn said he (Meyer) was a 'progressive reactionary'. There was excellent food, nice servants including a French maid and a butler from Kent. All the visitors were Anglophiles — one was even called an Anglomaniac by his wife; and all the men wore real English clothes and shoes and ties.

Wave Hill, New York, 26 June

Tonight Malik had his dinner, as usual a large affair with about fifty guests sitting at an immense table in a suite in the Waldorf Astoria. We had a lot of vodka and caviare, and at our places were no less than six glasses for various types of drink, all of which were Russian. My impression was that our hosts were trying to be more amicable than last year. There were certainly fewer obstructing thugs filling up the party — men with low brows and sinister expressions, and stunted, plump and unfeminine women. I sat next to Malik. We talk about Russian habits, his family, how the Russians drink tea, books, music, films, and any subject but politics. He is genial, but in moments of repose, or when taken off his guard, his face has a cruel, pinched and almost frightened look, which perhaps is not surprising.

From our conversations I have discovered a few quite interesting things. He is the eldest of five brothers, two of whom were killed in the War, two are alive, but the fifth is not mentioned. His mother, who is religious and goes to church, was uneducated but slaved to give him an education. She now lives on a small pension and his help: she was a teacher (of what, I cannot make out), and she writes. He never mentions his father. Malik has a handsome face and a fine bearing, so one wonders who his forebears were.

Wave Hill, New York, 13 July

On the Fourth of July weekend Gladwyn and I went up to Maine to stay with Rowland Burdon-Muller. Rowland is the kindest of men, a delicate bachelor of about sixty, and describes himself as 'an Edwardian dilettante of the Fabergé period'. Extremely intelligent, his one real fault is that he never stops talking. When he has no company he writes long letters to his friends or to his Senator. He collects Chinese objects, there being now quite a slump in Chinese things due to the conflict with Communist China. Rowland is looked after by an excellent French couple, he the valet, she the cook, so the food is delicious, as also the wines. He won't allow a bottle of gin or whisky in the house, and altogether the atmosphere is very civilized.

Since we came back, most of the week has been spent watching the Republican Convention on the television. It was most exciting to watch the whole business unfold before one's eyes – but what a business! I was shocked at the crookedness and levity. When the nominations were made there was a real pandemonium, with the vast crowds singing, dancing, shouting and behaving like naughty children. '*Ils sont complètement déchaînés*', whispered a French onlooker to me, and it certainly seemed so, though at the end the right man was fortunately chosen.[15] One feels that this great country ought to evolve a more worthy method of deciding such momentous questions. The leader in the *Tribune* yesterday was slightly shamefaced about it, but concluded, in a tone of defiance, 'We are like this. We like it!' Time they changed, I say, if they are to lead the world. And now we go through the same story all over again next week for the Democrats.

Chance conversations show that many people dislike the idea of a General as President; and, of course, the Americans don't like discipline. The lack of discipline is observed from the cradle upwards. I have recently been in contact with two small boys of five or six. One was Ed Morrow's child whom we saw when staying with him, and the other was brought here yesterday by his parents when his father was playing tennis.

[15] General Eisenhower was the Republican candidate.

Both were obviously sweet little boys at heart, but they were allowed to behave as badly as they liked, in fact they had no manners at all. They both became downright rude, and were not reprimanded. This emanates from a theory, evolved by a man called Dewey, whereby persuasion can be used, of a gentler sort, but no order given. At the Sulzbergers the other day the grandson was asked, 'Would you like to say how do you do to Lady Jebb?' No reply being given, the matter was dropped.

Wave Hill, New York, 19 July

On Wednesday I lunched with Janetta Whitridge at the Colony Club, and we had a most interesting talk about the Conventions. Gladwyn always thinks I am too critical and that the Conventions, though unconventional from a European standpoint, do in the end produce the right man for the times. Therefore it was gratifying to find that Janetta and her particular family were profoundly shocked by them, and felt very differently from her sisters, Mrs Winthrop Aldrich and Mrs Sheldon Whitehouse. Janetta has married into quite another milieu, Arnold being a quiet intellectual who was a professor at Yale and has lectured a great deal abroad. While we were eating Mrs John Foster Dulles[16] came and sat with us, and I told her how we had seen her on television. She said how exciting it had been in Chicago, and how the best party had been given by Elizabeth Arden.[17] When she had gone Janetta expressed her disgust that such a person as Elizabeth Arden should have been throwing a party at this supposedly solemn gathering to decide a vital question. She also criticized Dulles, whose political opinions have varied with expediency.

Wave Hill, New York, All Hallow's E'en (letter to MJ)

Everyone is getting excited over the elections. I have met several people who were for Ike and wore those 'I like Ike' buttons when I left in July, but have now switched to Stevenson because they were shocked at his association with Taft and McCarthy and others, and feel he is not

---

[16] Janey Avery, wife of John Foster Dulles (1888–1959). He was about to become United States Secretary of State.
[17] Founder of Elizabeth Arden cosmetics.

competent for the job. But some friends (the Ryans, for instance) are still firmly for Eisenhower, and are among those who repeat the most absurd and unpleasant rumours about Adlai. It will be a near thing.[18]

The other day we went to a farewell party for the Gunthers, who are off to Africa to do an 'Inside',[19] and who should we meet at this very intimate gathering but the Garbo. She wore a rather ordinary green daytime woollen dress, her hair was unkempt but short, her complexion curiously dark for a Swede, her lipstick slashed on very uncarefully. But she had a *je ne sais quoi* that was arresting and fascinating: she spoke in a deep male voice. Apparently she is enormously rich but never spends a penny if she can help it, wears ugly old clothes, particularly on her long walks in Central Park. She is a great buddy of Gaylord Hauser and lives on fruit juice; though she was drinking gin when I saw her. She likes to be known as Miss Brown.

Wave Hill, New York, 16 November (letter to MJ)

Anthony Eden[20] arrived considerably the worse for wear after a bad air journey and some recurrent internal trouble, but with rest and care made a swift recovery. Gravett doted on him – another example of the curious hero-worship he inspires – and nothing was too much bother. For some reason Gravett always referred to him as 'Mr Anthony'. On the other hand he showed the greatest contempt for Anthony's entourage, such as the detective, who in fact spent most of the time on the tiles in New York, and complained, 'I can't think why they don't give him a valet-detective like Lord Balfour used to have, someone who would look after his suits properly'. As to Evelyn Shuckburgh, he was merely 'the person Mr Anthony brought', or 'the one who sleeps in Miss Stella's room', and he was even blamed when the springs of a chair were found to be broken – 'the sort who flings himself on the furniture'.[21]

---

[18] It was a decisive Republican victory, with Eisenhower's 33.9 million votes to Stevenson's 27.3 million.

[19] John Gunther (b. 1901), married (secondly) Jane Vandercook. His series of books on regional current affairs had begun with his *Inside Europe*.

[20] Now Foreign Secretary once again under Churchill's premiership.

[21] Evelyn Shuckburgh, later Sir Evelyn (1909–94): Private Secretary to Anthony Eden. His *Descent to Suez* provides the leading British diplomatic diary of the period.

On the Sunday night we had a dinner of twenty for various American friends our guest wished to meet. Then yesterday we had a huge cocktail party for about four hundred, which I believe to have been a success as the company was reluctant to leave. All the Russians showed up with their attendant thugs. I had got the Baronial Hall nicely arranged after an exhausting battle with Gravett who was, as usual, full of pessimism, gloomy forebodings, and generally bad-tempered, though of course as the hour of the party approached he became efficient and co-operative and all went like clockwork.

Everybody is busy recovering from the elections, and some have even gone to recuperate in the country. People seem to take the attitude that all the mud-slinging must now be forgotten. I must say I agree with the Democrat who said, 'All I can say is "God save the President" when I think of the Vice-President'.[22]

Wave Hill, New York, 7 December (letter to MJ)

Just a fortnight ago I went out to a dinner party at the Whitelaw Reids who run the *Herald Tribune*. It was to be a surprise birthday party for his mother, Mrs Ogden Reid, who is seventy, and who thought she was coming to a quiet family gathering. There were at least a hundred people gathered to greet her, all waiting in the drawing-room, and our cars parked well away from the house for all to seem quiet. The red-coated musicians struck up 'Happy birthday to you', and then came the *pièce de résistance* – General and Mrs Eisenhower, and the band played 'We like Ike'. I found myself next to him at dinner, and got his signature for Stella's book. He had great vigour and drive and optimism, very simple and easy to talk to; but it was rather like sitting next to a very nice schoolboy. I was a little shocked at his lack of formality. For instance, when the musicians played his favourite or topical songs he sang lustily as he ate. They played something which was evidently intended for him but which he dismissed as being too highbrow: it was the Columbia University 'Alma Mater'.

---

[22] Richard Nixon.

1953

❧

Wave Hill, New York, 9 January (letter to MJ)

On Wednesday we lunched with the PM at Barnie Baruch's. Winston Churchill seems to have shrunk a lot and was very deaf in his left ear, which unfortunately was the side I was on, so conversation was a little difficult. But mentally he was extremely alert, and he had a charming old-world courtliness; he was dressed impeccably in a black suit. His skin is as pink and fresh and unwrinkled as a baby's. And he poured some champagne from his glass over the Virginia ham, and dipped the end of his cigar in his brandy. He made a little speech to the Mayor of New York, a slippery ice-creamer from near Palermo called Impelliteri, making a pun which the Mayor failed to see.

Wave Hill, New York, 18 January (letter to MJ)

We had a dinner party on Thursday for the Aldriches[1] to which two ex-Ambassadors to England came, Davies and Douglas, and among others the Luces. I am told Mrs Luce is not liked in Rome. She and her husband were both divorced before they were married, so the Catholics don't approve; whereas she is a recent and ardent convert to Catholicism, to the disapproval of most of the intelligent government people, who are anti-Vatican. Also, the Italians do not like being put on a par with Luxembourg, to which another female ambassador has been

[1] Winthrop Aldrich (1885–1974), married to Harriet Alexander. Was about to become US Ambassador to Britain.

sent. Clare Luce is very pretty, really lovely, but in a rather unreal way. She is like someone seen in fluorescent light, and doesn't look as though she were made of flesh and blood.[2] Mr Bing[3] was also at our dinner – we now call him Rudolf – and was glad to see the Waverleys again and to compare the Met to Covent Garden. Ava thinks that the minor parts are much better sung here than in England.

Wave Hill, New York, 3 February (letter to MJ)

I spent a most delightful weekend with my gourmet dilettante friend at Boston. Raymond Bonham Carter came to dine the first night. I don't quite know what he made of Rowland's memories of his Edwardian youth at Oxford, when he would come to London to go to the theatre wearing white tie and tails, hire an electric brougham with a footman on the box, dine at the Berkeley, and catch a 'special' back to Oxford. He described also his luggage for going abroad, his quantity of clothes and his jewellery. An aunt had married a stockbroker, who as such could not possibly be invited to the house, but 'one gave him lunch at Claridges'.

I flew down to Washington in Sir William Elliot's private plane, the Dove,[4] to stay with the Makins. After lunch Alice took us all over the Embassy. I must say I do not envy her that house. It is bad architecturally and decoratively, and full of second-rate furniture – dreadful bedroom suites from Maples or suchlike, sofas and chairs upholstered in common materials. No doubt it cost a lot, but it makes the Embassy look like a country club. I returned next day to Wave Hill with its friendly atmosphere and pleasing proportions, and the Jebb pieces of furniture and Jebb colour schemes.

The following night we underwent an awful ordeal, at which I just wanted to sink through the floor. There is an absurd fashion just now in New York of giving 'surprise parties'. In this case Mike Cowles was taken by his wife to dine quietly at a restaurant with his brother and

---

[2] When in Rome she nearly died from food poisoning, eventually traced to arsenic falling from the painted ceiling of her breakfast room.
[3] Rudolf Bing, later Sir Rudolf (1902–   ), Director of the Metropolitan Opera: a naturalized British subject who had previously directed at Glyndebourne.
[4] Air Chief Marshal Sir William Elliot (1896–1971): Chairman of the British Joint Services Mission in Washington.

sister-in-law, and came home to find lots of friends all hiding in the dark in the drawing-room. Above five of the men, including Gladwyn and Lou Douglas and Abe Burrows – who wrote *Guys and Dolls*[5] – were dressed in women's cotton dresses and wore blonde wigs. I didn't approve at all, and begged Gladwyn to remove his speedily. Lou Douglas then put on a false beard and did some comic turns of which I had never imagined him capable, kicking his legs up in the air and shouting in a most un-ambassadorial fashion. Bob Sherwood too sang and danced, and so did various other cabaret singers, and finally Danny Kaye arrived and was, of course, excellent and amusing. He has something extraordinarily attractive about him, with his sensitive face and touch of melancholy despite all his buffoonery. The Garbo was also there, looking untidy and aloof, but rather magnificent. By the time supper was to be eaten I persuaded Gladwyn to go home. I forgot to mention that all the carpets were black and long-haired, and our hostess has a black table-cloth and wears black glasses. It was all rather like a nightmare, not to be experienced again, I hope.

Wave Hill, New York, 22 February (letter to MJ)

I fell quite in love with the 'deep south'. Life in Georgia is delightfully civilized, and the lazy drawl no doubt comes from the relaxing climate: they seem as though they are too tired to finish their words, which makes them quite difficult to understand. I saw a lovely old house near Atlanta called Mimosa Hall. It was very like what I had imagined Tara in *Gone with the Wind* to be like, and was one of the few mansions not destroyed by General Sherman's ruthless ravages.

On our return we stopped at Charlottesville, where we saw Jefferson's famous university. Here there is a serpentine wall identical to that at Bramfield. When Jefferson was Minister to France in 1786, he came on a visit to England, and no doubt got the idea for it then. It was Jefferson who inserted the phrase 'the pursuit of happiness' into the Declaration of Independence, now thought by some to be unfortunate: perhaps it would have been better to say 'the pursuit of virtue'.

---

[5] The lyrics, not the music.

Wave Hill, New York, 23 March (letter to MJ)

We had a big dinner for the Edens one night, and one for the Butlers the next night. This, though exhausting, was an economy, as the flowers lasted for both evenings. At the Eden party old Trygvie Lie[6] did a monstrous thing, unheard of in the history of protocol, I'm sure. When he looked at the table plan he observed that Mike Pearson (Foreign Secretary of Canada and President of the Assembly) had been put on Clarissa Eden's right (she being a joint hostess) and he on her left in the second grandest place. So he pushed past Gravett into the dining room and altered the cards around. When later we went in to dinner, Mike made for Clarissa's right and sat down, but old Triggers turned him out saying his card was there. We couldn't quite understand what had occurred and so left it. Fortunately Mike Pearson didn't mind. Clarissa Eden[7] is a most unusual and interesting type, but I should imagine happier leading a life where she could meet her own intellectual friends rather than a lot of dull people to whom she has to be polite.

Wave Hill, New York, 10 April (letter to MJ)

Lady Astor is in New York and full of animation. Her now famous remark to that dreadful Senator McCarthy was made at a private party and repeated by someone to the press.[8] She says that she has had such horrible letters from his angry supporters that she is thinking of publishing them to show what kind of policy they advocate. I think McCarthy is a real danger. Somebody said to me the other day that he thought that within eight years from now McCarthy would either be President or be murdered: one must hope the latter.

[6] Trygvie Lie (b. 1896): the Norwegian Secretary-General of the United Nations. (Gladwyn had been the Provisional Secretary-General at the initial General Assembly in London in 1945.)
[7] Clarissa Churchill, second wife of Anthony Eden.
[8] 'What's that you're drinking?'; 'Whisky'; 'I wish it was poison'. In a way, it *was* poison, as McCarthy died of drink in 1957.

Wave Hill, New York, 12 April (letter to CN)

We have been busy this week with ceremonies of adieu to Trygvie Lie and of welcome to Dag Hammarskjold. The latter is a great improvement on the thick-minded gross-looking old Secretary General who has been here for seven years, of whom it is rumoured that when he resigned he was convinced they would never agree on a successor and that he would be sworn in again. However, he has gone, and his successor is a handsome interesting bachelor of forty-eight, at the thought of whom the ladies of New York are very excited. But I see he is serious-minded and an apostle of Schweitzer, and likes to climb mountains with a volume of T. S. Eliot in his pocket; so perhaps their high hopes will be dashed.

Wave Hill, New York, 11 May (letter to MJ)

When we returned from Florida we found we were to dine the next night with the Russians for their Security Council dinner – rather short notice, but as our relations with them are supposed to be so amicable, we went out of our way to attend. It took place at the Waldorf and was indeed a friendly affair with a great deal of toasting and professions of friendship and singing at table Russian songs such as 'Black Eyes' and the 'Volga Boat Song'. Vyshinsky raised his vodka and said 'buttons up' – meaning 'bottoms up'. It was a veritable orgy of vodka, caviare and roses. He handed me one of the dark red roses which, despite its prickliness, I shoved down my front. I then handed him one which he attempted to insert in his button-hole, but evidently the suits of Soviet officials, however high-ranking, don't run to *boutonnières*, so he had to put it in his pocket. He is a truly evil man, thin-lipped, horribly alert, and with cold steely eyes behind his spectacles. I asked him whether he had enjoyed the Indian film on the life of Gandhi. Vyshinsky said he had not agreed with the religious aspects of it, but when I said that I supposed there was very little religious feeling in Russia he hastened to assure me that there were many churches and people could go as much as they wished. He told me that he himself had been deeply religious until about seventeen, even assisting in church ceremonies.

Wave Hill, New York, 19 May (letter to MJ)

We went to Lancaster, Pennsylvania, with the object of visiting a curious religious sect called the Amish, people who have been there for nearly two hundred years and still pursue the same way of living as when they originally left Germany. They still talk a form of German, Platt-Deutsch. They farm, and are exceedingly thrifty and deny themselves modern luxuries such as radios, telephones or cars. The women wear black bonnets and stockings; and the men broad straw or felt hats, hair down to their collars, long beards if they are married – and the upper lip shaved, supposedly as a protest against the Prussian militarism from which they fled. As another protest they avoid the wearing of buttons, and rely entirely on pins. They drive around in little enclosed carts. Owing to intermarriage they all looked much alike, women not handsome, the men more so, but malodorous – perhaps their beards need a good wash. But they all had nice smooth happy faces, and I can say, with truth, that the happiest people I have seen in this country are the Amishes and the Hill Billies.

Wave Hill, New York, 12 June (letter to CN)

Last night we went to see the colour film of the Coronation. It is tremendously popular, and most people have to queue for hours. It must have been excellently rehearsed, for the whole ceremony went without a mistake or even a hesitation. How beautiful and dignified the young Queen looked, very like Queen Mary at times, I thought. Whatever it has cost, it has done wonders for British propaganda here: people could think and talk of nothing else, and are deeply impressed by our organization of such an occasion, the significance of the religious tradition, and the genuine enthusiasm of the crowds.

92 Eaton Place, London, 2 September[9]

I went up to Northumberland, the salient point of which was a visit to Chillingham. It is the most romantic place I know. Standing on the roof,

[9] In the flat of Thelma de Chair.

looking at the magnificent Northumbrian landscape, with a fresh soft wind bringing delicious scents, is to feel the magic of Chillingham. How strange it is to revisit a place one knew well as a child: it is all so extraordinarily familiar, and one realizes that one has really forgotten nothing. The steps, the stones of the courtyard, the door-handles, and all manner of details, seemed to be just as I knew they had always been, yet I had not thought of them through the years, but would have known if they had been different.

From Northumberland I went to Ardkinglas. There that beautiful great house was getting more shabby, damp and dilapidated, but all the same being run in a certain style – we sat in the saloon and dined by the light of silver candlesticks, and didn't have to wash up as we did during the War. The food was superb – great chunks of home-made yellow butter on the dining-room table, thick yellow cream, succulent fresh salmon, and those wonderful large and late Scottish raspberries. Everyone was so animated and laughed so much – this group of people living in this remote part of the Highlands where it rains so much that one's mackintosh is never dry, with cold draughty passages, and stone stairs cold to the feet, inadequate heating and plumbing, were all tremendously happy.

I went to Strachur to see Joan Campbell, whom I remember, when I was a child, as a tearing beauty. Her brother Ivar was quite astonishingly beautiful too, and in his kilt and blue jacket and blue tam o'shanter with a red bobble, and with his bright hair and blue eyes and brilliant complexion, he seemed to me like some bright-coloured bird of paradise. He eclipsed everybody with his looks and colouring and I thought him a god. He was killed in the First War, and Joan is now a soured dried elderly spinster, abominably dressed, sitting alone in her drawing-room and having high-tea for her last meal at six o'clock. But she still has good features and great distinction.

I also went to Dunderave and made a nostalgic tour of the castle and garden. It is supposed to be Lorimer's masterpiece, exquisitely restored and beautified with just the right touches by Aunt Lily for whom it was created.[10] It seemed full of her presence. We sat a little in the library among her books and embroideries and thought of old times, and how

[10] Dunderave Castle is across Loch Fyne from Ardkinglas House, and is the setting for Neil Munro's novel *Castle Doom*.

handsome she was. And I seemed to see Grandmama sitting on her window seat in the Hall of the Red Banner, sewing away and making astute remarks; or mixing drinking-chocolate at midnight in the little salon while we told ghost stories round the fire.

Yesterday I lunched with Ava Waverley, the only other guest being Isaiah Berlin.[11] He was in superb form, and we spent most of the time discussing the Eden marriage. Ava thinks Clarissa should acquire a more amiable manner, and remember to smile and shake hands. Isaiah thinks this is impossible for her to do. He thinks she has a sort of Edwardian view of life with big romantic attachments, and that she is not an intellectual, as I thought. But however ailing Anthony might become, he is sure she will stick to him.

92 Eaton Place, London, 7 September

We have just returned from a delightful weekend at Stanstead. Rab was in wonderful form, very amusing and also wise and interesting. I have seldom seen him in better spirits. Sydney too was in good heart, very abrupt and forthright and kind. The old Henry VII house looked so mellow and gave a great feeling of security. The garden with the yew hedges and roses, the old mulberry tree with yet another branch fallen, the moat, the birds singing, the rooks cawing, are all things I shall often think of when I am away in America. Somebody in a novel (I rather think it was Vera Birch describing Firle) writes how wood-pigeons seem to be cooing 'You've forgotten, you've forgotten'. At how many of the houses I have visited this summer – Chillingham, Old Quarries, Heveningham, Stanstead – have I paused to listen to their sad haunting notes.

[11] Isaiah Berlin, later Sir Isaiah (1909–   ). He had worked in the Diplomatic Service during the War, and was to become Chichele Professor of Social and Political Theory at Oxford, and subsequently President of the British Academy.

92 Eaton Place, London, 17 September

Yesterday I went to have a drink with Cecil Beaton in his charming house in Pelham Place, very Victorian in decoration. I particularly enjoyed the red flax walls and white woodwork with gold pickings. James Pope-Hennessy was there, and that strange dislikable baronet, Sir Francis Rose – such a beautiful name for an awful man. He had with him a swarthy young man of twenty-one, rather complacent, but not being able to speak a word of English. This youth, though seemingly a Marseillais whom Rose had picked up, was introduced to us as his son. Rose tells the extraordinary story that long ago he had a brief affair with a Spanish woman in a garden at a party. He never saw her again, but she died recently and sent the young man to Rose labelled 'This is your son'. Rose seems tremendously proud of, or rather, absorbed in, the boy. We wondered after they had gone if the whole story was a fabrication. However, Cecil fancied he saw some resemblance in their thumbs!

I rather wish people would wear brighter colours in England. And I wish people here were taught how to walk and sit better. But on Tuesday there was an impressive fly-past over London to commemorate the Battle of Britain. The noise was terrific and the sight wonderful. All the inhabitants of Eaton Place appeared at their windows or balconies, or on their roofs, and people on the pavements stood still, quietly watching and remembering thirteen years ago. It was altogether very moving and brought tears to my eyes. I thought to myself: what does it matter about smart clothes, bright colours, plumbing, and all that America can boast of? They could not have done what we did in 1940.

Wave Hill, New York, 1 November (letter to MJ)

Humbo is in terrific form, and I am passing him off very successfully as a good example of an eccentric English country gentleman – a type rarely seen over here. His wardrobe is in itself absolutely fascinating. He brought a large quantity of quite obsolete and extremely heavy luggage made of good worn leather, whose contents are worthy of reading aloud as in Consequences. They included his evening tails and decorations; his pink coat, top hat, boots, etc., for hunting on Saturdays; his bowler hat, black coat, boots, etc., for hunting on weekdays; his ratcatcher clothes for ordinary riding; a grey bowler hat for wearing on Sundays in the country; a large leather case containing outsize field-glasses for viewing the St Lawrence River from the ship; a smaller leather case containing an aneroid for use in the lift of the Empire State Building; Grandpapa's tie-pin and walking stick with 'Athenaeum' written in Greek on it; and the heavy leather writing-case which was made for Grandpapa when he went to Japan some fifty years ago. I successfully stopped him bringing his top hat and tails for day wear, but was unsuccessful in persuading him to invest in the most necessary garment of all here, namely, an ordinary dark suit, which would carry him through the day in New York and be suitable for cocktail parties and theatres. For this purpose he only has check tweeds which would be better in their Northumbrian background.[12]

[12] Humphrey Noble's imitation of the manners of an earlier generation also took the form of writing with a quill pen and sealing his letters. For this he had a normal seal, depicting his crest and the Brunel motto *En Avant*; and another seal for specially favoured recipients, depicting the first four bars of Bach's First Brandenburg Concerto.

1954

Connaught Hotel, London, 28 March (letter to MJ)[1]

I must tell you about our luncheon with the PM ten days ago. It was a very intimate affair, Lady Churchill being ill, and their daughter, Mary Soames, also. So we were only the Rowans from the Treasury, and the Private Secretary, Jock Colville. The PM was in wonderful form. He was less deaf and more animated than when I last met him in New York about a year ago. He talked most amusingly, and we stayed on till after three listening to him. He said among the honours given him by France was the privilege of being allowed to be carried home drunk without getting into trouble. I said I hoped he would come and let us see him exercise this privilege. His skin is quite extraordinarily youthful and could be envied by any woman – no wrinkles and so fresh-looking. I dare say the secret of this is going to sleep every afternoon, and not worrying.

British Embassy, Paris, 25 April (letter to CN)

We had a most comfortable and luxurious journey across and were met by various officials at Calais, and then had a delicious dinner on the train. When we reached Paris there was a huge crowd awaiting us on the platform – people from the Quai d'Orsay, our staff, French friends, and

---

[1] To Cynthia's great joy, Anthony Eden had appointed Gladwyn to be Ambassador to France, and not to succeed Sir William Strang as Permanent Under-Secretary of State for Foreign Affairs, as Gladwyn would have preferred.

the press. We then rolled along in a Rolls with outriders and arrived here, where some of the staff came and had coffee with us. I was very tired when I finally got into my gilt and canopied bed in the lovely red silk room, and slept very well there; indeed, I have ever since, nor seen any ghosts nor found the 'furniture watching me' as Maudie complained. On the contrary, it has all seemed most welcoming. Ever since then I have been trying to get the house arranged a little better. The downstairs rooms are all magnificent but need a little re-arrangement, since Empire furniture is rather cold and austere. Upstairs, the visitors' bedrooms are appalling, like a second-class hotel in Brighton with extremely old-fashioned and inconvenient bathroom arrangements. For the Edens' visit we managed to get two bedrooms quite tolerable with some of our own furniture, and I hope to get some better plumbing if the Ministry of Works will agree. The servants' rooms are shocking. We should never put anybody into such badly furnished bedrooms these days; and they haven't even got a sitting-room. So all that has to be seen to. I was surprised at the condition in which the Harveys left the house.

British Embassy, Paris, 5 May (letter to MJ)

On Sunday we attended the St George's Day celebrations at St George's Church (near the Etoile). We were received by Father Brandetti and an acolyte waiting ceremoniously on the pavement with a cross. We then processed into the church and were placed on ceremonial chairs – very important-looking, but with the disadvantage of our not being able to see what the congregation was up to behind us, and this was highly necessary since the service was different from anything I had been to before. It was real Popery. There were two clergy attendant on Father B, and a couple of acolytes, all dressed in beautiful red brocade copes, the material of which (so they said) came from Marie Antoinette's room at the Tuilleries; then there was the Bishop of Ely and a parson, and an old bishop of the Orthodox Church and a young Russian priest, both bearded. All these persons performed strange rites; they dressed and undressed, genuflected, knelt, sat, moved about, chanted the Gospel, embraced before Communion, and altogether it was most puzzling. The incense was swung at Gladwyn thrice, and he should have bowed in acknowledgement, but he obviously didn't hold with it. When the whole performance was over we all repaired to Father Brandetti's house next door and drank champagne.

British Embassy, Paris, 23 May (letter to CN)

We are in the midst of the Entente Cordiale celebrations and have the Charles Morgans staying here. There was a very long ceremony at the Sorbonne on Friday night. Fortunately our seats were luxurious arm-chairs, but some were sitting on hard benches and found it most uncomfortable. Charles recited his famous poem 'Beloved France' with tears in his eyes, and almost broke down, and of course the French adored it. Gladwyn read Anthony Eden's speech in his absence, and Schumann read Bidault's speech.[2] Then André Siegfried gave a brilliant talk on the English character; it was delightful, sincere and witty. After this we had some dancers from Aberdeen, the men in kilts, with very plain ladies in unbecoming white dresses with tartan sashes and all with reddish hair, reddish faces and necks, and protruding teeth. They really were not good enough, except for one famous dancer called Bobby Watson who performed a sword dance. This was followed by a superb work by Tallis for eight choirs. These were placed all around the circular hall, and the effect was stupendous. It was like being in heaven, with angelic sounds coming from everywhere. Instead of ending on this magnificent note, the Scottish dancers appeared again, Bobby Watson this time performing on the bagpipes and the others dancing a four-some and eightsome reel, just like in the saloon at Ardkinglas, and not as well done either, but evidently the French thought them wonderful.

British Embassy, Paris, 2 July (letter to MJ)

A few weeks ago we dined with the Windsors at their house in the Bois de Boulogne. We went in trepidation for we had been told that at a dinner the previous night the Duchess had obviously been drunk and behaved in a most embarrassing manner. However at her own party this

[2] Georges Bidault (1899–1983) was French Foreign Minister, and Maurice Schumann (1911–) was his Deputy, and subsequently Foreign Minister.

time she seemed perfectly all right, though a little excited and nervous, repeating herself the whole time. The house is pretty, but decorated in a very American manner. The dining room, whose boiseries have come out of an old château, contained two little alcoves arranged in a rather chi-chi way, with a cello and other musical instruments in one, and in the other a fan, a cloak, a mantilla, and a pair of white kid gloves. Quite amusing, but I wouldn't like it every day while I ate. We sat at a number of round tables. I was next to the Duke. He has lumbago, looks old and wrinkled with a baby face, very nervous, quick, with great charm, but of course immensely pathetic. After dinner a pianist played jazz rather softly in the drawing-room, not for us to dance, but for us to talk to.

We went to Oxford for the Encaenia ceremony.[3] Nowhere else would there be such delightful tradition, such witty speeches, Day-Lewis reading a particularly long piece in Latin recounting all the events at Oxford, rendering it quite beautifully and looking most handsome the while. Some of the other recitations were also excellent, especially that of young Arnander who recited Greek hexameters. Strange that the offspring of Folke Arnander, who was clever at arranging flowers in the Japanese fashion and would have liked to be an *antiquaire*, should be so brilliant.

British Embassy, Paris, 2 July (letter to CN)

The other evening we gave a return dinner for the Windsors. She had been careful not to take anything beforehand, or much at the dinner, so the evening went off well. After they had gone, a few of us, including Diana Cooper, went to the Petit Trianon where the Hameau was illuminated for a fête in aid of a charity – the first time there had been an evening party there since the eighteenth century. It was rather chilly, but very pretty, with fireworks, magic lanterns, and automatons – lifesize dolls in grottos bowing and curtseying or playing music. Then again, this week there was a garden party at the Bagatelle, which was delightful. Set on the rocks across the lake were groups of huntsmen playing nostalgic tunes on their horns and looking gorgeous in their red coats. The French know how to do this sort of thing so well.

[3] Gladwyn was being awarded an Honorary Doctorate of Civil Law by Oxford University.

British Embassy, Paris, 10 July (letter to MJ)

Last week we had a large luncheon for the Comte de Paris (the Pretender) and his wife.[4] She is good-looking and dignified, with a humorous expression in her eyes. They have eleven children, so the dynasty is unlikely to die out. Monseigneur has a royal manner, and most curious light blue-grey eyes, and a pointed face. I have heard it said that he is not his father's son, but since his wife is anyway a Bourbon, their children are at any rate descendants. It must have been a relief for this ménage that the progeny of Naundorf (who claimed to be the Dauphin in the Temple) have lost their case to claim legitimacy as the senior line of the Bourbons.

British Embassy, Paris, 18 July (letter to MJ)

At lunch today we were told by the Duchesse de Talleyrand about a most unfortunate gaffe made by the Duke of Windsor at the supper party following her son's wedding. He had spilt coffee over the dress of his next-door neighbour by making too hasty a gesture, and had been much comforted by the fact she was a Rothschild who could well afford another dress. After apologies had been made, and to start the conversation going again, he brightly remarked to her, 'Since you are a Rothschild, can you tell me which is the Rothschild with whom Pamela Churchill[5] is having an affair?' To which she replied, 'Sir, that's worse than the coffee; that's my husband!'

British Embassy, Paris, 18 August (letter to CN)

I am much better now, and in a few days will be quite all right again. It was a horrid accident, but over so quickly, and mercifully not worse. We

---

[4] Prince Henri d'Orleans, Comte de Paris (1908–), married to Princess Isabelle de Bregance. His claim to the throne of France was through the House of Orleans, though she descended from the more senior house of Bourbon-Bregance.
[5] Pamela Digby, former wife of Randolph Churchill and subsequently of Averill Harriman. In 1993 she was appointed US Ambassador to France.

skidded on the wet surface of a renowned bad corner which was not properly marked. A cavalcade of cars headed by a motor-bus was coming up the hill and the car behind the bus drew out, which caused Gladwyn to put on his brakes and skid. After a few days in Linz I was able to proceed to the Schloss in the Tyrol where we were to stay with the Arnold Whitridges.

British Embassy, Paris, 24 August (letter to MJ)

Last weekend we went out to Chantilly, the Coopers' house, which the American Ambassador and Mrs Dillon have taken for the summer months. I rather think they were disappointed in it, and I am sure that during their lives in New Jersey in the winter and Maine in the summer they had never come across anything like it. To begin with, the atmosphere was full of the presences of Duff and Diana, and the rooms full of their most personal possessions. Everything is prettily arranged and artistic, but rather thrown together. I am sure our friends expected a bedroom with twin beds and a bathroom with twin basins. Instead of which they found a wonderful romantic bed with a canopy and muslin draperies, and a bathroom where the lavatory was concealed by a silk curtain, where the taps were swan's heads, and where the plug was concealed by a straw hat and the soap hidden in an Empire crystal bowl.

1955

❖

Moulin Marachonne, Grasse, 28 August (letter to CN)

We are having a blissful time here.[1] This small house has a really lovely garden with lots of water rushing through it in small canals into the mill stream. The only slight inconvenience is that there is no electric light, since gas and oil lamps are never quite so good to read by.

An extraordinary collection of royalty, present or ex, are on the Riviera, including Queen Soraya. I have seldom seen a more disagreeable looking woman, with great pouting mouth, flopping back on her sofa with her legs and arms crossed. We have made friends with the ex-Queen of Italy (the one who was Belgian). She behaved very well in the War, and eventually escaped to Switzerland with her children. She is charming and very intellectual. But most of the people who come to this coast are vulgar rich Greeks and Italians, and, of course, the dreadful Dockers;[2] all cruising about in huge luxurious yachts, looking awful, and behaving as badly. I am told there is a lot of Communism in these parts, and really it is not surprising.

---

[1] A mill-house near Grasse rented by Gladwyn and Cynthia from Colonel Eric Dunstan for a summer holiday.
[2] Sir Bernard Docker (1896–1978), married to Norah Collins. He was Chairman of Birmingham Small Arms, and she was given to tactless remarks flaunting their ability to evade, by means of their yacht, the stringent exchange controls for foreign travel.

1956

❧

British Embassy, Paris, 7 May

Queen Elizabeth the Queen Mother came to Paris on Tuesday 13 March, the reason for her visit being to open the Franco-Scottish Exhibition at the Archives Nationales. She travelled with a large suite: her Lady in Waiting, Patricia Hambleden; her secretary, Martin Gilliat (very nice, charming, emotional); a detective; two dressers (for some reason, lady's maids of royalty are always called dressers); and a page (who was in fact a most obliging rotund footman and altogether helpful in the house). Her plane arrived at Le Bourget on a cold sunny March morning, and she emerged all smiles and nods and beams, dressed in pastel blue. On arrival at the Embassy we sat down to an intimate lunch, and afterwards went to change and dress for the opening of the exhibition.

The Queen Mother speaks excellent French and read her speech beautifully at the Archives. There were gathered among the crowd of French officials several people who had lent things to the exhibition. It was good to see John and Elizabeth [Noble's] familiar faces, and not so good to see Margaret Argyll's hard Elizabeth Arden face, looking as though she had just had a scrap with Ian; deservedly, she was not recognized by the royal visitor.

The first night we had a dinner party for the government officials. We were about sixty-six. Madame Dufy and Madame Anna came along to help me dress and my room (I was upstairs) was agog with helping hands, enthusiastic women, everybody very excited, and Gladwyn coming in at intervals telling me I would be late. Indeed I was, as half the dinner party was there already, but it didn't seem to matter. What did matter was that neither Mme Mollet nor Mme Pineau had come, or were intending to come.[1] Their husbands had arrived alone. Nevertheless they had definitely accepted and we have never been able to discover exactly what happened. There was now no time to worry or change the placement, so we just moved everybody up one. We then went into the State Dining Room, which looked very beautiful.

The next day there was nothing in the morning as the Queen Mother was to spend it in her sitting room, the Salon Vert, and receive there a few people she wished to see. I find her a puzzling person. So sweet, so smiling, so soft, so charming, so winning, so easy and pleasant. And yet there is another side, which sometimes reveals itself, rather mocking, not very kind, not very loyal, almost unwise. For instance, an old governess was to come, with her family, and this was mimicked and laughed at before and after: and yet I have no doubt that the famous charm was shown to the governess and that she went away enchanted. I have heard that Queen Elizabeth delights in mimicry, and particularly in doing herself using her charm. As another instance, before going to the Elysée to luncheon that day, Gladwyn told her how nice the President[2] was, and how much he admired England, as did also Monsieur Mollet. As I walked with her upstairs and along to her room she kept on exclaiming what a bore Monsieur Mollet had been with his loyalty. I was so surprised that I said, 'Did he say something that was annoying, or unpleasant, ma'am?'; and she replied, 'Oh no, he was very nice, but it is such a bore when people tell one that they like the English'. A very odd remark for an English queen.

Another un-royal habit of the Queen Mother is that she is very unpunctual. I am unpunctual myself, and could not sympathize with her more on this continual struggle in life; but I do expect royalty to be punctual on public occasions. We were about twenty minutes late for everything, and of course it upset all the plans. In this way we arrived late at Versailles to see the Petits Appartements, and by the time we reached the Commonwealth Party at the Grand Trianon everybody was beginning to get anxious at our non-appearance.

In the evening we had another dinner party of sixty-four, this time

[1] Guy Mollet (1905–1975) was the French Prime Minister, and Christian Pineau (1904–95) the Foreign Minister.
[2] René Coty (1882–1962): President of France 1953–8.

for friends and unofficial personalities. Diana was there, looking lovely in red velvet, and Daisy Fellowes being catty about her. The table had pink flowers and candlesticks, and nearly everyone wore all the jewellery they could muster, and tiaras, owned or borrowed, and the effect was glittering. Some of the old French jewellery was wonderful, particularly the very high tiaras worn by Aymone de Brantes and Brenda de Bourbon-Busset. I wore a white embroidered dress of Fath, and my diamond Empire wreath, and a white tulle scarf. After dinner the Queen retired briefly while about three hundred guests gathered below. We then processed through the drawing-rooms to the ballroom, and many presentations were made. It was difficult to pick out the right ones and avoid the wrong ones. I kept turning round, and somebody said that the Queen Mother and I looked as though we were skating, gliding and turning in a small space like Rose Red and Snow White, I being Snow White. Finally the Queen Mother went into the Salon Ionien, with the lovely pale blue satin covering on the furniture, and my two pale blue velvet covered tables. There she received the Nato ambassadors and ambassadresses, and special guests, and had a private buffet and champagne brought to her by her royal footman, who had also served her at dinner. Some old Frenchman once told me that up to the Revolution, if a nobleman went out to dine, he always brought his footman who would stand behind his chair and attend to his wants; so I suppose the presence of the royal footman was a survival of this old custom.

I am forgetting to describe my daughters. Vanessa in an embroidered dress of gold and blue on white, borrowed from Fath, wore the ornament with the pearl hanging down her forehead, that had belonged to Mother: Jean Oberle seeing her exclaimed, 'But who is this, Pauline Borghese?' Stella had her hair up and was in pale blue. Nancy Rodd had a little ruche round her neck rather à la Pompadour. Violet Trefusis[3] was in a tremendous Edwardian tiara and stomacher that had previously been Mrs Keppel's.

Next day, before going to the reception of the Association France-Grande Bretagne, I had a curious interchange with HM. I said I was afraid we might meet André Maurois. I knew that she had been warned that he might be there and had been advised not to be too amiable if he

---

[3] Violet Keppel (1894–1972), widow of Denys Trefusis, and daughter of Alice Keppel, who had been mistress of Edward VII.

was presented to her. We ourselves had not asked him to our reception, for the reason that he, who was always considered the great friend of England, the Frenchman who loved us and had written so brilliantly about us, had behaved badly in the War. Arriving in England when France fell, he soon decided to get to safety in America, where he gave lectures saying that Britain was finished. So I was amazed to hear her retort that he was an old friend, and had helped her with her speech to the women of France in 1940. I began to murmur about the War, but twigged that this line was not going down at all well, so quickly let the subject drop. That evening we were just fourteen for dinner, and it was most peaceful and pleasant.

On the final day, the acclamation of the crowd along the route to Le Bourget was great, and the Queen Mother's celebrated smile brought forth even greater cheers. She sat a little forward in her seat and did it all with grace and charm. Her only un-royal action was not to have put her gloves on till we neared the airport, which involved her in a frightful and no so graceful struggle to get them on before greeting all the dignitaries, blaming 'my silly maid' for 'giving me tight gloves'.

On Sunday 22 April Gladwyn and I, the Reillys,[4] the Service Attachés, and various important people, all found ourselves once more in the monstrously ugly VIP room at Le Bourget. We were awaiting the plane of the Princess Royal[5] who was staying with us two days before going up to Lille to receive a degree. As the Viking of the Queen's flight was sighted, we moved out on to the tarmac. The plane taxied to a halt, the gangway was brought up, the door was opened, but nobody appeared. There was a long pause while we waited expectantly, the men with their top hats in their hands. Finally the Princess Royal emerged, in full military uniform. This masculine-looking figure then came briskly down the steps in her solid low-heeled shoes, dark leather gloves in her hand, her chest resplendent with decorations, her lady-in-waiting carrying her handbag, and saluted the astonished company. Presentations were made, the traditional bouquet looked a trifle out of place, and we got into the cars. I drove with the Princess. A few Sunday crowds had gathered along the route to see who it was who was shooting past, pre-

---

[4] Patrick Reilly, later Sir Patrick (1909–   ), married to Rachel Sykes. Minister in the Paris Embassy 1953–6, and subsequently Ambassador to France 1965–8.
[5] Mary, Princess Royal (1897–1965), sister of George VI and widow of Henry Lascelles, 6th Earl of Harewood.

ceded by a police car, flanked by outriders and followed by officials.
And they must indeed have speculated as to the soldierly personage,
who yet from her contours seemed to be female, saluting rather
abruptly and conscientiously at intervals. Had they but known, it was, to
my mind, almost the most delightful and worthy member of the royal
family – I say 'almost', because the present Queen is perfection.

Princess Mary, I believe, had a wretched youth: strictly brought up,
bullied, and without even the chance of the occasional emancipation
enjoyed by her brothers when they could escape from their parents' vig-
ilant eyes. She was married off to Lord Lascelles, who was no longer
young and physically unattractive, but rich and with wonderful possessions. Some say he was horrid to her, others that she was happy with
him; but anyway he cannot have been a pleasant husband.

She is extremely shy, and was probably never helped to conquer this
defect. She is not unlike Queen Mary in appearance, and yet in her military cap she much reminded me of the late King. For some reason she
uses no aids to beauty, which is surprising as royalty always resort to
make-up. Queen Mary's face was exquisitely touched up and dazzling
even when quite old, and George VI towards the end of his life was distinctly made up at garden parties and such occasions. But the Princess
Royal spurns all artificial colouring, though she seems to wash her face
over with some sort of liquid powder which gives her a rather curious
hue. Her hair is greying, her clothes not becoming, and her shyness
makes her a little stiff and unforthcoming.

Yet very soon one begins to be aware of her sincere and good character and her many other merits. She is, above all, very conscientious, and
will always do the right thing. This shines out in her so strongly that,
even before reaching the Embassy, I was aware that this visit was going
to be much more simple than that of the Queen Mother. In lieu of
charm, here was a person who was anxious to help, brought up in the
old school, well-educated, intelligent, well-read, aware of what is going
on in the world and forming a sensible judgement on it all, and taught
by Queen Mary to appreciate objets d'art. Gladwyn was most
impressed by her knowledge.

When we arrived at the Embassy, Jasper was in the midst of it all,
barking excitedly in the background with Gravett trying to restrain him.
But his presence was a great success with the Princess, who approached
him with her hand clenched as all doggy persons know how, bending

down and letting him examine her thoroughly, and told us that she too had a black dachshund, called Punch. This completely won Stella's and Gravett's hearts. She won mine by her genuine admiration of the Embassy, and Gladwyn's by at once noticing, as we passed through the ante-room, that the Empire clock represented Hippolyte.

That evening we had a small dinner party, with the Salisburys, the Ismays, René Massigli, Georges Salles, Ava (who was also staying in the house), and members of the staff. Afterwards – and this was my bright idea – we went out in a procession of cars to see the illuminations (the important buildings of Paris being floodlit on Saturdays and Sundays), and all the party were enchanted.

Wednesday 25 April was the day of the degree ceremony at Lille, and the birthday of the Princess, and furthermore, Gladwyn's birthday. So presents were exchanged by the two Doctors in their robes outside their bedrooms in the passage of the Préfeture before going downstairs. Princess Mary looked splendid in her cap and gown, with a little Balfour boy as a page, and read her speech in perfect French. After a lunch party at the Rectorate she made a brief and impromptu visit to the museum on hearing that there were some fine pictures there; and on the previous day she had squeezed in a visit to the Louvre because I told her about the famous bronzes from the Place des Victoires which Queen Mary and King George had presented on their state visit. Later on a wet grey afternoon we saw the Princess fly off to Yorkshire. I felt really sad to say goodbye.

Stratfield Saye, Hampshire, 17 June

I came over from Paris on Friday to go to the Firle Ball.[6] Hartley Shawcross motored me down.[7] I was much depressed when he told me of rumours that we were to leave Paris when Ivone [Kirkpatrick] retires at the end of the year. Hartley said he strongly advised Gladwyn to come home soon and talk to Anthony about it. This, on top of feeling

[6] The ball given by Lord and Lady Gage at their Sussex house, Firle Place, for their daughter Camilla.
[7] Sir Hartley Shawcross, later Lord Shawcross (1902–   ). He had been Attorney-General 1945–51, and had also served as the Principal British Delegate to the General Assembly of the United Nations 1945–9.

ill, made me very sad. I have been living in paradise for two years and did not expect to be taken away from it quite so soon. I began to regret having left it even for a weekend. I love that beautiful house and want to see the completion of the improvements I am making to it. Then there is our happy household – Stella, in her pretty pink room with her work on *Vogue* and all her popularity; Jasper, cherished by Gravett and Berthe, and all the delightful walks on which I take him in the parks; dear Walter[8] and dear Mrs Walker in the office to greet one as one goes in and out. Then all the lovely clothes I wear from Fath, the hats from Reboux, and the entertaining; the getting-out of the Wellington plate on impor- tant occasions and thinking of different ways to adorn it with flowers and fruit; the arrangement of the lighting and the lighting of candles; the placing of ornaments; the summoning of Jacques Franck to help rearrange the furniture. Then the going out to parties with the knowl- edge that one was always going to find delightful conversation, deli- cious food and wine, often an exquisitely furnished house and spend a civilized evening; the sight-seeing, which is my passion, the discoveries – and all the dear friends! It is as though the bottom of my world might at any moment be taken away, which might indeed happen to anyone at any moment. I suppose it is a warning not to become too attached to material things; but mine was a particularly enchanting world, like living in fairyland, and it was all the more tempting to become attached to it.

So I didn't completely enjoy the dance at Firle, though there were many friends there and it was beautifully done. Moggs has got so many of her lovely Panshanger things there that it looks very different from what I remember in the old days when George (whom we used then to call by his first name, Rainald) lived there with his three sisters and an old aunt.[9] There were several friends from Paris there, and I had a long talk with John Christie.

At lunch today I sat next to John Waverley. I told him that Harold Nicolson had recently quite shocked me by saying that if it had not been for Winston we would not have gone on with the War when France fell; and Nancy Rodd had also said everybody in England would have given in (this conversation taking place in May when we were driving out to

[8] Major Walter Lees (1912–   ), Comptroller of the Embassy Residence, and estim- able adviser to Cynthia and Gladwyn on the intracacies of Parisian society.
[9] Henry Rainald ('George'), 6th Viscount Gage (1895–1982), married to Imogen ('Moggs') Grenfell.

Port Royal for Harold to get local atmosphere for his book on Sainte Beuve). John fortunately was able to refute this. He said Chamberlain's colleagues would not have let him give in, and that of course England would have carried on, Churchill or no Churchill.

British Embassy, Paris, 19 June

Gladwyn and Jasper (very wet) met me at Le Bourget. We talked in the car of those horrible rumours that have depressed me so much. It seems that Roger Makins is perhaps to go to the Treasury; and what with old Ivone's tiresome retirement imminent, that leaves two plums, the Foreign Office and Washington. Gladwyn would be disappointed if he did not get one or the other.[10] But how sad! I cannot think why the Treasury cannot run on its own officials. It is all because Harold [Macmillan] always has to have his favourite aides round him wherever he goes. And if Rab had not left the Treasury, Harold would not be there now.

It was in this very room, the Salon Vert (the lounge, as the Ministry of Works call it), that Rab sat pondering last November as to whether he should move or not. Anthony had offered him any job in the Cabinet he liked, he said, but the Lord President of the Council and Leader of the House of Commons was what he thought he would take if he left the Treasury, as he had been so little in the House during recent years, and felt out of touch with it. Also he thought it would be good training if he were to become Prime Minister. I asked him what Sydney would have wished him to do, and he at once replied, 'Oh, she would have urged me to leave. She thought I worked much too hard'. He also said that he did not want to do another Budget, which showed how sensitive he was to criticism of his last one. He then mused for a moment on whether Anthony could be double-crossing him. Of course, when the change did take place at Christmas he was deeply hurt when it was suggested he had to give up the Treasury because he was over-tired and had not recovered from his wife's death. He should, I feel sure, have carried on and tried to wipe out the bad impression made by his autumn Budget.

[10] The two front runners to succeed Sir Ivone Kirkpatrick as Permanent Under-Secretary for Foreign Affairs were Gladwyn and Roger Makins. In the event, Sir Frederick Hoyer-Millar, later 1st Lord Inchyra (1900–89), was appointed, to Cynthia's great relief but Gladwyn's disappointment.

When Harold brought in his Budget a few months later Rab was very bitter about it, and told Edward Boyle that he felt he could never speak again to the Governor of the Bank of England, because he had authorized Harold to do things that he had refused to Rab: (though Edward told me that when Rab asked for these things to be done, it would not have been expedient to grant them). So Rab went from the Treasury, and it was really because Anthony could not get on with Harold at the Foreign Office and wanted instead to put there somebody who he could control; so he gave the FO to Selwyn Lloyd, who has become a sort of 'bell hop' to Anthony.[11]

We went to the Menuhin concert this evening, and afterwards the Menuhins came back to supper.[12] He practises yoga, which gives him great relaxation and detachment, and he showed us how he stands on his head, which I long to be able to do. He played beautifully, but perhaps a little coldly.

British Embassy, Paris, 20 June

Dorothy Bennett came to lunch today.[13] She is a wreck of her former self; fat, untidy, bad teeth, bad memory. I remember her so well in the old days, when she was handsome and blonde and went everywhere because everybody loved Arnold, and accepted her. We used sometimes all to be in Paris together with Alfred Beit, for the Viennese opera or other events, and meet Ravel; and Arnold was the life and soul of the party with his wonderful remarks which he stammered out. He would sometimes spell a word if he couldn't say it; and I remember him saying that there was only one good bookshop in London, and that was 'B...U...M...pus'.[14]

---

[11] Selwyn Lloyd, later Lord Selwyn-Lloyd (1904–78): Secretary of State for Foreign Affairs 1955–60, and subsequently Speaker of the House of Commons.

[12] Yehudi Menuhin, later Lord Menuhin (1916–   ), married to Diana Gould. Violinist.

[13] Dorothy Cheston: mistress of Arnold Bennet (1867–1931), author and playwright, whose name she assumed.

[14] Arnold Bennett had been one of the first guests of Gladwyn and Cynthia after their marriage, in their small house in Chelsea, and had disconcerted them by waving away the inferior cigar offered to him, with '*Cela ne me dit rien*'.

British Embassy, Paris, 21 June

We had luncheon today ostensibly to entertain various people whom we had not thought could be included in the receptions for the Queen Mother. First and foremost, Pam Churchill: the *gratin* would have been horrified to see her at the evening party. However, when we asked her to today's lunch she said she could not come, or perhaps would not. Among those who did come were Paul Louis Weiller, whom a great many people cannot stand, but is a bosom friend of Diana's, and I imagine gives her wonderful presents of Dior dresses and mink coats. Diana herself came, dazzlingly radiant in a sage green silk suit and a Chinese coolie hat. Then there was Comtesse Elie de Ganay, well over sixty but in amazing preservation, very smart with a hat up at such an angle that it went right down on her cheek. She is a completely insincere character with a sugary-sweet manner and a metallic heart, and was Lord Derby's mistress.

Also present was Diana's great friend, Louise de Vilmorin. She is a subtle fascinating woman who gained a firm foothold directly after the War by a most ingenious method. Having spent most of the War in Berlin (she had married a Count Palfy), her position in Paris was precarious with the Allies victorious. Without really knowing the Duff Coopers, she got a friend to bring her along to a cocktail party here, at which she arranged to be taken extremely ill, so much so that she had to be carried up to a visitor's room. There she remained for a fortnight, during which time she made herself so enchantingly agreeable to Duff and Diana that Duff fell in love with her and Diana became her best friend, and she was invited to stay with them permanently. Given her reputation during the War, this did the Embassy much harm. She is certainly brilliant, but egocentric – all conversation must be towards her, all eyes on her. After lunch we wandered into the Salon Vert where Diana and Louise de Vilmorin recalled how in their time there had been a screen in front of the secret door, and how Duff would come in and peep round the screen, and then slip away if he saw any bores in the room.[15]

In spite of all the 'goings on' one must not lose sight of the fact that

[15] Louise de Vilmorin's domination of Duff and Diana Cooper is incontestable, though she did not acquire her entrée to the Embassy in the manner here described. She had already bewitched them when they first had her to stay at a time when she needed medical treatment.

Diana and Duff were blissfully happy together, that they always shared the not very broad Pauline Borghese bed, that he read her to sleep every night, and that when he died she said that the day she had dreaded for thirty-five years had come. Incidentally, with reference to the bed, Diana commented that if anyone said they had seen the eagle on the top of the crown, it was a sure sign that they had slept in the bed, as at present it can only be seen from there reflected in the looking-glass above the chimney-piece: (I write according to strict 'U' usage, and have been careful not to write 'mirror above the mantelpiece'[16]).

British Embassy, Paris, 26 June

This evening we had a dinner for the Comte and Comtesse de Paris at which the women wore tiaras. I had seen Marie Antoinette's sapphire diadem in the exhibition at Versailles last summer, and had wanted to see it worn. So Madame promised to wear it with the rest of the parure. She looked quite lovely and said, rather charmingly, that it did not make her feel sad to put it on. But on thinking it over, I wonder if Marie Antoinette would like it in the possession of the descendants of Philippe Egalité.[17] Had the Comte de Paris not made an unfortunate mistake during the War by siding with Darlan (he thought that if the monarchy were to be restored it should not be due to the Allies, as had been the case with Louis XVII), it is very possible that he could have been elected President in the last election, from which position a coup d'état might have been achieved.

British Embassy, Paris, 27 June

We dined at the Dillons. After dinner I sat talking to General Billotte and Norstadt, who has taken Al Gruenther's place.[18] Gladwyn thinks he

---

[16] 'U and non-U' had been Professor Ross's designation of what was or was not upper-class usage, and been taken up by Nancy Mitford and others in a best-selling book, *Noblesse Oblige*.

[17] Who in 1793 had voted in the National Assembly for the execution of her husband, Louis XVI.

[18] As Supreme Allied Commander of NATO forces in Europe.

has not got Al's strong personality, though Al did not always give the impression of being a great man. When I introduced him to Mother in the hall as he was just going out after seeing Gladwyn, he said in his noisy way, 'Spank Gladwyn for me!' Mother was completely taken aback by these first words from this great general. The explanation of his remark was that Gladwyn could not play tennis with him that afternoon.

British Embassy, Paris, 29 June

I spent a delightful afternoon at Compiègne. There was a ceremony for the inauguration of the Salle de Jeu de Marie Antoinette. In this I take an almost maternal interest, dating from the winter of 1954, when we went on an official visit to Lyon. I wished to see a silk factory where a hand loom was still in use. This, I was told, was almost non-existent, but finally Mme Frassenet, the wife of the Préfet, found one where I spent a most entrancing morning. On one of the looms was a perfectly lovely piece of white taffeta with a design of green leaves and red flowers, which was copied from a faded piece of stuff which had been part of a curtain from the Salle de Jeu at Compiègne, which the Beaux Arts were restoring. I asked if I might try a hand at weaving it, and so had the honour and joy of doing about a quarter of a centimetre of this exquisite material.

British Embassy, Paris, 30 June

Nin [Ryan] came to see me. She asked about the rumours of our moving. I told her that I would not be happy in Washington because I do not take such a great interest in politics, and Washington is nothing but politics.

We talked a little about Rab. She thought he seemed in a bad way altogether, talking endlessly about himself, his failures and difficulties, and recapitulating the recent moves and Budgets. I told her how when I saw him in London in March he had begun talking like this and said, 'Why do people think I am tired and run down: I'm very well, aren't I?' I replied that he would always give this impression if he talked about himself and his difficulties too much. He took this well, and wondered why he did so.

Pug,[19] the other evening, thinking we might be going to the FO, said he felt that the Conservative Party was 'not a happy ship' – good Pug language – and indeed it is not. He told me that Winston calls Selwyn 'Celluloid' (and I am afraid he used to call Rab 'the Rabbit').

This afternoon I made a delightful expedition with Madame de Lacretelle to the ruined Château de Beauregard, which is being demolished. We had both been reading the exceptionally good book (annoyingly enough, by Madame Maurois) on Miss Howard, the English mistress of Napoleon III. We wandered through the debris, picking our way among the scattered pieces of marble and plaster and broken glass; the fine staircase had lost its banisters, and the steps were piled up with rubble. I came away with a little souvenir – a fragment of a marble acanthus leaf – quite moved by the destruction of Beauregard.

British Embassy, Paris, 2 July

Tonight we had our annual dinner with the Windsors. The party was chiefly American and included Mrs Donahue, the colossally rich Woolworth woman who pays for a great deal in the Windsors' life. She is the mother of the homosexual Donahue for whom the Duchess conceived such a notorious passion two or three years ago, and during which she became rude, odious and strange. One had the impression that she was either drugged or drunk. She spent all her time with the effeminate young man, staying in night clubs till dawn and sending the Duke home early: 'Buzz off, mosquito' – what a way to address the once King of England! Finally Donahue's boy-friend is alleged to have told him 'It's either her or me', and so he chucked the Duchess. Since this extraordinary and unnatural affair, she has become quite normal, but always hard. However, the Duke adores her, there is no doubt of that.

Everything at the Windsors is a little over-done. Too many people disturbing one with cocktails and canapés; too rich a dinner (whipped cream served with the jellied consommé with caviare, whipped cream

---

[19] General Hastings Ismay, Lord Ismay (1887–1965): Secretary-General of NATO.

with the *loup flambé*, and horse-radish sauce whipped into cream); too many objets d'art on the tables; too many fancy arrangements of flowers; too many ashtrays being removed and replaced; altogether everything over-fussy.

The Duke told me that when he acceded the wastage and the graft at Buckingham Palace were shocking. Some of this had come to light when George V was recovering from a serious illness at Bognor. Parcels of food arrived there by special train, to be sent straight back to Buckingham Palace for those who remained behind but were unable to have their perquisites delivered straight to the Palace because the Court had moved to Bognor. He also told me that the French governess, who taught the Princess Royal such excellent French, had been an odious character who had gained a great hold on his father and mother. They relied on her far too much, and even allowed her to help in the translation of official papers. She made adverse remarks about the lords and ladies in waiting, so much so that when the Prince of Wales was at the Palace on sick leave towards the end of the War, old Lady Airlie had begged him to do something about the governess. All he could do was to take Princess Mary for a convalescent walk in the park, where he told her about the governess; whereupon she burst into tears, and everybody who saw them must have wondered what was the matter.[20]

British Embassy, Paris, 3 July

Diana has written a pathetic letter to me to 'intercede' about trying to get John Julius to Paris. She does not seem to like the idea, which Gladwyn put in his reply, that JJ should go not to the Embassy but to one of the other two delegations. I suppose she thinks there is more glamour at the Embassy. But there is no vacancy here, and anyway the question is whether he really wants to come to Paris at all, and be under the dominance of Diana. She said in her letter to me that last time she had attempted to interfere she had merely got him changed from Moscow to Belgrade, and that she would never forgive Clarissa after all Duff had done for her.

[20] The governess was José Dussau, an unmarried French Protestant.

British Embassy, Paris, 8 July

We went to luncheon at Royaumont with the Gouins. I remember going there a hundred years ago, taken by the Blanches, and there were masses of young people whom I did not know, and a huge tea, and a beautiful old mother, the Comtesse de Ségur, who is still alive and now just over eighty: she has not changed at all. It is a glorious building, partly ruined in the Revolution, partly occupied most comfortably by the Gouins, and partly a summer school for art and music. Upstairs is a huge room given over to the memory of Mme Gouin's brother who died in a concentration camp – I suppose because he was a Jew. He had been a pianist, and the room was full of manuscripts of Bach, Mozart, Beethoven etc., musical instruments, photographs and prints of musicians and composers, two pianos, and old books and objects that had belonged to him. What a charming idea, to dedicate a room to the memory of someone.

British Embassy, Paris, 9 July

Our last dinner of the very exhausting Paris season was with the Philippe de Rothschilds – in his house, because they keep separate establishments; a relic of when they were lovers, and Pauline thinks she will chain him better as her husband if he feels he still has his liberty.[21] It seems rather absurd after two years of marriage – or, alternatively, why marry? I was tired. Being rather livery after too many banquets, I could not indulge in the delicious food and Mouton Rothschild wine. Then General Catroux dropped a greasy fork which fell against my taffeta dress, and later, sugar dropped into Philippe's coffee cup made a few more marks. So I went home disgruntled as soon as we politely could.

Lansdowne Club, London, 11 July

I was to have gone to a luncheon party at Rab's, but we were all put off this morning as he was ill. So I went round to see him at 4.30, and found him

---

[21] Baron Philippe de Rothschild (1902–88), married (secondly) to Pauline Potter. He had elevated Château Mouton Rothschild to the status of Premier Grand Cru.

lying in the four-poster in which I so well remember seeing Sam during his last illness at Gatcombe. He looked fairly well, but as usual talked the whole time about himself. Once at Stanstead Miles and Richard [Butler] were at breakfast (myself wisely upstairs) and Richard was helping himself to eggs and bacon at the sideboard while Rab was soliloquizing at the head of the table. 'I think I'll give up politics and go and live in a villa some-where and write poetry'. 'Raise poultry, Pa?' came Richard's brisk matter-of-fact farmer's remark from the sideboard – the perfect antidote for Rab's mood. Molly came in later. August is getting worse, and one would wish it to end soon. If she were free, how wonderful it would be if Rab married her. It would be the perfect solution for both themselves and their families, and Sydney would, I feel sure, have given it her blessing.

I dined quietly with Gerry at Apsley House. Gerry keeps a large number of rooms on the ground and second floors though the rest has become a museum. He has quantities of treasures left, despite having given so much away. The basement is still wonderfully old-fashioned. There is a gloomy vaulted place with high windows which even in Gerry's youth was full of bunks, one above the other, where the footmen slept. We went down to the silver room, where we saw many things that were in the Embassy in the Great Duke's time. He nearly but not quite gave me a gold medal of Brunel, but it was inscribed to the Duke, so he quite rightly thought he had better not.

British Embassy, Paris, 15 July

Irene is engaged to a Frenchman, without money, but with a sixteenth-century château, a suitable age and a superb record in the War.[22] He could call himself a comte, but sensibly does not do so. I often think all the titled French are absurd to continue using their grand-sounding names and insisting on correct precedence, in republican France. Anyway, many of them have no right to their titles, having adopted them when the family bought a property, often of quite recent date.

[22] Irene Durlacher (1919–   ), about to marry Commandant Jean-François Clouet des Pesruches (d. 1957) and subsequently married to Anthony Hunter. She was Gladwyn's personal assistant in New York and, until her marriage, in Paris; and she later returned to him in 1968 for weekly secretarial assistance, devotedly keeping his affairs in order and befriending him into his extreme old age.

Walwick Hall, Northumberland, 14 August [23]

Today we visited Chillingham. We couldn't get inside, but managed to manoeuvre our way into the Italian garden, and from there it was easy to slip away and peer through the windows into the empty sad rooms that had once been so gay and comfortable. [24]

We went and looked at the church, now damp and obviously neglected. As I looked at the lovely Grey tomb I remembered so well sitting in that private pew between Mother and Aunt Molly in their beautiful Edwardian dresses and hats. They wore long kid gloves which they would sometimes take off to stroke our hands and calm us from too much fidgetting during the long sermons. Through the window one could see the sunny day outside, and the grass waving in the wind in the churchyard, and one longed to be finished with morning service. I remember Father, on a cold day, sitting by the lit fire, reading a book, a privilege we envied.

We also went to look at the cattle. [25] While Ian [Bennet] was trying to locate them we waited sitting on the hillside looking at the Cheviots, breathing in the glorious air. I thought of old days when as a child I had done the same thing, and I sucked a rush as one used often to do, and scrunched up in my hand a piece of Northumbrian bracken, which smells delicious, and felt I must at any moment see Mar and Marc and Bon, and that we would shortly be going back to the castle to have a huge tea with drop scones eaten off green-dragon plates in the bow window of the drawing-room.

Ardkinglas, Argyll, 17 August

John [Noble] met me in his aged but dignified Rolls at Arrochar, and after a lovely drive over the Rest [26] (now so easy and quick, unlike the hazards and excitements of my childhood) we came sooner than I

[23] Humphrey Noble's house on the Roman Wall near Hexham.
[24] Chillingham Castle was at this time owned by Charles Bennet, 8th Earl of Tankerville (1897–1971), but had become completely abandoned.
[25] The herd of ancient British white cattle.
[26] The Rest-and-be-Thankful pass, on the estate of John's brother Michael. When Michael was awarded a peerage, he toyed with the idea that he should take it as his title.

expected to the familiar approach to Ardkinglas, with the riverside and the great trees, and then turned into the open and saw the house, with dear Elizabeth to welcome me, and Daisy rather older and deafer, and Tasia looking like a manual labourer.[27] There seemed a lot of people staying, mostly young and wearing grubby blue jeans, altogether looking very wild but tremendously jolly. I am in what was Aunt Lily's room, and have a view over the loch. The lights of Inverary now shine as bright as the Champs Elysées, and lessen one's chance of seeing the ghostly Lorne Galley.

After tea today John took me up the glen. We left the car at the turning place and walked up to Inverchorachan, now deserted because no shepherd will live so far away. It was peaceful and beautiful, and one could forget about the horrible electrical scheme which is ruining the Larig burn, and is the cause of a smooth tarmac road to the Lodge, when there should be a nice bad twisty road full of holes. When a telegram came to the Lodge in the old days, a girl had to walk the three miles from Cairndow and back again, until Grandpapa gave her a bicycle. All the same, there is still a magic in the glen, and I believe that if one walked up by the river on a misty night, one might still hear the drums of Montrose's army, or see the lights that come up but never arrive.

Le Fresne, Authon, 31 August [28]

I came here on Tuesday and am thoroughly enjoying life in a French country house. To begin with, it is a very pretty house, square and white, with a chapel and a pavilion on either side, and further on a pair of little lodges, and finally a pair of old dovecots. The farm is nearby, and the sounds from it give a rural feeling to an otherwise classical plan. On the garden side of the house are old orange trees in great tubs, and delicious-smelling heliotropes planted among begonias. As I sit writing in my charming little boudoir, I see the long fish-pond overhung with limes. Then beyond the formal garden of yew trees are the lovely woods

---

[27] Daisy Powell-Jones (1885–1973), old friend and mentor of the family; and Anastasia Noble (1911–   ), leading British breeder of deerhounds and sister of John Noble. These two ladies had lived for many years in Ardkinglas House with John and Elizabeth Noble.

[28] The château of the de Brantes family.

where I go walking, wandering and losing myself in the avenues till I am lucky enough to get a vista again of the house and return in time for a delicious lunch at a quarter to one.

Inside Le Fresne I am completely happy, with its good library and pretty furniture and ornaments and pictures. The drawing-room is square with pale grey and gilt boiserie, rich port-red curtains, sofa and easy chairs, a fine Aubusson carpet, and a very good set of Empire chairs with their original brocade, all tattered and torn and not likely to hold together much longer. In the evening we sit around the large circular table with its green table-cloth and lamp at the centre. My bedroom is quite small, with a Louis XVI bed in an alcove, with red curtains, red walls, charming pictures, a door also of red, a dressing-table covered with old-fashioned muslin, and a view of the canal. Leading out of my bedroom are two small rooms; one my bathroom, and the other my boudoir. Here there is a nice log fire crackling away, and the chapel clock, with the bells that came from Chanteloup, has just chimed 7.15.

Every day we make delightful expeditions in Touraine. Yesterday we went to Chanteloup, having first steeped ourselves in the Choiseuls.[29] We climbed the pagoda and, books in hand, tried to discover the exact whereabouts of the château. From what was the garden, and now a rough overgrown field, I picked a little pink rose, which seemed to bring all the charm of the court of the Choiseuls at Chanteloup for a moment to life again, so fragrant was its smell.

Until Gladwyn arrived today there was just Aymone and her mother, Princesse de Faucigny Lucinge,[30] and her daughter Rosamée. Marguerite, such a brilliant girl, and only twenty-two, went into a convent at Easter; Aymone must miss her, for she was her favourite companion. But she is so happy that one cannot criticize the choice she has made. I believe the biggest wrench for her was to leave Le Fresne, and I seem to see her everywhere. Natty Lucinge is certainly a gay grandmother for a nun, with her bright-red hair artfully arranged, her lively mind, and amusing gossip: she is younger than her daughter.

[29] In 1770 Louis XV banished his Prime Minister, the Duc de Choiseul, to his estate at Chanteloup. The château was destroyed during the Revolution, and all that remains is the pagoda, dedicated, by the congenial Duc and Duchesse, to the ideal of Friendship.
[30] Natividad Terry y Dorticos, widow of Prince Guy de Faucigny-Lucinge.

British Embassy, Paris, 5 September

I had arranged to show some friends, including Mr Du Pont, inside the Elysée. The President returns tomorrow, so this was our one chance. A wonderful steward majestically showed us round both the good and the bad, and when he came to the Salon Bleu et Argent he was less interested to tell us of the well-known historical events that had taken place in this room, than he was to speak of Felix Faure's death on the canapé to the left of the fireplace. When the priest arrived he asked whether *'Monsieur le Président à toujours sa connaissance?' 'Elle vient de partir, Monsieur le Curé, par l'escalier de service'* replied the servant.[31]

British Embassy, Paris, 9 September

Mollet and Pineau go to London tomorrow, and Gladwyn too.[32] Walter Elliot came unexpectedly to dine tonight, and charmed me with his irresistible Scottish accent. But oh! how he alarmed me with his talk of war; of Violet Bonham Carter trying to get at Churchill to make him vote against Anthony's policy, of the likelihood of the government falling and the Commonwealth disintegrating. He also alleged that Neville Chamberlain deliberately wished to provoke war in 1939 by guaranteeing Poland. Gladwyn, who was Alec Cadogan's Private Secretary at the time, denied this. Gladwyn has just come up to bed, and though agreeing that the country is much divided about Suez and the situation grave, thinks that Walter Elliot is very alarmist, and often wrong.

British Embassy, Paris, 15 September

Selwyn Lloyd, who came over for the day, has just left. There was the usual rush downstairs, with secretaries carrying red boxes, and

[31] The priest meant *connaissance* in the sense of 'consciousness'; the servant thought he meant it in the sense of 'acquaintance', and so referred to the woman in whose arms the President had just died.

[32] For talks on the crisis precipitated by the nationalization of the Suez Canal by the Egyptian President Nasser.

detectives, and stenographers, and they all bundled into the cars, doors banged, someone got out because he'd forgotten something and the procession had to wait, and then they all swept off led by a police car. The courtyard was empty, the big lights turned out, and the great house was quiet again.

We had an early supper in the gallery with the windows open. The chestnut loomed large against the darkening sky, but there was a lovely moon coming up. Before dinner Selwyn and I walked a little in the garden. We talked of Rab. Selwyn thinks he is in a very bad way, almost pathological. When he goes on leave he wants Rab to look after the Foreign Office for a fortnight, which he thinks might help him mentally and do him good. The lights from the gallery glowed in a welcoming way, with the dark figures of the rest of the party silhouetted against them. Beeley rushed towards us over the lawn with a paper which he was made to read to Selwyn (with difficulty in the dark), and so our talk ended. It is said that Selwyn is no administrator, and that neither is Ivone; so the poor Foreign Office is badly looked after.

British Embassy, Paris, 16 September

Another glorious day. Nancy, Gladwyn and I went out for the day in the Bentley and picnicked on the edge of the Forêt de Compiègne. Nancy was at her nicest. Not catty, or trying to shock, or bored; but really her most charming genuine self, with far more sensible staunch views about people and life than her public or publishers would ever credit her with. She must now be quite rich, though I should imagine that her popularity might not last, her appeal being of such a frivolous fashionable nature. She says she pays half of what she earns in taxes, spends a quarter, keeps a quarter. She certainly spends very little, except on clothes. She came to live here because of Gaston, with whom she has the great bond of friendship and not, as I believe, the lesser bond of a love affair. He is always flagrantly in love with others, but returns to Nancy for this more lasting relationship. I expect she would not wish me to analyse the situation thus.

British Embassy, Paris, 27 September

The Edens and Selwyn and their suite have just left, and I must say I am quite exhausted. As usual, Clarissa and I spent the afternoon waiting for the men. We had quite a tussle with Clarissa about attending the dinner at the Quai d'Orsay and the luncheon party of Mme Pineau. When she heard she was to be let in for all this she said she would not come, and that she had just wanted to see me and do a theatre. However, she finally gave in, and behaved beautifully. Anthony was in fine form, waving, his head on one side, wreathed in smiles. Selwyn was a more pathetic figure, and ill into the bargain. We had to put him to bed and send for the doctor.

British Embassy, Paris, 17 October

We have just been to Irene's wedding near Angers. There were two services, and a great many speeches, a great many meals, far too many photographs and films, for the bridegroom is in the film business. Gladwyn returned by air to Paris with Bourges-Maunoury,[33] and I came leisurely in the Rolls. I arrived at the Embassy at about seven o'clock to be greeted by Vanessa and Walter who announced that the Prime Minister and the Secretary of State were about to come for the night. For a few minutes I thought it was a silly joke. To prove it they took me into the Bamboo Room where my secretary's desk had been moved, and at that moment the cars swung into the courtyard, and there was Anthony as large as life.[34] Thank goodness the excellent Walter had made all the necessary arrangements.

British Embassy, Paris, 24 October

In London last week we went to a party at the Austrian Embassy, and really I might have stepped back twenty years. Except that our hosts

[33] Maurice Bourges-Maunoury (b. 1914): French Minister of Defence.
[34] Eden and Selwyn Lloyd held a meeting of several hours with Mollet and Pineau at which all officials were excluded, and at which the concept of a secret collusion with Israel for an attack on Egypt was developed. Gladwyn was furious at this exclusion and (when he subsequently learnt of it) at the decision, and protested in writing to Selwyn Lloyd.

were the Schwarzenbergs[35] and not the Franckensteins, it all seemed exactly the same. Same embassy, same songs, same gilt chairs, same faces – rather older, it is true.

The next day we went to Ireland for a long weekend to stay in the Beits' most comfortable and luxurious house, Russborough.[36] They live there in great style, with many servants, everything done very well, and not a care in the world. We went to see two lovely houses. Castleton was the best, and typically Irish. Lady Carew read from sheets of type-written paper what we were to admire in the house. Everything was covered with dust and neglected and ill-arranged. From there we went to Carton, which has been much spoilt by having Lord Brocket's furni-ture and taste allowed in there. Desmond Guinness (Diana Mosley's son) is living there with his Austrian wife, and showed us round quickly as we had little time.

British Embassy, Paris, 30 October

Today we heard that Israel has invaded Egypt. Gladwyn was to have gone out this morning to be present at the unveiling of a memorial to 'the Unknown Jew', a beautiful idea to commemorate the millions who were killed by the Nazis. But the President called off. What bad luck that this ceremony should coincide with this Israeli attack.

British Embassy, Paris, 5 November

I returned here last night at about 6.30 and went into the library where I found Gladwyn, who was about to leave to see M Pineau, and then they were to go to London. Actually Gladwyn got back to Paris at about four o'clock this morning. He said that there were several demonstrations in the streets against the PM. Anthony looked as though he were sleep-walking, and the talks took place with people wandering in and out, and a general feeling of strain and unease.

[35] Prince Johannes Schwarzenberg (1903–78), married to Kathleen de Spoelberch.
[36] Sir Alfred Beit (1903–94), married to Clementine Mitford. He was an old beau of Cynthia, who had accompanied him on visits to the operas in Paris, Munich and Bayreuth in the 1920s.

I wish I could feel happy about the Anglo-French attack. I am sure it was the wrong thing to do – even if it succeeds. It was acting like a gangster, which we have always deplored in others, and the euphemism of calling ourselves 'police' was thought up a bit too late to take anyone in. I am afraid it has encouraged Russia to attack Hungary, also calling it a police action. I may say that Gladwyn was never consulted about it at all, which is typical of Anthony's dictatorship. England is strongly divided.

Highclere Castle, Hampshire, 10 November[37]

We came over on Thursday for the party at what the French call 'Bookingham', where were most of the government, including Clarissa, looking beautiful and amazingly confident. The Queen gave a most perfunctory handshake to the Russians, and some of the royalty left them out altogether, thus also leaving out the innocent Portuguese and others who were in the same room. Beforehand we dined at the French Embassy, and found it badly run – all very different from Massigli's day: Mme Chauvel came and rapped on the bathroom door to hand a towel, because there was none there.

We arrived here last night with Vanessa, rather late, but managed to bath and change before dinner. There are staying here just young Porchester and his pregnant wife, and the Blandfords. Susan is very pretty, Sunny not as bad or stupid as he looks. I believe his father, who is awful, bullies him the whole time. Porchy is a convivial much-married bounder, but a nice father, and I was quite touched to see him kiss his son goodnight..

Lansdowne Club, London, 13 November

I went to lunch with Rab at 3 Smith Square, and afterwards settled down to an intimate talk. Rab professed to be very unhappy about the situation. He said, 'I keep on asking myself, "When could I have resigned"; I said to my secretary, "I don't know when I could have been able to resign"'. All this, of course, in flat contradiction to his speeches in

[37] Seat of Henry ('Porchy') Herbert, 6th Earl of Carnarvon.

public, whereas in private he is quite outspoken in his criticism. I said to Rab 'between these four walls' that I could not help suspecting that the Franco-British attack had been cooked up by Anthony and Selwyn when they came over last month so unexpectedly for the night and had secret talks with Mollet and Pineau. Rab said he was returning from Scotland at the time, and was not told anything. When exactly was the Cabinet told anything, one wonders? Anyway, those who were told must have agreed, even if at the last moment. I admire Sir Edward Boyle's conscientiousness.[38]

Lansdowne Club, London, 14 November

I lunched at the Albany with Lady Lee and Lady Robertson yesterday, and again found loyal Conservatives imagining that everything must be all right. I ran into Tommy Davies outside the club, and found him also enthusiastic. When I remarked that all that had happened was that the canal was now blocked, he said, 'Oh, they can clear that in three weeks'. He maintained that the attack was anyway justified by Russian influence in Egypt: but all the facts were known back in July, and this was never given as one of the reasons for the attack.

My day ended with a quiet dinner and theatre with Ava. Here, in the privacy of her pretty little house in Lord North Street (just opposite Sybil's, so full of old memories) I gleaned a lot of gossip. Ava was evidently extremely worried – worried as to whom to back! She deplored Clarissa's ignorance and interference. It seems Clarissa is often present at private lunches and drinks and dinners, where important business has to be discussed with Anthony, and that she gives her opinion and advice. Worse still, Ivone has complained that she rings up Anthony at the last moment, tells him not to weaken, and interferes with whatever line has been agreed on. How dangerous all this sounds. Is it really a case of 'Infirm of purpose, give me the dagger'? Thelma de Chair at lunch, though ardent in her support for Eden, had told me she heard the situation described as 'Clarissa's War'. It made me think of the Empress Eugénie and her disastrous interference in politics. I thought

[38] Sir Edward Boyle, later Lord Boyle of Handsworth (1923–82); resigned as Economic Secretary to the Treasury in protest at the British attack on Egypt.

it significant that Ava has invited Edward Boyle to go with her to the Royal Box to *Otello*.

British Embassy, Paris, 16 November

Harold left early this morning.[39] His line was that we must all pull together and make the best of it all, disregarding that it was partly his responsibility that we got into such a mess. He gave a long intellectual dissertation on this being the end of an era, the end of Europe as we knew it, and that it was now to be the day of the Russians and Arabs and Orientals pushing westwards, and that life would be quite different for his grandchildren to what it had been for us, and that he had done his best. All rather unconvincing to me as an excuse for what happened. G said he thought that more people should have been consulted, who could have given expert advice. H replied, with a hearty pat on the back, 'I know, but we must all help now to make the best of it, and stick together'.

British Embassy, Paris, 25 November

We lunched at Chantilly today, and the Giles too.[40] We found there Juliet Duff, Judy Montagu, and a few others: Diana in what looked like a glorified dustman's hat, and wearing trousers. We had the hottest and most violent arguments. Fur flew. As far as I can make out, everybody, whatever their views, deplores the choice of Jamaica, and thinks that Anthony cannot return to be PM.[41] I bet he will: Clarissa won't let him not. It certainly must have struck most people as unfortunate that, while we in England and France are starting to feel the shortage of petrol, oil, salt, sugar and other commodities just as the really cold weather has

---

[39] Harold Macmillan, later 1st Earl of Stockton (1894–1986): Chancellor of the Exchequer and subsequently Prime Minister 1957–63.

[40] Frank Giles (1919–   ), married to Lady Katherine Sackville. *Times* correspondent in Paris, and subsequently editor of the *Sunday Times*.

[41] Anthony Eden, physically and emotionally exhausted after the ignominious collapse of his policy against Egypt, had decamped for a rest cure in Jamaica (at Ian Fleming's house Goldeneye), leaving R.A. Butler as Deputy Prime Minister.

Bramfield Hall, Gladwyn and Cynthia's house in Suffolk

Cynthia with Hugh Nelson-Ward, the 'King of Bath'

Nancy Mitford, the brilliant
English Parisienne

Helen D'Abernon,
Cynthia's ideal as a British
Ambassador's wife

Gladwyn Jebb and his antagonist Yakov Malik
at the United Nations Security Council in 1950

Wavehill, Riverdale on Hudson,
Gladwyn and Cynthia's residence in New York

Lunch at Wavehill: from the left,
Gladwyn, Bae Lloyd, unknown man, Cynthia, Selwyn Lloyd

Humphrey Noble, in the uniform of a Major in the Northumberland Hussars, making his ceremonial appearance as High Sheriff of the county in 1956

The courtyard of the British Embassy, Paris,
with the ambassadorial Rolls and the Humber used by Cynthia

Anthony Eden as Prime Minister, with his wife Clarissa

The Paris meeting of Eden and the French Premier Guy Mollet in October 1956, together with their Foreign Ministers Christian Pineau and Selwyn Lloyd, at which all diplomats were excluded

begun, Anthony has gone to Jamaica to rest and sunbathe, Dulles to Florida, and Eisenhower to play golf in Augusta. Anthony's departure was characteristic – smiles and waves and 'See you soon'.

British Embassy, Paris, 30 November

I went to the St Andrew's Day Dinner and sat between Pug [Ismay] and Kit Steel.[42] Pug kept saying that Anthony cannot possibly return as PM. There are too many jokes going round, one of them the wonderful competition offered by the *Daily Mirror* for the best solution to the Suez Crisis, the prize being a holiday for two in Jamaica. Meanwhile Ann Fleming, the wife of Ian who owns Goldeneye, in spite of being Clarissa's great friend, is having a tremendous walk-out with Hugh Gaitskell.[43]

British Embassy, Paris, 9 December

Two years ago today Sydney died, and it is also Rab's birthday. I telephoned him at Stanstead to tell him how much I was thinking of him and old times, and he seemed greatly touched. I could see it all so clearly; the sitting-room with the oriel window, and Sydney's pretty things around him; the chill of the old Essex house (neither Rab or Sydney could abide warm comfortable rooms); the late autumn garden seen through the lattice windows; the dogs barking. Many of us feel that if Sydney were still alive some events might well have been different. She was a great, good and strong influence, and just what Rab's character needed.

Tonight Selwyn arrived and seemed quite well and pleased with himself and anxious to brave everything out and pretend it has all been a success instead of a fiasco. Of course, this is to keep the Party together, but it is all very false. I prefer the French attitude which logically admits the failure of the enterprise.

[42] Sir Christopher Steel (1903–73), married to Catherine Clive. He was stationed in Paris as Permanent Representative on the North Atlantic Council 1953–7, and was Ambassador to Federal Germany 1957–63.
[43] Hugh Gaitskell (1906–63): Leader of the Labour Party and Leader of the Opposition.

British Embassy, Paris, 10 December

Selwyn told Gladwyn last night that nobody quite knows what will happen when Anthony returns. If he keeps on as PM he will drive everyone mad, so impossible and difficult he is these days. Yet if he goes, it will be hard to find the right person to replace him. Harold is not entirely popular, and Rab has blotted his copy-book. There is nobody else worthy of the position. So I suppose that in spite of his temper and ill-health and dictatorial methods, it will in the end boil down to Anthony staying, in order to preserve the Conservative Party.

I have been rather clever about the heating. I arranged that it should be kept specially low in order that all these visiting ministers should not complain that we were making no attempt to economize. Now Gravett tells me that the S of S finds the house very cold. So, with great pleasure, I can say that, at his request, it will be made warmer. Selwyn, just before dinner, said he felt ill, so we got the doctor, who gave him a shot of penicillin. This is the third time he has come here ill due, I suppose, to worry and overwork. Now I must go to bed, as I am dropping with sleep, the fire is going out, and the room is full of men's smoke.

British Embassy, Paris, 11 December

Harold arrived, and dined in. The Heads[44] came too, and we took them to a translation of a bad American play, a first night, or we would not have gone. Harold went to bed, wisely. He is at one moment full of optimism about the success of the famous attack; and then at another moment will talk endlessly in a sort of intellectual pessimism – the end of the white man, the end of Europe, the end of the Commonwealth and Empire, and the fault of the Americans, who don't care. Lady Dorothea Head too was anti-American on every point, even as regards plays and books; he less so. She is quite amusing, but by the end of the evening I found her rather absurd: he is not a very clever man. In fact, I get more and more anxious about the fate of the country with this Cabinet to run it. There must be better men available in the Party.

[44] Antony Head, later 1st Viscount Head (1906–83), married to Lady Dorothea Ashley-Cooper. Secretary of State for Defence.

British Embassy, Paris, 12 December

We sat for a long time after dinner in the small dining-room, round the large tureen and the candles. There was just Harold, Selwyn, Denis [Laskey], Gladwyn and myself. Over port and brandy Harold held forth. The great thing for a country was to be rich as we were in the nineteenth century, he mused; and why should we not give up spending millions on atom bombs, why should we not give up Singapore, sell the colonies, sell the West Indies too to America, and just sit back and be rich? Later Head came in and sat with us, and tonight we were more impressed by him. The news was bad, because it seems we are not to be allowed to clear the Canal, due to American opposition to us. Harold then soliloquized that he might resign and get himself appointed Ambassador to Washington, because he felt he could deal with them. I said politely 'What a good idea, because you are half American', but I could sense Gladwyn's amused contempt at the suggestion. A message came in from the Prime Minister; when it was shown to Gladwyn he remarked, 'That shows he has absolutely no idea what is going on'. No comment came from Selwyn or Harold. Head was quite emphatic in disagreeing with Harold about what to do next. It struck me that the experts, such as the Ambassador, are not being consulted enough; but I whispered to Gladwyn afterwards when we were alone for a moment in the Salon Vert, that I thought he might handle Harold better. I feel he has to be allowed to air his curious theories, and must be flattered and listened to, and not be interrupted; and then other suggestions and ideas can gradually be inserted, so that he begins to enlarge on these quite happily, as though he had thought of them originally. If one bluntly argues with him, I can see he could turn nasty. There is an almost cruel look now and then on this otherwise handsome and exquisitely-mannered person. I suppose this might be the flaw in his character, and why people say they can't trust him. Still, he is very able and brilliant.

All this business, the crisis, the great ones conferring into the early hours of the morning, the messages and replies, the speeches composed, all form just another chapter in the history of this old house. Gladwyn told me just now that the PM's message was what he intended saying at the airport on his return on Friday – that it would all have been a tremendous success if it had not been for the Americans. Not quite the right moment to say this.

British Embassy, Paris, 18 December

In the midst of all this unpleasant news, a frivolous event was organized
at the Musée Grevin, where a wax figure of 'Major Thompson' was
unveiled by Pug and myself – we were the godparents, in fact.[45] The
Major was immaculately dressed with Briggs umbrella, gloves, bowler
hat and regimental tie complete. I presented him with an artificial red
carnation, and he is to have a fresh copy of *The Times* delivered to him
every day, which I hope is then passed on to someone who will read it.

British Embassy, Paris, 31 December

Christmas went off happily and successfully. For charades, at which
Nancy and I remained as spectators, 'Goldeneye' was, needless to say,
one of the words chosen. In another word, Gladwyn was Ike greeting
Nehru and the Mountbattens. I thought the Naval Attaché looked a
little embarrassed when he had to portray his chief, but was obviously
relieved when subsequently he saw somebody acting the Prime
Minister.

---

[45] *Les Carnets de Major Thompson*, depicting the life and opinions of a blimpish
Englishman, had great success in France.

1957

British Embassy, Paris, 4 January

We were just about to start our Christmas staff party when Gladwyn was called to the telephone by Rab. Not to impart any political news, but merely to say that the Duchess of Kent had asked him to fix it that her sister and Prince Paul of Yugoslavia should be invited to the Embassy, there having hitherto been strict instructions to exclude them from any of our activities here.[1] Gladwyn said that Rab must put the matter to Selwyn, and also consult Buckingham Palace. I myself consider that it would be no great gain if we had to be friendly with 'Prince Palsy', as Churchill called him, as he is pretty awful, and she is apparently not much liked. But I suppose it would make things easier with the Duchess, who stays with them when she comes to Paris. The Queen Mother too is tremendously friendly with him.

British Embassy, Paris, 9 January

Gladwyn heard tonight from the Foreign Office that Anthony has resigned. The papers today had pictures of the Edens going down by train to Sandringham yesterday, all smiles. The reasons given for this resignation are entirely those of health. It is a pity he did not go long ago, for he has been in a really bad state of nerves almost ever since he

---

[1] In March 1941 the Government of Yugoslavia, of which Prince Paul was Regent, had signed a pact with the Axis powers, despite the Regent's pro-British sympathies. This had paved the way for the Axis occupation of the Balkans.

became Prime Minister. During the Suez crisis he was continually taking benzedrine, and by the time it became necessary for him to depart for Goldeneye, he was in such a bad way that he didn't make sense. I imagine that the general public know nothing of this, and think that his bad health has been brought on by his operations of four years ago. But I would say that he had completely recovered from the operations, for he seems to have been able to eat, drink, and do anything he wanted. I imagine he inherited an odd and violent temper from Sir William Eden; and he has a strong streak of feminine temperament, and relies on praise and flattery. As Pug said, 'Some men need drink; others need drugs; Anthony needs flattery'.

Will he be succeeded by Rab? or Harold? or somebody like Heathcoat Amory about whom there could be no controversy? I would like eventually to see my dear Sir Edward Boyle in Downing Street, with his brilliant brain, his conscience, and his humane outlook.

British Embassy, Paris, 10 January

This evening we heard the news that Harold is Prime Minister. I suppose it was the obvious choice. Rab must be feeling disappointed, and I think that in this house we are all rather sad. Ava said that as he is only fifty-four there is plenty of time for him, but one never knows in politics. I would have liked to see him at Number Ten, but best of all I would have liked to see Sydney there. She was indeed of immense value to him, and with her going his star has gone too.

British Embassy, Paris, 12 January

Evidently many people, even those in favour of Macmillan, question the manner in which he was chosen, considering it undemocratic. Naturally the opposition are making a lot of this. Gladwyn thinks it might have been better for Rab if he had resigned with Edward Boyle and Tony Nutting.

While Gladwyn and Stella went, on this cold Saturday afternoon, to a football match (at which Scotland won), I went to the Louvre. I spent a long time wandering about the museum and visiting parts which I had never been to before. This would have been delightful had it not been for the discovery that a great deal of the Louvre has no electric lighting whatever – typical of French economy. It is indeed vast. I thought what a long distance the Empress Eugénie must have walked when she was escaping from the Tuilleries, hurrying along the whole length of the palace till she reached the far end of the Louvre.

British Embassy, Paris, 15 January

We had a dinner party of twenty-eight tonight at two tables in the State Dining Room, and very cold it was too, in spite of stepping up the heating, drawing all the curtains on to the gallery, and lighting the candles. It was a farewell party for the Steels, who go to Bonn, and for our Naval Attaché who is leaving us. But it ended by also being a farewell for the Dillons,[2] who arrived with the sad news that they are leaving within a fortnight. They will indeed be a loss to Paris life; they are great friends of ours, and Gladwyn and he have worked most happily together. Gladwyn made a very charming and witty speech.

When we were talking quietly together after dinner, Doug Dillon commented vehemently on Selwyn remaining as Secretary of State. Dug said, 'I understand England doing what she did, but what cannot be understood or forgiven is the way she did it'. He told the story of Winthrop dining with Selwyn on that famous Sunday night when Selwyn assured him no action was going to be taken. As Doug said, rather than lie, Selwyn should have made some excuse to get out of meeting Winthrop. Understandably, this rankles deeply with the Americans. Of course, if Selwyn had been dropped, it would have looked as though the new PM had not approved of the Suez policy.

Meanwhile, Anthony and Clarissa are staying at Chequers, slipping in to Downing Street by the back door to supervise the removal of their things, and shortly they will leave for Australia and New Zealand, sharing a cabin and bathroom, all the better suites having been booked. One wonders how the disappointed couple will fare. He ill, difficult, nervous, vain, martyred; she disappointed. Both will miss the comforts

---

[2] Douglas Dillon (1909–   ), married to Phyllis Ellsworth. United States Ambassador to France.

and glory and adulation they had got accustomed to. I cannot imagine what they will even talk about. She is an intellectual, and might be glad to return to seeing her old friends. But his one interest has for long been politics, and only foreign affairs at that. Beatrice[3] told me last September that when he was a young man he sometimes sat on the floor and read Persian poetry to her. But then he soon became absorbed in politics, which bored her. And now poor Beatrice is dying of an incurable disease. Many people thought that she was very good with Anthony, and reminded him about people he should be nice to, and was a great help in that way, in spite of disliking his career. She said to me that she supposed he and Clarissa got on because they were both rather inhuman.

British Embassy, Paris, 18 January

We had a luncheon party for Princess Alexandra. She is a very nice charming good-natured girl, with excellent manners, and behaving most correctly. She has not got her mother's beauty, but is pleasant to look at. Gladwyn had on his left Princesse Isabelle de France, whom he found a particularly delightful and intelligent young woman, who leads a useful and democratic life; in fact he thinks that the education of the Pretender's family contrasts favourably with that of the younger members of our own royal family.

Harold made a tremendous speech yesterday, full of pep, saying we were a great power, that everybody must work hard, that it was ridiculous to say we were finished. He is quite right to take this line, but it is further proof of the sickening hypocrisy of politicians. Only a few weeks ago, in this very Salon Vert, he was giving us a long tirade on how the European civilization had come to an end, that England was finished, that western man's day was over and eastern man's day was dawning, that he had tried (via the Suez attack) to save the situation for the sake of his grandchildren (a great deal is made of these grandchildren, I notice), but all to no avail, because the white man is doomed.

---

[3] Beatrice Beckett, first wife of Anthony Eden.

British Embassy, Paris, 19 January

Edward Boyle is appointed Parliamentary Secretary to the Minister of Education and, as the Minister is in the Lords, Edward's post is an important one. In accepting he states, 'I do not unsay one word of what I said last November'. Cheek by jowl comes the appointment of Julian Amery, Harold's diehard, ultra-right-wing, Suez Group son-in-law, as Parliamentary Secretary in the War Office. So Harold is cleverly roping in all sides.

British Embassy, Paris, 23 January

We lunched today with the John Millers. He was *Times* correspondent in Washington, and, after the 1953 election there, Haley fired him for being too pro-Democrat. We were alone, and I was amused to hear his account of lunching at 11 Downing Street with the Macmillans the day before the PM departed for Goldeneye. Harold, indicating St James's Park with a wave of the hand, began a monologue on how all this world would not exist any more, that it was the end of life as we know it – in fact the same theme as we heard in Paris shortly afterwards. Harold, by the way, has trimmed his Edwardian moustache.

British Embassy, Paris, 2 February

I went with Muriel [Gore] and Gladwyn to see the Theatre at Versailles which has just been restored. It exceeded all I had imagined. It is a symphony in blue, and so exquisite and brilliant that it is like something in fairyland. Everybody connected with Versailles is furious that the opening performance, which is to be when the Queen comes, is to be an afternoon and not an evening one. This is because the Grand Gala has to be at the Opéra, which can accommodate so many more of the boring people who don't wish to be done out of their right to attend. But it would have been perfect had we all been in evening dress in that lovely setting, and also so fitting, since it was inaugurated nearly two hundred years ago for Marie Antoinette.[4]

---

[4] Constructed in 1770 by Louis XV on the occasion of the marriage of his grandson to Princess Marie Antoinette of Austria.

British Embassy, Paris, 16 February

During luncheon today Michael Palliser[5] telephoned from Rheims, where he had gone with a visiting Parliamentary Delegation, to say that poor Leslie Hore Belisha had died suddenly while making a speech before a banquet. His wife having recently left him, and his having no intimate friends, it was difficult to know who to get in touch with. A member of the Delegation mentioned that he believed he had become a Roman Catholic about a year ago (he was fond of going into retreats), so the Archevêque, who had discreetly retired from the sad scene thinking that the defunct was a Jew, returned to say the appropriate prayers. Later in the day his secretary flew out and averred that he was still a Jew; so the Chief Rabbi of Paris rang up the Protocol here to announce he was sending his representative to Rheims. Anyhow, he will be safe in a Catholic as well as a Jewish heaven, and, as I understand that there was a Protestant pastor attending the banquet, perhaps he murmured a few prayers too.

The large and distinguished company were faced with the problem of whether to sit down to the wonderful repast which had been prepared in their honour. To do so appeared unsuitable under the circumstances; but the problem was cleverly solved by omitting the pâté de foie gras, and changing the meal from a banquet to a luncheon.

British Embassy, Paris, 17 February

Maurice Edelman called before lunch to tell us a little of the sad story at Rheims. We then began talking of the political situation, and Edelman told us something of great interest. Yesterday he had seen Mollet, who frankly stated that it was he who had suggested the whole thing in general terms to Anthony. This was quite a shock for Edelman, and I must say it was rather a surprise to me, for I had always imagined that it was Pineau who had thought it up, not Mollet. Maurice Edelman said that he really believed that the PM had been unbalanced. He had

[5] Michael Palliser, later Sir Michael (1922–   ), married to Marie Spaak. First Secretary at the Paris Embassy, and subsequently Permanent Under-Secretary of State for Foreign Affairs 1975–82.

travelled up with him to Llandudno for the Conservative Conference, and Anthony had then talked of a plan for Iraq invading Jordan, something very different from what took place a little later.

British Embassy, Paris, 24 February

André de Staerke came to lunch with us quietly.[6] We talked of the Spaaks, and we also talked of Simone Dear. Years ago, in the War, I worked under Sybil Colefax at the Hospital Supplies Depot, which was in the Hambledens' old house in Belgrave Square. We were all dressed as nurses in white veils and overalls, and Sybil, knitting hard when walking among us, used to retire to her office and do all the telephoning, postcards and planning that her famous entertainment entailed. Machining away next to me was a pretty little Dutch woman called Mrs Dear, well off, a friend of Paz Subercaseaux who also worked there, and with a rich husband and house in Lisle Street close by.[7] Sometimes, if she was away, she let me use her electric machine, which was bliss, and I whizzed away at it and could make pyjamas and shirts all the quicker. She told me that M Spaak was a great friend of hers; and I began to hear all sorts of stories about this friendship from Paz. Mme Spaak and the children were in Belgium, so Spaak had consoled himself with this adoring young woman who burnt with a fierce and passionate fire of admiration. Now Spaak is coming to take Pug's place on NATO, and is thinking of placing Simone and the adopted child at Versailles. Gladwyn and I firmly told André that he must stop all this. It would lead to endless gossip here, and would be most unpleasant for Mme Spaak and her family.

British Embassy, Paris, 24 March

On 5 March we left for a tour of Western France. These tours are exhausting, and calculated to make one feel ill. Gladwyn and the junior

[6] André de Staerke (1912–   ): Belgian Ambassador to France.
[7] Simone Dear married Paul Henri Spaak after his first wife's death. Paz Garcia Moreno (1900–93) was the wife of Leon Subercaseaux, and had been one of Cynthia's closest friends.

Naval Attaché had to return to Paris from Nantes after our final dinner-party, spending four hours on couchettes, because Harold, Dorothy and Selwyn were arriving next morning early. The new PM had insisted on coming then, and Gladwyn was forced to cut short the tour. At first this visit smacked of another Suez Plot, for the PM and S of S intended to lunch alone at the Hôtel Matignon with Mollet and Pineau, and have secret talks. No doubt it was legitimate to let them see each other for a short time alone, as they must have wished to discuss how everything had gone wrong. But Gladwyn was not going to let the same dangerous procedure repeat itself, and had told the FO he was not going to stand for it. It really would have been disgraceful if there had been more secret plotting.

The PM looked tired, and rather different with his altered moustache. He has charming courtly manners. Dorothy Macmillan is kind, spontaneous, warm-hearted. After the luncheon I had arranged in my absence, for her to meet some of the Embassy wives, she allowed herself to be whisked off by them to the Victoria Home Jumble Sale. Clarissa would never have agreed to spend a Saturday afternoon in Paris thus.

British Embassy, Paris, 31 March

I returned last night from London. After my influenza I found running around London tiring, and we also had some late nights.

The first night we went with Ava to the gala performance of the ballet. There was what I thought to be a superb performance of *Petroushka*, though the critics do not seem to have praised it to such an extent. I lunched with Christopher and Betty Hussey, and we discussed the article on the Embassy which he will do for *Country Life*. We had a dinner at the [Terence] Maxwells at which we met, for the first time, Lord and Lady Swinton. They are a very vulgar pair. He bounderish, but rather good-looking; she loud-voiced and rude. I am told that Rab and others stay with them in Yorkshire because he is a pillar of the Conservative Party, and has the best shoot to be found (on her money).

The next evening we had a much more agreeable dinner with the Von Hofmannsthals at their pretty house in Connaught Square. They had asked Vanessa too, and there were Shirley and Henry Anglesey, a

Professor Ayer,[8] an intellectual, and an American couple. It was great fun. We next lunched with the Eccleses, where there was a lot of political talk, and Duncan Sandys, the S of S for the Commonwealth, was present. On our last night we dined with Pam Berry.[9] Bob Boothby was there, in great form and most amusing. We had just heard that Bobbity had resigned over Makarios being released, which is a blow to the government.[10] The other subject of conversation was the revelations on Suez in the *Figaro* this week. Though not all quite accurate, it must now be regarded as a fact that there was collusion; and if so, Anthony lied to the House of Commons. Here I must say how excellent I found the food in these private houses: all the lunches and dinners we went to were small, very gay, charmingly done, and with delicious food.

We went to the Boat Race with the Waverleys on Saturday morning. On our return journey after the race I sat at a table for lunch with Nin Ryan, Mary Roxburghe, and Edward Boyle. Edward said he thought Dulles had not behaved so badly over the Canal Users' Association as everybody made out. He had seen the telegrams. We also talked of Rab, who continues to talk of nothing else but how he had expected to be offered the Premiership, and whether he should have resigned. Gladwyn saw Gaitskell, who said that, to his amazement, Rab had told him that of course the Suez attack had all been planned. Many people, including his admirers, think he should see a psychoanalyst.

British Embassy, Paris, 14 April

Everything conspired to favour the Queen's State Visit.[11] The spring was about a month early, so that the trees were green, the chestnuts in flower, tulips out, lilac out, lilies of the valley out, roses showing their leaves, and birds singing. Then the sun shone which, of course, made all

[8] Professor Alfred ('Freddie') Ayer, later Sir Alfred (1910–89): philosopher, later Wykeham Professor of Logic at Oxford.
[9] Lady Pamela Smith, wife of Michael Berry, later Lord Hartwell (1911–   ), proprietor and editor-in-chief of the *Daily Telegraph*.
[10] Robert Cecil, 5th Marquess of Salisbury (1893–1972). As Leader of the House of Lords, he resigned on the issue of the release from exile of Archbishop Makarios of Cyprus.
[11] Although the visit had been arranged before the Suez crisis, it now assumed an added importance in healing Anglo-French recriminations.

the difference for the comfort of the waiting crowds and the beauty of Paris.

Our preparations started ages ago, well before Christmas. I had thought that since the Queen was the guest of the French, and staying at the Elysée, there would be little organizing for us to do, but I was much mistaken. I was admirably aided by having two excellent secretaries: Lydwine d'Oberndorff,[12] who had come to me this spring; and Diana Bowes-Lyon,[13] whom Walter had persuaded to take the job for six weeks. She was an ideal choice; very efficient, quiet, artistic, and being a cousin of the Queen she knew her tastes and likes and dislikes, and could also ring her up or write to her, and thus find out what we wished to know quickly and without fuss.

We arrived at Orly and had the usual long wait. Gladwyn went out with the President and all the leading people to greet the royal visitor, while I was lined up with the Commonwealth ambassadors and ambassadresses. I must say here what a happy family relationship we have together: I think it puzzles the French. The Queen wore a beige wool suit, with mink trimming round the neck, and rather disappointing brown accessories, which I did not think quite grand enough. Frankly her clothes – though praised tremendously in the English papers with such remarks as 'Paris gasped' or 'The Queen in her Hartnell dress stole the show' (a silly remark, because she in fact *was* the show) – were not very beautiful, and did not compare with the French clothes. Cecil Beaton wrote to me afterwards; 'The Queen triumphed over Hartnell's bad taste'.

To my mind she is almost perfect. She is small, well made, well proportioned. She has dark hair, blue eyes, and a lovely English skin. Her features are not classical, but she is much prettier in real life than in photographs. She has an exceptionally charming soft clear voice, high pitched and pitched just right, like a singer, and with an almost bell-like quality. Her French is excellent and her accent astonished everybody here. She has not got the Queen Mother's well-known charm and smile, but I think that this is as it should be. She is not out to charm all and sundry. She has better qualities than that. One feels the presence of a

[12] Lydwine Von Oberndorff; later married to Sir Peter Petrie. He was subsequently Ambassador to Belgium.
[13] Diana Bowes-Lyon, later married to Peter Somerville.

very fine character, simple, kind and good; always anxious to do the right thing; a person who would never let anyone down. And yet quite shrewd and quick about all that is going on. She is quite a 'chip off the old block', in that there is much like Queen Mary or the Princess Royal about her, for she is definitely royal. She is rather serious in her manner, and does not smile much; but when she does it is a lovely radiant smile. To quote Cecil B again in his letter, 'she scored a bull's eye every time she smiled'.

When I say she was almost perfect, I only mean that I cannot help regretting that she had not got more interesting interests. Apart from horses and racing I could not discover anything that interested her, such as the arts, or gardens, or books. This seems to apply equally to Prince Philip.

Prince Philip is handsome and informal, creating an easy democratic atmosphere in the wake of the Queen. He likes to pick out people in the crowds at a party; to ask who they are, find out about them himself, crack jokes with them, get lost in the general mêlée, have everybody waiting for him, and finally catch up again with the Queen and the advance guard. This informality makes him very popular. He shines out as a breezy sailor who has known what it is not to be a royalty. I would say that he handles a difficult position in a remarkably successful way, and I cannot think that any other person, whom the Queen might have married, would have done as well.

When everybody had been presented, we all got into our appointed cars and processed into Paris amid shouting excited clapping waving crowds. The Empress Eugénie said that the cheering of crowds was 'the most intoxicating sound the human ear can hear'. Though not wishing to detract from the cheers of the Parisians, I could not help thinking, as they shouted '*La Reine, La Reine*', how their forebears had hurled their insults against their own *Reine*; and as we passed the Place de la Concorde with all the fountains playing, I remembered the guillotine.

After arriving at the Elysée, the Queen came down looking very charming and dignified without her hat or jacket, and we went into lunch. As I was one off her, I could notice that she eats very little, and in fact she had asked for the meals to be short and not elaborate. This was a wonderful idea, enabling us to emerge from the festivities with our livers in good order, though perhaps some of the French felt they had been done out of their rightful banquets.

After luncheon I had the afternoon off, as I was not involved in the ceremony at the Arc de Triomphe or the Diplomatic Corps reception. Dressing time came all too soon. Marie Louise, from Antoine, came to do my hair; and Madame Dufy and Amélie from Fath came to put me in my full dress of lime-coloured satin. We put Aunt Amie's wreath well forward, and I was very pleased at this and fancied myself rather like the Empress Eugénie: Vanessa too had encouraged it, but neither Gladwyn or Walter approved. A huge dinner at the Elysée, and then the Opéra, where there was a not very remarkable performance of a ballet by Lifar.

I awoke at eight with my breakfast for what was to be our heaviest and most responsible day, as our reception was to take place that evening. Oh! the letters, the telephone calls, the disagreeable messages we had from those who were not asked; the confusion over those who were to have supper upstairs and who cried off in the morning and were on again in the afternoon; and those supper guests who just failed to turn up. But I didn't worry one jot: it was all left in such admirable hands. Mrs Walker (despite a terrible temperamental scene and touchiness) did two beautiful silver wine-coolers on my console-tables on the staircase with great sprays of flowers, and lovely pink and red roses in the gilt baskets on the Queen's and Prince Philip's supper tables (me at the one with the Prince, the President at the Queen's). Pauline Borghese's table centrepieces were wonderfully effective in the Salon Blanc et Or, which was almost entirely lit by candles except for a faint glow of electricity in the lustre. We had two tables of eighteen, which just fitted in allowing for crinoline dresses and the Nuncio's almost equally voluminous skirts.

In the Salon Jaune were tables of six, each presided over by one of the Commonwealth ambassadors, with my artificial fruit in large Edwardian silver vases (or *bonbonnières*, they are perhaps). Rather at the last moment I had what I thought was a brilliant inspiration, to have the fruit arranged in the emblem of each country. This was achieved, not without search for maple leaves, mimosa ferns etc. (I only hope they were noticed.) In the ante-room was a round table of men only, presided over by Gladwyn. Altogether we were eighty for the supper parties, being served from the private dining room. Downstairs were a thousand who were fed at a huge buffet running the length and ends of the State Dining Room, admirably decorated with the four large silver candelabra and the tureens. On the consoles were the wine-coolers filled with flowers. There were two small buffets at the ends of the galleries, and another large one in the Victorian Room. I think there were about sixty 'extras', and the huissier from the Elysée to announce. Then we had a Hungarian band in the hall, in the well of the staircase, a gesture to recent events in Hungary.

On the morning of this Tuesday we left the Embassy at ten to go to the Elysée and have our usual wait there. The Queen came down in a dark blue suit with black accessories, which I thought not quite important enough for the ceremony at the Hôtel de Ville, particularly as all the rest of us were dressed up as for a garden party, ready for the lunch and theatre at Versailles. As usual inside the Hôtel de Ville, the crowds invited to hear the Queen speak were rather uncontrolled. And when she and all the leading people moved down from the dais to go into a private room where the presents were displayed and champagne drunk, everybody who could push hardest squeezed in with us. When we were walking down the stairs of the Hôtel de Ville, Gladwyn and I were much amused (and annoyed) to see Paul Louis Weiller, very erect and solemn and looking all wrong in his tails, marching along just behind the Queen and even in front of Prince Philip. Had one not known the truth, one might have supposed he was an important official, whose presence was imperative to see her Majesty off the premises. Naturally he got himself thus into all the photographs and film coverage. We had not invited him to our party.

From thence we drove to Versailles, where the Queen and Prince Philip were shown into the Petits Appartements. We then went into the Galerie des Glaces where we were to lunch. The tables were decorated with pink roses placed in Empire tureens and vases which I recognized as coming from Malmaison. One saw all sorts of people: Diana in a huge white hat, Vanessa and Stella in borrowed hats and dresses looking very smart. Then we all trooped along to the exquisite theatre, the Queen sitting in the armchair at the centre which is where Louis XV always sat. When the delightful performance of *Les Indes Galantes* was over we had to make a quick getaway and line up in the cold wind under the colonnade of the Grand Trianon to receive the Queen. This Commonwealth party over, we returned to Paris.

After a reviving bath I had a boiled egg and toast on a tray. Then Monsieur Antoine came to put up my hair *à la grecque* and fix on Mother's tiara; and again Mesdames Dufy and Amélie put me into my

huge crinoline dress of volants of pleated white tulle with red velvet
bows at the back. Soon after nine o'clock I was ready, gloves on, the
white tulle scarf over my shoulders, and I left my room to join the fray
below, for many people had started to arrive. I started down the red-carpeted staircase while the Hungarian orchestra was playing a Viennese
waltz. It sounded so pretty and romantic, and I could see in the hall
below the guests in their uniforms and decorations, their bouffant
dresses and their glittering jewellery. I then started receiving in the ante-
room. It was cold, because all the doors had to be open as people were
coming in in such shoals, and the north wind blew straight into the
house, so I had the fire lit.

The Queen, together with the President as well as Gladwyn and
many of our guests, had been on a boat on the Seine, seeing all the fireworks and illuminations. She arrived dressed in a sheath dress, very glittering, and it suited her beautifully. She had a white fur cape which she
wisely kept on till the President arrived. Then there was the usual pro-
cessing through the rooms, starting from the ante-room, then the
Ionian Room, the Victorian Room, the length of the ballroom, returning by the galleries and into the State Dining Room, I following with
Prince Philip. I had been told not to make too many presentations, since
supper must not be too late for the President, who was an old man who
wanted to get home. I don't believe the Queen took in a single word I
told her about my beautiful historic bedroom, to which I took her
before supper, but she suddenly saw Jasper in his evening collar, and at
once bent down and he gave her his paw. When we returned to the
Salon Vert where the President, Prince Philip and Gladwyn were
waiting, she sat down and said to Jasper, 'Come on up', which he
promptly did. I may say that Berthe and Gravett have never ceased to
talk about this conquest.

The supper was, I think, just right for the occasion: cold salmon,
chaudfroid of chicken, a salad, oranges and lemons filled with sorbet, and
a wonderful Bollinger. The meal was not long, so that when we got
downstairs again and the President had left, another tour of the rooms
could be done before the royal party went home. The difficulty was to
get rid of all the guests. They lingered on, and at half past one Cecil
Beaton was still sketching Diana Cooper and Anne Norwich in the
Ionian Room. He then wanted to do me, but I was too sleepy, and after
a few minutes posing, went to bed.

I think there was a good representative gathering that evening at the Embassy. The *gratin* looked well in their family jewels: Baronne Elie de Rothschild wore the most superb emeralds, which I think were Brazilian crown jewels.[14] Madame Fath represented couture; Boussac and Suzy Volterra racing; and for culture and the arts we had Jean Cocteau, Francis Poulenc, the Aurics, Mauriac, and alas! Maurois. All the women on the staff looked their best, and with their husbands were the greatest help.

Next day the Queen and Prince Philip arrived here soon after ten and were greeted by the cheers of the Chancery children grouped in the hall. The ground floor was crammed with different delegations who were to be presented, including representative groups of Resistants, and the British Legion were lined up in the garden, where a military band was playing on the lawn. Then M Joffet, of the Ville de Paris, and René, the gardener, were presented, and the Queen planted a weeping cherry tree. We then drove to La Celle Saint Cloud to lunch with Monsieur Pineau.

On leaving La Celle Saint Cloud we found ourselves suddenly making a quite unexpected detour to show the Queen some of Boussac's racehorses, and I wondered whether Boussac had bribed the outriders; at any rate, it gave HM the greatest pleasure. We then proceeded to Flin to see the Renault works in the most modern factory in France. This was the only thing I was not happy about, for there was a sullen atmosphere of hostility on the part of the workers.

In the evening we went to the Louvre, which had been transformed, to where an oval salon had been created out of one of the sculpture rooms, and hung with pictures. The dinner that followed in the Salle des Caryatides was memorable. Tremendous trouble had been taken; statues moved, velvet curtains hung over the windows, small orchestra in the gallery. We then returned to the oval room where a charming incident occurred. It was discovered that the Queen had never been to the Louvre before, and therefore had never clapped eyes on the Mona Lisa. About a quarter of an hour later two men came staggering in carrying this celebrated picture, and leant it very informally against a chair for a close and intimate inspection. Then began the most unpleasant episode of the whole visit – even more disagreeable than the Flin factory, for we were in danger of being squashed. There were to have been two thousand guests

[14] Liliane Fould-Springer, married to Baron Elie de Rothschild (1910–   ).

at the reception, but this had been weakly augmented to three. It soon became the most dreadful pandemonium which nobody could control. Bouffant dresses were squashed flat as pancakes, and old ladies dropped their bags which were trampled underfoot. I heard Lady Margaret Hay anxiously say to the Queen, 'Are you all right, ma'am?', and she replied, 'Just'. I am forgetting to mention the press with their horrible cameras and flash-light bulbs and television lighting, all milling around us and contributing to the general discomfort and disorganization.

The last day, Thursday, there was a great departure from the Elysée, and we drove to Le Bourget and then flew to Lille in the Viscount. Gladwyn and I, Monsieur de la Chauvinière and General Ganeval, sat the four of us together; and on the opposite side of the gangway sat the Queen and Prince, their suite somewhere in front through a door. On this journey I could notice how happily devoted the royal couple were to each other. They laughed and joked and chatted in a most easy and natural manner.

There was rather a long pause in the Préfeture before lunch. To help matters I got the Préfet, Monsieur Benedetti, to tell his amusing story of his visit to England in charge of a delegation of Préfets. Like all the French, they had appreciated the English breakfasts, though not the other meals. Then they were taken to some County Council where the Town Clerk made a long and boring speech of welcome as they were offered tea. It was here that they were introduced to *les crumpets*. So delicious were these that the Frenchmen quite forgot about the speech and began to eat them with relish, emptying the plates, seizing them from another table; and they were so absorbed in this new dish that he had to call his flock to order, and make '*des grands yeux*' at them. Everyone thought this very funny, and I heard afterwards that on her return the Queen sent him a present of crumpets.

Afterwards we started off again, beginning with the flower show in the Royal Place de Gaulle, then to La Vieille Bourse, where there were people dressed in medieval clothes, and trumpeters with tabards. From there we went to Roubaix, to the clothing factory of Monsieur Prouvost[15] and on to the Lainière, an enchanting place where they had built little streets of shops to show their goods when manufactured. This over, we all drove to the airport and, goodbyes said, we saw our royal couple enter their plane and fly off home.

[15] Jean Prouvost (b. 1885): industrialist and newspaper magnate.

Dear Diana Bowes-Lyon left the next day. Then, saddest of all, Walter Lees left us, to go and work for Niarchos. I couldn't bear to say goodbye to him but told him to slip away without my knowing when. Everybody was glad of a good rest; the house went back to normal, and so did our lives. But wherever we went we heard praise of the Queen, and what a happy time her visit had given to everybody, and touching tributes came from all walks of life.

This is the third anniversary of our arrival here. Three blissful years we have had in this wonderful Embassy. How lucky we have been to have had the experience.

Abbaye de Lescaladieu, Hautes-Pyrenees, 9 August

We are staying in the most delightful and romantic place. An old abbey, dissolved during the Revolution, made into a château in 1824, and now converted into a hotel during the summer months.

I made a visit to Lourdes. At first I was shocked at the commercialism of it all – endless little shops called St Patrick, the Little Flower, etc., selling trinkets and statuettes; quantities of hotels; crowds of people swarming along the streets, or buffer to buffer in cars; a vast new underground cathedral being built. I regretted that the little village of Lourdes, with its famous grotto, had not been left in all its simplicity, with pilgrims and tourists lodged nearby, leaving the holy site as it had been when Bernadette saw the vision on the hill-side. But all this vulgarity becomes altogether justified when one sees the processions coming away from the grotto, a seemingly endless file of the devout, the maimed, lame and sick, some in wheelchairs, some in stretchers on wheels, some limping, some led, some bandaged, some holding up their hands to keep the sun off their eyes, some wiping away their tears, some supported by relatives or nuns or monks. The expression on their faces was that of ecstasy – 'the peace that passeth all understanding'. Particularly I shall remember a very handsome elderly well-to-do woman, obviously English or possibly Irish. She sat in her wheel-chair very upright, and her beautiful face was lit up with a spiritual glow. One could not help envying the joy of these people. What was impressive was that whether they had been cured or not, they had found true happiness.

Hôtel du Palais, Biarritz, 14 August

The management here have given us a wonderful suite of rooms, with a lovely sitting-room giving on to a terrace, and the Atlantic rollers roaring in one's ears and health-giving breezes filling one's lungs. I must say it is bliss, and I think that Biarritz has every advantage over the Côte d'Azur.

I have been very neglectful of my diary since the Queen's visit. Complete exhaustion set in, but could not be indulged because the Paris season was upon us, and a series of visitors descended upon the Embassy.

In the beginning of May the Alexanders[16] came to open the Hertford Hospital. He is charming, and also deeply spiritual, which one would not have imagined on initial acquaintance. That awful couple, the Dockers, somehow got themselves invited to the opening ceremony, and she became very drunk. When I left she was trying to make a speech and attract the attention of the crowds.

Rab came to stay, bringing Sarah on a long-promised visit. What was delightful was that he had entirely got out of his usual rut. There was no going over the past, no recriminations, no might-have-beens. He was the old Rab of Sydney's days, and little Sarah dealt with him as abruptly and successfully as her mother.

The Oliviers gave a very successful performance of *Titus Andronicus* to which we took the Jean-Louis Barraults.[17] Maxine Audley, who acts Tamara, came to lunch. Evidently nobody likes Vivien Leigh backstage. Since she loses her tongue so soon in the play, she is always interfering and telling the others how they should be acting. She is odious to the two unfortunate young men who have to rape her, accusing them one moment of being too rough and having broken her rib, and the next time of being too gentle. They go in fear of her, knowing that she could spoil their chance of a future engagement. Larry everybody loves, but he knows how much depends on them being together and puts up with her difficult personality. Anthony Quayle, the brilliant Arab in the

---

[16] Field Marshal Harold Alexander, Earl Alexander of Tunis (1891–1969), married to Lady Margaret Bingham. Formerly Supreme Allied Commander Mediterranean Theatre, and Governor-General of Canada.
[17] Jean-Louis Barrault (1910–), actor and producer, married to Madeleine Renaud (1900–), actress.

play, tells the story that on their wedding night the Devil appeared, telling them he admired them both tremendously and was going to do everything in his power to help them on to great success. They replied that they were not going to be taken in by him, because he would want them to sell their souls. 'Oh no', he said, 'there's only just one little thing you'll have to do – stick together'. Paul Louis Weiller gave a luncheon for them and the cast at his house at Versailles. I sat between Maurice Chevalier and Sadri Khan, the other side of whom was the notorious Nina Dyer, and they were fondling each other the whole time. She looks rather oriental herself, and very feline. It is said she was the Begum's find originally.

Alain de Rothschild's ball was quite the prettiest of the season. Jacques Franck had decorated the Rothschild house, using some very pretty Sert panels in the dining-room, very like those that Mother has at Bath. A lovely Chinese kiosk had been put up in the garden. A day or two later we went to Elsa Maxwell's party at the Restaurant Laurent, an experience not to be repeated. About two hundred people were squeezed into the room, the waiters could hardly hand round the food, the band was so loud that one could not hear anything that was said, and the dance-floor so small that one could not move on it.

At the end of May we attended the unveiling of the Memorial at Dunkirk by the Queen Mother. It was quite the hottest day of the year, and the ceremony was exhausting under the blazing sun. Fortunately I had put on a large hat and had a fan. Monty sat next to me. Instead of being got up like the Duke of Gloucester, he was in a light-weight battle-dress such as he might have worn at Alamein. The strange little man did not cease boasting of this: 'I wear what I like. I don't mind what other people say or think. I just do as I want to do'. I asked him to come and see us in the Embassy, and he said he would love to come along and not when there were crowds of other people. I said we would invite Nancy Mitford for the fourth, and what would he like to eat? 'Rice pudding', replied the Field Marshal.[18]

We went to the Grand Prix, I sitting in Mme Suzy Volterra's box, and

[18] Field Marshal Bernard Montgomery, 1st Viscount Montgomery of Alamein (1887–1976): Deputy Supreme Commander Allied Forces in Europe 1951–8. Gladwyn and Cynthia had first had Monty and Nancy to lunch *à quatre* in 1951, after Monty had remarked to Gladwyn, 'Read a novel the other day. Hardly ever do. By a woman. *The Pursuit of Love.*'

visiting the paddocks with her. Pierre Lyautey tells me that in the old days, if one ran into a man the day after the Grand Prix, he would be dressed in a straw boater and brown and white shoes, and would apologize for being found in Paris at all, hastily explaining that he was about to catch a train. On no account must it be thought that he was remaining in the city, or people would suppose that he had no château to go to.

Mme Jacquinot gave a dinner-party of about eighty. She is enormously rich, and married Monsieur J because there was a good chance that he might be elected President.[19] I sat next to Monseigneur [Comte de Paris], for the second time that day. What with the success of his coming to live in France, and the great interest he takes, and the heady enthusiasm at the royal wedding (there were cries of '*Vive le Dauphin, Vive la Dauphine*'), he begins to have some hope that he might play a more important part here. Being left-wing politically, he aspires only to be a Prince-President, not a King. He confided to me at this dinner that, should he ever come to power, he would have to show strength and firmness, because that is what people needed.

Later in the evening a very odd thing happened. There had been some chamber music after dinner, and at about one o'clock some people started to say goodbye, but not the Comte and Comtesse de Paris. Seeing that about twenty people had left, I went up to the Comtesse and asked to be excused, and then began to say goodbye. The Duchesse de Noailles then made the staggering remark, 'What! are you leaving before our King has left? We waited for your Queen!' I was so astonished that I wondered if I could have heard aright, whereupon she repeated it. I was trying to collect myself, so as not to retort rudely, as I was much tempted to do, when fortunately Mme Catroux, who was standing next to the Duchesse, said tartly, 'That's not at all the same thing'. 'My King', my foot! What a silly woman. Saying this sort of thing would certainly help to dish quickly the Orleanist cause.

In London in July I went to tea with Dorothy Macmillan. Number Ten presents a very different appearance under the new regime. It now seems a very cosy place with an easy happy atmosphere. She showed me round the house and pointed out its extraordinary inconveniences, which are many, for it really is a rabbit warren. But it has great charm.

---

[19] Simone Lazard, married Louis Jacquinot (b. 1898). He had been a presidential candidate in 1953.

She herself is quite the nicest person in the world. Abominably dressed, and not caring two hoots about it, she radiates kindness and enthusiasm, and is very amusing. The next evening I went to Glyndebourne with the Beits and Sachy [Sitwell], to see *Ariadne auf Naxos*, which was beautifully sung and, though an absurd story, has the most lovely music in it – I think – that Strauss wrote. It was difficult to recognize in Glyndebourne as it now is the house that Mother rented from John Christie in the summer of 1929. I remember so well being there. What a different world that was, with lots of servants, long evening dresses every night, everything cheap and easy to get.

On the Sunday we made an expedition after my own heart from Stratfield Saye. It was to the tombs of the French imperial family in the Memorial Chapel at Farnborough, which Gerry and Frank [Pakenham] are interested in preserving. After seeing the tombs I begged that we might stop and see the house where the Empress Eugénie had lived. It was now a convent school, and the Pakenhams knew all the ropes of how to get in, addressing the nuns as 'mother'. So in we went, leaving Gerry rather cross in the car, for he had not thought it worth getting out to see what he considered to be a house of a bad period. However, I found it enchanting, particularly as we were shown round by a very old French nun who had known her: where she sat and worked, where she received Queen Victoria, where the Winterhalter group had hung, where her bed had been placed. Almost the most fascinating moment was when I asked whether our guide had ever seen the famous curtsey that, with its circular movement, seemed to be addressed to each individual in the room. The old nun said, 'Oh yes, it went something like this'; and she started by turning her head to the right and slowly brought it round to the left as she curtsied. So now I feel I have seen the circular curtsey, which was grace personified. Ethel Smythe, seeing her make it to Queen Victoria at Balmoral, described it as being like a field of corn bent gently down by the wind and coming as gracefully up again.

I went to Beatrice Eden's memorial service at St George's Hanover Square. Poor Beatrice. It is a pity she could not be persuaded to go back to Anthony. She told me, when she came to see me just over a year ago, that she was once or twice almost tempted to do so when he used to come and see her in New York, but then he would always go and say just the wrong thing, which put her off.

I lunched with the Scarbroughs in their delightful house in St James's

Palace, to meet the Duke and Duchess of Gloucester. He looks a real
Hanoverian, not very bright, but hearty and conscientious. There was
always the wonderful story of him in Cairo, when his staff took him to a
night club and he took to the floor with the leading houri. One of his
equerries managed to manoeuvre himself and his partner close enough
to hear the conversational interchange between these two incompat-
ibles. After a silence of some minutes, the Duke was heard to say, 'Ever
been to Tidworth?'[20]

Fenton, Northumberland, 20 August

We were greeted by a crowd of barking dogs and Tony Lambton, with
his hair all blown out in the wind and looking quite extraordinary.[21] This
Victorian house is most comfortable, with fires lit in every room and
the food excellent. Tony has an intelligent mind, and is shrewd and tren-
chant about people in a cruel way. He had been Parliamentary Secretary
to Selwyn, and thought S had been very stupid with Dulles long before
Suez. There are lovely things at Fenton, but best of all I liked the Red
Boy, Master Lambton, as poignant as ever in the frame that Lawrence
chose for it.

Glen, Peeblesshire, 27 August [22]

From the visitors' book we discovered that I had not been here since
1918. I remember it very well. The large house party, people coming and
going, Sir Oliver Lodge, Sir Edward Grey, Mary Strickland (very beautiful), Letty Benson (then Lady Elcho, and recently widowed), Bibs
Plymouth (not then married), old Lady Wemyss, Biddy Monkton (then
Lady Carlisle and not as nice as she is now). Christopher on leave from
the Navy; David, who was at that time charming; Stephen, fair and frail-
looking, artistic, always dressing up in scarves or any feminine attire. It

[20] Tidworth Barracks, on the edge of Salisbury Plain.
[21] Antony Lambton, Viscount Lambton (1922–   ), married to Belinda Blew-Jones.
On the death of his father in 1970 he disclaimed the earldom of Durham and other
peerages for life.
[22] As guests of Lord and Lady Glenconner.

was all gay and noisy and fun. Then in the midst of all this I got a horrible cold and had to retire to my four-poster bed for a day or two, and kind Bessie Belloc-Lowndes came to see me the whole time. I felt dreadful when I got up, and not at all like rejoining the noisy house party.[23]

Christopher [Glenconner] has much improved the house. I have a lovely four-poster bed, and am looked after by a nice Scotch maid who was with Pamela Grey and talked about her with affection. 'She was always the same', she said; which belies all the unkind things that acid Clare says about her mother. Clare, brought up in an intellectual atmosphere, soon discovered that what she really liked in life was something quite different – horses, cards, and the kind of men that go with them. Today the men went shooting and we went to join them for lunch in the traditional fashion: fortunately it was fine enough to eat outside instead of in the keeper's stuffy cottage. As we were waiting, drinking our sherry, Clare told us how once, when Margot Oxford[24] was getting particularly impatient with her sister-in-law Pamela, who was boring them all about her love and understanding of birds, she slipped in with, 'I'm damned fond of a robin myself'.

British Embassy, Paris, 18 October

Sir Thomas and Lady Beecham came to lunch this week, she ghastly, he as amusing and brilliant as ever. He kept us laughing the whole time. He began talking of the George Moore letters to Emerald [Cunard], and evidently did not agree with the idea that their friendship had in fact been a love affair: 'I always understood that George Moore was a case of didn't kiss but told'.

[23] The hostess of this house party had been Pamela Glenconner (shortly to marry Sir Edward Grey), together with her sons Christopher, David and Stephen Tennant. Her sister, Mary Wemyss, was the mother of Irene ('Bibs') Charteris and Mary Strickland, and the mother-in-law of the widowed Violet Elcho, who later married Guy Benson. Oliver Lodge (1851–1940) was a physicist and a psychical experimenter, who greatly influenced Lady Genconner. And Marie Belloc-Lowndes (1868–1947) was an authoress, and sister of Hilaire Belloc.

[24] Margot Tennant (1864–1945), married Henry Asquith, later 1st Earl of Oxford and Asquith, Prime Minister 1908–16.

British Embassy, Paris, 24 October (letter to CN)

Nancy Mitford's book on Voltaire has just arrived, and I imagine it is not much liked here because yesterday it was reported that a huge heart had been chalked on our garden gate, and on it written 'Voltaire does not love Nancy'. I wonder who could have done it. Gravett went and rubbed it out.

British Embassy, Paris, 8 November

We went to London for two days, chiefly to go to the Buckingham Palace Diplomatic Party. We stayed with Gerry at Apsley House, the last of the great London houses.[25] We thought that he would be going to the party, but he says he has been dropped. I told him that we would be arriving sometime after midday; but we were extremely punctual and reached Apsley House at about four minutes to twelve. We rang the bell and Gerry opened it, and I rushed forward joyously to greet him but was responded to by a furious frowning face and an angry whisper, 'There is a meeting of forty bishops, generals, and admirals for Wellington College going on, and you're early'. He then reluctantly let us in, but said that as the meeting was taking place in the library, we would have to reach the lift by going through the basement. This was a lengthy and laborious process, we all carrying suitcases and knocking them at every corner and door; down the stone back stairs and along dimly-lit passages. We finally reached the lift and the second floor and the delightfully old-fashioned bedrooms: heavy half-tester beds hung with faded chintz, couches, po-cupboards, long bell-ropes, and, of course, mahogany round the baths and lavatories. There was a good layer of dust in the cupboards. The Great Duke himself had always liked to occupy the most simple bedroom, and as far away from his Duchess as possible. At Stratfield Saye he slept at the far end of a ground-floor wing, and here at Apsley House it had been almost a cubby-hole on the ground floor too, with several doors and one gloomy window with hardly any light.

[25] He had generously given Apsley House and its treasures to the nation, though retaining part of the house as his London residence.

British Embassy, Paris, 12 November

We returned on Friday with Gerry. The next night we had a cocktail party for Gerry consisting mostly of curators from the various museums. Varlet came from the Louvre. There was a tremendous rumpus at the time of the Queen's visit because he refused to lend some furniture, including the *bureau du roi*, to Versailles, having wanted to become curator there instead of Van Der Kemp. But the President insisted that the stuff should go, and ordered a van to be sent for it. Varlet's reason for not sending the furniture was that he feared it would never be returned; and this is exactly what has happened. Later in the evening we went to the Folies Bergères at Gerry's request. He said, 'I am a simple English gentleman living near Reading, and when I come to Paris I want to be as gay as possible, and have the club seats at the Folies Bergères and be as close as possible'. So Nancy was persuaded to come, and Gladwyn was dragged reluctantly, but as the seats are extremely comfortable he managed to have a good sleep. On Monday I took Gerry and Ralph Dutton to Fontainebleau. We had a really enchanting day there, with the curator to show us round, and we saw everything, he opening up more and more rooms until it became so dark that we could hardly distinguish anything. The final thing we saw was the dilapidated Napoleon III theatre, all hung in tattered yellow satin, the scene of all those plays and charades of the Second Empire.

British Embassy, Paris, 18 November

Gladwyn left last Tuesday for a fortnight's tour of the Sahara, in a private plane laden with excellent wines, food and delicacies. Everybody seems to think it clever of him to absent himself from Paris at this moment, for we are in bad odour here over the Tunisian arms affair.[26] The French behaved tiresomely, but we even more so, and Gladwyn had tried to postpone the unfortunate move as long as possible. The day it broke I was supping with the Princesse de Robech after the concert by

[26] On 15 November Britain and the United States undertook to supply token consignments of arms to Tunisia. The French Government held that this was tantamount to arming the rebels in Algeria.

her elderly decayed-looking pianist lover. I noticed I was being rather cold-shouldered; but I sat by chance next to Quaroni[27] who said that Italy had been much in sympathy with us over our action and had been tempted to do likewise, 'in fact' (here with an appropriate gesture) 'we were just waiting on our oars'. A day or two later I saw him again and he said that, seeing what a mess England and America had got into, he felt he had been right to advise his country to do nothing. All very Italian, trying to be the cleverest.

Meanwhile our unpopularity certainly increased. Or rather, it was decided that the English must be shown how unpopular they were. So extra police were added every day to guard us. By Saturday there was a rumour of a demonstration against us and the American Embassy, and when I returned from that annual homely function, the church bazaar, the police were all around us and lorry-loads of soldiers stationed right round the block. Colonel Robertson decided it would be desirable to shut the great doors at dusk.[28] From time to time I went into the library and peered through the window, but could see or hear nothing. Gravett, thoroughly enjoying it all, went as far as the Place de la Concorde and just missed the demonstration which had taken place outside the American Embassy.

British Embassy, Paris, 26 November

Gladwyn returned from the Sahara, by which time the storm was less violent. On Monday the PM and S of S and their appendages arrived to try to set things right. They wanted a working dinner and hoped to leave afterwards, but if the talks went very badly they would not want the dinner, and if the talks took a long time they might wish to spend the night. What a confusing prospect for a hostess. One thing I did insist on was that the 'working dinner', which Harold had thought should be a light cold meal, must be a hot and *beau menu*, knowing that nothing would put the French in a better humour than really delicious food and wine. So, prepared for every eventuality, we went ahead with plans, and there was duly a dinner for twenty-four and the PM's party stayed the

---

[27] Pietro Quaroni (b. 1898): Italian Ambassador to France.
[28] The doors were normally left open, there being then no fear of terrorism.

night. They dined in the Ionian Room and, to enable the talkers to talk to the right persons intimately, we had four tables of six, with the four cherub centre-pieces from the Borghese plate with candles on them. Apparently Gaillard greatly admired them and the room. But otherwise the talks were rather sticky. Afterwards they all packed off back to the Hôtel Matignon[29] where matters improved a little, enough for them to be resumed next morning. Again the dilemma, possibly they would all lunch in, or possibly on the plane. In the end the relationship became even more cordial, and after many false starts we were told that they were heading for the Embassy and we were finally able to sit down to lunch at about half past two, after which the whole box of tricks departed.

British Embassy, Paris, 2 December

This was an important weekend for me for it was my first St Andrew's Night Banquet as President of the Caledonian Society of France. Lord Dundee (whom we knew as Jim Wedderburn, and then as Lord Dudhope, in spite of which discouraging name he managed to claim successfully the earldom of Dundee) was Scottish Guest Speaker, and Maurice Schumann the French Guest Speaker: the Dundees and the John Nobles stayed with us. We all looked very fine as we started off for the Hôtel du Palais d'Orsay, the men in Highland dress, the ladies with sashes and tiaras. I wore an 'ancient' silk Campbell sash woven by hand by the Edinburgh Craft Centre — Campbell because, though it is not quite correct to wear one's grandmother's tartan, it is infinitely prettier than the Mackintosh which I can wear, the Nobles being a sept of the Clan Chattan. I wore my lime green satin dress that I had for the Queen's visit. We processed into the ballroom to the strains of 'Bonnie Dundee'.[30] When the haggis was brought round I had to pierce it with a dirk and say whatever one says in Gaelic and hand the piper his whisky. My speech included my own favourite remark of the Scot who said,

[29] Residence of the French Prime Minister.
[30] 'Bonnie Dundee' had been the heroic seventeenth-century Jacobite, John Graham of Claverhouse, Viscount Dundee. The present Earl (no relation of John Graham) had earned the sobriquet 'Bunny Dundee' from his speeches in the House of Lords on the subject of the rabbit population.

'I've been to Paris; and I've been to Peebles. But for pleasure, give me Peebles'.

Next evening I had to give the prizes for fancy dress at the Embassy Club Ball. It is strange what disguise will do for some people, particularly the introverts. Dick Faber,[31] generally so serious and shy, transformed into a Victorian dandy in grey tail coat and top hat and red whiskers to match his hair, had become gay, easy, debonair, in fact greatly improved in appearance and manner. Mr Neville, the man responsible for redoing the electricity here, wore spectacles and a false nose and was dashing about in an almost abandoned manner, very different from the quiet Yorkshireman we generally see about the house. Mr MacLehose,[32] with a beard and a jewelled turban and without his spectacles, was most handsome as a maharajah. Marie Palliser looked enchanting as a matador, having made it up herself that morning; and Diana Beith[33] looked eighteen in a kilted skirt and a glengarry.

British Embassy, Paris, 19 December

We have just finished a week of great activity, another of the occasions when this old house seems to come to life, show itself at its best, and make history. Last Thursday it began with the arrival of Selwyn, Denis Laskey and a detective. On Saturday morning the Prime Minister arrived with two private secretaries and another detective, and Mr Maudling[34] was around too, and had to have a room at his disposal. So we were pretty full up, with the PM using the library, and Selwyn Lydwine's room, and all the typists in the private dining-room and security guards posted at various places in the house.

On the night when a big men's dinner was given here, every possible precaution was taken including even more police, and a French plain-

---

[31] Richard Faber, later Sir Richard (1924–   ): Second Secretary in the Embassy, and later Ambassador to Algeria.

[32] Murray MacLehose, later Lord MacLehose of Beoch (1917–   ): First Secretary in the Embassy, and subsequently Governor of Hong Kong.

[33] Diana Gilmour, wife of John Beith, who was Head of Chancery at the Embassy.

[34] Reginald Maudling (1917–79): Paymaster General, and subsequently Chancellor of the Exchequer and Home Secretary.

clothes detective was to sit at the window of Gravett's sitting-room, looking down to the entrance in the Faubourg St Honoré to see that everything was all right when the important personages arrived and departed. I had dined alone with Jill and Edward Tomkins, and returned home fairly late to be told by Gravett that some of the party had gone and the rest were upstairs talking. As I was going to bed Gladwyn came in and said that he could not find where the drinks had been put, so I told him to telephone Gravett who could only just have gone to his room. This was the beginning of an extraordinary incident – and the drinks were all the time in the ante-room.

When Gravett's telephone rang he had not yet arrived in his quarters, and Lucio, the Italian footman, went to answer it in a night shirt. The detective, who must have been drunk, hearing the noise, opened the door and brandished his revolver; and, for some curious reason, he had removed the antlers hanging from the wall of Gravett's sitting-room and put them round his neck, presenting the strangest appearance. Thus he bore down on the telephoning Lucio, saying he was there to protect 'Monsieur Macmillan'. Lucio, true to the traditions of his country, turned and fled, pursued by the detective. Thus the incongruous pair arrived in the front hall, where Gravett was with the night guard. With British stolidity, Gravett reacted differently to Lucio. ''and over me antlers', he shouted angrily, disregarding the revolver. At this moment Gladwyn from the staircase called to Gravett to bring the drinks, and hearing a commotion behind the coromandel screen, came down to see what was happening. 'Don't come downstairs, sir! We've a madman 'ere who's asking for the Prime Minister'. Then Colonel Robertson appeared on the scene, and the antlers and revolver were seized from the drunk detective, and the police were told to get two plain-clothes men to come and assist him out, so that there should be as little publicity as possible. Gravett said afterwards that his antlers had been damaged, and the night guard had a hernia, and poor Lucio the fright of his life. The next day there was a full apology from the French police, and we all had a good laugh; particularly as the British detective really responsible for the PM's safety was sound asleep all the time on the second floor.[35]

As for the great men attending these 'summit talks', Adenauer could

---

[35] The laugh was all the merrier because the story was unscooped by the press.

not leave his hotel as he was too full of antibiotics after his recent flu, and Eisenhower had recently had a stroke.[36] I thought that Harold Macmillan looked well, and I don't believe that Selwyn had to have the doctor once, so our team did not do badly. Harold is always very charming and courtly. He likes to sit on after lunch or dinner drinking his wine or brandy and talking about all sorts of subjects. He told me that Ronnie Knox, who had been his tutor, had come up to London for some particular occasion shortly before he died, and Harold insisted on him staying at Number Ten. The next morning he took him to Paddington in his car to put him on the train for Mells, and the stationmaster had turned out in his top hat and everything was arranged in the greatest comfort. As Harold bid goodbye he said, 'I hope you have a good journey'. And Ronnie Knox replied, 'I am going soon on a very long journey'. So Harold bowed his head, realizing that he knew.

The last day I suggested that the PM and S of S and all his retinue come and have drinks in the Salon Vert. So we had a charming little party with all the secretaries, and people popping in for last minute alterations or instructions, and hangers-on, and Stella to give support. Then off they went, goodbyes were said in the hall, coats and hats and pouches were hastily seized, names were signed in the book, and all the cars swept out of the courtyard. Gravett turned the lights low, and remarked that somebody had left his hat.

---

[36] Konrad Adenauer, Federal Chancellor of Germany; and Dwight Eisenhower, President of the United States.

1958

❖

I have not written a word since February, and so much has happened since then that I must try and remember some of the most important things with the aid of my engagement book.

On 8 May we had a party for the first night of Glyndebourne's Paris performances, after *Le Comte Ory*. John Christie came to stay and was an eccentric guest. He arrived off the ferry and demanded a plate of porridge for breakfast, which was just what we had not got. He was always disappearing when wanted. He wore a wonderful Coke bowler. And when he left a key was found tied to an old handkerchief, right at the back of a drawer in his bedroom. It turned out to be the most precious key of the safe at Glyndebourne, too precious to be entrusted to anybody at home.[1]

During the second half of May the French political crisis was blowing up and had reached gale force.[2] The atmosphere was intense, alarming, and there was a feeling of 'touch and go' about it, though at the same time people were curiously calm and went about their business as usual. I was told that the French no longer have it in them to make revolutions, and that all that they are really concerned about is their holiday entitlement. Yet we were on the brink of a civil war, and, had things taken a bad turn, I am sure that their mercurial Latin

[1] He also remarked loudly in the foyer before the opera, 'I don't like the French. Never trusted them'.
[2] The Fourth Republic was in its death throes, enfeebled by the crisis in Algeria. Waiting at the bedside were the Communist Party, and the solitary figure of General de Gaulle.

temperament would have burst out. The great doors of the Elysée were kept shut and it was surrounded by police, and there were vans of armed police and troops and Gardes Republicaines concentrated particularly in our *quartier*. The Embassy also was guarded, though we were not this time the butt of public anger. Many engagements were cancelled, the papers published the wildest rumours, and were frequently censored. One English paper mistook the carloads of families leaving Paris for the Pentecost weekend for refugees fleeing. Mother, reading this in Bath, at once got ready her spare rooms for us. Michael Foot insulted President Coty in one of his articles, and was detained in the Ministry of the Interior and expelled from France next morning. Randolph Churchill rushed off to Colombey-les-Deux-Eglises to try to see General de Gaulle. Failing to do so, he telephoned Gladwyn from there, telling him how there had been an electricity cut in the village when he arrived, and how the General's house was guarded by huge dogs and he could not get admittance because he had no identity card, though he waved his war disc in their faces; and there was only one bar, 'and what's more, there's only one Eglise'.[3]

When de Gaulle was accepted[4] on Thursday the 29th there was great rejoicing, and I heard the shouts of the excited crowd outside the Elysée. Later they congregated in the Champs Elysées and sounded their horns till all hours of the night.

British Embassy, Paris, 19 October

We had a dinner in the Salon Ionian in honour of the Menuhins' wedding anniversary. The chef excelled himself with a sweet shaped like a violin. Diana M gave an amusing account of their recent journey to Moscow. The lavatory of their suite had been out of order, but Yehudi, a most useful handyman, mended it.

---

[3] But Randolph did manage to force his way past the night guard into the Embassy for a late-night talk with Gladwyn, the flustered guard dramatically announcing him at the library door as 'Mr Winston Churchill'.

[4] By the National Assembly as Prime Minister, pending the constitutional changes that inaugurated the Fifth Republic, of which he became the President 1958–69.

British Embassy, Paris, 6 November

The Churchills came for the night, as he was to receive the Croix de la Libération from General de Gaulle.[5] Sir Winston arrived with Anthony Montague Browne, and with a male nurse-valet and a detective. Clemmie arrived a little earlier from London. That evening we had a small dinner for them. We met in the library where there was a fire, and inaugurated 'the lettering' and the putting back of the green carpet.[6] There was alarm at one moment that Randolph would barge in on the proceedings, and no one knew what his parents felt about it. It turned out that his mother had not spoken to him for two years. In the end he was allowed to come in after dinner and was in a mild and sentimental mood, kissing us all, and even his mother called him 'dear boy'. Sir Winston, having recited a good deal of the 'Lays of Ancient Rome' to me and Odette[7] at dinner, was in excellent spirits. He was afterwards placed in an armchair by the fire in the Salon Blanc et Or, and all the pretty ladies came and sat at his feet, so he was, as Diana said, like a pasha in heaven.

The next morning we sallied forth for the ceremony at the Matignon; it was to be out of doors, and fortunately the weather was fine. Gladwyn and Churchill were to get into the first car, but the old man stood waiting at the doorway looking at his wife, and finally reproached her with 'Clemmie', whereupon she kissed him, which was what he had been expecting, and he was not going to go off without it. She chatted brightly – 'Winston is very moved' – as we got into our car. She is tactful with him. Coming home after the luncheon, when I sat between them in the car, he said, 'And did I go round very slowly when I was inspecting the troops?' – which indeed he had, almost staggering at each step, which made anxious watching – and she replied, 'Yes, you did

[5] In 1947 Churchill had received the Medaille Militaire from the hands of the French Prime Minister, Paul Ramadier: de Gaulle, offered the same distinction, had refused it.
[6] The elegant library had been designed by Charles de Beistegui to house the collection of books which Duff Cooper had given to the Embassy. Cynthia and Gladwyn had now reinstated its carpet and curtains, removed by the Harveys, and had arranged for the frieze to be decorated with a Latin inscription recording Duff Cooper's generosity.
[7] Odette Wallace, wife of Jacques Pol Roger: Churchill's last inamorata, and for decades the bountiful provider of champagne at the annual Duff Cooper Literary Prizegiving in London.

it beautifully slowly, looking at each medal'. At the luncheon I sat on de Gaulle's left and discovered that it was quite true that he has Scottish blood. Harold Macmillan once told me that long ago in Algiers, when the General was being particularly obstinate, he had said to him, 'Really, you might be Scottish, a son of the manse'; to which the General replied that he had, in fact, a Scottish great-grandmother.

Spending a good deal of time with Clemmie, I was much amused to hear of her youth in Dieppe and of her friendship, when fifteen, with Sickert. Jacques-Emile Blanche was shocked to find Sickert going around with this respectable young girl when she was in Paris at the Sorbonne, and sent her home at his own expense in an electric brougham. We went to tea at the Elysée on the way home – the last time we were to be entertained there by President Coty – and then our guests left from Le Bourget. Winston said to Gladwyn, 'I always found conversation difficult, and now I find it impossible'.

1959

❦

British Embassy, Paris, 27 February

We made a visit to Rome. I had not been there since 1935, twenty-four years ago, and therefore I suppose I should have been more prepared for the tremendous changes. The first shock, on arriving by plane, was to find the Campagna gone, for it has largely been built over. We drove to our embassy, no longer the charming house in the Via Venti Settembre with the large garden, but instead what used in our day to be the German Embassy. Here it was that we would be received by our friends the Von Hassels, who entertained a lot – music parties, fancy-dress parties for their daughter and son, lunches and dinners. He was a fine type of German, with the customary sword slashes on his cheeks, and she a nice, simple, but cultured woman, the daughter of Von Tirpitz. They loved music, and collected Primitives. He met his end in the July 1944 plot against Hitler.

So when we crossed the threshold of our new embassy, we were full of memories of it as it used to be. Apart from our personal recollection, there were plenty of sinister stories about the place since then. Poor Princess Mafalda, who had not concealed her anti-Nazi feelings, had been invited to lunch by the then German Ambassador: as she was leaving, and her car was just outside the gates, she was seized from it by the Gestapo, and eventually died in a concentration camp. How extraordinary that the British should have chosen to occupy this particular building when they could have had the choice of so many historic palazzi.

The Clarkes[1] could not have been kinder, and provided a car for us.

---

[1] Sir Ashley Clarke (1903–94), married (firstly) to Virginia Bell. Ambassador to Italy.

The narrow streets, once such fun to wander along, are now exceedingly dangerous with cars and Vespas, and it was quite frightening to cross a road. Roman society used to be so chic and elegant, but now everybody seemed to be poorly turned-out, and I felt overdressed in my Paris clothes. Gaston was also most kind to us.[2] I dined at the Palazzo Farnese several times, and he often took me sightseeing. He sighs for Paris, but is unlikely to be moved. Two years ago he asked the General, then in retirement, to recommend him for a post. This was something the General particularly disliked doing; and, having made an exception for Gaston, he is highly unlikely to recall him now. However, Gaston has occupied himself most happily in rearranging the Embassy in perfect taste, and he is an excellent host. I believe he is anxious to marry (never Nancy, mark you, but Ethel de Croisset chiefly, or Caroline Murat and others). Personally I think he does better as a bachelor.

We lunched with the De Margeries. Roland is in as good form as can be expected from somebody who is ambitious and clever, and an atheist, who has to spend his time putting on uniform and going to the Vatican. Jenny, on the other hand, is perfectly content, and is said to be furthering the career of her son, who is a priest.

I must say I did enjoy seeing it all again, and all sorts of old friends, including Iris Origo, on whom I called in the palazzo where Vittoria Sermoneta used to reign, and Zanotti Bianco, who came to dine. I had by then moved to Molly Berkeley's apartment in the Palazzo Borghese, and was happy to be in old Rome, with a lovely view of old roofs from my bedroom window, and devoted servants, who stayed up to let me in, and brought me a hot foot bath when I strained my foot by walking too far. But I understand how Gaston misses Paris. Rome, though so beautiful, is as full of silly gossip as ever, and has something about it that would not make me want to live there. Oh the joy of getting back to wonderful Paris. As I flew back, passing over the moated Ormesson, I thought how this is the best city of all, and how lucky I am to be here.

---

[2] Gaston Palewski (1901–84): French Ambassador to Italy 1957–62, residing in the Palazzo Farnese; and subsequently French Minister for Scientific Research 1962–5.

British Embassy, Paris, 25 April

Here is a saga worth recalling. It proves, had anybody doubted it, how vain Anthony Eden is, and how difficult Clarissa is.

Act 1 Scene 1. I go to London in the middle of March to discuss plans for the Queen Mother's visit, and am invited to the first night of the Comédie Française and to a supper party at the French Embassy. Here I see Clarissa who tells me she has just written to ask if she and Anthony can come and stay. Secretly dismayed, I say how delightful that would be, and she warns me that they are difficult guests, since Anthony is such an invalid, but that they could easily go to a hotel.

Scene 2. I return to Paris and find the letter, which suggests their coming at the end of April, an impossible time for us because of our royal visit.

Scene 3. After much thought I write back a welcoming letter suggesting their coming for one of several weekends or any time in June. The point of this was that we had a shrewd suspicion that Anthony really wanted to come, not to see the pictures, as he avers, but to see Mollet and to square Bourges Maunoury before his book comes out, so that it would tally with what he himself is writing about Suez in his memoirs. It would obviously be awkward, at the present delicate stage in our negotiations, to have our former PM staying here and intriguing with those who were in power here three years ago.

Scene 4. A telephone message from Anthony, very amiable, that all the same they wanted to come at the end of April, but would go to a hotel and come and see us. I heaved a sigh of relief that everything had been so amicably settled.

Act 2 Scene 1. About a week later comes another call from Anthony saying that they would like to come and stay after all, after the royal visit, but during a week and not at a weekend. Taken unawares, I find myself in an awkward position. We particularly wanted to avoid the embarrassment of having politicians of the old regime coming here when those of the present one might be coming to see Gladwyn. I tried to stall by saying that ministers might be coming to stay, and murmured about the difficulty of making them comfortable and giving him the rest he needed whilst all the week-time entertainment was going on. I thought I had persuaded him, but at this point Clarissa removed the receiver from Anthony's hand and was as rude as only a red-haired person can be. She said that they had stayed with the Dixons in New York during the middle of a week, and Anthony could always have his food on a tray if he couldn't attend our lunches and dinners, and ended up by saying they would go to a hotel and rang off abruptly.

Scene 2. Gladwyn now wrote a letter to Anthony, which, to please Anthony, should have been flattering, complimentary and affectionate. But Gladwyn was not prepared to be any of these things to the man who had lied to him. So he wrote to say that the Rolls and his private secretary would meet their plane, and that he hoped they would lunch or dine with us, and that if they came on the Thursday or Friday they would find Rab here, who was coming to speak at the St George's Dinner on the 23rd.

Scene 3. This news, that Rab was able to stay in the house and they not, was obviously a bombshell with the Edens. Ignoring the fact that Rab had been invited months ago, and that I had got permission from the Queen Mother for him to stay on till Sunday (as had originally been intended before the royal visit was ever suggested), Anthony complained to Norman Brooke. The latter telephoned to Gladwyn telling him that A was being very difficult and touchy, but that for political reasons it would be better to try and placate him. As Philip de Zulueta[3] was passing through Paris next day, he came to discuss it with Gladwyn.

Act 3 Scene 1. I say *'Paris vaut bien une messe'*, and that we must do our best and try to give this curious interlude a happy ending.

Scene 2. Gladwyn telephones Anthony and says what on earth is all this about? Rab had been asked ages ago (and anyway, Rab is not likely to have to be carried out on a stretcher, which was another thing we feared might happen with Anthony); that it was absolutely true that ministers were coming to stay; and (brilliant inspiration) that he, Gladwyn, might have to go to Geneva – 'Oh, I never thought of that', said A. Finally Gladwyn says he will meet him off the plane himself.

Act 4. Happy ending. We do them proud, meet them in two cars, take them to the Vendôme where I had sent flowers, give a lunch party for them. I take Clarissa to a party, they are in a good mood all the time; I am even photographed in the *Daily Express* kissing Anthony. So the powers that be can feel we did our best.

[3] Philip de Zulueta, later Sir Philip (1925–89): Private Secretary to successive Prime Ministers 1955–64.

Bramfield, Suffolk, 1963

I write this in retrospect, and I suppose I have forgotten some of the details and incidents. The impression that still remains very clear after four years is the flagrant behaviour of Princess Margaret.

Our royal guests were to take us in on their way back from a visit to Rome, and the ostensible reason for the Queen Mother coming to Paris[4] was to inaugurate the Floralies Exhibition at the newly-completed modern building at the Place de la Défense. It was to be a glorified Chelsea Flower Show, with all countries vying for prizes, and as England is the cynosure for anything floral, and David Bowes-Lyon is President of the Horticultural Society, it seemed to follow that Queen Elizabeth should honour the occasion with her presence.

So far so good; and delightful and suitable plans were being laid when, as far as I can remember, there came a letter telling us that the Queen Mother hoped very much to bring Princess Margaret with her. This put a different complexion on the whole scheme. It meant that things to amuse the Princess would have to be thought up, and people who would not bore her would have to be invited. Her reputation, when staying in embassies and government houses, was not an encouraging one. The reasons for her coming gradually revealed themselves during the weekend. They were twofold: to get her hair done by Alexandre, and to fit a Dior dress.

We went to meet them at Orly. The Queen Mother was radiant as always. She was followed by the Princess in a distinctly ordinary coat and skirt, and looking far from radiant. This was partly explained by the fact that she had been dashing around in Rome in a smart set introduced to her by Judy Montagu, and had had hardly any sleep. For what was described as a quiet unofficial weekend in Paris, our royal visitors brought a singularly large retinue. There were the Queen Mother's two dressers, her detective, her footman, her hairdresser, her lady-in-waiting (fortunately, Patricia Hambleden), and her equerry, Martin Gilliat. Princess Margaret had a dresser (the famous Ruby), her footman, her detective, and her lady-in-waiting, Iris Peake. Quite a number of people to arrange for.

The Queen Mother's sparkling and delightful manner is all the more

[4] In April 1959.

winning because unexpected. To be greeted with 'How lovely to see you again' at once puts everything on an easy footing. Princess Margaret seems to fall between two stools. She wishes to convey that she is very much the Princess, but at the same time she is not prepared to stick to the rules if they bore or annoy her, such as being polite to people. She is quick, bright in repartee, wanting to be amused, all the more so if it is at somebody else's expense. This is the most disagreeable side to her character. She is very small, but somehow not nearly as exquisite or pretty as the Queen, despite beautiful eyes.

When, after the cocktail party, we went to dress, Princess Margaret asked me whether it would be 'short or long'. I knew that this trivial detail had often been a stumbling block; that if it was decreed that we would all wear short dresses, she would embarrass everybody by making an entry in the most sweeping of ball dresses, and vice versa. So, as the occasion was not a particularly formal one, I had given out that the Queen Mother was certain to wear a long dress, and that I should do the same, but that Princess Margaret might well wear a short dress, so that either would be correct. In fact she did wear a short dress which, as one Frenchman commented, 'began too late and ended too soon'.

We were about sixty for dinner in the State Dining Room, at small tables, Queen Elizabeth being at the centre table with Gladwyn. Afterwards we went to the ballroom to see a performance of Les Frères Jacques[5] on a stage at the garden end. When we escorted the royal party in from the gallery all the rest of the guests had sat down; and, being French and republican and democratic and independent, and with nobody giving them the lead to rise, they remained as they were. Queen Elizabeth, with perfect manners and comprehension of the situation, just smiled amiably and moved towards her chair. Not so Princess Margaret. She exclaimed imperiously, 'Look! they've sat down!', and showed that she was displeased. It had been planned who she should have on either side during the performance, but she would have none of this, and, having been amused by Jean Cocteau, insisted that he should come next to her. She took such a fancy to him that she would hardly talk to anybody else the whole evening. René Massigli, until recently Ambassador in London, came up to me with 'I really must have a word with the Princess. Can you arrange it?'. So I took him up to her, and

[5] Four black-tighted, white-gloved, bowler-hatted *chansonniers*.

tried to edge him in to the little group where she was and to catch her eye, but all to no avail. She was well aware of my tactics, and determined to ignore them. In the end I gave up.

On Sunday matters moved from bad to worse. When we all mustered for church (at the Anglo-Catholic St George's Church, to celebrate St George's Day) it was clear from the Princess's expression that she was very much put out by something. When we returned home, the plan was to change into country clothes and all go to the Ganays' at Courance, and then to tea with Mme Sommier at Vaux-le-Vicomte. To amuse Princess Margaret a lot of young people had been invited at both châteaux, all eager to meet this celebrated girl who had become a very popular figure in French eyes from her much-publicized romance with Townsend, and her spirited behaviour. So it was upsetting when, as we entered the Embassy, the Princess came towards me and told me she had a cold and therefore could not come with us. Simultaneously she began clearing her throat, cooked up a few coughs, and said that her voice was going. The Queen Mother turned to me rather sadly and sweetly and asked whether it would matter very much. Naturally I said that although everybody would be dreadfully disappointed, health was so important that if she felt ill of course she must not attempt to come. I suggested cold cures, a doctor, hot-water bottles, and was told that she had everything and would go straight to bed. There seemed a slight look of relief all round that the matter had been settled so swiftly. Telephone messages were sent to the châteaux, lunch was ordered for the Princess, and the most disappointed person so far appeared to be Iris Peake, who was not allowed to leave her royal mistress, and was still clutching the bouquet presented to Princess Margaret on leaving the church, which the latter had received with noticeable ingratitude, holding it by the stalks, with the heads of the flowers almost touching the pavement, and swinging it thus to Iris.

Meanwhile a quick change had to be made out of our church-going clothes. While I was thus hastily dressing, my old maid Berthe announced triumphantly that she had been able to telephone Alexandre, the famous hairdresser, and arrange for him to come after lunch to do the Princess's hair. '*La ladies maid*' had asked her to fix this up. Clearly Princess Margaret's cold was a fake. As I was to drive alone with Patricia Hambleden, I thought I must tell her of this discovery. She was not in the least surprised; it was the sort of thing that they were always confronted with. Perhaps she knew it already. If the Princess had after all been forced to come against her will, she remarked, she would have been so disagreeable that it would have spoilt the day for everybody. She went on, 'You will see that this tiresome incident will have no effect on Queen Elizabeth at all. She will enjoy her day as much as though it had never happened. Nothing will disturb her happiness'. I wondered to myself whether it might not be better if her happiness had been disturbed, and that Princess Margaret had been firmly dealt with. In answer to my question as to whether the Queen Mother had always been as happily philosophical as this, even as a girl, Patricia said, 'Yes, I think she always had this quality. And a sort of serenity, and of being unhurried'.

Our day was delightful and successful despite the absence of the Princess and the intermittent rain which gradually became drenching. No clodhopping was necessary at Vaux-le-Vicomte because our tour of the gardens could only be done by car, all around the wonderful parterre and the great fountains which were all playing and shooting up water as strongly as it was pouring down.

We returned to the Embassy, and I went with the Queen Mother to see how the Princess was. Her elaborate coiffure showed that something rich and strange had been done to her. Nevertheless the farce of the cold was still kept up, and the difficult girl had not yet decided whether she would come down to dinner or not. As nothing could be said or done by me, I went to have my bath and dress. While I was in my bath the house telephone rang and Patricia rather apologetically asked me who important was coming, as HRH wished to know. I told her that there was, in fact, a list in all the rooms, that I was in my bath and could not at the moment remember all thirty people, but that ex-President Coty was coming, and the Prime Minister and Foreign Minister.[6] Then came a rapping at the door from Berthe to tell me that '*la ladies maid*' said that the Princess had no hot water in her bath. I told the Comptroller who promised to look into it. I telephoned back to Patricia who rather wearily told me that her own bath had been beautifully hot, and that she thought I shouldn't worry too much about what the Princess said. Soon after this Princess M made up her mind to come down for dinner.

We must at least give her credit for being a good actress, for she

[6] Respectively Michel Debré (b. 1912) and Maurice Couve de Murville (b. 1907).

played the role of somebody with a loss of voice effectively, even though her occasional cough, more difficult to simulate, was less effective. The turn would have been quite impressive if she had remembered to keep it up. But now and then she lapsed and became perfectly normal, to the amusement of those who knew what was behind it all, and the puzzlement of some of those who had been going to meet her during the day, such as the Marquis and Marquise de Ganay. But what was really remarkable was her lack of desire to please.

The dinner itself was, as it turned out, one of the most unusual we have ever given on an important occasion. At one moment, fortunately at a fairly late stage of the meal (we were in the Ionian Room), we had the unprecedented sight of the Queen and Princess sitting there with no man on either side of them. The cause was that M Debré, the Prime Minister, had been called to the telephone on some urgent matter, and almost simultaneously President Coty was taken ill with what we feared might be a heart attack, so Gladwyn escorted him to the adjoining room and sent for a doctor. By the time the doctor arrived, Coty felt better and regained colour and refused any medical attention, so was able to return to the table. It was a point of honour with the dear old man to do so, for he was extremely upset at defaulting in the presence of the Queen Mother.

As if all this was not enough for one evening, there had been another perplexity before dinner. At 7.30 a telephone message had come from General Catroux[7] to say that he had a cold and could not come, but that Mme Catroux would come all the same. The naughty old man, aged about eighty-four, is having an absurd undignified love affair with a pretty young woman called the Marquise de Dalmatie, which sounds fantastic enough. She is a poet, anxious to shove into good society. The old boy is besotted by her, and even gave her the Légion d'Honneur, though he carefully chose a moment in September when nobody was in Paris. She plays havoc with him and, because she had not been invited to our dinner, she made a terrific scene which was too much for the military eighty-four year old to resist. So, after the fashion of the royal twenty-eight year old, he pleaded ... a cold! Flowers and profuse regrets and apologies duly came next morning, but I knew what had gone on behind the scenes.

[7] General Georges Catroux (b. 1877): Grand Chancellor of the Legion of Honour.

On Monday morning Princess Margaret was returning to London after an early fitting at nine o'clock for a Dior dress. As I was to accompany the Queen Mother to the Floralies Exhibition, I asked whether I could say goodbye, and she told me to come to her room at ten o'clock. So I duly tapped on her door, and found her in a beautiful sweeping négligé. I asked her how she was feeling, and she said much better. As I curtseyed I could not resist remarking, 'I'm so glad, ma'am, that having your hair shampooed did not make your cold worse'.

We lunched at the Elysée. Curiously enough, Madame de Gaulle looks not unlike the Queen Mother, but not so pretty or charming. We had tea in the Salon Blanc et Or, where the Queen gave me a beautifully bound edition of Redouté Roses. Later she left by air, as serene and happy as ever.

British Embassy, Paris, June 1959

Last night we dined with the Giscard d'Estaings in the Ministère de la Finance.[8] It was so amusing to see our dear friends, so young, so elegant, she so exquisitely small, in this amazing building which is a riot of Second Empire. Immense rooms, draped portières, great high ceilings, everything decorated everywhere with gilt nudes, garlands, ornamentation, frescoes. Napoleon III at his most flashy, but really very splendid all the same. It was a large party at several tables, and afterwards more people came and we did our tour of the place, and sat about on charming '*indiscrets*'.[9] Prince Napoléon[10] and his wife were there. Brenda Bourbon-Busset, who is always very '*vieille France*' with the Comte and Comtesse de Paris (giving a great many '*madame veut-elle*' this and that, and curtseys, and candles to greet them with) seems to be turning her allegiance to Son Altesse Impériale, on the grounds that he is far less Left than the Comte.

[8] Valéry Giscard d'Estaing (1926–   ), married to Anne-Aymone de Brantes, daughter of Aymone de Brantes. French Finance Minister, and subsequently President of the Republic 1974–81. The sumptuous suite here described is now incorporated into the Louvre Museum.
[9] Pieces of furniture comprising two armchairs whose backs together form an S shape, enabling the occupants to converse in close proximity.
[10] Prince Napoléon (1914–   ): head of the imperial family, descended from Prince Louis, brother of Napoleon I.

British Embassy, Paris, 13 September

Gladwyn and I have been wandering in the garden, gazing at the almost full moon to see whether we could detect the Sputnik, due to impact at about 10.20; but the moon looked as chaste and fair as ever. The flowering shrubs and trees and roses we have put into the garden have now grown to a respectable size. The sad thing is the dying of the dear old chestnut tree. Everything was done to save it, but to no avail. It stands there without any leaves, bending over in spite of the steel hawsers attached to the next big tree, looking like an aged man who can no longer stand straight and is about to die. It was probably planted before the Revolution, when the formal garden was changed to an English garden, for it figures in early pictures and prints, recognizable by its slightly bent silhouette and its forked trunk.

British Embassy, Paris, 9 October

Gladwyn and I enjoyed the election, for we went to the *Daily Telegraph* non-stop party at the Savoy. I returned here late tonight alone, because Gladwyn has gone on to stay with Rab at Stanstead. The Conservatives are in – too well in, it seems.[11] A stronger opposition would have been better, they say. Michael Berry fears that the party will get arrogant, and Kim Cobbold[12] and Bobbity [Salisbury] were among those who thought that on the whole a Labour victory might have been better for the country in the long run. Some believe that Hugh Gaitskell will form a sort of Radical Party with his followers, and that the rest of the Labour people will go far to the Left. Christopher Chancellor, now taking over Odham's Press, didn't approve of any party and seemed to be enjoying a good hate all round. A good love all round emanated from beloved Pug [Ismay], who seemed horribly wheezy and exhausted in the smoke-laden air. Through the thick atmosphere there then approached a portly figure, whose face had two such chubby cheeks that the rather

[11] With an overall majority of 104 seats.
[12] Cameron Cobbold, 1st Lord Cobbold (1904–87), married to Lady Hermione Lytton. Governor of the Bank of England, and subsequently Lord Chamberlain.

solemn mouth had hardly any room to break into the smile it wished to make. This was Francis Rennell, having suffered a sea change, possibly by having his brother Prod to live with him, which must entail many late nights with the whisky. Dean Acheson's moustaches were as jaunty as ever; Mrs Acheson, as always, tragic and beautiful. But I really must stop enumerating them all, or I would never end.

British Embassy, Paris, 11 October

I motored out to Chantilly today, arriving, as usual, with a bottle of gin, the Sunday newspapers, my tapestry and Jasper. Besides the habitual hangers-on, the Pattens and the Gileses, there was Ronnie Tree, hot and red and inarticulate as ever; whatever he tries to say bursts out from him with unwarranted vigour. Some say he is much neglected by Marietta, who is altogether absorbed in the Democratic Party. André de Staerke discussed sex, to make us believe, I fancy, that he is a *coureur des femmes* which I rather suspect him not to be. Diana is thinking of bringing a lawsuit against the *Evening Standard* for an offensive mention by Sam White in his 'Letter from Paris', *à propos* of Nancy's new novel about the Embassy, called *Don't Tell Alfred*. She telephoned Beaverbrook who said, 'The brute. I'll sack him'. Sam White alleged that Diana had resented the Harveys replacing her. This was not true, because Duff had been a Conservative political appointee, and had never expected to stay on after Labour got in, considering himself lucky to stay on as long as he did. Diana had indeed called them the 'Horrible Harveys', but this was because they had despoiled the famous library which Duff and Diana had created, and to which so many of their French friends had contributed generously. When we came here in 1954 the green carpet was being used as a runner in the passage upstairs and in the lavatory, and the fine old velvet curtains were lying quite forgotten at the upholsterers, and the busts were stored in cupboards. I am glad to say that all this has been restored.[13]

---

[13] The feud between the Coopers and the Harveys had been the great scandal of its time in Paris, and Sam White's article was hardly libellous, as neither was Nancy Mitford's characterization of Diana Cooper as Lady Leone in *Don't Tell Alfred*.

British Embassy, Paris, 12 October

Gladwyn had a long talk with Selwyn this morning. The latter stays where he is, at any rate for the present, which will be a disappointment to some who aspired to the Foreign Office, including, I suppose, Rab. Gladwyn also talked about his future. It seems we shall stay here for the present, and later on there is a possibility that he should become a sort of political adviser to the Foreign Office, which he would much like to do. This gives us a breathing-space here for a little which is, for me, a great relief.[14]

British Embassy, Paris, 26 October

Myself: 'Gravett, could you find that paper of Saturday that had the photograph of Mr Butler on his honeymoon?' Gravett: 'Do you mean the one of 'im in a paper 'at?' Myself: 'No, I mean the one of him paddling'.[15]

Lansdowne Club, London, 2 November

I dined with Edward Boyle at the Carlton Club. From the walls of the huge dining-room eminent men looked down from enormous canvases – the venerable Lord Salisbury (according to Edward, he could be very funny), Dizzy, and a tall willowy Lord Balfour in a long frock coat that made him look even taller. We had a delicious English meal which included partridge with bread sauce, something I hadn't had for years. He too felt that Sydney had been good for Rab, and went into a long dissertation about an essay on Othello, which portrays Othello's idea of himself, and not Shakespeare's idea of him, which is what we admire. In the same way, there was 'Sydney's Rab' and 'Rab's Rab'.

---

[14] Gladwyn was approaching the official retirement age of sixty in April 1960.
[15] The widowed R.A. Butler, now Home Secretary, had married Mollie Montgomerie, widow of August Courtauld, and the honeymoon was being spent in Rome.

British Embassy, Paris, 10 December

We are in the midst of the wedding arrangements,[16] on top of which the Mountbattens came to stay, but they are such well-organized guests that they were no trouble, except that we had to have a large dinner and luncheon for them. She could still be lovely were her face not so wrinkled. Her stance gives her round shoulders, a sunk-in chest and protruding stomach. But she looks splendid in evening dress and bejewelled. They seem happy, working actively for their respective causes, 'all passion spent'.

British Embassy, Paris, 14 December

Stella looked exquisite and ethereal in a lovely Lanvin stiff-satin dress, simple but beautiful. She wore my Empire gold and crystal tiara on her hair dressed by Alexandre, with clouds of white tulle. Everything went off well, crowds came to the reception, and lots of relations from all parts of the British isles, ancient and young, made the trip to Paris. I dare say a surprising marriage like this may turn out far better than a more conventional one. Anyhow, it is all Bohemian and happy-go-lucky and suits Stella.

[16] On 12 December Stella married Joel de Rosnay (1937–   ), at the time still a student. He subsequently became successively Scientific Attaché to the French Embassy to the United States, Director of Applied Research at the Pasteur Institute, and Director of Development and International Relations at the Cité des Sciences at la Villette; also the author of several books on interdisciplinary science and a leading lecturer and commentator; a Chevalier of the Legion of Honour.

1960

✤

British Embassy, Paris, 15 May

The summit conference has just started and started badly. Khruschev threatens to leave on Tuesday unless an apology is given for the spying American plane.[1] He came this afternoon to see the Prime Minister. I asked Gladwyn how things had gone, and evidently it is all rather depressing. I saw K leave. There were faces at every window and police on the roofs. In the courtyard an army of motor-cyclists and police cars and, besides all our cars and chauffeurs, K's huge car driven by a man who looked like a gangster. For his departure the car roof was removed and he sat on an uncomfortable looking jump-seat to be better seen.[2] He looked horribly well.

The house has been completely rearranged. The PM has for his sitting-room the Salon Blanc et Or, converted into a more masculine setting with a desk and comfortable chairs. This afternoon K sat in the armchair with his back to the light, Harold opposite facing the light; a vase of spring flowers, placed on a low green table, was thought to form a calming hedge between them. The Salon Jaune is the PM's secretaries' room; the private dining-room the typists'; Selwyn in the library; and his Private Secretaries in the Wellington Room. The Ambassador retires to his room in the Chancery musing on the complications and dangers of the summit, as compared to the merits of good old-fashioned

[1] The Paris Summit Conference between Eisenhower, de Gaulle, Khruschev and Macmillan collapsed at the outset on this Russian demand, shattering the hopes of Macmillan that the Cold War could be ended by means of a negotiated settlement.
[2] In his memoirs Gladwyn recorded his astonishment at seeing 'the Ruler of all the Russias on the off-side strapontin', whilst Marshal Malinovsky occupied the back seat.

diplomacy when matters could be discreetly discussed between the envoys themselves.

British Embassy, Paris, 17 May

Things are going from bad to worse, and it looks as though the summit will end before it has begun. Gravett says, 'If only they had served tea yesterday to Khruschev, it would all have been all right'. These are days of coming and going; crowds outside in the Faubourg waiting patiently; and sometimes two figures to be seen sitting down in the garden out of earshot – Harold and K, Harold and Ike. The PM started yesterday early by going to an eight o'clock breakfast with Ike. After a day of exhausting and abortive discussions he came home from the Elysée late at night and went on talking into the early hours in the Salon Blanc et Or. He was by now in the depths of gloom, so Gladwyn said, fearing that war was imminent and talking of his grandchildren. Gladwyn takes the view that the situation is not so bad, that Khruschev never wanted the détente, and that we are merely back in the Cold War again, even though it is now called Peaceful Co-existence.

This morning Ike came to the Embassy. After coffee in the garden, he went for a drive to Marne-la-Coquette in an open car, and walked in Norstadt's garden, and then returned here. This curious expedition seemed to give a momentary relief to the anxious onlookers. I thought that the President looked very old and ill and finished.

I went out to dine and, coming out of my bathroom, found the head security man and the military police on guard because Gromyko was in the library. When I came home after midnight I found a note from Gladwyn to say that all was over.

British Embassy, Paris, 18 May

Khruschev came again this morning and was booed by the crowds. Ike came in the afternoon and was clapped. The Americans handled the unfortunate business about the plane in a rather unadroit way, though they were unable to apologize because American opinion would not allow it.

British Embassy, Paris, 19 May

After lunch at the Elysée, the British delegation departed. The PM looked less depressed, the S of S fairly jaunty, Derek Hoyer Millar phlegmatic, John Russell dressed as for a race meeting, Michael Wright and some bespectacled younger men unknown to me such as Alan Campbell. Suddenly all these seemed to vanish away, together with the detectives, military police, security guards, extra waiters, and the place became quite empty and rather untidy looking.

Gladwyn said de Gaulle seemed very calm and Olympian, slightly annoyed at K's vulgarity. He says that the atmosphere of the Cold War has fewer bacilli in it than that of the détente.

British Embassy, Paris, 9 June

Today we had the garden party, and all could admire the great change that has taken place in the garden over the last few years. Instead of a bare indifferent lawn dotted about with old trees, there is now a beautiful vista of clumps of syringas, lilac, roses, catalpas, a paulownia, a judas tree, a mulberry, the royal cherry trees, all terminating in the vase we gave which stands out against the rhododendrons. Then the borders are a mass of colour, and everywhere one can pick something sweet smelling – lavender, rosemary, catmint, lemon verbena, santonina, geranium, mint.

British Embassy, Paris, June–July

Our last June here. The time flies by horribly quickly, and I wish I could halt it. Only three more months here, then only two and soon one, and then we shall be gone. I feel so strongly attached to this house and garden that I am almost part of it. I get to know it more and more intimately and a curious awareness has sprung up in me. I touch the panelling, the furniture, caressingly enjoying the feel of the carvings and the surfaces. I would not be surprised if I haunted this place! Almost every night we have dinners in our honour, speeches, compliments, emotion, presents. Then I got the flu, felt dreadful, lost my voice.

Thursday 7 July was the night of our farewell party. I stayed in bed till the last possible moment, got up, dressed, and had M Antoine to come to do my hair. A false chignon helped considerably. I came downstairs to the ballroom feeling pretty awful, and had to have some whisky. Everything was beautifully organized by Judy[3] and the staff. Dinner was at small tables in the State Dining Room. At my table were Courcel,[4] the American Ambassador, Valery Giscard d'Estaing, and Diana. After dinner Joxe[5] made a charming speech, to which Gladwyn replied, and then I staggered to my feet and managed to get out a few words ending with a quotation from Madame de Sevigné, '*On ne guérit pas de Paris*'. We moved to the ballroom where a small band was already playing and there was dancing. The cold night prevented me from wandering in the garden, which was a pity as it had been floodlit with much artistic thought. At about one o'clock I suddenly felt completely exhausted and had to rush off to bed.

Oh dear, how sad it is to be leaving, and so much still to do in the house. I have continued with my researches about it, and keep on finding out more. I got John Hope, our Minister of Works, to come for a weekend to impress on him the value of everything at the Embassy, also Sir James Mann from the Wallace, so I hope that in future nothing ghastly can be done to it as it has been in the past.

The Debrés gave a large dinner for us at the Matignon, and Couve [de Murville] gave another at the Quai, all very splendidly done.

British Embassy, Paris, 24 August

Mme de Gaulle came to tea today. She is a charming, natural, simple woman, with a pretty smile, no chic or allure, but most agreeable. Altogether not the rather bigotted and prudish character that she is sometimes made out to be. She is the ideal calm wife for the General. She talked about her time in England during the War, and of her poor daughter who died. She said that the General was like the old man in the

---

[3] Judy Dugdale, Cynthia's social secretary, later married to Sir Guy Millard, subsequently Ambassador to Italy.
[4] Baron Geoffroy de Courcel (1912–92), married to Martine Hallarde. Subsequently French Ambassador to Britain 1962–72.
[5] Louis Joxe (1901–91), formerly Head of the French Foreign Office.

fable of La Fontaine about the donkey and the young man and the old man, and took no notice of what was said about him. Then she left to collect him and go to Colombey-les-deux-Eglises.

Bramfield, Suffolk, 1961

We left Paris on 20 September. The most notable of the final parties was the great honour paid us by the General, who gave a dinner for us for about a hundred and forty guests at the Elysée on 14 September. The giving of a farewell dinner to a departing ambassador was in any case unprecedented, and this was furthermore done in great style, with the Garde Republicaine, the mounted guards, the courtyard floodlit, and music during dinner. But what was even more unusual was that, apart from the officials, a large number of our friends were invited – from society, the arts, the intellectuals, and the press. Many of them had never been asked to the Elysée before, and their delight was evident on their faces, so that there was an atmosphere of enjoyment and interest such as is conspicuously lacking at most Presidential parties. The guests included Nancy Rodd and Odette Pol Roger, both fervent admirers of the General; the Elie de Rothschilds, Prince et Princesse de Polignac, Marc de Beauvau Craon, the de Waldners, the Malraux, the Baumgartners, the Joxes, Brenda and François de Bourbon Busset. Madeleine Renaud (he could not come, as he was acting) represented the Left, and it was particularly nice of the General to have asked them; as also Jean-Claude Servan-Schreiber, who was asked: 'But whose side are you on?'; to which he replied, 'A hundred per cent for you, *mon Général*'.

I wore my pale blue dress with the embroidered bolero, and Vanessa wore a coral dress. We arrived at the Elysée almost too early, and were ushered into the central salon where were the General and Madame de Gaulle with their entourage. There we had an aperitif while through the doors we heard a babel of voices, becoming increasingly sonorous, which indicated that the bulk of the guests were massing in the adjoining drawing-room. Finally we were arranged in a row – the President, Mme de Gaulle, Gladwyn and myself; the great doors were flung open, and in came all the invitees. When the stream had passed through to the dining-room we processed in. I sat on de Gaulle's right with Malraux on my right and Mme Debré on de Gaulle's left. Gladwyn, opposite, was on Mme de Gaulle's right.

Then one of those superb Elysée dinners was served at this very brilliant table.[6] The table-cloth was embroidered with gold fleurs de lys, the plates were Sèvres. Conversation with the General went swimmingly. He has a pleasant, gracious, almost royal manner, a caustic sense of humour, and no sentimentality whatsoever. His sight is bad, though he does not like wearing spectacles in public, which has sometimes nearly led to accidents. Avoiding politics, as I always do, we talked on all sorts of matters. We discussed the French language, and all the English words and slang that had crept in. So the General reeled off a whole string of slang and abbreviations – '*Je sais qu'on dit S Lugo pour S Lazare*'. I said, 'I know one says "*d'acc*" pour "*d'accord*"'. 'One must never say that', he and Mme Debré cried in one voice horrified, 'because one must never even say "*d'accord*" but "*je suis d'accord*"'. This light talk kept the conversation going gaily until the moment came for speeches. The General rose and made a speech full of praise for Gladwyn, and with a charming tribute to me. Then Gladwyn got up and made a beautiful speech, full of emotion, with tributes to the Resistance and all that the General had stood for.

We then left the great Salle à Manger, again to music, and went to the drawing-room, where the general animation and excitement came to its height. Now was the opportunity for those who had never had the privilege of meeting the President, including Aymone de Brantes, who was closeted with him in a quiet corner of an adjoining salon. Finally the President proceeded to take his leave of us, and we all moved away from the salons. On the doorstep of the Elysée Joxe gave me a quotation from de Musset, which I wish I could trace or get accurate, something to the effect that '*Les plus jolies choses n'arrivent pas deux fois dans la vie*'.

On our last evening we had the more intimate members of the staff to dine. Nattie Faucigny-Lucinge was also to have come, but she cried off owing to ill health, and died at Christmas. She was a dear and faithful

[6] Cynthia was no gourmet, and her diaries seldom describe her food. One of the maxims inscribed in her commonplace book was 'It isn't the menu that matters, it's the men you sit next to'. In point of fact the menu at this memorable dinner was: Consommé Royale; Suprême de soles Champenoise; Selle de Pauillac rôtie, Bouquetière de légumes, Coeur de laitue; Soufflé glacé aux fraises; and the wines, Château Haut-Brion 1955, Château Mouton Rothschild 1951, Pol Roger 1949.

friend, and invaluable to me as I could consult her on matters that could not be discussed with anybody else. Though perhaps over eighty, she was young in spirit and appearance. One time I was travelling up from Cannes to Paris in the Mistral on a hot August day. There was an empty seat opposite me, and of all curious coincidences, who should board the train at Marseilles and occupy it but Nattie. The long journey passed most agreeably thanks to her enthralling gossip and racy conversation: old scandals, old liaisons, old romances. And then descriptions of the old days of the Belle Epoque: the chauffeurs who waited up till six in the morning to bring her home; the *vie de château* in the summer months, the private theatricals, which moved on after a long stay to perform in some other château. But she had accepted modern life philosophically; and I have myself minded less leaving Paris now that she is gone from that enchanting scene, because she seemed so much part of it, with her quickness, her intelligence and impatience, her always red hair, her retroussé nose and her warm heart.

1961

❦

Royal Crescent, Bath, 24 February

The chief event at breakfast this morning was getting a letter from Clarissa Eden, literally as well as metaphorically out of the blue, since it was written from an island in the West Indies, where, she says, they have no telephone, no electric light, and no doctor. But why should she have suddenly written me a friendly letter asking us to choose any weekend in the summer to come and stay at Pewsey? I can only imagine that Gladwyn's speeches in the House of Lords, and letters to *The Times*, must be in accordance with Anthony's own views, particularly as G strikes out against the government's lack of policy. It appears that the Prime Minister is just not up to anything, that he cannot make up his mind. It is said that he has never been quite the same since the failure of the Summit last summer.

Albany, London, 1 March[1]

We lunched with the Birkenheads to meet the PM and Lady Dorothy. Freddie appeared to be off the bottle and drinking lemonade, and consequently not so amusing but much better. The PM was in as good form as his tiredness and disillusion will allow. Dorothy, as always, completely natural and delightful. It is rumoured that she continues to see a lot of Bob [Boothby]. Indeed, when he dined with us the other night, he was indiscreet enough to tell Gladwyn that 'Dorothy says that Harold cannot make decisions any more'.

[1] Cynthia and Gladwyn were renting Alan Pryce-Jones's set of chambers in Albany.

Albany, London, 2 March

Jamie Hamilton[2] told me that when Henry James first became a British subject he was asked what it was in the British character that made him take this step. After a typical moment of hesitation while he chose the exact words, he replied, 'Their decency and their dauntlessness'. A superb reason.

Stafford Hotel, London, 1 May

Our weekend with the Edens was extraordinarily agreeable! I had gone in trepidation. As it was they were both tremendously pleasant and far nicer as hosts than guests. She good-tempered; charming; intelligent as always, of course, but most civilly so. He amiable and considerate. Of course, as Gladwyn kept on repeating in the privacy of our bedroom, he is not a clever man; and his real interest is only politics, to which he harks back all the time. Talking of the Hoare-Laval pact he was saying how disgraceful the secrecy of it had been, so Gladwyn quietly asked, 'Had the Ambassador been informed?', remembering what had happened at the secret Paris talks over Suez. Anthony didn't rise to this.

Clarissa has made the house very pretty and comfortable. Everything was carefully thought out, and great trouble was taken. The food was delicious, yet keeping within Anthony's special diet. We walked in their grounds and in their romantic wood, lay in comfortable chairs, and various people came to dinner. Our host spent much time resting; Clarissa says he gets more and more tired. One thing that he does not lack is money, thanks to his autobiography. (Of which Churchill said, 'I hear Anthony has written a book with the help of a man called Hodge. Do *you* want to read a book by Hodge?'[3]) Anthony told us that there was no truth in the story that Mussolini in his famous interview had been rude to him, and made him walk the whole length of the room before he looked up.

---

[2] Hamish ('Jamie') Hamilton (1900–88): founder of Hamish Hamilton, publishers.
[3] Alan Hodge assisted Eden only in part of Volume 2 of his autobiography.

Stafford Hotel, London, 17 May

We have at last acquired a flat. It is in Whitehall Court, overlooking the
river; in real-estate parlance, it is on the 'upper ground floor'. There are
three good rooms with french windows, and a balcony running the
whole length. Ruth found it ambassadorial. Ava says it has atmosphere.
Mother thinks it a very dignified address. It is solidly built, has high ceilings, will take our furniture, and has the merit of being close to the
House of Lords.

Stafford Hotel, London, 31 May

We went to the dinner at All Souls in honour of Dag Hammarskjold,
staying the night with the Berlins. It was in the Codrington Library, by
candlelight. That curious friendship between Dag and Bill, his one-time
chauffeur, has blossomed into the latter becoming his bodyguard and
personal assistant.[4] Thus he appeared in an immaculate dinner-jacket
and was highly placed at dinner. When we came out after this delightful
evening, having all paused as we crossed the quad to admire the architecture silhouetted against the sky, we discovered that Gladwyn's car
had gone out of action. For a moment we thought of Bill, who would
have mended it in a trice, but he was now too grand to be asked.

Stafford Hotel, London, 18 June

We spent last night with John Foster in his lovely moated house near
Oxford. It was crammed with people. John is a strange person. He only
drinks water, but water in quantities, by the bucketful. It has an almost
intoxicating effect on him. He poses as a Don Juan, but there is a school
of thought that this is more talk than action. He is huge, handsome,
unkempt, unwashed, clumsy in his movements, eats enormously. He
has an almost exaggerated devotion to somebody he calls 'auntie' but
who is not his aunt at all.

---

[4] Bill Ranallo, who was shortly to die with Hammarskjold in the air crash in the
Congo.

Stafford Hotel, London, 20 June

The Berlins and Ava dined with us before going to the concert at Syon. Ava arrived a good half an hour late. She rattled on about who was going to get what in her will: 'Harold will have Lord North Street, Hugh my two china parakeets'. The concert was lovely, though a trifle cold and slightly marred by occasional roars from jets at Heathrow. A strange pair collided with me in the semi-darkness, causing a near fall on the part of the very blousy woman who was being supported by a kindly man. I suddenly realized that they were Christabel on the arm of poor kind Ralph Dutton. But Christabel grown fat and bloated and puffy. Before I could stop myself after this sudden encounter, I found myself saying, 'Oh Christabel, I didn't recognize you!', and then hastily adding, 'in this half-light'.

Whitehall Court, London, 27 July

This was our first night in the new flat, and Gladwyn must needs give a cocktail party for 140 for the signatories of the Common Market.[5] For two days before I exhausted myself trying to get the place fairly straight, and it really looked good considering. The drawing-room is pale grey with blue curtains and a carpet of a sort of Nattier shade.

Bramfield, Suffolk, 13 September

I have just returned from launching a luxury motor yacht at Lowestoft. I was chosen for this because the owner, Mr Flack, a self-made man and ex-army sergeant, now colossally rich through his real-estate business, is a passionate admirer of I K B and the yacht was to be named the *Isambard Brunel*. 'The Auk'[6] was there. Mr Flack served under his command, and has brought the old Field Marshal into his business. Also Dickon Lumley, who is helping Mr Flack, being anxious to make money; 'lovely stuff', he calls it.

[5] The signatories of the Common Market Campaign, later merged in Britain in Europe, of which Gladwyn was the President.
[6] Field Marshal Sir Claude Auchinleck (1884–1981).

Mouton, Gironde, 29 September

We flew to Paris, and then caught the swift comfortable train from the Gare d'Austerlitz to Bordeaux and settled down to a delicious lunch. We arrived in a warmer climate, and motored about an hour to Mouton. As we approached through the vineyards we could see the château illuminated, and soon we were being welcomed by Pauline and Philippe [Rothschild]. While drinking my cocktail in the delightful Second Empire drawing-room, all red and gold, and crowded with amusing objects and embroidery, I suddenly observed that my feet were standing on the bosom of Queen Victoria, for the amazing carpet depicted Napoleon III receiving Queen Victoria. The guest apartments are across the courtyard from the Petit Mouton, where our hosts live. We never dined twice in the same room, and each meal had a new flower arrangement on a different-coloured table-cloth which swept out on the floor like a lady's train. As for the food and wine, they were unsurpassed, and ruinous to the liver.

The object of our visit was really for the Rothschilds to approach us as to whether their superb museum, of everything connected with wine from the earliest times onwards, could possibly be opened by the Queen Mother. They have collected it for years, and now it is ready for the public. It is full of beautiful objects, and tapestries, and Pauline's exquisite taste is much in evidence. We were pretty well the only people, apart from museum officials, to have seen it. Whether the Queen Mother will come remains to be seen.

Whitehall Court, London, 4 October

We dined with the Droghedas in Lord North Street, in the house that Brendan Bracken bequeathed to them. He is very intelligent and rather neurotic; she still has a good figure and great elegance, is very musical and a good pianist. Steven Runciman was there, and I reminded him how once, in the Cloisters in New York, we were gathered around the famous Chalice of Antioch, and Rorimer was telling our suitably-awed group that it might have been the Holy Grail. Steven broke the silence, in a matter-of-fact voice, with, 'I knew the man who made it'.

Whitehall Court, London, 26 October

Dined with Pam Berry, voluble as usual, and wild in context. There was a lot of talk about how wonderful Supermac was, but she was referring not to Harold but to Macleod. Hartley [Shawcross] was there, as could be seen on arrival by the presence of his red-satin-lined cloak in the hall – such a curious flashy form of attire. Humphrey bought one at Harrods in which to attend the reopening of the Vienna Opera. Unfortunately, when he stayed with us in Paris on his return journey, Madame Coty died, and the red-lined cloak could not be worn, being far too festive.

Whitehall Court, London, 8 November

We dined with the Lambtons. Daisy Fellowes, looking old in white, was there. The conversation was amusing but wonderfully malicious. I have seldom spent an evening of such denigration, as is almost bound to happen when Tony and Daisy are together in a room. Everybody mentioned was tossed and gored. Best friends and enemies were all treated alike and Boofy Gore, of whom Tony is reputed to be fond, came off as bad as anybody. All the Cabinet were torn to pieces, of course. Maurice Macmillan, it appears, has green teeth; Katie, his wife, new teeth, and all of them bad. Loelia Westminster's book, which has had such success, was ghosted. One hardly dared leave, for fear of what would be said. Daisy was the first to go, and at once the chorus began, 'She's too old to wear white', 'How she has aged', etc.

Petworth, Sussex, 26 November

We came here for a shooting weekend; the party consists of the Spanish Ambassador and Ambassadress, Antonia and Hugh Fraser, and Robin McEwen. The house is wonderful, and kept in excellent order by the National Trust. Pamela[7] is charming and gives a tremendous impression

---

[7] Pamela Wyndham-Quin, wife of John Wyndham, later 1st Lord Egremont (1920–72). His father had given Petworth House to the National Trust.

of beauty. She is far more effective than many beauties, graceful and willowy.

John has an inclination to drink, and even a little makes him sway about on his feet and slur his speech. This, I am told, sometimes gives an unfortunate impression at important functions given by the Prime Minister, whose unpaid Private Secretary he is. His being employed in this capacity is an instance of Harold Macmillan's love of stately homes and wealth, and, of course, of first class shooting. Our PM, who is cynical at heart, is torn in two by his simple Scottish crofter descent and his marriage with the daughter of a duke and the amenities of places such as Chatsworth. He also owes a deep debt to John Wyndham who, in Algeria during the War, not seeing very clearly, rescued from a burning plane what he took to be a person, but which might equally have been a sack of papers, or potatoes, or what you will, and this bundle proved to be Harold![8] And there is more to the appointment than this, because John is shrewd and sensible, and has an approach to life that is probably a good healthy ingredient in the entourage at Number Ten – or, rather, at present, at the Admiralty. As host and chatelaine at Petworth, this couple is charming and hospitable.

In conversation about the Edens, I was surprised to discover that John had never heard the rumour that Anthony was the son of George Wyndham. There certainly is a resemblance, which is particularly striking in the bust of George Wyndham at the Musée Rodin. When we stayed with the Avons in the spring we somehow began talking about this, and Anthony said he didn't really know the truth of it at all; but that when he went to Australia first, somebody had said to him, 'Your voice is exactly like George Wyndham's'. Clarissa avers that he would much prefer to be his father's son, and it must be said that Anthony could have inherited his violent uncontrolled temper equally from Sir William Eden or George Wyndham.

[8] This is an exaggerated account: Harold Macmillan managed to scramble out of the cockpit window by himself.

1962

❧

Whitehall Court, London, 10 January

We went to a lovely concert in the Festival Hall, with music performed by Menuhin and Nadia Boulanger. Yehudi's brother-in-law Louis Kentner was sitting with us. He is such an amusing and clever little man, and a great contrast to Yehudi, who is serene and spiritual. Kentner said, 'I am a practising Jew; I am a Jew and I am always practising'. He once said, 'There are two things that one must never do in life. One is incest, and the other folk-dancing'.

Whitehall Court, London, 7 February

Ruth Lee lunched with us quietly today to meet Selwyn Lloyd. Selwyn uses Chequers a lot, because the PM prefers to go to his own country house. Ruth says that the original clause suggested that it should be offered first to the Prime Minister, and then to the Chancellor of the Exchequer. Anyway, Selwyn greatly appreciates it, as was evident from all his eager questionings which she was delighted to answer. She told us that when she first came to England and wanted to put heating in the bedrooms of their then country house, she was told that if she did so no English person would come and stay. An absurd correspondence in *The Times* lately revolved around the difficulty of reading in bed at night in unheated rooms. Wonderful solutions were suggested, such as shawls, skiing clothes, two holes made in the bedclothes for one to put one's hands through, reading by torchlight under the bedclothes, learning Braille, etc.

Enid Jones, talking of Diana Cooper, said that it was Desmond MacCarthy who first remarked that she had the wrong looks for her character. With her almost gipsy-like ways, she ought to have been a dark beauty. Enid imagined that Diana must always get a start when she looks at herself in a looking-glass, because it cannot be the face she expects to see – exquisitely fair and white, and sometimes almost expressionless. Enid said that during the War, when Diana was down at Bognor milking cows and feeding chickens and getting up at six thirty in the morning, she told Enid that about once in three weeks she liked to go to bed as an animal, without washing or combing her hair or doing anything.

Whitehall Court, London, 9 February

Violet Hammersley[1] came to see me, looking wonderful, swathed in some voluminous garment such as nobody else wears, a black lace mantilla over her head, and accompanied by a duenna (her old maid). The maid remained on the settee in the passage and was given *The Times* and cake and tea, while Violet and I settled down to a delightful talk. I wonder how old she is. Somerset Maugham says that when they were children long ago in Paris he and she were the same age, but with the years she has become much younger than him.

We talked a lot about the Mitford family, whom Violet had known intimately when they were children on the Isle of Wight, and had remained a great friend of theirs. *A propos* of Nancy and Gaston, and Unity and Hitler, and all the sisters and their so-called amours, she maintains that they are not really amours at all, because none of them have what the French call *tempérament*, and I think she is right. Mrs Ham averred that they were all '*des honnêtes femmes*'; and when somebody had asked her what '*une honnête femme*' was, she had said, 'Not a bitch'.

She told me something I had never exactly known, and that is who Tom Bowles (the father of Lady Redesdale[2]) was. A Mr Milner Gibson, who lived at Hardwick Hall near Bury St Edmund's, had a child by either the cook or the midwife, and the boy was given the name of Bowles, it

---

[1] Violet Williams-Freeman (1877–1964), widow of Arthur Hammersley. She had lived in Paris as the child of a British diplomat.
[2] Mother of the Mitford sisters.

being his mother's name. The Milner Gibsons brought him up and gave
[...]cation, and he eventually became an MP. I told Mrs Ham
[...] he had French ancestry on her mother's side, and
[...]ld her that her great-grandmother was buried in
[...]olet says that this was Mrs Milner Gibson, who
[...]d lived and died there; in any case, she was not
[...] he mother of Tom Bowles.

[...]guished origination of Lady Redesdale is thought
[...] Lord Redesdale was always ticking the family off
[...] nstead of writing-paper, and mantelpiece instead
[...] l mirror instead of looking-glass: (though mirror
[...] Shakespeare, and is merely one of those French
[...] our language).

[...]n, *12 February*

[...]*wanni* tonight, and afterwards had supper in the
[...] Savoy. Ted Heath was of the party.[3] A complete
[...]ualities. I wonder whether he could become Prime
[...] he is one of those mentioned. He has a funny
[...]f giggling and shaking his shoulders up and down
[...]her endearing, but odd. Yet perhaps no odder than
[...]g.

[...]*don, 19 February*

[...] tells me that he thinks Nancy Rodd writes beautifully. He says she never wastes a word. I said I like colloquialisms in
novels, but I like better English in biography. I don't like to read,
'Voltaire was miles above doing this'. Raymond didn't seem to mind,
and he also admires the way that her popular style makes her a lot of
money. He says that he is himself sixty-six and would like to rest a bit
now, but has to go on writing to make money.

[3] Edward Heath, later Sir Edward (1916–   ): Lord Privy Seal, with Foreign Office
responsibilities, and subsequently Prime Minister 1970–4.

MORNING KATE
HOPE YOU ARE FEELING BETTER. Pls
TAKE CARE I FELT LORRY ABOUT
FLOOR H
H WILL SORT IT OUT
SATURDAY

Whitehall Court, London, 5 March

The Eshers[4] and Tom Goff to dine. Oliver as witty and sparkling as usual, Antoinette as unwitty and unsparkling as usual. He must have married her for her money, as well as being quite fond of her, for owing to her he has had the life he enjoys – comfort, beautiful things, leisure, and the pursuit of dilettantism. He teased Tom Goff about the scope for harpsichord sales if we join the Common Market, saying, in his booming voice, 'Gladwyn, this is an aspect that you have not studied, and obviously far more important than tomatoes'.

Scotney Castle, Kent, 9 March

We are staying with the Christopher Husseys in a wonderful early-Victorian castle. Lofty rooms, broad staircase, parquet floors, Turkey carpets, swivelling book-cases, half-tester beds, po cupboards with pos inside (so rare), and 'Hallo Largesse' in all its crude colouring, hanging on the landing.[5]

Saltwood Castle, Kent, 10 March

From one castle to another, a far more beautiful affair, full of priceless things and all that great wealth and fastidious taste can buy. I have, I admit it frankly, often laughed at the Clarks, particularly Jane, with her absurdities and ambitions, and of late her failing in taking 'a little too much'. But now as hosts they could not have been more delightful or kind and natural.

There were staying the John Hopes[6] and Gerard André;[7] the latter as inscrutable as ever, the former in what I can best describe as 'a bad way'. We wondered what could be the matter, Liza on edge and he so dis-

[4] Oliver Brett, 3rd Viscount Esher (1881–1963), married to Antoinette Heckscher.
[5] A harvest scene in Norfolk.
[6] Lord John Hope, later 1st Lord Glendevon (1912–   ), married to Elizabeth Maugham. Minister of Works.
[7] Gerard André (1910–   ): a diplomat with exceptional social contacts, who was retained for twenty-four years in the French Embassy in London.

tracted. Was it that Somerset Maugham had altered his will and left money and pictures to his boy-friend Searle? Apparently he dislikes John Hope.

In all these country houses we stay in, television seems to play a big part. At the Clarks we were bidden to be dressed by 7.15 in order to see a Perry Mason thriller before dinner. Otherwise the atmosphere was of a high intellectual level.

Saltwood Castle, Kent, 11 March

At breakfast today John Hope was in such a strange state of agitation that he could hardly talk, and kept on suddenly leaving the dining-room without any explanation. The Hopes left before luncheon to go and see their children at school. While we were having coffee the Italian butler came in with a bunch of keys on a long chain, which he had found in Lord John's room. This, of course, explained (or so we thought) the poor man's disturbed behaviour, for the keys were to his precious cabinet box. Gerard André at once offered to drop them at Chelsea Square on his return tonight, but Gladwyn interposed with, 'He can't, because he's a foreigner. I must do it'. So a discreet message was sent to the Hopes' boy's school, and after dinner, when Gladwyn had dropped me, he took them round to John. A drink and a chat about the Common Market gave a mentionable reason for the late night visit.

British Embassy, the Hague, 16 March

Yesterday afternoon we arrived here by air to stay with my cousin Paddy Noble and his wife Sisi, for Gladwyn is speaking here tonight.[8] Paddy is kind, affectionate, deaf, an excellent husband and father, but a heavy bore. In a post like the Hague he is a good ambassador, for he is far from stupid, though there is little to do. So he is able to pursue to his heart's content his favourite occupation, a genealogical study of the Noble family, all written out in his neat Italian hand.

[8] Sir Andrew Noble (1904–87), a first cousin of Cynthia, married to Sisi Michelet. He had succeeded to the junior Noble baronetcy, that of Noble of Ardkinglas.

I went to see the Anna Frank house in Amsterdam, which is deeply moving. It is ghastly to think that all those eight Jews lived here in constant fear, silent, on tiptoe during the daytime hours.

British Embassy, Rome, 17 March

My being here is, I must admit, due to Ava. She had invited herself — as she invariably does — and Ashley, having acquiesced, had afterwards quailed at the thought of having her on his hands for ten days. So, saying he was busy during that time, he suggested that she brought a friend, and I was delighted to help out, and to get away from feeling depressed about poor Mother's long drawn-out illness and second childishness.

British Embassy, Rome, 18 March

Gaston came to dine, and Violet and Horace Seymour,[9] the latter got so old suddenly and making a queer grimace whenever he had finished a sentence. In spite of this he is very charming. He used to be known in the Diplomatic Service as Silent Seymour. Once an important foreign lady sitting next to him at a dinner party asked him in exasperation if he ever spoke at dinner: 'Never', he replied.

British Embassy, Rome, 19 March

Ava went to talk to Diana at Judy's, and I went to fetch her afterwards. Judy [Montagu] lives in the oddest little house on Tiber Island. Diana was packing in a small bedroom reached only through the kitchen. I had often heard of Diana's packing. There was no paper to be seen, and a great quantity of crumpled clothes being stuffed into some imitation leopardskin cases. We shoved, pulled, heaved, sat on the luggage. Diana says she now dresses at Cresta shops, and so does Judy. We went to drop our coins in the Trevi fountain, and Diana came with us. I was chris-

---

[9] Sir Horace Seymour (1885–1978), married to Violet Erskine. Formerly Ambassador to China.

tened in water from Trevi, in the family silver bowl.

In the evening we went to a brilliant dinner at the Palazzo Farnese, the dining-room splendid with its illuminated frescoed ceiling and all the candelabras on the long table. The rumour is that Gaston wants to marry Violette de Pourtalés.[10]

British Embassy, Rome, 20 March

I lunched with D'Arcy, who is in the same palazzo in which the D'Abernons used to live. D'Arcy has become so very good-looking. Always very distinguished and complicated and inhibited, one wonders what his private life and desires have really been. Perhaps just what he told me at luncheon, that he would have liked a wife and two charming children who would never have got any older. He has great friendships among women, such as the Queen Mother. And yet I think his real interest has been in young boys – the boys he used to photograph, and the boys of his adoption society. I am certain that all this is completely innocent; perhaps he was, on the whole, afraid of women, and found himself more relaxed with youth. He has such a fitting name for his appearance – D'Arcy Godolphin Osborne; and one longs for him to become Duke of Leeds. Our conversation somehow wandered to religion and death, and I found he thought much the same as I did.

British Embassy, Rome, 21 March

I don't know who put her on to it, but Ava professes to be making a study of Caravaggio. We ask people which churches have a picture of his, and there is a lot of sending for pencil and paper and writing it down. Today at a luncheon party at the Embassy Orietta Doria was present with her very likable little (much smaller than her) husband from Bristol, who now calls himself Frank Doria, but is really Mr Frank Pogson. He has jollied her up a lot, but alas the union is not blest, so that the great name of Doria will, I suppose, go to some other remote

---

[10] Violette de Talleyrand-Perigord, married to Comte James de Pourtalés, and subsequently to Gaston Palewski.

branch. After luncheon Orietta suggested that we look at her picture gallery, which she would open up for us. Ava, not aware how famous it was, seemed reluctant to fall in with this plan, and stipulated we should do it hurriedly, staying only a quarter of an hour. Then, while skimming through it, her attention was drawn to three magnificent Caravaggios, and her whole attitude changed. 'Does the French Ambassador know of these? May I bring him to see them?', and so on. I drew her attention to two lovely Claudes which did not interest her one jot; but afterwards, when she had studied her guidebook, I heard her describing them as the two best Claudes in the world.

British Embassy, Rome, 22 March

Ava and I went to a consistory, for which we had been given very special seats. We arrived particularly early and were rewarded by being in the front row, as near to the holy of holies as it was possible to be. It was tremendously impressive, with the gorgeous costumes and ancient procedures, and the Pope[11] carried on his chair just as emperors were carried long ago, and flanked by the feather fans, and everybody clapping. On one side of him was Prince Colonna, and on the other side should have been Prince Orsini; but a family scandal had lost him this hereditary right, at any rate for the moment. The Pope, benign and jolly, was in pink. And one of the cardinals was in grey, being a Franciscan. There was a wonderfully ascetic personage who directed everything; this was Dante, the Pope's Private Secretary. What makes this sort of occasion so very different to those performed in our own country, is that ours are so much more formal and solemn. We could observe the quips and jokes being made among the immediate entourage of the Holy Father, and himself smiling away with evident pleasure at it all. An aged cardinal was unable to abase himself to kiss the Pope's toe; and an Orthodox prelate was arrayed quite differently to the others, with a black toque with a veil down his back: these provoked particular merriment.

[11] Pope John XXIII.

Hotel Arcadia, Brussels, 27 April

We flew here on Wednesday and straightaway went to dine with Spaak at the Ministry of Foreign Affairs before Gladwyn's lecture. Gladwyn told Spaak that the British Government was being too complacent about the negotiations about entering the Common Market, and it was difficult to make them realize how uncertain it all was. Paul-Henri said it would be a disaster if we did not get in. After Gladwyn's lecture we returned to our hotel and found Eric Bessborough, Francis Rennell and Taffy Rodd having drinks – Francis overblown, and Taffy, the youngest of all the Rodds, lined, white haired, balding, black-spectacled, unrecognizable. However, he was organizing this cultural meeting we had really come for, and doing it very efficiently despite his aged appearance. The shining light at this gathering is Prince Bernhard. He is brilliant at dealing with people – quick, subtle, good-humoured, intelligent. The young Princess Beatrice is sweet, with her father's humorous expression.

Cliveden, Buckinghamshire, 30 April

We flew to London Airport yesterday, and motored on here. Bill Astor's newest wife is a model called Bronwen Pugh, and she is extremely good-looking and intelligent and agreeable in every way, with an unusual calmness which I fancy comes from having studied Buddhism. Altogether she must be the ideal person to manage Bill, who is reported to be difficult, and behave strangely to his wives.

SS New Amsterdam, cruising to the Norwegian Fiords, 23 July

Vanessa's wedding was on 5 May.[12] The bride looked lovely, and the church at Bramfield was a perfect setting, and the splendid old bells, rung by Walter Lovett and his assistants, were jangled in time-honoured fashion. We walked back to the house for the reception, and then

---

[12] Vanessa married Hugh Thomas, later Lord Thomas of Swynnerton (1931–). His first major historical work, *The Spanish Civil War*, had been published the previous year.

Andrew [Vanneck], handsome and saturnine, gave the toast standing on the staircase, immaculate with his button-hole. Mrs Berry's home-made cake, the best in the world, was cut and eaten, much champagne was drunk, and Antonio, our Spaniard, rushed in and out of the guests offering food and drink, and expected us all to dance. Finally the bride and bridegroom left, driven by Kerridge, our local taxi driver, with hardly sufficient time to get to London Airport.

On the morning of 22 May Coué, the strange servant at the Crescent, told me that Mother was very ill. I went at once, and she died in the night. The end, of course, was a merciful release. But when all was over, the nurses gone, the house to be sold, the possessions to be quarrelled over, I felt that this was almost the saddest part. The funeral in the Abbey was beautiful, and just what Mother would have loved.

On Tuesday 29 May we had a dinner for the new French Ambassador and Madame de Courcel, our great friends from Paris. It was at the Turf Club. We invited a cross-section of representative life in London. Apart from Harold and Dorothy [Macmillan], there were John Wyndham and Pamela, Frank and Elizabeth Longford for the Labour Party, Mark and Leslie Bonham Carter for the Liberals, Michael and Pam Berry for journalism, K and Jane Clark for art, Lord and Lady Plowden for intelligence, Gerry Wellington for old sake's sake, beloved Diana because she had been Ambassadress in Paris, Raymond Mortimer for literature, Andrew and Debo Devonshire – for nepotism, perhaps;[13] and last but (certainly in her own opinion) not least, the all-important, much feared, redoubtable, intriguing, and yet dear old friend, the Vicaress of Bray, our entirely inimitable Ava Waverley.

How convenient to dine at a club, particularly when the PM is a member. For when he refused the excellent cuisine I suggested cold ham and chutney, which was produced with such celerity that it almost seemed as though the waiter had it up his sleeve. The PM told me that the Turf was a wonderful haven for him. He could come and sit down at a table alone, and eat his lunch without anyone bothering him. He said that during the War some old member had come and sat down in the dining-room, and an old boy looked up and asked, 'Any news?'. And the

---

[13] Andrew Cavendish, 11th Duke of Devonshire (1920–   ), married to Deborah Mitford. Parliamentary Under-Secretary of State for Commonwealth Relations in the government of his uncle, Harold Macmillan.

other replied, 'Bad news. That bounder Montgomery is chasing Rommel at Alamein'.

We dined one night at Admiralty House. At the end of the evening, after the more important guests had gone, John Wyndham, quite tight by now, took off his coat, revealing bright red braces, and pretended to be a matador to Quintin Hailsham's bull: all this rowdiness going on in the middle of a very dignified drawing-room with the enigmatic Prime Minister watching, and not displeased. I call John his *eminence gris*, because he certainly has an influence on Harold, and is nearly always rather drunk.

On the weekend of 20 June we went to Paris, which was looking glorious in the only warmth we seem to have had this summer. On the Friday we dined with Nancy. Her house, number 7, Rue Monsieur, is set between courtyard and garden, as all charming old houses in Paris should be. As we walked across the courtyard we saw, through the tall french windows, her pretty room lit up. Nancy, elegant and witty as ever, was alone. We went into the feminine drawing-room with its pink taffeta curtains and rather sparse but choice furniture, and lamps draped with muslin petticoats and ribbons, and with three windows which gave on to the garden wide open to the warm June night. I went out into the dark garden with the deep blue sky above and the distant hum of traffic, and thought how peaceful and civilized it was, and how wise of Nancy to live there. She says, nevertheless, that it has grave disadvantages, for her landlord's children come hurtling up and down the stairs – indeed the chandelier tinkled as we spoke – and play games in the courtyard. We then sat down to an enchanting evening of good food and gossip *à trois*. An enjoyable quarter of an hour was spent in hearing criticisms of our successors at the Embassy.

We had been trying to contact Gaston who, according to Nancy, was very busy and elusive. Through his secretary at the Ministère de la Marine we were trying to fix up going to drinks with him on the Monday evening. Then on Saturday morning came a telephone message from the secretary in a sweeter tone, telling us that perhaps we might meet the Minister at dinner on Sunday night at the Comtesse de Pourtalés'. Sure enough within five minutes the telephone rang and Violette de P invited us to dine with her quietly *en tout petit comité* with no mention of her husband. Of course, I imagined it was to be at the château where I had known them of old. But she then explained that she was at Le Marais, which she had inherited recently when her mother – Gould, Castellanne and finally Talleyrand – had died. I wondered if anybody could drive us there, and later a message came that M Palewski's car would fetch us at seven.

Aware of the gossip about Gaston and Violette, and influenced by Gladwyn's desire to talk to Gaston and mine to see a fabulous château, I thought that the best thing to do was to make a clean breast of it to Nancy, explaining that we had been asked there because it seemed too difficult to meet Gaston in Paris. This she appeared to understand, and, if there was a trace of sadness in her voice, she quickly covered it by saying that the Marais was well worth seeing.

When the car arrived, a handsome young man, not dressed as a chauffeur, drove us off and announced that he was taking us *chez M le Ministre*. 'What, to Rue Bonaparte?' asked Gladwyn; to which the driver with a broad grin answered, 'No, to Le Marais'. When we got there we gasped at the sight of such a huge and glorious château. It was almost on a par with Vaux le Vicomte. And I had never even heard of it, let alone seen it. We got out of the car and were admiring its splendour, our eyes wandering to the terrace, the fountains and vistas, when far far away beyond the water two figures were to be seen hurrying along. They were obliged to do the complete length of the balustrade, there being no possible short cuts, and we soon recognized them as being Gaston and Violette returning from an idyllic walk. She was dressed in a cotton frock, and I had come in my cocktail clothes – can one ever hit it right! We had been told, before leaving, that the Alphands and others would be there, whereas it turned out to be just ourselves and Violette's daughter.

Violette is nice, but very simple: not amusing, or interesting, or pretty, or well-dressed. She is unconcealably in love with Gaston, and he with her. Or is it, as I afterwards remarked to Nancy to make light of the evening to her, that the darling old colonel is in love with advising and organizing the redecoration of a wonderful château? After all, he had just about completed work on the Palazzo Farnese when he was moved back to Paris, and he would be awfully bored with nothing artistic to plan. He was full of ideas as to what should be done, and Violette lovingly agreed to everything. Altogether we spent a delightful evening. Gaston motored us home.

Luton Hoo, Bedfordshire, 7 July

Staying with Harold and Zia Wernher[14] is like staying in a royal house-hold. Though half the house is converted into a museum, what remains is run on pre-War lines. A retinue of butlers and footmen and house-maids, a superb cook, huge rooms filled with beautiful pieces of furni-ture, wonderful carnations and plants, a profusion of Fabergé, and altogether all delightfully Edwardian. A royal touch, which I did not twig at first, was the keeping of all clocks a quarter of an hour fast: and one was, as I soon did twig, expected to be horribly punctual. There were staying the Salisburys, the Spanish Ambassador and Ambassadress, and the Adeanes. On Sunday morning we all set off for church in style, dressed as I haven't been dressed in the country on a Sunday for many a year. When we got there we were all told where to sit, and Betty Salisbury said afterwards, 'I've never before known place-ment in church'.

Stratfield Saye, Hampshire, 15 July

At our weekend here were the Sachy Sitwells and Harold Nicolson. He is much shattered by Vita's death, for it was a marriage of perfect under-standing: he a homosexual, she a lesbian. Poor Harold is very debili-tated, what with this bereavement and a stroke or two. We went to a concert in another lovely house, the Vyne. What an amusing, clever, rather vulgar, rather gross, person Oliver Chandos[15] is: sensitive to beauty, yet schoolboyish in his sense of humour.

On Sunday we did the usual tour of Stratfield Saye, which I always enjoy, including seeing the Great Duke's false teeth and washing-glove. Gerry's grandson, Elizabeth Clyde's son, came over for lunch.[16] He is typical of the rising generation in a conventional family. He is a beatnik, and wears his hair long (he is at the moment acting in a Shakespearian play, but it never seems to be kept much shorter). In his favour he has a

---

[14] Major-General Sir Harold Wernher (1893–1973), married to Countess Anastasia Michailovna de Torby.
[15] Oliver Lyttelton, 1st Viscount Chandos (1893–1972): had been a member of the War Cabinet.
[16] Jeremy Clyde (1941–   ): actor.

good deal of charm and attractive looks; and that old satyr, Harold, was aware of this the instant he set eyes on him, and made what can best be described as a bee-line for him.

Whitehall Court, London, July

We dined with the Eccleses, and the Butlers were there. He tremendously pleased with himself, as indeed is justified: for, as a result of the great purge, Rab has been given a good chance of being the next PM.[17] Selwyn has fallen by the wayside, and the general opinion is that he has been scurvily treated. His first appearance in the House was greeted with prolonged cheering, whereas Harold was greeted with an eloquent silence. I wonder whether a shake-round such as this is likely to make the Conservatives more popular. Pam [Berry] was saying the other night that, when she was canvassing, what everybody seemed to want was a younger man at the head.

Whitehall Court, London, 11 September

Tonight there was a Commonwealth reception at Lancaster House. Gladwyn, with characteristic courage and energy, was in his element bearding the important personages and telling them that it was essential that we should join the Common Market. Some of the VIPs appeared to be having so much champagne that they were unable to take in the important points he was making. Then in came Hugh Gaitskell, who has 'wrought the deed of shame' in a speech at the Labour Party Conference, espousing the cause of the Beaver, and even using the maudlin phase about not 'selling the Commonwealth down the river'.[18] He looked sheepish, as well he might. Bob Menzies was as jaunty as ever, with Dame Patty always the perfect genteel correct partner to this

[17] On 13 July, the 'night of the long knives', Harold Macmillan dismissed seven out of the twenty-one members of his Cabinet.

[18] Cynthia must have written this diary entry subsequently, despite the given date. It is true that Hugh Gaitskell had just issued a statement opposing British entry into the Common Market on the current terms proposed. But his denunciation of it at the Labour Party Conference only took place on 3 October.

vital cunning old boy.[19] John Wyndham, wonderfully drunk, either sitting on the floor at one's feet, or lurching around, suddenly lifted me into the air. My last vision of Lancaster House was of a tight Bustamente and his very new wife going down the staircase. I thought of the stories I had been told of the magnificent parties at Stafford House, with Millie Sutherland looking like a goddess, standing at the head of the stairs to receive her guests.[20] She was like a lovely light, people said: it seemed to radiate from her. I think she was Bohemian enough to have enjoyed the odd mixed lot at tonight's party. What lets it all down badly is, of course, the undistinguished atmosphere created by that horrible monster, Government Hospitality.

Whitehall Court, London, 6 November

I had drinks this evening with Virginia Surtees, and one might well ask who she is, for she has changed husbands and names with astonishing rapidity. She left poor Ashley Clarke for David Craig, the Rome representative of BEA, and after about a year left him for solitude and the pursuit of the pre-Raphaelites. She has a compact but large-roomed flat arranged charmingly with all her pre-Raphaelite things, and she has a terrifying bull-dog, and affects to have at last found happiness. She is an attractive but strange woman, or perhaps I should best describe her as a leprechaun, for she doesn't seem quite to be made of flesh and blood.

Whitehall Court, London, 23 November

Lunched with K [Clark] and Jane at the Café Royal Grill, which still retains its delightful 1880 decor. Red plush seats, elaborate gilt carving, mirrors, painted ceiling, it is all that remains of this famous restaurant, patronized by Oscar Wilde and Whistler and all their set. Jane made an extraordinary remark. She said that a week ago she had seen Osbert

[19] Sir Robert Menzies (1894–1978), married to Pattie Leckie. Prime Minister of Australia 1939–41 and 1949–66.
[20] Millicent St Clair-Erskine, wife of the 4th Duke of Sutherland. He had been the owner of Stafford House, subsequently renamed Lancaster House.

Sitwell lunching here with Malcolm Bullock, and she had gone up to Osbert and said, 'You're Bosie; I'm boozy'. I feel sure that Osbert must have made some pungent comment afterwards. The Ashley Clarkes were at luncheon, for he has married again, to a nice quiet secretary, who will probably be a far better wife than Virginia – somebody kind and pleasant who will see that he can enjoy his music and his pursuit of art.

Bramfield, Suffolk, 25 November

We had today a warning to ambitious hostesses, and a reminder of the golden rule that ambassadors should not be embarrassed socially. We were invited to lunch at Blickling to meet Courcel, who was staying there for a shoot. The previous evening Thelma Lucas[21] telephoned Gladwyn to tell him that the Bristols were to be there, and that she hoped we would not mind, and that everybody was devoted to Juliet Bristol. Gladwyn said he didn't mind, but as we motored along I reminded him who Lord Bristol was – one of the four Mayfair young men who, before the War, had perpetrated the crime at the Hyde Park Hotel in which a jeweller from Cartier was hit on the head and nearly killed.[22] Blickling is a wonderful house, and I think Thelma likes its grandeur, though she has not made it comfortable.

Hôtel Bristol, Paris, 3 December

We have just returned from a weekend at Le Fresne, which somehow I had never expected to see again. It was at the invitation of Valéry and Anne-Aymone Giscard d'Estaing, and I must confess that I did not altogether enjoy seeing this lovely old château – one of my favourite places, and where I had invariably found charm and peace – being run

---

[21] Thelma Arbuthnot, married (firstly) to Somerset de Chair, and (secondly) to Sir Jocelyn Lucas. She had rented Bramfield Hall, and now had the tenancy of Blickling from the National Trust.

[22] Victor Hervey, 6th Marquess of Bristol (1915–85), married (fourthly) to Juliet Fitzwilliam, who subsequently married Somerset de Chair. Cynthia is incorrect in asserting he was involved in the attack on the Mayfair jeweller, though he had served a term of imprisonment for embezzlement.

in quite a different guise. It was Valéry's big shoot, though in point of fact there was hardly anything to shoot, and the bag was about five brace of pheasants, a hare or two and a jay. Certainly not worth standing about in the woods on a bitterly cold day. To this non-existent *battue* had been invited an extraordinary mixed party.

There was the Prime Minister, M Pompidou, a fat, commonish, jolly, but shrewd fellow, who has the appearance of being Jewish but is in fact a typical Auvergnat.[23] Madame Pompidou was pleasant but awkward-looking and unattractive: I regret to say she is considered an English type, with her fair hair, large build, prominent teeth, and bad carriage. Then there was Diana de Mouchy; charming, but unemotional and practical. And Herzog, who managed wonderfully out shooting, having lost his fingers and toes through frost-bite.[24] There was a Belgian count and his Austrian wife (I never got his name), he a typical heavy-minded Flemish type, blond and with a perpetual smile. Most astoundingly, there were the Ribes. She is the daughter of the Beaumonts and is reputed to be one of the best-dressed women, as well as having a reputation for exhibitionism. Her shooting clothes were fantastic: a Cossack hat, and a leather fur-trimmed Cossack coat, very long, and Russian boots. Indeed, all the women had got themselves up in strange attire, excepting the Duchesse de Luynes who, with the Duc, was also of the party.

We started our shooting day on Sunday with '*le breakfast Anglais*' in the dining-room. And instead of having a shooting lunch, there was a snack of hot soup and sandwiches and wine and coffee in the woods, eaten round a bonfire. This, at least, was well organized, and made a charming scene. We all sat around on shooting-sticks or tree trunks. The food was on a little table, and the beaters grouped themselves a short way off: they did not have a bonfire but seemed to become sufficiently heated by their wine, for sounds of merriment were soon heard. Meanwhile our party was rapidly showing signs of gaiety, and frivolous chatter flowed freely. Jacqueline de Ribes, seated on a fallen tree, had the Prime Minister sitting on her knee, and no light weight can he have been,

[23] Georges Pompidou (1911–74), married to Claude Cahour. Prime Minister of France and subsequently President 1969–74.
[24] Maurice Herzog (b. 1919): French High Commissioner for Youth and Sport, and conqueror of Annapurna.

though he remained there long. (One cannot conceive Harold Macmillan sitting at a shooting party on the knee of some renownedly fast married woman!) I returned to the château before the next fruitless drive started, and enjoyed the peace of the dear old house without the gang. We all dined at six, and then Gladwyn and I motored back to Paris.

Whitehall Court, London, 11 December

I caught the 10.30 train to Manningtree to go to Phil Nichols's funeral.[25] It was an intimate affair, with only family and close friends there. Everybody present cared, and there was not a worldly face among them. The pretty little old church, the country churchyard, the very well-chosen service, the intimate address from the vicar who had been a real friend of Phil's, all combined to make it a deeply moving occasion. A gentle rain fell, which made me fancy that Lawford itself was weeping for someone who had loved the place all his life.

I seemed to be burying a good slice of my youth. I remembered the old days there, light-hearted and irresponsible, and all the love affairs! Irene getting engaged to the solid George Gater (dubbed by Anne the 'Rock of Ages'), and now himself a completely helpless wreck, recognizing nobody. And Anne doing what tantamounted to an elopement with Harry Strauss, because his having once been in love with Irene made it impossible for her to broach the subject to her family. And Robert, gifted, unbalanced, exhibitionist, never quite *persona grata* with the rest of us as he was so embarrassing. I remember him at old Mr Nichols' funeral, rushing forward and kneeling melodramatically beside his father's grave, and the others being so annoyed, for he had not got on well with his father. And Phil, charming, delightful Phil, happy and unhappy, oozing charm: here we were seeing him buried. Afterwards we went to the house. It stands, melancholy and lonely at the end of a long avenue, and is not unlike Bramfield in architecture. After hot soup and sherry and sandwiches and coffee, we all left to catch the London train.

25 Sir Philip Nichols (1894–1962) had been married to Phyllis Spender-Clay. Formerly Ambassador to the Netherlands.

1963

❦

Bramfield, Suffolk, 19 January

We heard on the radio this evening that Hugh Gaitskell has died. Fortune plays an unpredictable role in the manner and timing of our deaths. Hugh, so sharply criticized, the butt of many cruel remarks, mistrusted by his own party for being too much of a Winchester and Oxford man, and mistrusted by the Conservatives for being Winchester and Oxford and yet Labour – Hugh could hardly be described as a popular figure. Yet such were the circumstances of his death that he went out from this world in a blaze of glory. He would certainly have been the next Labour Prime Minister, and was in the prime of life; and while he was dying the public waited tensely between each bulletin, almost as if it was the passing of a monarch.

Biddick, County Durham, 27 January

We came up here on Thursday evening, leaving King's Cross at five and dining on the train. I love the journey north, which reminds me nostalgically of my childhood and the fuss and excitement of the expeditions to Jesmond. The snowy cold weather intensified as we progressed, as it always seemed to long ago, bringing hopes of sleighing and tobogganing. We passed the old landmarks – Grantham, Selby, York with its portholes, Durham (too late to see the splendidly situated cathedral), and finally arrived rather late at the familiar old Newcastle Central Station, where a large estate waggon met us.

At Biddick we were welcomed into a brightly-lit house. In the drawing-room a large collection of sepia prints had been cleverly arranged in four or five oval groups, which gave a most charming effect. Lovely old chintz curtains and a bright needlework carpet also made it a pretty room. In every room a comforting fire of coal and wood was blazing away; these were lit first thing in the morning and kept going all day. It was a joy to turn out the light and from my four-poster watch the firelight flickering, a sight I believe I had not seen since we last stayed with the Lambtons, at Fenton, a few years ago.

Next to the pleasure given by these almost obsolete fires, I do enjoy a family atmosphere. After five daughters Bindy at last produced a son, called Ned; but all, male and female, are equally loved and welcomed at birth. An ideal nanny reigned in the happy nursery, which had all the proper old-fashioned appendages of nursery life, including a cuckoo clock. This was one of the most delightful aspects of the visit; though for Gladwyn, I suppose, it was the superb shoot.[1]

What is never so agreeable chez les Lambtons is the sort of person who is also staying, and the silly malicious conversation. Indeed, it could not really be called conversation, of which the rule (as, I think, Mrs Montagu said some two hundred years ago) is to return the suit, as in whist. What happened here was that anybody who could think of something disagreeable to say about friend or foe or public character, would throw out a remark, as if a stone into a pond, hoping to make as big a splash as possible. Then somebody else with even more out-rageous intention would fling in an even larger stone. And so on, always uninteresting, unconsecutive, unconstructive, at every meal, and always just plain nasty. I really cannot remember all the absurdities, though the Snowdons were called the Poison Dwarfs, or the Royal Midgets. Amongst those staying was Charles Rutland, one of the nicer people there, and the Peter Wards.

Throughout all this bandying about of cattiness, Tony lent back, hunched in his chair, occasionally capping the remarks with relish. He is a strange figure, with his slight slouch and his dark spectacles and his very long legs, which enable him to stalk along. He makes an almost melodramatic silhouette, with green velvet jacket, green boots, green hat worn at an angle. There is something slightly feminine and small-boned about him, but above all he is *racé*, a *grand seigneur*, with excellent

---

[1] Gladwyn was a crack shot.

manners, and a perfect host. He is a superb shot and loves the country, and is always out of doors, winter and summer, followed by his dogs. Rather mad, I would say, like all the Durhams. But Bindy is sane and warm and motherly and a wonderful person for making her home comfortable.

Given all these ingredients of the party, the nicest time was when we were alone with Tony and Bindy on Sunday, the others having gone off after breakfast. Then one could talk, and it was peaceful, and the little girls (all dressed alike) were charming and amusing. But, of course, the departed guests had to be dissected. Perhaps it was not fair game to criticize the Ward family, because of the dreadful curse that shadows them.

The story goes that the present Lord Dudley,[2] when he was Lord Ednam and married to a charming woman, Rosemary Leverson-Gower, went to visit a temple of some obscure sect in Egypt. He and his party made themselves offensive by giggling at the holy rites and making a lot of noise and taking photographs. So much so that they were turned out, and the High Priest came out on to the steps of the temple and delivered a terrifying curse on Lord Ednam and his family. The words were so dreadful that when Millicent, Duchess of Sutherland (the mother of Lady Ednam) heard of it, she arranged for someone to go out and pacify the High Priest and offer him money for his temple and try to lift the curse: but to no avail. Soon afterwards the Ednams' little boy, Jeremy, was killed by a lorry when his tricycle ran down the hill on Albert Bridge and he didn't stop in time (the fault of a careless governess): we lived in Royal Avenue at the time, and I remember the horror of the tragedy well. Then in 1930 Lady Ednam was killed in an aeroplane accident coming back from France, I think Le Touquet. Peggy Munster, née Ward, had a little boy of two who was drowned in a few inches of water in an ornamental pond in the garden while his mother had gone indoors for a moment to answer the telephone. An older boy, some years later, died from being hit by a cricket ball on the playing fields of Eton. Peggy's sister, Lady Stavordale, lost two sons; one in a bicycle accident, and the other shot in Cyprus during the troubles there. Nicolette, the third sister,[3] married to Michael Hornby, felt so strongly about the curse that she insisted on having some special service of

[2] Eric Ward, 3rd Earl of Dudley (1894–1969).
[3] The three sisters were first cousins of Lord Dudley.

exorcization when Susan Hornby married Sunny Blandford: but their first baby died after about a year. Then Honor, the sister of Eric Dudley, lost her only child when she was having an operation for appendicitis. And Dickie, another sister, married to Con Benson, lost her daughter Sally in a riding accident. The only person who continues unaffected is Lord Dudley himself, though much disliked and much despised.

Bramfield, Suffolk, 9 March

I made a most unfortunate and unrewarding visit to Paris. With the exception of my first evening, when I went out to dinner at the Bordeaux Groults, I spent my entire time in bed with flu at the Bristol. At the dinner everybody was talking about the death-knell given to Britain's application to membership of the Common Market by the General's veto.[4] Billotte, who was there, had written an article in some paper, addressed to Gladwyn and entitled '*Ne pleurez pas, Milord*', after the words of an Edith Piaf song. But everyone felt the situation must somehow be mended, with time and tact. But then on the Monday morning we heard that Bidault had given a television broadcast on the BBC, which seemed to the French to be yet another retaliation in the tit for tat interchanges that have been going on for weeks, beginning with the unsatisfactory talks at Rambouillet. The French, with their controlled television and radio, do not comprehend that the BBC is an independent body. The Ramsbothams[5] came to see me, and his pronouncement that the British entry was dead struck me as being unnecessarily pessimistic.

Whitehall Court, London, 22 March

There is a good deal of talk going on about Profumo, Minister of War, being involved in some form of sex scandal, arranged by Bill Astor and

[4] In January President de Gaulle had publicly stated that France would oppose a British application to join the European Economic Community.
[5] Peter Ramsbotham, later Sir Peter (1919–   ), married (firstly) to Frances Blomfield. Head of Chancery at the Embassy, and subsequently Ambassador to the United States.

concerning a missing model. Profumo made a statement in the House of Commons today clearing himself of having seen the girl since December 1961. He is nice, but a poor creature to get himself embroiled in all this.

Nostell Priory, Yorkshire, 6 April

As Gladwyn was lecturing in Leeds last night, we spent the night here with that curious eccentric, Roland St Oswald, who had asked us to come and see his Palladian house of which he is justly proud.[6] Built by Paine from the plans of Palladio (which had never been used), altered by Adam, adorned by Zacchi and Angelica Kauffman and Joseph Rose, furnished by Chippendale, it certainly is rich in treasures. Like many people who have inherited beautiful possessions without having previously had much knowledge or ever developing any real aesthetic sense, Roland reeled off several statements which could not possibly be true. Every table and chair, of whatever style, became the handiwork of Chippendale.

This huge place is run, with fairly good results, in a most unusual manner. From the St Oswalds' house near Algeciras are brought a batch of local peasants, young men and women, who live in dire poverty in Spain and are glad to come to work in the cold grey West Riding. After several years they are returned home, and another lot are rounded up. We were told that this market is now ruined because the peasants make for the big wages in Madrid. Nor do I blame them, for at Nostell these wretched Spaniards were treated in a feudal fashion: bullied, chivvied, shouted at, and even made to dust something they had left undusted on a Chippendale bracket in the dining-room after dinner in front of us all. They appeared to be terrified of their overlords. I myself was quite frightened of Lady St Oswald, a Pole who must have been beautiful and was still good-looking, the deterioration being not from age but from ill-health, and also, I feel sure, from sheer hardness. She is the second wife, and probably suits Roland far better than poor Laurian Jones,

[6] Roland Winn, 4th Lord St Oswald (1916–84), married (secondly) Marie Wanda Jaxa-Chamiec. Nostell Priory (now National Trust) contains over a hundred pieces firmly attributable to Thomas Chippendale.

whose marriage ended soon after the honeymoon. He being rather brilliant, difficult, original, odd, needs somebody strong-minded and unafraid of him. They obviously are very happy together.

Whitehall Court, London, 10 April

Yesterday I lunched with Ava, the only other person there being Gerard André from the French Embassy. Ava is fond of lunches *à trois*. If I am the third, as I often seem to be, she knows me well enough to be able to ignore me slightly and concentrate on the important guest, from whom she may wish to extract some information of consequence whilst not subjecting him to anything so obvious as a *tête à tête*.

I enjoyed watching Ava's technique. She builds up her position of importance with a network of lies. Those who swallow it unquestioningly show a lack of discernment. Yet one cannot easily escape being fascinated by her story. I fancy a pin would without difficulty prick the bubble, but nobody quite seems to dare. Who is Ava to set herself up as somebody of such tremendous influence? I even heard her say, after asking Gerard about the President's refusal of our joining the Common Market, 'Why didn't you ask *me*?' And she suddenly threw out, 'You know, the President writes to me. I find his handwriting very difficult to read', to which Gerard politely agreed that the writing was not easy to decipher.

We know perfectly well that when she tells us that Harold telephoned her on Sunday afternoon on some vital issue, that it was she who, by sheer persistence, got through to him at last, riding rough-shod over his secretaries, family and servants, and the shrewder among us suspect that in all probability she never spoke to him at all. Once one starts doubting, the whole house of cards rather pathetically falls down. Oh those sagas about Ava's friendships with the eminent. We are led to suppose that they are partly political, partly intimate, possibly (according to her hinting) even amorous; but always she is making history, she is invariably being consulted, giving advice, arranging for a meeting with the right person, passing on a message to a higher authority. Naturally it is easy for her to talk about the dead without fear of being found out; Lord Lothian, the Duke of Alba, Smuts, can all be freely quoted. When it comes to the living, she has to be more careful. But, after all, she is an old friend, and I have always accepted her as she is, with her ambitions and absurdities and inconsistencies and, I must not forget, her extremely rewarding company and intelligence.

Bramfield, Suffolk, 15 April

I remember Moly Sargent saying shortly before he died, with all the cynicism which served to conceal the deep passionate emotion of his innermost feelings, that the Common Market was a subject which was taboo until Gladwyn retired and returned to England, since which it had suddenly become a matter of national importance, and we were all urged to further the cause. Now Moly is dead, and British entry is virtually dead: and the subject is again taboo. It seems that it is the wrong sort of cry on which to win an election, and must be dropped until the atmosphere seems propitious. Thus when Gladwyn persuaded Ted Heath to attend the Annual General Meeting of his Britain in Europe Campaign, Ted's speech made no acknowledgement of their activities, and he would on no account allow his speech to be reported. The whole policy must sink into oblivion because the wretched ignorant and unsuspecting electorate might object! Perhaps they are not so ignorant as is thought.

Whitehall Court, London, 26 April

We went to the ball at Windsor to celebrate Princess Alexandra's marriage.[7] I had never been to a party at Windsor: indeed, nobody living had been to an event of such magnificence as this, the last great ball there having taken place early in the reign of Queen Victoria. The castle was floodlit and looked most impressive as one approached. The interior, though grand, was less formal than Buckingham Palace, and the atmosphere was one of enjoyment and gaiety. The place was stiff with visiting royalty, largely 'ex' and a few pretenders. All the throneless personalities appeared to have saved from their wrecks jewellery that eclipsed that of the reigning families. The triple diamond necklace of Princess Paul of

---

[7] To Angus Ogilvy, later Sir Angus (1928–).

Serbia was a glorious affair, and I believe Russian. The Comtesse de Paris wore the parure of sapphires belonging to Marie Antoinette: other jewellery of Marie Antoinette being worn by the young Duchess of Northumberland, who laughs the whole time in a rather childish fashion. The heroine of the evening, Princess Alexandra, was charming, simple, warm-hearted and friendly, moving about hand in hand with Angus.

The conglomeration of royalty was perfectly understandable because they were mostly close relations of the bride. And even exiled kings and queens cut better figures than much-divorced British families. Tony [Snowdon], seen by us all for the first time in his Windsor Uniform, looked more like a bell-hop than ever; people called him the shrimp cocktail.

The whole evening was delightful; seeing many friends and many glamorous strangers, and such glorious things. Fortunately I was able to find Francis Watson, who gave me a tour of all the rooms. The contents of Windsor Castle are fabulous. Francis said that no other collection anywhere can compare with what the Queen possesses. All largely due to the taste of the much-abused George IV. I didn't feel like dancing more than once, so it was enchanting to pass the time seeing the beautiful furniture and pictures. The flowers too were superb, azaleas at least ten feet high, and all bloom and no leaves. The gold plate on the buffet in the Long Gallery was splendid. What with talking to friends and sight-seeing, we left very late, and I did not get to bed till three.

On the morning of the wedding we left in very good time and drove along the empty Whitehall, lined with people. It took us only about a minute to reach the Abbey, and so we had a very long wait before the ceremony started. We were placed quite well, in the lantern, and could catch a reasonably good glimpse of the processions. The ceremony was heralded by a great procession of church dignitaries who made a magnificent group. Then the bride arrived in white lace. The bridegroom has an unusual face. I have never known him not smiling or being kind and helpful; but his broad jaw and the lines that come down from his cheekbones give a curious impression of strength and almost of fierceness, which could be frightening were one not certain that he has the nicest of characters. The real love that the young couple had for each other was deeply moving. The smiles seemed to melt all the stiff formality and traditional pomp of the royal wedding. Even the large

impressive face of the Archbishop of Canterbury could be seen breaking into a benign smile beneath his great mitre. What was most touching
was the way the bridal pair looked at each other when they were making
their vows: I had never seen this before. The Queen was obviously far
more pleased over this marriage than she had been over Princess
Margaret's, and one could hardly help comparing the two occasions.

In the evening Nancy Rodd and Malcolm Bullock dined with us in
the flat. She did not seem at all well, and was depressed and quiet. But
Malcolm rattled away happily, telling us all his little anecdotes and vulgar
stories and gossip. Apropos of the Vassall case and Profumo and the
Keeler girl and various other scandalous happenings that have been
awkward for the Conservatives, Bob Boothby had said that it would be
a 'funny thing if this government were brought down by sex'!

One of the amusing incidents of the wedding was when all the visiting royalty went for an outing to Syon. Helen, Duchess of
Northumberland, who has contrived to hang on to the famous Marie
Antoinette pearls, was standing in the hall when suddenly the string
broke and the pearls scattered far and wide on the marble floor. So all
the party went down on their knees to retrieve them, muttering 'Ach,
poor thing' (thinking of the unhappy Queen), when the Duchess said
'Ma'ams' (pronounced in the good old-fashioned way as 'marms', and
making for a very odd plural), 'it is of no matter. They come from
Selfridges!'

Whitehall Court, London, 29 May

Tonight we went to the Opera Gala with the Queen Mother. We could
not refuse such an invitation, so I had to dispose of my own party as
best I could, but they all seemed able to get dinner or supper elsewhere.
The party consisted of Lady Spencer, Malcolm Bullock, the John
Hopes, and Major Griffin, the first and last being in waiting. Though
offered champagne cocktails immediately, the atmosphere was rather
formal and the conversation subdued.

But this was only to begin with. Suddenly there seemed a movement
in the air, a widening of our circle, a rustle of skirts, and in came, with
the greatest of informality and the highest of spirits, the Queen
Mother. Sparkling with diamonds, in a pink tulle crinoline, and breaking

any ice there might have been, she exuded an excited joy that was almost unqueenly. I didn't remember, in the old days when I saw more of her, such a terrific amount of fun. Was it, could it, have been the champagne which flowed lavishly the whole evening, I wonder? What was interesting was that such is her power to charm and dazzle, that it does not seem to matter one whit that her inherent stoutness is now completely out of control. The disproportion of her figure is all the more astonishing these days when everybody fears fat for health reasons if not from vanity. Not her. Obviously she relishes her food, her sweets and her champagne, and is not going to spoil her enjoyment of life by bothering about diet and exercise.

In her winning manner she led us into the small dining-room adjoining the drawing-room, and urged us to help ourselves from a delicious selection of cold meats and salads which was on a side table. We put our food on exquisite china plates and all sat down. Our hostess spread a particularly large napkin (far larger than ours) over her ample knee; the scarlet-liveried footman kept our glasses filled; the atmosphere became gayer and gayer. Queen Elizabeth was enjoying herself and so were we.

I think she would have been happy to spend the whole evening thus, but we were gathered together to go to *Figaro*, and soon it was time to be off. Furs were wrapped round our shoulders (the QM hilariously saying that she was envious of my white fox because it was better than hers). Gladwyn, Malcolm and I got into the second car, which was entirely lined in dark-blue plush, and we sped along through the traffic which was held up by policemen, arriving at Covent Garden in about three minutes. The Droghedas, David Webster, Diana and one or two others, were there to receive; and after a few pauses for conversation, we took our seats, G sitting on the right of the Queen Mother and looking so impressive (I was told) that it seemed almost as though he had taken over the country. The lights were lowered, the exquisite overture started, and those of us in the box who loved Mozart settled down to enjoy the opera.

And did the Queen Mum enjoy it too? I wonder. She sat straight as a ramrod and completely still, not moving a muscle, which must require a good deal of self-control. I thought from where I sat that I could detect a little weariness, a little sadness, in her profile. The moment there was an opportunity for applause and comment her gaiety returned. We must make as much noise as we could clapping, John must shout encore loudly, she giving him the note by singing it, and was suddenly caught doing so after the applause had stopped, so that those near us must have heard. This gave her much merriment.

In one entracte we had the rest of supper in the back of the usual royal box; in the next we met the artists. Then, when the performance was over, back we went to Clarence House for more champagne, more chat, more laughter. At one moment she did a sort of African dance with John. I fancied that Lady Spencer and Major Griffin didn't think it all quite so funny. Being rather serious-minded and conventional people, perhaps they feared that their high-spirited mistress might go on thus till all hours. However, soon after one o'clock a move was made and we took our leave. It was an evening of luxurious comfort, great charm, and rollicking fun.

Whitehall Court, London, 5 July

We spent last night with the Bessboroughs at Stansted to go to the Chichester Theatre, and saw a superb performance of *Uncle Vanya*. The cast was remarkable: Michael Redgrave as Uncle Vanya, supported by Laurence Olivier and his new wife Joan Plowright – a complete contrast to Vivien Leigh, rather plain, straightforward, pleasant to all, and an excellent actress. Also Max Adrian, Fay Compton (who, as the old mother, spoke with a French accent, a clever touch), and Rosemary Harris. With the projecting stage one had the impression of being part of the family whose poignant drama was being unfolded. We went backstage afterwards and Larry Olivier gave us champagne out of a toothglass. Then a lovely drive across the downs by full moon, and an excellent supper before going to bed.

Whitehall Court, London, 11 July

The Greek Queen's state visit went off worse than was even antici-pated, and involved our own royal family in scenes of booing. Gladwyn, driving out to dinner, found himself in the midst of a massing crowd in Parliament Street, shouting 'Down with Queen Frederica!' He lowered his window and asked a few of them what all the fuss was about, and found them curiously ignorant and vague.[8] Obviously they had been roped in to demonstrate.

I lunched today with the Birkenheads and found the Avons there, as handsome, young, and healthy a couple as one could wish to see. God forbid that he finds himself well enough to return to politics. The conversation these last weeks (even months) has been almost altogether devoted to the Profumo affair, and no luncheon party would be complete without some new stories being contributed. I had a success with mine, about the French taxi driver who said to his fare, 'I'm sorry for poor Mr Macmillan who didn't even take advantage of the girl'. I heard from the Avons that it was that very inadequate Chief Whip, Redmayne, who telephoned Profumo on holiday in Venice to tell him that the truth had been discovered and he must return. Some people have said that it was Valerie who told him he must confess, but this is evidently not so.[9]

My great boast these days is that I was at one time a patient of the notorious Ward. He bought the practice of Dr Douglas when that best of all osteopaths returned to Paris in about 1948. Ward was far inferior, and altogether I disliked his jaunty conceited manner. I never came across him again until we spent a night at Cliveden last year, where he occupied the cottage which Bill [Astor] let him have for purposes which have now become apparent. We heard then about the Russian, and the open house kept by Ward; but there was no indication of any sexual scandal, no naked tarts swimming in the pool. In fact it was all highly correct. And even when out for a long walk with Sir Gilbert Laithwaite, who is eminently respectable, and we penetrated inside the cottage because I was tired and wished to sit down, I had no idea what really went on there. It was dusty, untidy and rather sordid, and I seem to remember having some sherry out of a grubby glass.

The great scandal follows close on the Argyll case. The 'headless

[8] Greece was in uproar following the murder of the left-wing deputy, Gregory Lambrakis, and the resignation of the Prime Minister; but the London demonstrators were mostly unilateral nuclear disarmers.

[9] On 22 March, John Profumo, Secretary of State for War, denied having an affair with Christine Keeler, a call-girl associated with Colonel Ivanov, the Russian Naval Attaché. On 5 June he admitted it, and resigned. On 8 June Stephen Ward was arrested and charged with living on immoral earnings; and on 3 August he died from an overdose of drugs. The government of Harold Macmillan was irrevocably shaken and wild and pernicious rumours circulated, such as that an unnamed Cabinet Minister had served, naked and masked, at a dinner-party.

Cynthia's daughters Vanessa and Stella at the British Embassy, Paris

The British and French Premiers,
Harold Macmillan and
Michel Debré, meeting in Paris
in 1959, surrounded by officials:
from the left, Maurice Couve de
Murville, Louis Joxe, Jean
Chauvel and Gladwyn Jebb

Harold Macmillan's wife Doroth

Cynthia, as ambassadress in Paris, dressed for a grand reception

The failed Paris Summit of May 1960:
De Gaulle, Macmillan and Eisenhower – but no Khruschev

Robert Boothby, Gladwyn's Best Man

Geoffroy de Courcel's arrival as
French Ambassador in London
in 1962, with his wife Martine:
Gerard André behind them

Edward Boyle, Cynthia's regular
companion at concerts and opera

Jeremy Thorpe, as leader of the Liberal Party in 1970,
sandwiched between Edward Heath as Prime Minister and Harold Wilson as Leader
of the Opposition

Cynthia with
Yehudi Menuhin

Gerald Wellington, longstanding
friend of Cynthia and Gladwyn

men', said to be Duncan Sandys and Douglas Fairbanks Junior, are supposed to figure again in the Profumo affair. More photographs are promised and two other Cabinet ministers may be involved. The newspapers are crammed with detailed reports of the proceedings, and *The Times* becomes pornographic reading.

Bramfield, Suffolk, 15 August

I wonder why I ever leave here. Time passes peacefully, gently, in this pretty old house. The roses in the garden are lovely, and the chintzes in the house are lovely. The sun pours in. When it rains, all the different greens of the huge trees in front of my window look like something growing at the bottom of the sea, sodden in water. When the rain stops, the fresh smell is as delicious as that produced under the warmth of sunlight: the smell of box on a sunny day is to me nostalgic. The yews are not to be clipped this year because of the cold winter we had. Our aged cook gives me excellent summer puddings, tarts, bread-and-butter pudding, roasts – brought to me on a tray by dear motherly Mrs Lovett, who comes in from the village any time she is wanted, and is the salt of the earth. She has worked in the house since she was a girl, and knows it all intimately. The old almshouses, which I tried to buy to preserve, have been sold to a London speculator, who will build new houses on their site. It is a pity, because, though modest, they were part of old Bramfield.

Bramfield, Suffolk, 16 August

Mary Potter came to lunch today. I knew her long ago, with Clare MacKail and the Nicholses, as 'AT', for she was then Mary Attenborough, who had won the top prize over all the men and women at the Slade. Her husband, Stephen Potter, left her about ten years ago, her children are grown up, and she lives at Aldeburgh and paints with great success. She is a tremendous friend of Benjamin Britten and Peter Pears. In those circles, I observe, the former is always alluded to as Ben. We had a charming gossip.

Bramfield, Suffolk, September

We have returned from a Swan's Hellenic cruise. The lecturers included Sir John Wolfenden, an extrovert but perhaps really an introvert, and his more solid wife; Sir Mortimer Wheeler, an exhibitionist with his loud voice, extravagant gestures, his vanity, his vulgarity, his anxiety to attract, his wavy moustache and long wavy hair, all rather pathetic in somebody well over seventy. Maurice Bowra was the lion of them all, partly because he roared the loudest, knew his stuff brilliantly, was convivial, a sort of jolly father figure. We were like disciples hanging on the lips of this big-bellied teacher who boomed out his lectures in that peculiar Oxford intonation, invented by himself and imitated by many, notably Osbert Lancaster. But of all our lecturers the one who gave us the most impressive and poetic talks was a charming Professor Stanford from Dublin, a man of great modesty and refinement, and with a beautifully chiselled profile.[10] He chanted to us in Greek in the manner he believed the ancient Greeks had recited the *Iliad* and the *Odyssey*, a rhythmic chanting on two notes a fifth apart, in effect something like plainsong, which itself probably originated from some similar form of chanting. One morning on deck, Gladwyn read Jebb's translation of Sophocles, Maurice read the Greek as he believed it to have been spoken, Professor Stanford chanted it, and a young Greek guide read it as it is pronounced in modern Greek. 'That was very dignified', said our schoolmaster friend, Mr Manning.

We had on board an extraordinary Jewish family from New York called Schwartz. Swarthy parents, both attorneys, had produced a precocious little boy who was the image of his father. The likeness was made even more noticeable by their dressing identically. Solar topees; black shirts; black shorts; black socks, shoes that one might have played football in, with some yellow about them. This curious get up made one think that they might be ants, or rather bees, dressed as people, for there was something not quite human in the darkness of their colouring, their woolly hair, and their curious way of holding their arms when they walked, as if they were prepared to walk on all fours. They were tribal. The great object on all the expeditions appeared to be for Mr Schwartz to photograph young Brian. So during any lecture at a good site, the boy

---

[10] Bedell Stanford (1910–84): subsequently Chancellor of Dublin University.

had to manoeuvre himself into a suitable place while his adoring father clicked away at the camera. This was sometimes rather disturbing for us. Thus Brian was immortalized with all manner of famous backgrounds, such as standing to attention in the cave where St John wrote Revelations while the chaplain was reading the holy words to an inspired audience. But the most curious photograph of all must have been at Delphi when he was made to climb up behind the headless statue of Aphrodite, and where her head should have been was Brian's head, peering over from under his solar topee. The effect was very odd indeed.

From Venice Gladwyn and I went to Florence to stay with Marjorie Scaretti. It was cold and pouring with rain as we motored up and up into the hills some sixteen miles. Finally we climbed the highest hill of all, the road flanked with cypress trees, and after many hairpin turns landed in the courtyard of Il Trebbio, an old restored fortress. I can understand how it was designed as a summer place, and that in the hot Italian sun the severity of the furnishing might be cool and pleasant. But we had the misfortune to spend two days there in the most appalling cold rainy weather, and therefore everything seemed dark and damp and depressing, almost prison-like. It was very reminiscent of an old dank castle on the west coast of Scotland. The rain slapped down continually on the paving of the courtyard, and above this sound came that of doors swinging in the wind or being slammed. Worst of all we could not see the glorious view which was the whole point of the place. We were in a great cloud.

Bramfield, Suffolk, 12 October

There have been great happenings this week. On Tuesday the Prime Minister was struck by one of the most convenient and timely acts that God has ever thought of sending. It came in a painful form: an immediate operation for the removal of the prostate gland was suddenly necessary. In the morning there had been some pain, and he asked his Cabinet colleagues whether they wished him to resign, leaving the room for them to decide his fate. He wept when he heard their verdict that he should stay. In the evening the pain became violent and he was whisked to the King Edward VII Hospital in preparation for an operation. He then renounced his leadership without ignominy and on a wave of public sympathy.

It isn't the first time that a Prime Minister has had to resign because of ill health. But this time the circumstances were particularly dramatic because it took place just on the eve of the Conservative Party Conference. With all the party workers gathered together in Blackpool, the place has naturally become a hive of political speculation. And with all the star turns in the Cabinet vying as to who can make the best speech and achieve the most enthusiastic applause, one would almost imagine it to have become a contest as in the last act of *Meistersinger*.

Reggie Maudling made little impression, which will disappoint Gladwyn, who had hitched his wagon to this star. He thought he had hidden gifts, was the right age, had a nice wife, and would lead us into the Common Market. Quintin Hailsham had an almost hysterical success, by which he was so fired that he immediately announced his application to renounce his title and seek a seat. This struck some as being premature, and the 'QH' badges worn by his supporters were felt to be in bad taste. Lord Home, it is said, made such a first-rate speech that now people are urging him to apply for the House of Commons. Then this afternoon Rab had his big moment. The audience and commentators are deeply impressed and his stock has risen high, and his chances seem pretty certain. He should be the obvious choice for Premier were he not such a strange enigmatic man.

He was the only one of the orators who I saw on television. He looked unattractive physically. Bald, rounded, a flabbiness of flesh, weary, rather old and tired, and an aura of sanctimoniousness. He needs toning up – cold baths, cold draughts, exercise, anything to make the blood flow quicker, the heart beat faster, the flesh become firmer, the inscrutable face to look alert. Having said this, I recognize his excellent brain and political astuteness. It would be a terrible blow for him if he does not make the grade this time. Indeed, it is now or never.

On Wednesday night at dinner at the Colytons Bob Boothby seemed convinced that it would be Rab, and I imagined that this must have come straight from the horse's mouth, or rather, the mare's mouth, for he had lunched that very day with Dorothy Macmillan. The Colyton dinner was for John Gunther, who is updating his *Inside England*. 'What are you going to say about us?', I asked, for certainly the murky waters we are in do not make for a story one would wish to have recorded. 'Tell the truth about us', said Bob, ready to depart in his crottle tweed coat with a red carnation rakishly peeping out, and looking for all the world like a Whig statesman. The truth about Bob had better not be told.

The next night at dinner I sat next to Lord Mancroft. He said of Bob Boothby that he was 'immoral, amoral and unmoral'. I expect it is true that if he had not been these things he could have made a wonderful Prime Minister. That rich velvety voice is very winning. I wonder whether Harold realizes how much she sees of her old love, and whether she realizes that what she says to him may well be passed on to Wilson, of whom Bob sees a lot.

Whitehall Court, London, 16 October

Still no news. It would seem to be a deadlock, but Reggie Maudling is creeping up in popularity. Tonight Gladwyn rang up Bob Boothby, who had gone out. His secretary indicated that he too was now for Maudling, and then let drop the remark, 'Lady Dorothy has just left'. Some ministers would resign sooner than have Rab or Quintin, but Home doesn't really want the job, though would doubtless accept it if there was no other solution.

I heard from Thelma Lucas that when the Butlers arrived at Blackpool they gave themselves airs and were very gracious, confident that Rab was to be PM. Tonight we saw Selwyn at the Turf Club, where we were dining. He had been to see the PM today. It must be amusing for Harold to lie there in hospital sounding all these opinions and finding, as yet, no consensus as to who should take his place, when for four months people have been wanting him to resign. There is a joke going round that he has decided to come back!

Bramfield, Suffolk, 18 October

It is to be Lord Home. Failing Maudling, I suppose this is the best choice, though Gladwyn thinks his health is not strong enough. He is absolutely honest, very intelligent, and very nice. The papers make a ridiculous fuss about him being the 14th Earl, as if this affected his ability or character. In fact I think he will be more democratic than his enigmatic predecessor, who went in for nepotism in such a big way. Poor Rab! What a disappointment it will be for him. He once told somebody that he had had three great disappointments in his life: one being Sydney's death, the second not being made PM after Suez, and the third he would not say. I believe it to have been not becoming Viceroy of India, which had always been his ambition. From his sick bed Harold has made John Wyndham a peer, which I think is an excessive reward. As long ago as the Summit Conference Harold said that he would like to revive the title of Egremont, which John would have inherited had there not been illegitimacy in the family.

Whitehall Court, London, 22 October

Lunch at Mary Roxburghe's today. I sat next to John Foster. He is pleased about Home. He said he thought it must be the first time that a Prime Minister has two brothers who have been to prison. William Douglas-Home went for honourable reasons: he refused to carry out a command in the war which meant killing people unnecessarily. Henry D-H was 'drunk in charge'. All this would be a very good response to the accusation that the new PM 'doesn't know how the other half lives'.

Whitehall Court, London, 28 October

We have just returned from a delightful visit to Ireland. We flew to Dublin on Friday and spent the night with the Beits at Russborough. They are extremely rich, childless, and live a pleasant life of luxury and dilettantism. On Saturday we drove to Wexford for the Festival. We saw three operas – *Don Pasquale*; *The Siege of Rochelle*, by Balfe; and *La Gioconda*, by Ponchinelli. All very well done in a little cinema seating about 250. Certainly the Gioconda proved a little too loud with singers in full voice. But it was amazing what can be achieved with a tiny stage. We went behind afterwards and were astounded by the lack of space. Altogether it is a most enterprising undertaking, all financed, I suspect, by Alfred, and inspired by a Wexford anaesthetist, Dr Welsh. As Compton Mackenzie said in his speech on the final night, one wonders why Edinburgh wishes to build an opera house when they already have a theatre which is enormous as compared with the Wexford cinema.

Our return journey from Wexford to Dublin airport was most uncomfortable. Raimund [Von Hofmannsthal's] brandy flask, from which we all had nips, was a help. Everybody felt pretty tired by the time we reached London, and for Gladwyn and me it was a horrid thought that we had to go on the eight o'clock plane to Paris tomorrow morning, rising at 5.45, and with the possibility of not being able to leave owing to fog.

Hôtel Bristol, Paris, 29 October

Well, we got here all right despite delays. This evening G and I dined alone with Baronne Edouard de Rothschild in her beautiful house in the Avenue Foch. This was to be a simple affair, but the Rothschilds cannot do anything plain, and it consisted of six courses. We had soup, fish, delicious partridges, asparagus, cheese, sweet, fruit. All this in Germaine's lovely dining-room with her famous Fragonards and Goyas looking down on us, and we ate off her wonderful Sèvres. Her house is filled with exquisite objects. They had been taken by the Germans during the War, but practically all had come back. Afterwards, when Gladwyn had gone, seeing that I was interested, she took me upstairs to see her private rooms, which were filled with exquisite things on a smaller scale than downstairs. I thought I had never seen such a collection of fine workmanship, nearly all of the Louis XVI period. Such lovely inlay, finely chased with gilt mounts of a suppleness that nobody could achieve now, and the prettiest little tray-tables of porcelain. And two Fragonards in her bedroom. And up there also, in a room lined with books, she writes about her collection and studies philosophy. She is a most sweet kind woman, and I thought how civilized it all was, her sitting there in her white mink jacket by a log fire, surrounded by such beautiful things, and her mind occupied with deep problems of life. We talked till late about the Jewish question, and religion. She has a daughter who lives in Israel.

Whitehall Court, London, 13 November

We set off for our dinner at the Turf Club, delayed by Gladwyn not finding his studs, and arrived after some of the guests were already there. We were to be twenty-eight, sitting at two tables in the big room upstairs, where a coal fire was burning. As if this was not enough, out of the blue there came a charming couple, greeted warmly by Gladwyn and, I hope, not too dismayfully by me. It was the Carringtons,[11] and I had not expected them. Fortunately we were able to squeeze two more places at one table.

Directly we had finished we had to get a move on in order to reach St James's Palace and receive the party.[12] Here too the fires were burning in the huge grates, and the rooms looked splendid. There can be no more becoming background than red and gold and white. The band played and the throng arrived: the distinguished rich, the vulgar rich, the officials, the relations, the friends, the beauties, the oddities, the unknown. I, Gladwyn, and Hugh Hertford, stood in a row in front of a blazing fire at our backs, and I was quite wondering whether we could not move elsewhere when we were told we must go to receive the Queen Mother and Princess Margaret, who were arriving by what was known as the hole in the wall, a door leading straight in from Clarence House.

From the passage leading from Clarence House there first appeared two corgis, followed by the Queen Mother, all sparkles and spangles and smiles, insisting on them being given their evening run from the door leading to the garden. As usual she looked radiant, smiled to all, said the right thing to everybody who was presented to her, and altogether ensured the success of the party. One can count on that! Princess Margaret looked very pretty in a turquoise blue dress, with a beautiful turquoise and diamond tiara and necklace to match, and was fortunately in a good mood. Tony had a sun-lamp burnt brown complexion, and his hair had been tinted in a curious new colour. Sachy Sitwell afterwards described it as peach, but I would say more apricot.

Meanwhile I and Gladwyn were with the QM trying to bring forward the right people to be presented, and ward off those that were unsuitable.

[11] Peter Carington, 6th Lord Carrington (1919–), married to Iona McClean. Secretary of State for Foreign Affairs 1979–82.
[12] A charity reception in aid of the Hertford Hospital in Paris, hosted jointly by the Marquess of Hertford and Gladwyn.

We circled around, delved into the crowd, seized on the reluctant shy, who nevertheless were delighted after the ordeal was over, and searched for those who had given generously. Mr Sunley, our trump card, who had given the Hospital £100,000, seemed sober, which was a big relief as he was to be rewarded with special thanks from Queen Elizabeth and was to sit next to Princess Margaret at supper. Paul Getty was presented, which I afterwards regretted upon hearing that, though he had brought two or three friends with him, he had sent a mere five pounds to the cause.

Many French friends came over, braving the November climate of London. Even Violet Trefusis came, just for the night, planting herself firmly in the royal path. Most people had taken much trouble with their appearance, and got their tiaras out of the bank, and so the scene had great brilliance and beauty. Also it had gaiety, which is always a little difficult to achieve in a large formal party. Everybody appeared to enjoy themselves thoroughly, from the Queen Mother downwards.

It is interesting to watch her technique. Her stout glittering form moves slowly and gracefully through the crowds. One brings forward the person to be presented and tries to give some clue as to who he is or what he does or where he comes from; maybe one can't illuminate her much. She gives her hand, and then seems to pause an instant, after which she somehow contrives to say a few words which invariably are exactly fitting to the occasion, in fact, the right thing. She looks enchanted to be talking to the person, and visible pleasure glows from his face. The conversation may be short or long, never too long, but the difficult moment of bringing it to an end is brilliantly achieved. She just moves on slowly with a charming smile and a lingering look of reluctance at parting. So there is no more shaking hands, bowing or curtseying to be done, and the person who was presented is left with the happy impression that the Queen Mother would have liked nothing better than to remain. It is a great gift.

After this those specially selected were all to go into the room beyond the Throne Room where were two large supper tables of eighteen or twenty. Here I badly missed the supporting staff on whom I could rely at the Embassy. Half the people expected had not realized we had sat down, and were still chatting away in the drawing-rooms: but all was well in the end, the tables filled, cold supper and more champagne served, and it was well after one when the royal party made a move back through the hole in the wall, apparently well pleased with the evening.

Whitehall Court, London, 26 November

I lunched with Tom [Goff], cosily and alone. His is one of the only London houses I go to which has been occupied by the same family for getting on for seventy years, and not converted or divided. 46 Pont Street has remained delightfully unchanged, with its good rooms and polished staircase, and Lady Cecily's beautiful needlework and Tom's musical instruments.

In the evening we dined with the Colin Andersons in Hampstead. They live in Admiral's House, which has all the charm of a country house, lovely air and garden, but too many steps for my liking. One goes up several flights to reach what they call the gallery. Here they have an amusing collection of Victoriana, including Holman Hunt's 'The Awakening Conscience', which we studied while Colin read an article by Ruskin describing it. How I like a picture that tells a story!

Whitehall Court, London, 28 November

We gave Ava dinner at the Turf. She was in a mellow mood. She capped my story of Ralph Anstruther reminding Anthony Meyer that the rule is 'a hard collar and hat when the court is in London', by telling us that her father always wore a top hat when the House was sitting. I then remembered that Sir Claude Phillips, who was, I think, art critic or music critic of *The Times*, and somewhat of a dandy, used to call on my mother bringing his hat and stick and gloves right into the drawing-room, and placing the hat, with the gloves in it, under his chair like a po. Apparently it was a sign of great advance in friendship, if not intimacy, when a hostess invited her visitor to leave his hat in the hall.

Whitehall Court, London, 2 December

We dined at the French Embassy tonight. It was a large dinner of thirty-four (at tables of about eight or ten) in honour of Rab. I sat next to Rab, a thing I had not done for two or three years, and I found it difficult to know what to talk about. Having known him so very well in the old days, but realizing that many of our links were severed, and that it would be awkward to discuss politics, I wondered what to say. But we somehow contrived to chat lightly about a number of unimportant things. His appearance is – I almost hesitate to use the word – repellent. He has become far fatter and looks almost oriental, I would say like a mandarin. Gladwyn swore that he was unshaven with a 'five o'clock shadow', but my short-sighted eyes didn't detect this in the candlelight. Mollie was looking handsome and well-dressed, and was extremely amiable.

Whitehall Court, London, 3 December

My few essays at cooking have not, as yet, been exactly successful. Gladwyn, having decided, with his habitual exaggeration, that we were spending 'thousands and thousands of pounds' on having breakfast sent up to our flat, has taken to doing it himself, sweeping aside the kind offer from the Irish maid to do it for us. The devastation in the kitchen is great, but the breakfast, I must concede, is better than anything produced by Whitehall Court.

Whitehall Court, London, 5 December

Vera Bowen[13] arrived for lunch, and then we went to a ballet matinée at Drury Lane. I was on the committee, and so on the receiving line for the Queen Mother. Margot Fonteyn and Nureyev danced *La Sylphide*, an exquisite *pas de deux*; she frail, ethereal and romantic, and he the perfect partner, dressed in Highland costume. His every movement is made with a natural grace. Our other male dancers give excellent well-drilled performances, but Nureyev expresses a deep poetic feeling with every part of his body. He is like a reed in the wind, swaying this way and that with a suppleness not to be found in Anglo-Saxon dancers. Vera, whose reminiscences of ballet and knowledge of all that goes on behind the scenes are fascinating, says that Nureyev is quite impossible. His behav-

---

[13] Vera Polianova (1889–1967), widow of Harold Bowen. She was a Russian with many friends in the world of Bloomsbury, and he had been an orientalist; and it was in their house that Cynthia had first met Gladwyn in 1927.

iour is so unpredictable that she is prejudiced against him to such an extent that she will hardly praise his genius. She avers that Diaghilev would never have stood for absurdities such as flinging off his shoes, as Nureyev did in his solo performance. When I asked how he compared to Nijinsky (who I remember seeing when Father took me to the ballet as a child), she said that Nijinsky was every bit as good a dancer but was properly disciplined. Perhaps stupidly, I rather enjoyed the lack of discipline. Nureyev is something not quite human, and I don't expect him to conform to the rules.

Whitehall Court, London, 11 December

The subject that rages violently at the moment is the resignation of Lord Mancroft from the board of the Norwich Union. The directors persuaded him to go because they feared losing business from the Arab states because he is a Jew. The consequent storm has been so great, with questions in the House, that they have now offered him reinstatement; but he has refused, to my mind most wisely. As one approaches Norwich one is greeted by a large sign proclaiming 'Norwich, a fine city': this slogan is now being repeated with a different inflection.

We went to Pam Berry's dance at the Savoy, and squeezed with difficulty into an immense crowd bobbing and jumping about to a frenzied rhythm on a far too small yardage of parquet. I danced half way round with Gladwyn and then persuaded him to extricate me from this terrifying mob. Fortunately we landed ourselves right in front of Edward Boyle, so thankfully I sat down with him, fortified by champagne. We discussed Harold, whom Edward analyses as a middle-class man with a veneration for the aristocracy. He told me how at a Cabinet meeting, when the status of that too-small county Rutland was under discussion, Edward had stated that the Rutland children were deprived of things such as speech and drama therapy. Whereupon Harold, in his most Edwardian manner, threw out 'What Rutland needs is more gamekeepers'.

This evening we went to the Duff Cooper prizegiving, at Enid Jones' house. It is a charming annual gathering of more or less the same friends and acquaintances. This year the winner was a modest young American woman who had written a book on Keats. She had come over from New York to be given the prize by Bruce.[14] Raymond [Mortimer] spoke too. How sad the passing of the years is on such occasions. There was Diana, noticeably less beautiful this winter, for she is not well; and Harold Nicolson, generally enjoying himself and drinking quite a lot, now greatly aged by his last stroke and anxious to make for home. On the other hand John Julius' beautiful little boy was old enough to appear, wearing a delightfully old-fashioned sailor suit; and then there was Vanessa, enormous with child. So though the older generation may wane, the younger one is close at hand.

Whitehall Court, London, 12 December

Gerry Wellington's grandson, the son of Liza Clyde, went on the stage and became a real Bohemian, with long hair and beatnik clothes. In spite of having been to Eton, he kept such curious company that, in his august grandfather's words, 'He does not know a single gentleman'. However, suddenly Gerry has good cause to be proud of the young man, for he has somehow jumped to the top of the pop-singing poll and is earning huge sums of money. He and a friend called Chad (in reality Chadwick, but names must be abbreviated to sound matey) are earning £120 a week singing at Hatchetts in Piccadilly.

When I suggested that we should go and see him, Gerry was pleased enough to organize a party, treat us to a princely snack of oysters, champagne and caviare at Apsley House, and then convey us in a huge hired car first to a 'musicale' and then on to Piccadilly. So we all trooped in to Hatchetts, rather overdressed compared to the rest of the company, for it is not a night haunt of great distinction and Gerry's Iron Ducal manner didn't seem to belong at all. However, as we were tucking into our supper, he became more relaxed and was ready, with an almost boyish air of embarrassment, to enjoy the programme.

The two pop singers wore light grey Edwardian suits, and each carried a horrible invention, hideous to look at and hideous to hear, an electric guitar. From the back of the guitar, like a long tail behind them, an electric cable connected with an amplifier on the floor. In front of them was a microphone, which was placed at a rather lower level than

---

[14] David Bruce (1898–1977): United States Ambassador.

the proper height of the singers should require: perhaps it was considered more attractive for them to adopt a slightly stooping position, as if they were whispering something intimate into the mouthpiece. To tell the truth, their singing was more like whispering. Thus they bent forward, with their heads together, and made suitable rhythmic movements with their bodies and feet, and gave us sad songs, and gay songs, and cynical songs, and evidently everybody was delighted. It certainly was not great art, but it was rather charming, particularly because they were such very nice boys. Chad was bespectacled and modest, and Jeremy most endearing with his charm of manner and youthfulness.

Bramfield, Suffolk, 31 December

I walked up to Mrs Berry's cottage in the late afternoon to take her her Christmas present. It was so cosy, with the bright warming gas light, which she buys in containers and which keeps her independent of power cuts. A good coal fire was burning in the sitting room, the kettle was on the hob, and I thought how comfortable she made herself and how content she was. She has good fresh Suffolk air, good food, no frigidaire, an excellent vegetable and flower garden, plenty of energy, enjoys her grumbles, fervently supports the Conservative cause and the Church, and has the gift of superlative cooking.

It being the day for New Year resolutions, so few of which are now kept, I am going to limit mine to one important determination: tomorrow I shall start my book. I must plan out my time for working at it, and stick to it.

1964

❖

Well, I have made a start. After much preparation, and rather in trepidation, I put pen to paper very late on Friday. To make a beginning seemed to me to be the most difficult thing of all. But I found that once I forced myself to concentrate, which I did at all hours, while walking, dressing or eating, ideas came into my head. So I sat down at my writing table with an empty note book in front of me and suddenly, to my intense surprise, my pen began almost running away with me. I could hardly get it down quick enough. I made a few obvious corrections as I went along, and altered things round a bit, but I haven't yet dared read through what I have so far written. I am such a novice and wonder whether I should carry on like this. I see clearly that I must have regular hours for working, and stick to them. Even early rising may have to be faced!

Tonight on television we saw the Pope's visit to Jordan and Israel. We saw him trying to walk along the Via Dolorosa, buffeted, jostled, hemmed in on all sides, even lifted off his feet, and all this from enthusiasm. It was a pathetic example of how hysterical a crowd can become, and one could not help reflecting how little difference there is between anger and joy.

Bramfield, Suffolk, 13 January

On Saturday the Waveney Harriers met here. It was such a pretty sight, and I enjoyed seeing all those typically English horsey people, with their

wonderful lingo. We gave them port and sherry, sausage rolls and biscuits, in the hall. Hunting has become quite mechanized, and I was not
prepared for all the huge horseboxes drawn up in our park, nor for the
amount of followers in cars.

Bramfield, Suffolk, 17 January

I went to Cecil Beaton's sixty-sixth birthday party. I spent a long time
talking to Diana, and John Wyndham. At least, Diana was doing the
talking, delightfully and always stimulatingly, ensconced in an arm-chair
in the corner in her beautiful black satin dress, her fair hair and white
skin standing our like a light against Cecil Beaton's black velvet walls.
She sat there entertaining us with her stories and comments, giving
sometimes graceful gestures with her arms to illustrate a point, and
sometimes just slapping her thighs heartily, her legs well apart. There is
a down-to-earthiness about her. John, looking far younger than his
forty-three years, was pretty drunk, but coherent enough to say that he
should give up the bottle.

There were all sorts of elegant and attractive socialites there, and
what I took to be one of the Beatles: long black hair, fringe down to the
eyebrows, drainpipe trousers, boots. I was told it was no Beatle but
young Lord Londonderry. Just as extraordinary was a fair beatnik who
turned out to be one of Bridget and Jock McEwen's sons. His hair was
so long that it could almost have been plaited. Cecil B was in his red
velvet suit.

On Wednesday we were bidden to a party at Number Ten in honour of
Erhardt.[1] At first I thought that the old house looked much the same,
with the old leather porter's chair in the hall, and the red baize doors. But
when I got upstairs I thought the decoration extremely bad and over-
done, endless money having been spent on elaborately draped pelmets
and on materials that were intended to match the silk on the walls, but
didn't. There were masses of Germans there, and all our ambassadors to
Germany and various politicians. Gladwyn had a short talk with the
Chancellor, and the PM afterwards said he was sorry G had not had a
longer talk with him, but 'that awful little man Wilson monopolized him'.

[1] Ludwig Erhardt, Federal Chancellor of Germany.

Bramfield, Suffolk, 27 January

A delightful weekend with the Francis Watsons as our only guests. He is one of the world's best experts on French furniture, and knows a lot about pictures and objects, so I could not enjoy his company more. His wife and he are devoted to each other but bicker endlessly. She commits the unforgivable sin of taking over the story he has already begun, and would have told far better than she ever could; and she interrupts him with trivial details when he is in mid-stream. All husbands and wives should somehow settle such points in private so that the story-teller, once he has embarked on his story, has a free hand. I must say that I have never been able to get Gladwyn to curb himself in this way. He breaks in, picks up the thread, weaves it according to his fancy, laughs falsetto at the climax, and is quite unaware that I am left sitting silent and that all the heads which were turned on me have switched over to the other end of the table as if watching tennis, politely waiting for the end of the story from Gladwyn.

Bramfield, Suffolk, 1 February

I was asked to tea with the Princess Royal. She and Phyllis Balfour were alone. We sat and chatted in her charming apple-green drawing room, quite small but wisely furnished. When tea was announced we went into the dining-room next door. It looks on to the garden facing south, and the Princess thought it would be nice to have tea by daylight as it was such a springlike day. We sat there till it was almost dark and we could hardly see. There was a lovely pink glow in the pale aquamarine sky from the sunset, and from where I sat, opposite the window, I had a charming view of the trees of St James's Park beyond the wall of her garden. Then, as the evening darkened and the lamps of the Mall were lit up, a sort of gentle melancholy descended on us, and conversation flagged. The sound of the traffic seemed to come from an outside world very remote from the quiet civilized room of the old palace where I was sitting with this quiet civilized princess. How interesting that in our royal family this type of real benevolence and integrity, such as is found in the Queen and the Princess Royal, runs side by side with the type of which the Duke of Windsor and Princess Margaret are examples.

Whitehall Court, London, 6 April

Tonight we went to a dinner given by the Franco-British Society for Courcel. I sat next to Bob Boothby and was treated to a mass of fascinating gossip, a good deal of which was directed against Harold Macmillan. Harold, he says, is the coldest of fish; and he was, not unnaturally, furious about Dorothy's affair with Bob. I suggested that this had arisen because Bob was the antithesis of Harold, to which Bob replied in his rich porty voice, 'Yes, I was the antidote'. Harold told them that he would never, never divorce her. They could go off together to India or anywhere they liked. Bob asked him to be kind to Dorothy and not to make life too difficult for them. Harold made her go and live with his own mother who, I believe, was an odious woman not liked by any of her children: she was alleged to have coloured blood. Bob said that only one of Dorothy's children was his.

Harold knew everything about Profumo in that unfortunate affair, even though in July last he told the House of Commons that he had not known the truth. Bob said that Harold had particularly wished to have Redmayne and the others question Profumo in the hope that the whole matter might have been hushed up.

Then Bob, very confidential, said he wanted my advice on a private matter. He has become a great friend of Harold Wilson, who he sees about once a month. Harold Wilson has told him that when he comes to power he feels he can deal with Soviet Russia and America, but is much concerned about Europe, particularly France. To counteract this Wilson has tentatively suggested to Bob that he might be the ambassador who could win over the General! Of course, Bob would have to lead a correct life, with no disappearing into Montmartre! I was amazed and amused and somewhat shocked. How could our dear old friend with his appalling private life, his drink, his thoroughly unreliable character, ever fill that role with any success or dignity? Fortunately his health would almost certainly prevent him from taking it up. I murmured congratulations, and told him that I had once read that Lord Lytton was the most popular ambassador that we had ever sent to Paris because the French liked somebody who had a Bohemian streak. This pleased the old rogue immensely.[2]

[2] There is no evidence that Harold Wilson had ever suggested this to Bob Boothby, and it is more likely that Boothby was fantasizing.

Whitehall Court, London, 20 April

We were asked to dine at the American Embassy tonight, having never been to a big dinner or luncheon there since the coming of the Bruces. This is odd because, after all, Gladwyn was four years in New York and is an eminent figure over there. Apparently they do not ask people out of duty, and MPs on both sides of the House have complained. So I imagined that amends were now being made about us. However, on arrival it proved that we were invited purely because the party was in honour of the Rothschilds; and the other guests were almost entirely those we had had in the flat the other night,[3] plus a good many pansies and decorators and figures from the artistic world. In among this *galère*, like a fish out of water, was Duncan Sandys, who was not even given the proper precedence due to a minister. All very odd and ignorant.

Whitehall Court, London, 12 May

We have just returned from dining with Norman Collins to meet Harold and Dorothy Macmillan. Harold was much changed, was physically and mentally slower, and more than ever in an Edwardian dream, harping back to the golden age before the First War. When I praised him on a recent speech he had made (how one flatters people at dinner parties! it is quite despicable – partly good manners, partly that weakness 'the desire to please', partly to help out), he said that he had suddenly felt tired half way through and realized that he couldn't go on as he used to. He had that unhealthy glow that comes from a sun lamp, a fatal sign that does not deceive the eye. He is terrified of women, though he covers it up by kind remarks and enquiries that surely deceive nobody. We talked of his old friendship with Geoffrey Madan; of Oxford; of the First War; and of the new book about Rupert Brooke. At the close of the evening, to my great embarrassment, he came up to me and said, 'I must now say goodbye to my charming hostess'. This is typical of his lack of touch with reality. As for Dorothy, she was, as always, splendid: plainest of clothes, hair washed but nothing done to it, solid, and very animated with her good-humoured laugh – the very

---

[3] A dinner party at Whitehall Court in honour of Philippe and Pauline de Rothschild.

opposite of her complicated many-sided husband. Harold stays, when in London, either at his club or with Maurice. She had got a room at the Dorchester.

Whitehall Court, London, 4 June

Clarissa Avon dined tonight. We were just six; Tony Lambton, Ann Fleming, and Leslie Hartley. Tony, as always, made a succession of catty remarks, and Clarissa was reduced to helpless schoolgirlish giggles and snorts, even having to wipe away tears. I had never seen her like that. Apparently it happens very rarely, and is good for her and relaxes her, so Ann told me later. I gather that for the others the evening was in consequence a great success, though Gladwyn and I agreed we had found it a bit boring.[4]

Bramfield, Suffolk, 18 July

Our most important function this season was the dinner we gave in the flat for the Queen Mother on 30 June. G wished to ask all sorts of unusual people, but I felt that what she really desires on such an occasion is to be among friends. In the end I won. We had Gerry, the Salisburys, the Devonshires, the Spencers, the John Hopes, and K and Jane Clark. To this was added, by Gladwyn while in Dusseldorf, the Alexanders, which swelled the numbers to sixteen.

This was almost too many for our flat, particularly as the QM likes to be all together at one table. In fact, it presented quite a difficult problem, and endless enquiries had to be made for a table, broad and not too long, which would allow the important personage to sit at the centre of the table with sufficient room, not only for her legs but for her crinoline. Robin Brackenbury the Old Etonian caterer, who provided the food and waiters, finally unearthed one at a warehouse at Kingston. It was in three parts, which he guaranteed would be nailed firmly

---

[4] On 19 June Ann Fleming wrote to Evelyn Waugh: 'Lady Avon has suffered earache for several months, but Lord Lambton's leg pulling of Lady Gladwyn reduced her to such ill-mannered and prolonged laughter that she was miraculously cured'.

together. But when it came, on the afternoon of the day, the three portions had no means of being kept together. Fortunately Whitehall Court has a house carpenter, who appeared in a trice and was soon hammering away and the horrible object became one firm board.

Our guests arrived, as instructed, sharply at 8.15. To our surprise the Spencers, who were to accompany the Queen Mother, arrived on their own and told us she was coming alone, which they said was a great compliment. Gladwyn was waiting outside in the street, and I greeted her as she came out of the lift. She came forward with her winning manner. Reminded of Gravett, whom she had known in Paris, she said exactly the right thing to him, and to dear Mrs Dowsing, eighty-three years old, who, with others had come along for the evening. But her first words on entering the flat pleased me more than anything she could have said. She exclaimed, 'But it's like a country house', and repeated it with delight. Indeed, as one comes into our hall one has a vista through the drawing-room windows to the catalpa trees, their large leaves cool and green, and with glimpses of the river glinting in the evening light.

We had for dinner a mousse of salmon; veal in marsala, with rice and peas and salad; and a sweet consisting of raspberries and strawberries in a melon, with whipped cream. We drank pink champagne. Everybody appeared to enjoy the evening immensely, particularly the guest of honour, who chatted away with the greatest gaiety.

Andrew Devonshire says that she misses being Queen. We were discussing her great capacity for enjoying herself, which I feel is largely because she lives in the present and doesn't worry about the past or the future even when she should be doing so. Tommy Lascelles used to call her the 'imperial ostrich', but said that of course it was just the right attitude for her to have, since the late King was so highly-strung, anxious, and uncertain of himself. Andrew said that one should see her treasurer leaving Clarence House holding his head in despair because of her extravagance, perhaps having brought a new string of racehorses. As for the Castle of Mey, which cost a huge sum to restore and where she only goes for a fortnight every year, she now says, 'I can't think why I ever bought the place'.

Bramfield, Suffolk, 25 August

On our Scottish holiday we went to Cortachy,[5] which had been taken by
Philippe and Pauline Rothschild, and where we lived for five days in the
lap of luxury and comfort. The food and wine were superlative, and
also the conversation. The lifestyle was delightful: lunch at two; tea at
six-thirty; dinner at nine. The charming Spanish maid who called me
would tell me that the weather was too bad for me to wake up, and that
she would bring my breakfast later, that is, about ten o'clock. Pauline,
who takes houses in Denmark and Scotland during the summer, to flee
from sun and heat, nevertheless had the central heating on full blast,
and fires in every room. Scottish neighbours coming to lunch or dine
were appalled at such warmth and had to take off their coats and ask for
windows to be opened. And Pauline's fancy dress intrigued them. In the
daytime she might be found in brown satin breeches, brown lace stockings, brown leather jerkin deeply decolleté, two long rows of outsize
pearls, hair long. At night oriental tunics, or elegant négligés from
Balenciaga, wrapped and held precariously by one hand, without fasten-
ing. Cortachy has been reduced in size and excellently arranged by the
Airlies. It is a lovely place, full of history and romance. Our bathroom
was in a turret, and immediately below the famous drum which is kept
in the cap room. I couldn't resist unlocking the concealed door in the
bathroom and creeping up the narrow corkscrew staircase into the attic
where I found the drum, to be heard drumming when an Airlie is about
to die, neglected on the sill of an open window, exposed to wind and
rain.

We had lunch at Balcarres with David and Mary [Crawford]. Here
was about the biggest contrast to Rothschild-Cortachy as could possibly be imagined. The riches in the form of works of art, pictures, furniture, objects, were incalculable. The comforts nil. Mary's bedroom was
singularly unalluring. There was a dog kennel; the twin beds had no
coverlets; the quilts were not a pair; old clothes, stockings, general
untidiness everywhere. The food, plain, homely, unattractive, was certainly good for our stomachs after the art of the Rothschild's chef; and
the draughtiness and lack of warmth (the one ill-burning fire with damp
logs having fallen apart) were almost welcome. Everybody says that if

---

[5] Cortachy Castle, Angus, seat of the Earl of Airlie.

David were to sell just one good picture he would be able to live in comfort for quite a time or be more generous to his family.[6]

David is quite the most delightful person I know, and with tremendous knowledge of his subject. Mary is most intelligent, though she makes the worst of her appearance. Of so little importance to her are her looks that when she lunched at Cortachy the other day one eye was half shut and her cheek black and blue and swollen. She had been hit in the face by a horse, but had not complained in any way, or been to see a doctor.

On the way south we stayed at Compton Wynyates, a cousin of Gladwyn's having married Lord Northampton – second marriage for her, third for him.[7] He is nearly eighty and quite amazingly handsome and alert, but rather deaf. I could dream away my life very happily in that peaceful old house, lying in its hollow. Neglected for nearly a hundred years, it was restored in mid-Victorian times in a manner that can well be criticized. But it remains a most impressive and moving place, the epitome of peace and continuity. Through the open lattice windows came summer evening sounds: rooks and wood-pigeons in the high trees, lambs on the hillside. It must have been thus for centuries in the old brick house.

Bramfield, Suffolk, 6 September

I am doing *The Ring*, and went to *Die Walküre* last night, taking Tom Goff. We used to go to Wagner together in the old days. It was a splendid performance, and gripped one with emotion as strongly as ever. The audience seemed transported with great surges of feeling as the music soothed, calmed, uplifted, roused, caressed, seduced, thundered, and carried one along with it. I thought the clothes of *Rheingold* and *Walküre* hideous, and too removed from time-honoured tradition. No lock of hair to cover Wotan's blind eye, no helmets or shields for the *Walküre*. And when the great doors of Hunding's hut opened we saw no lovely forest, but instead it became clear that the house was practically out of

[6] In the year after his death, his widow did sell Duccio's 'Crucifixion' for £1m, and lived on the proceeds.
[7] William Compton, 6th Marquess of Northampton (1885–1978), married (thirdly) to Elspeth Whitaker, a second cousin of Gladwyn.

doors already, with loose beams flung across and looking like the new houses at Stevenage, designed by the present Lord Esher, after a gale had blown off their roofs.

On Friday Gladwyn went to Paris for the day on a matter of great interest and importance for which I must be given some credit. When we were in Paris some two months ago we gave Nancy and Vincent Labouret dinner in a little restaurant in the Rue de Bourgogne. Gladwyn showed only too clearly how frustrated and angry he felt at the General's refusal to let England join the Common Market, and was distinctly critical about de Gaulle. Vincent said that it was a pity that Gladwyn was so vehemently embittered against the President, and he could well understand his disappointment, but that G was considered at the Elysée as being the only English person who could make any impact on de Gaulle and be capable of bettering the situation. The next morning I telephoned Nancy, really to apologize for Gladwyn's dejection about the state of affairs, and Nancy said that Vincent, as he took her home, remarked, 'Why doesn't Gladwyn go and see de Gaulle? He could see him any moment he wanted. I suppose he knows this.'

I passed this exciting information on to the old man, who perked up at the possibility of saying his say to the fountain head. He murmured something about having to do it through the proper channels and the danger of getting spokes put in his wheels by jealous unimaginative civil servants and politicians. But, surprisingly enough, the scheme was passed by those in high places: even Rab, from his fence, admitted good might come out of it. And after much delay and difficulty in selecting dates, the meeting actually came off this last Friday. By a fortunate stroke of luck Bob Dixon was still away on his holiday, so the coast was clear.

It wasn't a bad performance for a sixty-four year old to sit for an uninterrupted stretch of over two-and-a-half hours of *Rheingold* on the Thursday night; get back to the flat for a light supper; be called at 7.30; snatch breakfast at eight; at 8.30 drive himself down to London Airport to catch the ten o'clock plane to Paris; see people in the Embassy; lunch with Peter Ramsbotham; go round to the Elysée for his great interview; return to the Embassy to write down his impressions of the President and what exactly was said; dine; catch the late plane back; picking up the Bentley and drive himself home to the flat around midnight. The next day he left at ten for Bramfield to try and shoot partridges in the afternoon.

He said he found the General tremendously changed. Far more so than he expected, not having seen him for four years. His recent operation must have taxed him greatly. He was no longer the tall impressive man we knew, but appeared to have shrunk, got thinner, and everything about him sagged, and he looked grey and ill. There was none of his old roguishness and flashes of humour which were such a charming side of his austere character. The deep voice no longer boomed out fine phrases. There was lacking the punch and the vigour. G was quite shocked at such a marked alteration. The General seemed pleased to see him and was amiable. But obviously no real impression can be made now which would lead to a change of outlook. However, they had an interesting walk, and I do think that the General enjoys meeting somebody who stands up for the other side, since he privately holds in contempt those who do not do so.

1965

❧

Bramfield, Suffolk, 18 August

As I am writing my book on the Embassy, I have neglected this diary badly.

Churchill's funeral at St Paul's[1] was most impressive. From where we sat, nearly under the dome, we saw beautifully. The splendid heralds in their brilliantly-coloured tabards, carrying Churchill's emblems draped in black crêpe, were a wonderful sight. Most moving of all were the body-bearers, who carried the enormously heavy coffin with perfect timing, their heads leaning almost tenderly against the great swaying burden on their shoulders. But the television lighting takes away much of the mystery of such an occasion. At the Duke of Wellington's funeral gas lighting was first introduced, and must have been far more impressive. Even better would have been the torches and candles of Nelson's funeral, leaving so much of the great cathedral in darkness.

Whitehall Court, London, 22 June

We went up to Chatsworth last night for the ball – Stoker's coming-of-age celebrations.[2] It was the greatest fun. I had a new dress for it, made up from a length of rose-coloured diaphanous silk from Burma. Nancy, knowing that I wanted to see the house and contents more than the

[1] On 30 January.
[2] Peregrine Cavendish, Marquess of Hartington (1944–), son and heir to the Duke of Devonshire. His mother Deborah was a sister of Nancy Mitford and Diana Mosley.

people, wisely suggested our going very early to the ball. Others, such as the Courcels, did not get into the house till after midnight, so long was the queue of cars. So we had a delightful time wandering around seeing all the beautiful things.

The Mitford sisters looked splendid in their dresses and jewellery, but their faces were positively scrubbed clean, with not a speck of make-up. Oswald Mosley was there, now looking fat, smiling, benign, grey-haired, grey-complexioned. Harold was shuffling about, reminiscing about his father-in-law the Duke. Diana was there, saying she wasn't enjoying it. Crowds and crowds of smart people came from London, but the presence of local types, of the dull sort found in any county, showed the niceness of Debo's character in not leaving anybody out. In every room, guarding the treasures, was some homely retainer, who seemed to be enjoying the event as much as anybody. Dancing was in a gallery filled with marble busts draped and festooned with greenery. If I had a criticism of Chatsworth it would be that the main rooms are on the upper floor, and thus rather removed from nature.

1966

❧

Whitehall Court, London, 16 February

We have just made a pilgrimage to Sissinghurst to see Harold Nicolson, now seventy-nine and a pathetic sight after several strokes, and very glad to greet Tommy Lascelles, Osbert Lancaster, Gladwyn and me, with our gifts of wine and brandy. The old Scorpio has no sting left in his tail. He is sweet towards the world, ashamed of his infirmity, grateful but impatient with his male nurse, who calls him Harold. To encourage him I tried to persuade him to start his diary again. I told him it could be just reminiscences, Nigel having said that there would be nothing to put in it. Having suggested this, I really feel I must keep up my own diary.

We spent last weekend with Gerry. Gerry is my oldest greatest friend, though he is completely unsentimental. He wouldn't miss me if I were dead; he is too practical for that. He likes to go out with me to the opera or sightseeing because I am appreciative and gay, and we correspond the whole time and have great fun. He is a bully, and hates frailty or illness: a very British product.

The whole weekend Gerry alternated between being lion and lamb. 'What!', great falsetto roar, 'you think *this* or *that*?'; and then, suddenly, as mild as milk and acquiescing to everything. After many displays of fury he let me wear the famous George,[1] framed in huge diamonds, which Charles I gave to Bishop Juxon on the scaffold, saying 'Remember'. Tom Goff unfortunately made some remark about the mistakes made by Charles I, which annoyed Gerry and provoked a terrifying scene. Gerry is quite remarkably young-looking for eighty. Active, animated,

[1] The pendant of the Order of the Garter.

plenty of hair on his head, which makes such a difference, blue eyes that can still flame with anger or twinkle with amusement, and a charming youthful manner and voice.

British Embassy, Paris, Whitsuntide

I have just spent nearly a week in my old home.[2] It is sad to see how much it has deteriorated. The curtains are never drawn at night; the windows are left open whatever the weather; everything is undusted and badly arranged.[3] A dinner of eighteen or twenty was given for us. Its appalling shortcomings were, I afterwards discovered, due to it being organized by a grim woman who acts as comptroller and has no idea of how an important dinner should be chosen. The food was shaming. Consommé with two little devilled croutons in each cup. Then one chicken wing each. No salad. No cheese to follow. It was puzzling to see a double row of spoons and forks placed, contrary to all rules of elegance, in front and not at the sides. For the strange menu now consisted of a chocolate mousse, so hard that one needed almost to hack at it with a sledge-hammer (Philippe de Rothschild had to smash my portion out for me), and after that strawberries and cream. Even more unfortunate was that Philippe's exquisite Mouton, sent to the Ambassador as a present and down on the menu, had been forgotten in favour of another red wine.

Bramfield, Suffolk, June

The Grimonds stayed for the weekend and we made it a Liberal occasion.[4] I begin to wonder what Jo would do without Laura. She is splen-

---

[2] As the guest of Sir Patrick and Lady Reilly.
[3] On 1 June, Nancy Mitford wrote to her sister: 'The Embassy. I don't know if you ever saw it in Cynthia's time? She had decorated it too beautifully, with people from the Louvre, found which bits of furniture went there in the days of Pauline, etc. Now, modern airport furniture, modern pictures, of dripping entrails, yards and yards of them, covering those huge walls . . . It's as though Chatsworth had been redecorated by a dentist from New York'. (*Letters of Nancy Mitford*)
[4] Joseph Grimond, later Lord Grimond (1913–94), married to Laura Bonham Carter, daughter of Violet Bonham Carter. Leader of the Liberal Party, which Gladwyn had joined in 1965.

did in the way she keeps him on the right tack. But his appearance always wins through, even if there is something a little soft about him.

Whitehall Court, London, 4 August

Tonight we had a party for Jo. Liberal champagne too! Unfortunately I had all the cards sent out with Grimond spelt with two 'm's. After an onslaught from Gladwyn, I thought I would write to Laura apologizing and asking her to intercede with him. A lesser man might have minded, but not our Leader. Violet came, looking distinguished, Jeremy Thorpe, and lots of Liberals we did not know.

Whitehall Court, London, September

In Munich,[5] stung by a plausible high-collared military German, who assured me that none of them knew about concentration camps, I felt I must go and see for myself. Dachau is only seventeen kilometres from Munich, about the same distance as Ruislip from London. I got one of the wives from the Consulate to accompany me, and hired a car. We had a nice young student as a driver, and I suggested he should come in with us, which he was pleased to do. It was very moving, with many large photographs, some of them too grim to look at. I came away feeling that the only thing that matters in life is human dignity.

In Vienna we stayed at Sachers, just opposite the opera; and as I was alone during the evenings, I went by myself on both nights. Strange to think that in all my life I had never been to the opera alone. *Zauberflöte* was beautifully done, with none of our Covent Garden bad taste: Papageno and Papagena were not made into vulgar comic characters, but half bird, half human, creatures of fantasy. The magnificent *Meistersinger* has set me up for a long time. Ted Heath was in Vienna. A cold fish.

---

[5] Gladwyn had been appointed the Liberal member of the parliamentary delegation to the Assemblies of the Western European Union and the Council of Europe, which involved several official visits to European cities.

Whitehall Court, London, 14 October

Today I went to Hastings for the celebrations for the nine-hundredth anniversary of the Battle of Hastings. I drove in Martine [de Courcel's] car, and we had interesting talks. She is a psychologist, and is calm and shrewd. She is very Anglophile. She said that in France there are far fewer people who stammer or stutter than in England, and she thought that this was due to our upbringing and complicated views on sex. Sex is treated in France in a far more sensible and logical way. But I reminded her that our whole tradition is more romantic and less practical than the French.

Whitehall Court, London, 6 November

After going to the last night of *The Ring*, Edward [Boyle] and I went to supper with the young Paul Channons, who I find very nice. Talking of diaries, and the publication of Harold Nicolson's which has been so heavily expurgated, Paul said that he might publish his father's up till the last war. I thought it too soon, for there would be so many people alive who would be offended. For instance, what would Diana's reaction be to read that Duff only resigned in 1938 because he was about to be fired, not having been a competent minister?[6]

[6] Though this allegation does not appear in the published Channon diaries.

1967

❦

Whitehall Court, London, 20 February

A party here after ten to meet our new Leader, Jeremy Thorpe.[1] A huge crowd came and drank much champagne. Paul Hislop took Yehudi Menuhin for a Liberal candidate; David Frost kissed Violet Bonham Carter; Lord Gardiner, who looks so impressive when dressed in his Lord Chancellor's robes, came; but neither George Brown or the Prime Minister did – just as well, I thought. Jeremy won't be as good as Jo, whose wonderful looks, voice, and integrity, were a tremendous asset to the Party, especially on television. Jeremy is a bit of an actor; in fact, he would have made a marvellous actor. His imitations of Harold Macmillan, Harold Wilson, Rab, Bobbity, even Jo, are terrifyingly funny; and best of all is that of Ted Heath saying 'out of the House'. Admittedly Ted has behaved rudely to Jeremy, walking 'out of the House' when Jeremy took his place there as Liberal Leader.

Whitehall Court, London, 30 May

We lunched with Mrs Epstein from Chicago at Claridges, the fourth being that most vain of men, A L Rowse.[2] I have never heard such conceitedness as poured from his lips. Gladwyn thinks he is mad.

[1] Jeremy Thorpe (1929–   ): Leader of the Liberal Party 1967–76.
[2] A.L. Rowse (1903–   ): the popular historian.

Bramfield, Suffolk, 3 June

Diana arrived in John Julius' car. She went straight away to bed. Not because she is ill, but because she spends all her time at home in bed. If she isn't asked out, she doesn't bother to get up or to eat. She writes all her letters in pencil, sitting cross-legged in bed.

Bramfield, Suffolk, 4 June

Today we had our buffet lunch. Thirty-six and all sitting down, though they had to collect their food which consisted of smoked salmon, *chaud-froid* of chicken, cheese, strawberries and cream. Three tables in the dining-room, two in the study, two in the drawing-room, the buffet in the hall, cocktails on the lawn. The butler, recommended by the local cook, turned out to be an angry young Liberal with whom Gladwyn had exchanged disagreeable remarks in a correspondence about Mr Newby, the hopelessly bad Liberal candidate we wish to see replaced. However, this was put right with a little flattery.

Whitehall Court, London, 19 July

I went to listen to the Abortion Bill in the Lords, which our excellent young Scottish member, David Steel,[3] presented in the Commons. A crowded house, swarming with bishops and large-familied Roman Catholic peers who gave impassioned vent to their feelings about the sanctity of human life. Far the best speaker, I thought, was Lord Soper. As in the Homosexual Bill last week, he spoke excellent good sense, standing out in contrast to the awful Lord Dilhorne, who seems to me to be so prejudiced and retrograde that I feel quite angry when I see his unattractive bulky figure rise up.

[3] David Steel, later Sir David (1938–   ): Leader of the Liberal Party 1976–88.

Whitehall Court, London, 20 July

Princess Alice came to dine.[4] She is quite the prettiest old lady I have
seen, and so charming. She was telling us about Queen Victoria: how
she laughed heartily, throwing her head back and laughing till she was
blue in the face, and showing her gums and very small teeth. Her
cheeks were wonderfully soft when, as children, they kissed her.
Princess Alice said that as a young woman she had been terrified of
finding herself next to King Edward, who always let the conversation
drop after the first sentence, and then impatiently rattled his knife and
fork on his plate. So difficult was he that she even sought advice from
Mrs Keppel, who reassured her that he was always like that and she
must not mind.

Bramfield, Suffolk, 30 September

Last night I had an adventure. Edward Boyle took me to *The Three Sisters*
at the Old Vic, which was quite the most exquisite performance I have
ever seen. When we came out it was raining cats and dogs, and there
were great pools of water everywhere. It was impossible to venture out,
particularly as all we had for protection was Edward's mackintosh.
Everybody seemed stranded, hoping that it would soon abate. Finally
the doors closed, the lights went out, and the theatre crowd thinned as
the rain grew less intense. I suggested to Edward that he should walk to
Waterloo Station and get a taxi there, and come back for me. Off he
went, I waiting by the doors to be under cover, till there seemed practically no one left but myself.

Suddenly a man approached me, rough, thickset like a miner or a
docker, middle aged, rather handsome, wearing a cloth cap. He asked
me what had been going on; had there been some social gathering? I
said there had been a play. He then became abusive in a terrifying bitter
manner, and asked me if I knew that there was a gas chamber waiting
for people like us, and it was near Waterloo Station. I was quite
alarmed, for obviously he was a little drunk, but so fierce. But suddenly

[4] Princess Alice, Countess of Athlone (1883–1981): granddaughter of Queen
Victoria.

two guardian angels appeared as it were from nowhere, a young man and woman. They swiftly and silently flanked me, not saying anything, but, as guardian angels should, just smiling reassuringly. The rough man was by now pouring forth a tirade of abuse all mixed up with memories of the Black and Tans, which proved him to be an embittered Irishman, and I was the butt of it. He was positively macabre now in his gloating over what was going to happen in the gas chamber. As he tried to get close to me, the male angel firmly slipped himself between us.

At last the taxi turned the corner and out got the large form of dear Edward. Seldom have I been so glad to see him. I said to my protectors, 'Come quick, and we'll give you a lift', and we scrambled into the taxi to the bewilderment of Edward leaving the man shouting abuse on the pavement. They were an American couple from California, and I wish that, in my profuse and heartfelt thanks when we parted at the Savoy, I had said how such kindness and staunchness redeems the unpleasantness of such an occasion. 'In a better world than this I shall desire more love and knowledge of you'.

Whitehall Court, London, 7 November

To Attlee's memorial and burial service in the Abbey, a far more simple and dignified affair than the flashy service we attended the other day for Malcolm Sargent. From where I sat I could observe the PM[5] behind his lectern getting ready to read the lesson, moistening his lips and casting up his eyes. There is an inhuman quality in him, and an almost terrifying vanity. I am told that his wonderful memory is almost a disadvantage, and that people who work for him become fascinated by him rather than liking him. He has a carefully-learnt and well-produced delivery, but the effect it makes is quite unconvincing.

[5] Harold Wilson, later Lord Wilson of Rievaulx (1916–95): Prime Minister 1964–70 and 1974–6.

Bramfield, Suffolk, 19 November

A peaceful weekend spent mostly gossiping by a lovely glowing log fire, brilliantly stoked by Nancy.[6]

Nancy's day is: called at nine with breakfast; comes down about eleven and walks hard; lovely talks at meals and in between walks – tremendously lively and amusing. But the whole weekend the conversation had to be played in her key, that is to say, always making a joke about everything, however serious, or indeed poignant, the subject might be. Hilarious jokes, very witty and funny. And then moments of sadness, and moments of niceness about people, but somehow lacking real depth of feeling, yet aware that there is a feeling which comes from emotions deeper than a Mitford can know. Consequently the sadness is almost more pathetic, almost wistful. Exquisite elegance in clothes, face clean, dry, distinctly wrinkled. No scent. I would say almost spinsterish. No abandon, no sensuality, no emotion. I noticed that her eyes seemed to worry her later in the day; she would shut them, or put her hands over her face. At ten, if not before, to bed and to sleep soundly till 9 a.m. No sleeping-pills, but sound, sound sleep. Then why doesn't she look rested and refreshed?

I begin to see the disadvantages of being punctual. The anxiety of being late, which grows on me, would be eclipsed by another anxiety, that of being far earlier then necessary. This pacing about all ready, booted and spurred, long before the taxi is due to come and fetch us for the train, this waste of precious moments, all this is contrary to my nature and philosophy. Anyway, I can't change my nature now.[7]

Whitehall Court, London, 20 November

My birthday. Not my lovely midsummer birthday of 'thirty-nine', but my real birthday. Born at 6.30 (I think, or was it 7.30?) on a dark cold late

---

[6] From Bramfield Nancy wrote to Gaston Palewski: 'This is the Gladwyns' pretty house – no party so it's very restful, which I needed', and 'Everybody is on about Chip's diary – you can't think how vile & spiteful & *silly* it is.' (*Letters of Nancy Mitford*)
[7] The only occasion when Cynthia was known to have risen and dressed excessively early was in old age, staying at the Embassy in Brussels, in a room that had on the previous night been occupied by Margaret Thatcher as Prime Minister.

November morning on the outskirts of Newcastle-on-Tyne, very very delicate, looking blue – not a blue baby with some heart complaint, but blue from lack of circulation. I was so likely to die that I was quickly christened in the nursery in Trevi water, brought from Rome by Aunt Lily. My mother was not to know how delicate I was. They knew she had liked the name Angela, but they thought it sounded too much like a little angel about to go to heaven. Then they remembered, fortunately, that she also liked the name Cynthia. I didn't die, and am still here, and sometimes I wonder what I have done with this second chance in life.

Whitehall Court, London, 27 November

Just returned from a weekend at Firle; such a lovely house, and still so well run. Mogs [Gage] gives every attention to comfort. It must be something she inherited from her mother, Lady Desborough, that great Edwardian hostess. As always, Mogs produced her mother's wonderful albums, enormous bound volumes full of the names of famous people who had stayed at Taplow, their signatures written in bold confident writing with thick firm dashes under them, an effect only to be got with quill pens, surely. These splendid old florid signatures are accompanied by pasted-in photographs of the more favourite visitors. Mr Balfour, again and again; Lady D'Abernon, exquisite, imperious; her beautiful sisters; Lady Lytton (now over ninety, and her mind gone) looking too pretty and winning for words; all sorts of charming young men; the Grenfell sons; and all the names one heard so often spoken of as the *jeunesse dorée* of the pre-First War years. Lady Desborough lost all three sons, one in an accident.

On Sunday Rainald [Gage] drove me over to see Lydia Keynes.[8] She is said to be extremely odd now, and won't see people; and if she does she can become queer and nasty. She agreed to see me for twenty minutes, but we stayed longer, and she was delightful, her old self. Now seventy-six, she looks, as all ballerinas do, remarkably upright. Her face was weatherbeaten but shining with health, and she was animated and amusing. She showed me how she could still kick her leg right up in the air, and though she had one finger in a stall, she made some exquisite

---

[8] Lydia Lopokova (1892–1981), widow of Lord Keynes.

arm and hand movements for us. She is tiny, far smaller than I am. She looked just like what she was originally, a Russian peasant. She seemed to have on masses of skirts and jackets, and on her head was a fur hat round which was tied a veil with a rose in front. We talked about ballet and old times, and Vera's death. Her hall was cluttered with boots, shoes, clothes, a tremendous confusion. George [Rainald Gage] was anxious to get me away lest Lydia's good humour didn't last.

Whitehall Court, London, 1 December

I went down for the day to see the Avons in their new house. I was met at Salisbury by Clarissa looking very pretty and *gamine* with her red hair cut short like a boy, and driven in thick mist to Alvediston. We couldn't see the downs, but the house is charming; a red brick farm house, much nicer than Pewsey. Anthony was in bed with a cold. I find her a delightful intelligent companion. I had never thought the marriage would be so successful when it began, and I think its success is due to Anthony being such a physical wreck, arousing her maternal instinct. I cannot help feeling that she would have got bored with politics, with his vanity and his sycophantic young men, and having to be polite to lots of people she didn't like. She never was good at this. She told me that A is annoyed about Nicholas doing nothing. He gave him half the family trust, so he is very well off. But he is not very interesting, and his tastes are unintellectual, like those of Beatrice, though she had far more character.

Hôtel Prince de Galles, Paris, 6 December

At lunch we spoke of Madame Mendès-France who died the other day, of her sweetness and Egyptian beauty. She had eyes that seemed to go round the side of her face. Abbelin said of her, '*On a rien à lui reprocher*': of how few people can that be said. She was a sensitive artist, and told Clarissa (they were both wives of Prime Ministers at the time) that if she were to continue to paint as she would like, it would absorb her so much that she would have to leave her husband and children.

I went to a reception at the Embassy for the Western European

Union. It was in the downstairs rooms. Four French Ambassadors to England were there. Geoffroy de Courcel, Chauvel and Massigli; but the most charming of them all was the eighty-six year old Corbin, born in 1881. Not only was he so on the spot, but so beautiful with his distinguished features, wax-like complexion, and white hair. He looked like somebody from the *ancien régime*, and stood out against some very mediocre personages. That snake Sam White, from the *Evening Standard*, swarthy and sinister, was strangely amiable to me. I wonder why?[9]

Hôtel Prince de Galles, Paris, 7 December

I arranged to show Norman St John Stevas round the Embassy, but discovered that he was only really interested in Pauline Borghese's bed, of which, in fact, I wanted to get the measurements. So with a tape-measure Norman and I struggled to lift up the bed clothes to get the accurate width of the mattress. It must have presented a scene worthy of Feydaux had anybody surprised us in the act.

Whitehall Court, London, 20 December

Gladwyn, returning from Christmas shopping laden with parcels, and searching for a taxi, saw one arrive at Whites out of which got Cyril [Connolly]. So he got in and, while driving along, he saw a piece of paper on the seat. He took this to be a bill which had fallen out of one of his packages. But when he got home he saw it was addressed to Mr C Connolly, and could hardly help reading the few lines written underneath the statement: 'I supplied you with a bookcase at a low price, and am tired of trying to get you to pay. You ought to be on the black list'! Typical Cyril.[10]

---

[9] Sam White (1911–88), Paris Correspondent of the *Evening Standard*. In 1955 he had deeply offended Cynthia by publishing an article about the refurbishment of the Embassy bedrooms and bathrooms, under the headline 'Lady Jebb Bans the Bidets'; though it was his turn to be offended when he was satirized by Nancy Mitford as Angus Mockbar in *Don't Tell Alfred*.

[10] In 1928 Gladwyn and Cyril Connolly had planned to share a flat in London, but the plan was superseded by Gladwyn's engagement to Cynthia.

1968

❧

Whitehall Court, London, 29 February

I had a long talk with Geoffroy de Courcel, obviously furious over Gladwyn's continual broadsides, particularly that in the *Daily Telegraph*.[1] Gladwyn, I ventured, is rude. 'It's not his rudeness I object to', he said, 'it's because he isn't giving the truth'. 'Of course he is!' I said, 'But he has a love-hate for de Gaulle'; to which Courcel angrily replied, 'A hate-love'. And with dear Martine, such a delightful friend, with whom until recently I used to lunch together, and go to exhibitions, with Martine I see I am now on the worst of terms. All on a matter of principle. Sometimes I wonder that Courcel, with plenty of money, and not a career diplomat, does not resign. They cannot really agree in their hearts with what de Gaulle has done.

Whitehall Court, London, 13 March

Letty Benson told me of how much, as a child, she and her sisters had admired Lady Lytton (Pamela Plowden), to whom Winston had proposed marriage. She turned him down, telling him he was a 'timid mouse', which was an odd remark. Perhaps she thought that his self-confidence, which everybody found intolerable in him as a young man,

---

[1] Britain's formal application in 1967 for membership of the EEC had been effectively vetoed by President de Gaulle. During 1968 Gladwyn conducted a regular campaign against the French policy and the 'Bonapartist bombast' of de Gaulle, culminating in his book *De Gaulle's Europe, or Why the General Says No* (Secker and Warburg, 1969).

sprang from timidity. Letty remembered coming down reluctantly to make a fourteenth at a luncheon party, and her mother, the Duchess [of Rutland], coming out of the study with Winston, who was telling her of his being refused. Letty also said that old Lady Wemyss was the nicest person she ever knew. She was wonderful when Letty's husband was killed, coming to her room at Stanway in the middle of the night because she instinctively felt she needed comforting. I asked Letty about her mother-in-law's affair with Wilfrid Scawen Blunt, and she said it was indeed true, and that Mary Charteris was his daughter. It had happened in Egypt, despite it being in the middle of his great love affair with the beautiful Duchess of Leinster, Lady D'Abernon's sister.

Whitehall Court, London, 19 March

To Puffin Asquith's memorial service. A beautiful choice of music, with Menuhin playing the Bach chaconne and the passacaglia at the end. Just before it began an extraordinary diversion took place. I can best describe it as if two barrels of gin were rolling up the aisle of St Margaret's, uncertainly moving from one side to the other as they advanced between the crowded pews. They were, in fact, two human barrels: a huge Christabel Aberconway on the arm of the huge Leslie Hartley.

Whitehall Court, London, 21 March

I went on this cold wet first day of spring to Charlotte's for a lunch in honour of Martine de Courcel. As frequently happens, Charlotte [Bonham Carter] disappeared for a long time as soon as we were assembled. And, as usual, we complained of hunger between ourselves and wondered whether she had gone to another party. Eventually she returned and led us below to the dining-room, where we were made to sit on chairs arranged round the walls, while she herself dispensed ungenerous helpings of indifferent food. The Ambassadress will not easily get over being offered a meal which to her was a sort of après-ski snack, beginning with tiny cups of consommé, followed by a mousse of some sort, a meagre salad, and a gâteau.

Whitehall Court, London, 27 March

Mary Soames came to lunch armed with a huge book in which she was going to write down all the answers to her questions about the Embassy.[2] She is extremely nice: a buxom good-looking young woman of forty-seven, honest, eager to do the right thing, a good mother and wife. Her faults are to laugh and talk too much. She makes a lot of noise.

Whitehall Court, London, 14 May

Tonight to the Italian plays at the Aldwych, *Naples by Day* and *Naples by Night*, very evocative of Neapolitan life, but a little slow in places. I sat immediately behind Tony Snowdon, dressed in his white polo-neck jersey, his now auburn-coloured hair dressed in two handsome waves, the perfection of which seemed to preoccupy him very much. After the supper at the Italian Embassy, even though the crowds thinned out, Princess Margaret would not leave. She kept on approaching the door, and just as we were encouraged to think she really was about to take her departure, she suddenly went back into the centre of the room and became engaged in animated conversation – all just to tease and annoy. Diana said she remembered staying at Hatfield when Princess Margaret (then unmarried) was there; and how, after dinner, she was adamant in refusing to play or sing, until eventually a move to bed was made, at which she went and sat down at the piano till four o'clock.

Whitehall Court, London, 16 May

To Harold Nicolson's memorial service in St James's Piccadilly. It was a joint affair for him and Vita, as Vita never wanted one when she died. Neither of them had any religion, and Gerry was perfectly right to say that it should have taken place in a room. Far the best thing was John Sparrow's excellent address. Those devoted letters of Harold's which have now been published don't quite ring true. Vita was a happy

---

[2] Mary Churchill, wife of Christopher Soames, later Lord Soames (1920–87), who was about to become Ambassador to France 1968–72.

uncomplicated lesbian; Harold was a not entirely happy and very complicated homosexual. In fact Vita confided to her friends that he was asexual, a sort of Peter Pan afraid of growing up. Raymond wrote a rather sentimental obituary, but by far the best was by Alan Pryce-Jones, who said that 'there was always an imp on his shoulder'. I have always said that he was 'puckish'.

Bramfield, Suffolk, 16 June

The Menuhins arrived Friday afternoon, great preparations made here for their visit. They are strict vegetarians, so a stock of unsprayed vegetables, fruit, nuts, rose-hip tea, maté tea, honey, and a sort of porridge called muesli, was laid in.[3] He rushed off to rehearse, whispering something about Diana having been ill. Diana's trouble, obviously, is nerves. She never stops talking, is brilliantly amusing and several jumps ahead of everybody else, but completely exhausting. No wonder Yehudi practises yoga, and stands on his head, and assumes a sort of detached serenity.

They left on Saturday morning armed with a vegetarian picnic, and I went over to the Maltings[4] for the concert in which Yehudi played with his wonderful nobility. No earthiness there, which I personally feel is faintly wanting. Afterwards we went with them to Ben Britten's for drinks.[5] When the Menuhins left, Britten and Pears and several others came out on the porch to see them off; and this coincided with a most refreshing and delightful happening – the arrival of Rostropovich.[6] I have never seen such glorious Russian bear-hugging as went on, such kissing (even I got kissed); and George Malcolm – lugubrious and embittered of expression, and wearing the longest tails I have ever seen, right down to his ankles, which made him look as though he were in a funeral procession – had a little warm-hearted emotion infused into him by an abandoned embrace from Rostropovich. Altogether it was an unforgettable scene.

[3] And thenceforth became Cynthia and Gladwyn's invariable breakfast foods.
[4] The newly built concert hall used for the annual Aldeburgh Festival.
[5] Benjamin Britten, later Lord Britten (1913–76): composer.
[6] Mstislav Rostropovich, the Russian cellist, elated by his return to Aldeburgh under permission of the Soviet authorities, greeting Benjamin Britten, Peter Pears, the tenor, and George Malcolm, the accompanist.

Bramfield, Suffolk, 23 June

This was our big weekend, starting by attending K Clark's lecture on
civilization on Friday morning in the Jubilee Hall. K's lecture was, in
Gladwyn's opinion, and I agree with him, too much pandering to an
audience of sycophantic old ladies who titter delightedly at his little
jokes, and are enchanted to be flattered by that charming manner and
his subtle way of implying that they know almost as much about art as
he does. Gladwyn feels he is too distinguished a man to waste himself
on this sort of thing.

Diana, motored down by Philip Ziegler, arrived at about six, Philip's
car having broken down on the way, and he full of admiration at her lack
of annoyance at a greatly delayed journey. She arrived wearing a huge
hat and carrying another, looking astonishingly beautiful for seventy-
six. She brought with her that extraordinary little animal which she calls
Doggie, a chinchilla, more like a rat or a doe or anything but a dog;
somebody called it a 'hairless Mexican'. It went with her everywhere,
even to the concerts, concealed under her coat (which, she says, like all
her clothes, was Daisy Fellowes' and ten years old, but looked marvellous on her). I must again reiterate on Diana's amazing personality. Her
animation, her interest in everything, her energy even when plodding
round Aldeburgh in the rain, her contribution to every occasion, her
desire to make the best of everything, her unselfishness (wanting to
take the least good seat at the puppet show, taking the back seat in a car),
and her humility.

Whitehall Court, London, 24 June

To Norman St John Stevas's extraordinary party in an extraordinary
house in Hampstead on a pouring wet night. Lots of little rooms on
three or four floors, Victoriana, brass beds, oddities, a lavatory that
flushed blue water (which Mark Bonham Carter displayed to the Italian
Ambassadress), a bar in the dining-room, a Hungarian band, a lot of RC
clergy, the Bishop of Southwark, and a good many parliamentarians.
Gladwyn found it boring, so about one we left, dropping Diana on the
way. Diana discovered she had forgotten her latch-key, and hoped that if
she rang the bell, her maid, Drunken Mary, would hear. She refused to

let us get out to see she was all right, but Gladwyn surreptitiously watched her get in. I do admire the way this once-fêted beauty manages alone.

Whitehall Court, London, 27 June

Tonight to Jeremy Thorpe's wedding celebration party in Burlington House, with him in white tie and tails, which seemed to be too 'square' and out of touch. It is to be hoped that his nice wife will influence him about dress, for he likes to look like a man-about-town of the late nineteenth century – high stiff-winged Edwardian collars, chimney-pot hat, and clothes quite different to everybody else. I hear that Lord Byers has begged him to be less distinctive in dress, and not to be so flippant with his irresistible imitations. Of course, he should have been an actor. But no party in England is at present content with its leader and really, of the lot, I prefer Jeremy.

Whitehall Court, London, 2 July

Gladwyn, having always averred he admired Randolph [Churchill], and having liked him so much that he didn't attempt to come to my rescue when Randolph imagined one night at dinner that I was contradicting him and lost his temper in a terrifying way, yet Gladwyn couldn't be bothered to go to Randolph's memorial service this morning. It was, as such services go, rather nice, with sentimental hymns and Harold MacM reading 'There is a time for all things' very effectively, with the old ham actor's skill in dropping and raising his voice. But it was a bit too much having to pray for 'Thy servant Randolph, and the example he set us'!

Whitehall Court, London, 11 July

Ben [Nicolson] came to lunch after we had just been listening to a talk on Couve de Murville, now Prime Minister, in which it was alleged that his hatred of England sprung from being unmercifully teased by the

Nicolson boys when he was their tutor. Ben said that when they took him to see Knole, his only reaction was to say that they have far finer and grander houses in France.

Whitehall Court, London, 31 July

I went to Walwick. Humbo sleeps a lot, and is very dignified and calm. I had one or two wonderful talks with him about old times. He was much older than me, of course, and could remember much I didn't know about, often with great clarity. He told me how he had stayed with Neville Lytton[7] to play tennis (real tennis, of course) at Crabbet, and finding the whole family dressed in Arab costume; and how Neville adopted the French dress for tennis – a frilled shirt, silk trousers drawn in at the ankles, and shoes with a red line across them; and how he watched the ball with an almost fierce concentration.

I shan't see Humbo again, and I am glad to have got so close to him at the last, and to have sensed something of the more interesting person-age he might have been had he married somebody more stimulating, to keep him up to the mark in life.

Today I went to Hermione Cobbold's at St James's Palace to see her mother, Lady Lytton. She is about ninety-five, has hardly a wrinkle, and a beautiful neck-line. But her memory has begun to go badly; and, as I wanted to ask her about the Paris Embassy, it was not a very successful visit from that point of view.

I stayed about three quarters of an hour, and then walked home across St James's Park through the rather vulgar crowd of sightseers, tired cross parents and tired cross children sucking lollipops, all looking singularly unattractive. Then I suddenly saw approaching a beautiful smiling elderly woman, on the arm of a companion. It was none other than Clemmie Churchill. Really, she looked most handsome and young for her age. I said, 'I know where you are going, because I have just been to see Lady Lytton, who is having a little rest before you arrive'. Clemmie said how grateful Mary was for the help I had given her about the Embassy.

---

[7] Neville Lytton, 3rd Earl of Lytton (1879–1926). Cynthia's interest in the Lytton family stemmed from her study of Neville's father, Robert Bulwer-Lytton, 1st Earl of Lytton, Ambassador to France 1887–91.

Whitehall Court, London, 13 September

One of the things I enjoy about my book is all the people I meet who may give me useful information. Today I went to see Reggie Bridgeman, now in his eighties and once a bright star of the diplomatic service, for a long time in Paris under Bertie and a short while under Crewe. This interesting man was a friend of all sorts of people, such as the Comtesse de Noailles and Jean Cocteau. He married, while in Paris for the second time, a woman with Communist views, though this was not the cause of his downfall. In Persia he went to a brothel disguised as a holy man, so Curzon decided he must go. He then went to India, stirring up trouble against the Empire. He now lives in Pinner, whither I went by train from Baker Street. I was met by a distinguished old man, very thin, very well-bred and with manners and speech belonging to another age. He was so charming and intelligent that I could not help feeling that the Foreign Office had lost a brilliant diplomat despite his eccentricities.

Reggie Bridgeman told me about Bertie, who must have been an extraordinary Rabelaisian character.[8] Some of the stories about him are almost unprintable, such as when he asked a distinguished member of his staff, who wore particularly high stiff collars, 'Do you manure the tail of your shirt to make your collar grow?' Another official reminded Bertie so much of a bird, that he used to say, in the FO, that when he left the room he always expected to see a white mark on the floor.

Whitehall Court, London, 1 October

I have just returned from a weekend at the Embassy. Gladwyn had gone to Strasbourg and was to join me. I arrived on a sunny morning, and as I came into the imposing hall all formality vanished, for Mary was

[8] Francis Bertie, 1st Viscount Bertie of Thame (1844–1919): Ambassador to France 1905–18. Cynthia's chapter on him concludes: 'When asked why he, who spoke fluent French, had never perfected the accent, he replied, *"C'est pour montray que j'ai la flotte Anglayse derrière moi."*

running down the grand staircase to greet me with open arms. I was whisked into the Salon Vert, where were the charming nineteen-year old daughter Emma, a nanny (no house is complete without one) and two dogs, and then, just what was needed, a bottle of champagne was opened. It was a wonderful warm welcome on my returning to the old house, and the whole place seemed sunny and happy, with everybody anxious to please and make a success.

The next morning Mary and I put on overalls and went over the whole house — cellars, attics, everywhere. We found glorious Empire furniture stored with common office desks, and chairs piled on top; rolls of carpet and silk lying on the floor covered with dust from the installation of the new central heating. The chaos was appalling. Quite exhausted, we all forgathered in the Salon Vert before lunch, and the Soameses had the kindness to invite Phyllis Bontoft, the head telephone operator, who was moved to tears at this honour, particularly as she had suffered ever since we left. After lunch we motored to Versailles and took a brief walk in the woods between showers. Christopher, a highly-strung man despite his obesity and jolly manner, was very upset by the delays of traffic. Both he and Mary are most anxious for all to go well, but I sense an underlying nervousness in him which I hope will not prevent them from really enjoying themselves.

Whitehall Court, London, 8 October

After lunch the skies seemed to come down and it became pitch black. The doorbell rang, and I shouted 'Who is it?' An indistinct voice answered and the bell was angrily rung again, so I shouted, 'I won't open unless you say who you are. You might be a thug with a stocking over your face!' The voice then said he was the Big Bad Wolf, thundering on the door the while with fury. Then a note was thrust through the letter-box and I at once recognized the handwriting and opened the door. There stood Gerry, looking like a drowned rat in his cheap thin green mackintosh from which the water was dripping on to the floor forming a pool, with another pool from his umbrella. 'It's you', I said; 'Well, come in'. To which he made the memorable reply, 'Well, I'll come in, but I won't take my clothes off'. A most egregious remark, I told him, for a gentleman to make when calling on a lady alone in her flat in the middle of the afternoon. He had come to invite me to lunch next day, and discuss our trip to Ireland for the Wexford Festival.

Whitehall Court, London, 28 October

This afternoon I got back from a happy but exhausting six days in Ireland. Our return journey from Wexford to Dublin was a worthy climax to all the fun and music, for our car load consisted of Gerry, Diana, John Julius and me (Gladwyn having left at about 6 a.m. with two musicians and a music critic), and we sang all the way. It was nearly a hundred miles, and we enjoyed ourselves so uproariously that the long somewhat tiring drive passed in a flash. We sang arias from favourite operas, and German and French songs. John Julius sat between Diana and me and conducted us. 'There's a good one coming up', Diana said: it was the '*Konig von Thulle*'. Gerry excelled at '*Die Rose*', '*Die Lili*', '*Die Taube*', etc. There was hardly a song left unsung. As we drove through Dublin, Gerry became embarrassed by all the noise we were making. He turned pompous, showed all his double chins, said we must stop; and then, suddenly remembering something particularly good from the *Geisha Girl*, which even Diana and I didn't know, started off again. When we reached the airport we were quite sad as we were about to do *Lucia di Lammermoor*. Gerry, sometimes irrepressible, can be touchy. He was cross by the time we reached Heathrow, and wrote to apologize.

Boston, Massachusetts, 2 November

Miles and I left for Boston this morning, the object of the trip being to see Stella. We were met in brilliant sunshine by Stella and Joel and the two little girls, and drove to their delightful house. It is built by Lutyens, and is something like a miniature Bramfield. The interior decoration produced a childhood nostalgia for me, for the panelling and paintwork were dark, and the kind of detail and carving very like what I remembered at Jesmond and other places. In the evenings when the fire was burning and the lamps lit, it looked so cosy and gave a feeling of pre-First War security.

It was delightful to see the children running about this roomy house instead of all on top of each other in the flat in which I last saw them.[9] Stella has made it so pretty: everything in my room was pink, even a pink paper rose above my bed. Cecilia (aged five) said, 'I know what Grandmama's favourite colour is. It's pink'. Whereupon Miles said, 'No, it's black and white', for my great fault in the eyes of the family is never to see anything grey. Stella was a wonderful hostess, and entertains in a most civilized and successful way, with a French cook got in to do the food. She has such charming friends too, American and French, and the French in particular were extremely intelligent and handsome young men, very healthy-looking and manly compared to the old type of young Frenchmen. The charming son of the Yturbes was evidently an habitué of the house. Then there was the son of the Rougemonts, who looks extraordinarily like a tall healthy Napoleon, being descended from Caroline Murat. Obviously Stella is tremendously popular.

Whitehall Court, London, 25 November

I lunched alone with Martine at the Embassy. Sensible and balanced woman though she is, she is more like a French peasant on two subjects: the Belgians ('*il est Belge*' defines everything that one might criticize about that country); and the French Protestants (HSP means *Haute Société Protestante*, and she feels about them something like what I feel about the British Roman Catholics).

Whitehall Court, London, 27 November

Mary Links came to lunch today to give me some help on my bit on Lytton. She told me an extraordinary thing about her mother, Lady Emily Lutyens and the old clergyman, Elwin, who called her the

---

[9] Stella's three children are Tatiana (b. 1961), Cecilia (b. 1963), and Alexis (b. 1967).

Blessed Girl. About three months before Lady E died, and when she was perfectly clear mentally, she told Mary that Elwin sometimes made her lie down on the floor and he lay on top of her! I said to Mary, 'I can't make use of that!', but I record it here in my diary.[10]

---

[10] In *A Blessed Girl*, Lady Emily Lytton, wife of Sir Edwin Lutyens, published some of the almost daily letters written between herself, when aged from thirteen to twenty-three, and her father's married friend Whitwell Elwin (1824–1900), parson and squire of Booton, near Norwich, fifty-eight years her senior. In Cynthia's words, 'From the bleakness of Norfolk the eccentric old priest had kindled a flame in the girl's heart which must have warmed the cockles of his own'.

1969

❧

Bramfield, Suffolk, 1 January

Saw the New Year in this morning in the traditional Noble fashion. A very small party consisting of Vanessa and myself, and James Murray,[1] who really is, as we sing, 'the friend we can trust'. For he came all the way down from London, arriving at Darsham at 6.52, and having to walk from the church porch (where we had left a torch) because of the snow and ice, changed into a dinner jacket, and we had a lovely candle-lit evening with a roaring log fire in the drawing-room, and sang the old songs, 'There's a Sound of Joy and Singing' and 'Here's to the Year that's Awa''. Having been ill I didn't go out to burn the calendar, but we mulled some claret and drank healths. Then James had to go back to the Foreign Office because of trouble about an official in Peking, and left the house at twenty to eight in the black morning, having swallowed his thermos-full of coffee, torch-lit himself again to the church porch where Smith was waiting to take him to the 8.01 a.m. train.

Bramfield, Suffolk, 4 January

I see that Mogs Gage has died, which makes me very sad. Gladwyn, composing a letter to poor George, asked me how the Rossetti quota-

---

[1] James Murray, later Sir James (1919–): Head of the Foreign Office Far Eastern Department, and subsequently Ambassador to the United Nations agencies in Geneva.

tion went, 'Better you should forget and smile, Than that you should remember and be sad': but I told him he really could not quote this directly after somebody had died.

Annapurna Hotel, Khatmandu, 11 February[2]

This is a wonderful country. One really feels on top of the world, the air pure and thin and invigorating, the people dignified and active. Their way of life appears to be entirely natural. But however much one admires the absence of stresses and strains and unnatural habits, the poverty and dirt are dreadful. There is much consumption, infant mortality and goitre, and quite a lot of lepers. Khatmandu is much like what many English towns would have been in medieval times, with narrow streets with projecting upper storeys. Everybody says that in about five years much of the old part of Khatmandu will be swept away.

We went to see the Kumari goddess, a young girl who has to be physically perfect and able to face calmly the horrible ordeal of divinity: she has to spend a whole night in a pitch dark room surrounded by six decapitated buffaloes' heads. When she is twelve she rides round the town in a hugh high coach. We called for her to appear, which she did at a second floor window. She was beautifully dressed in rich pink stuff, and her eyes were heavily made up. She behaved just like a goddess should, standing calm, aloof, expressionless, inscrutable. This is how kings and queens of old must have looked, supremely conscious of their divine right, without any of that bowing and smiling that modern royalty affects.

Bramfield, Suffolk, 23 February

Gladwyn and I got back here last night after three days in Paris for the Western European Union meetings. While we were there the Soames affair burst on the world, in a paragraph or two inserted in an article on WEU in the *Figaro*. It disclosed that Christopher had misinterpreted his

---

[2] On a visit to India and Nepal with Miles and Vanessa.

talk with the General on 4 February.[3] I hadn't seen the passage until I happened to talk to Nancy on the telephone after breakfast, when she left fly at the 'horrible British' with such venom that I expostulated 'No, no, Nancy', whereupon she put down the receiver, which made me feel guilty because she was suffering from sciatica and in great pain.

For the rest of our visit rumours were rampant about what actually happened after Christopher's talk with the General, and I suppose we shall learn something of the truth when the subject is debated in the House of Commons. I was at first inclined to think that Christopher had been at fault by wanting to bring off a coup in order to make a splash and achieve something important at last. When he was here last summer, Gladwyn and Michael Palliser tried to drum into him that he must not expect a change of heart in de Gaulle, and that all that could be done was to wait for his decline or departure. But when Christopher, an ambitious politician, got to Paris, he was determined to have a success to his credit. Pat Hancock told G the other day that C expected to deal directly with the Foreign Secretary and Prime Minister instead of going through the usual channels at the FO, and that he, Pat Hancock, had to go over to Paris to tell him he could not do this.

G says that all the points that Christopher reported were really things that the General has always said. He cannot see how Christopher can stay on in Paris under the circumstances, as obviously the General will not see him again. But Gaston, with whom I managed to have a word about this Franco-British storm, said 'Wilson has behaved abominably'; so the wrath is vented more on Wilson than Soames.

Whitehall Court, London, 25 February

G says now: If he had been Soames he would not have sought an interview with the General, but would have waited till the latter made the initiative. In any case, when the General began to air his views, the right thing to do would have been to ascertain whether such propositions

---

[3] On 4 February de Gaulle allegedly told Christopher Soames that the major European powers should manipulate the smaller ones. The British government decided to report this to all the European Community members, and, when news of it broke, to reveal the details to the press. A major diplomatic breach with France ensued.

were serious, and, if so, to demand the presence of somebody to make
notes.

Bramfield, Suffolk, 1 March

Still apropos of Soames, Diana, just back from Paris, says that de Gaulle
has spoken of Christopher as *'ce pauvre Soames'*, which implies that he
exonerates him. Driving down last night, Gladwyn maintained that
Wilson was right to tell the allies, and that no honourable government
could do otherwise. But G also said he would not be surprised if
Christopher does resign. He is such a hero of the Tories, having been let
down by Wilson, that 'they would shoot somebody to get a vacant constituency for him'. If Christopher got back into politics now, he would
be in the Shadow Cabinet and in running for Secretary of State.

Whitehall Court, London, 1 April

Today we entered a world so completely different to anywhere else that
it was like an excursion into dreamland, nostalgic and unreal. The
moment we drove into the courtyard of Buckingham Palace the ordinary life of London, the bursting crowds, the harassed faces, the bus
queues in the cold wind, the dearth of taxis in the rain, all seemed extraordinarily remote. Smiling courtiers, Masters of the Household, eager
equerries, charming ladies-in-waiting, all contributed to make the guests
feel at ease in the grand setting. Upstairs in a beautiful room, the Music
Room, overlooking the garden, we all gathered and were given drinks.
We were altogether thirty-one for luncheon. Then in came the Queen,
very pretty and smiling; the Duke of Edinburgh, handsome and smiling
but with a hardness which cannot be concealed; the charming Prince of
Wales with his desire to please, his tentative interest in everybody, his
wild-rose colouring like his grandmother, his sensitivity contrasting
with his father's lack of it; and finally Princess Anne, a thoroughly nice,
almost handsome, English country girl, healthy and sensible and with
no complications. It was tempting to wonder how these four human
beings sort themselves out in private life.

The guests of honour were from Nigeria, the women beautiful in white gauze embroidered with gold, the men equally spectacular, one of them wearing a yashmak, which caused great curiosity as to how he was going to eat: he lowered it to his chin. I sat next to Prince Philip. He is well-informed, very Germanic, very active.

Whitehall Court, London, 28 April

De Gaulle has been defeated. That is the great news; and not having written in my diary for some time, I must quickly resume it to record this. Gladwyn says they've killed his fox. I really wonder what he will do, for the President and his policy have been a godsend to G in retirement, a tremendous challenge which is just what he needs in life. This morning at 7.15 he was (over the telephone) put on the air in Jack de Manio's 'Today' and was very good. And tonight, up in Newcastle for a lecture at the University, he was hoiked out of his dinner to do a television interview hooked up with Schmidt in Bonn and Con O'Neill in London, and was very effective.

Hôtel Bristol, Paris, 28 June

This was the day of the great Paris Embassy ball, which has caused such excitement. All sorts of people went over from England, and tried to get their friends invited. The Embassy was transformed, with apricot-coloured tarlatan draperies ornamented with gold paper bay leaves curtaining the galleries, a dance floor between the two wings with a raised stage for the band at the garden end, surmounted by more apricot festooning. The garden was all floodlit, all the steps were covered with felt and scattered with cushions with gold paper bees on them, so that people could sit anywhere. Buffets in the ball-room and dining-room, supper tables in the galleries, tremendously elaborate floral arrangements everywhere. No expense spared. It was all marvellous, but the house and contents are so beautiful in themselves that I don't think they needed embellishing with decorations such as this. Princesses Anne and Alexandra were staying in the house. Gladwyn had a long walk with Edgar Faure.[4]

---

[4] Edgar Faure (b. 1908): French Prime Minister 1955–6.

Plas Newydd, Anglesey, 29 June

Reached London early afternoon, got an hour of blissful sleep, then repacked for Wales, travelling on the sleeper from Euston.[5] The Templers were on the train.[6] She is obviously a good army wife, but an unworthy companion for such a splendid hero. She is like a twittering bird, making tiresome remarks the whole time and then looking round quickly from side to side to observe the result. We were met at Holyhead and drove to Plas Newydd where, after an excellent breakfast, I had a bath and changed and began to feel rather less exhausted.

Everybody here is apprehensive about bomb scares and manifestations. The Duke of Norfolk came to drinks before luncheon. We hear that the Earl Marshal and the Constable of Caernarvon Castle hate each other;[7] the former is the most excellent and efficient organizer of ceremonial, and the latter is only concerned with television publicity. In the afternoon the men went to rehearse while we drove around, and then went to a cocktail party given by the Household Cavalry at Vaynol, where Lady Templer was in her element. Back for late dinner; Henry [Anglesey], the Field Marshal, Gladwyn and Lord Plymouth quite exhausted by the rehearsals. Templer told us that the Duke of Norfolk and Snowdon are by now on such bad terms that it is no longer a question of them not speaking to each other, they cannot even bear to look at each other.

Plas Newydd, Anglesey, 1 July

We left for Caernarvon at 11.15 sharp, drove to the car park where we women picnicked, the men having been dropped in the town. I found myself extremely well placed in the third row behind the Cabinet. The only disadvantage was that we got the full sun whenever it came out, and we had been particularly requested not to wear shady hats or to

[5] To stay with Lord and Lady Anglesey for the Investiture of the Prince of Wales at Caernarvon Castle, at which Gladwyn was to represent the Liberal Peers.
[6] Field Marshal Sir Gerald Templer (1898–1979), married to Ethel Davie.
[7] Bernard Fitzalan-Howard, 16th Duke of Norfolk (1908–75), Earl Marshal of England; and Antony Armstrong-Jones, 1st Earl of Snowdon (1930–), Constable of Caernarvon Castle.

bring umbrellas. The Queen and Queen Mother were the only ones allowed to carry parasols. Thus when towards the end of the ceremony it started to rain, there was a great rustle of plastic macs and hoods.

The processions were wonderful, and the array of diplomats opposite me must have been amazed at the fancy dress of some of those partaking. The Druids would have looked far better had not their garments been made of nylon. Gladwyn, in the procession of peers, looked particularly distinguished, with hair rather longer than usual; and Maurice Aberdare, tall, dark-complexioned and grey-haired, was splendid – in a long black cloak with a silver emblem on one side – as a Prior of St John of Malta, though looking like the Prince of Darkness. The Constable of the Castle wore a self-designed uniform of bottle green, which would have been very suitable for a commissionaire. His complexion was bronzed (I fancy it was made up for television) and he was darting here there and everywhere.

Finally there came the Queen, Prince Philip, and the young Prince, who won everybody's heart with his charm and diffidence and perfect behaviour. Henry Anglesey, who carried the Sword of State, told us of the very human incidents which he observed just as the procession was forming, the sort of thing that might happen to anybody. Firstly the Queen complained that a pin was sticking into her, and this had to be removed from her new dress. Then she and the Duke of Edinburgh had a marital quarrel. Probably unnerved by fear of something dreadful happening, she agitatedly remarked that she hoped the text of what she had to say would be on her seat; and Prince Philip (probably cross because he was not in the lime-light) answered rudely that he had no idea, and that it was her show not his. After a little bickering they started off. The tense look on the Queen's face may partially have been explained by her going down with flu the following day.

Whitehall Court, London, 16 July

Lunched with Ralph Dutton. The form never varies. I am invited at about a quarter to one to his flat. I am invariably late because I start late, and then the taxi never remembers whether 95 Eaton Square is on an eastbound or a westbound one-way street. In the flat, full of choice objects, we have double martinis, and then go to the Coq d'Or and have an excellent lunch of fish and white wine. After which we go to look at the pictures in Sotheby's or Christie's, or to an antique shop where he often buys something at a high price. He has nobody but himself to consider, and his Hampshire house and its contents constitute the pleasure of his life. Much of the house was destroyed in a dreadful fire some years ago, but he rebuilt it even more to his liking and has had all the fun of buying more beautiful pictures and furniture.

Whitehall Court, London, October

In the latter part of July I began to feel horribly tired, with aches and pains everywhere and appalling headaches. I then became terribly ill with a high temperature; for about three days I couldn't eat, and then I went yellow. After blood tests this was diagnosed as hepatitis. I was in bed for about ten days, and then my temperature went down and I started getting up. The virus had been eliminated entirely by diet, no drugs at all. The disagreeable part of this recovery is that I am not allowed any alcohol whatsoever for six months, and am still on exceedingly plain food. G goes about telling people that I am 'on the waggon', giving the impression that I have been forced to join Alcoholics Anonymous. The distinguished-looking elderly porter at Whitehall Court came up to me and confided that he had also had to give it up. When I asked him if it was liver trouble he said 'Oh no; I was a whisky-bottle a day man, and lost two businesses.'

1970

❧

Bramfield, Suffolk, 17 January

I went this afternoon to Heveningham for the last time before it is either
bought by the government or pulled down. It was echoing and deserted,
and seemed very melancholy on this bleak January day. I wondered what
Sir Gerard Vanneck, who built the house, would have thought had he
seen Britta and me in the servantless house making tea in the kitchen, the
family about to abandon the place and go to live in Australia.[1]

Whitehall Court, London, 22 January

I went to a huge party at the Dorchester for Schumann's visit, to what
looked like an excellent meal, though I could not partake as I am still on
a diet. I sat between Eric Bessborough and Jeremy Thorpe. I am afraid I
do not think much of our leader. His buffooning becomes a bore, and
when he is serious he is horribly gloomy. Then he is always boasting of
some wonderful coup he is about to bring off. Tonight it was that he had
found a millionaire who he believed would pay off the Liberal Party
debt. It was practically in the bag and we would know in two days. But
Gladwyn says he has been talking of this for years. His next idea was to
get Forte to buy Heveningham and turn it into a Georgian centre, and
everybody would go there and see what Georgian life was like. He got
very excited about this, but I purposely discouraged him, as it seemed
just one of his wild ideas.

---

[1] It was purchased by the Government and then resold to private ownership in 1982.

Whitehall Court, London, 5 February

Lunched *à quatre* with K Clark at the Albany. Jane was in the country allegedly nursing a sick dog. Very good lunch served by K, that most practical and well-organized of men, and excellent talk, a feature of his entertaining of which our host is extremely conscious. It would be even better if it were all spontaneous, and one didn't feel that praise was expected. I have never been entirely at ease with this strange brilliant personality.

Whitehall Court, London, 17 February

I lunched with Jeremy Thorpe at his flat in Ashley Gardens. Our leader is certainly the strangest of the party leaders, and I sometimes wish we had our handsome Jo Grimond back, with his magnificent presence and resonant voice. Of course the great sum of money which was 'practically in the bag' has failed to materialize. From being something like £150,000 it is now reduced to £10,000, if it materializes at all.

At this luncheon Jeremy and I were involved in a little incident which was for a moment embarrassing. He has an annoying habit of telling me rather silly little anecdotes slightly against Gladwyn, which are not even funny and turn out to be untrue. I suspect he does not really like G, and is envious of his indifference to what people think of him, as J is over-anxious to please, being hypersensitive about the impression he makes. So when today he again began telling some footling story about what G had done or said – a story which ridiculed G while, at the same time, he was assuring me how devoted he was to G, how tremendously he admired him, and then, in another volte face, slid in that Caroline (his wife) never could make out whether G recognized her or not – I really felt he must be stopped. So I interrupted with 'Really, Jeremy, there's no point in all this you are telling me. It's not true, not funny, annoying for me, and altogether a waste of breath. I expect the Leader of the Liberal Party to behave as such, and to be a person with whom I can have a serious interesting conversation'. He at once became particularly contrite, and was frightfully anxious to put things right, showed me everything in the flat, insisted on taking me home (though somebody else had offered to do so), was most effusive in praise of Gladwyn, repeating how greatly he admired him, and on the drive back to Whitehall Court did his best imitations of Violet Asquith [Bonham Carter] which he knows I always laugh at. That same evening a letter arrived at the flat, in a curiously large handwriting for a man, full of abject apologies. I fear that his nice practical wife, who has given him the much-desired son, is not a clever woman and does not help him much with his inferiority complex.

Whitehall Court, London, 25 February

Today was Gladwyn's motion in the Lords on the changes in the BBC's radio programmes, particularly in the Third Programme, which I urged him to table and so felt very responsible about the success of the debate. It went very well, there were seventeen speakers, G spoke very well, so I felt gratified. What a strange man Lord Annan is. Anxious to keep in with the government, he rose to his feet to state that he wondered why the BBC had bothered to announce the changes, since had they not done so they might have got away with it; a most deplorable argument, as orchestras might have been disbanded without anyone knowing. I could see the jaw of that philistine and uninspiring figure, Lord Hill, who had been responsible for it all, drop in astonishment.

Whitehall Court, London, 3 May

To the Menuhins' box at the Albert Hall for Yehudi's Beethoven concert, and afterwards to sup with them at a Chinese restaurant in Knightsbridge. I didn't really like all those endless courses. There seemed no reason why the meal should ever come to an end. It was like Indian music. At his Memorial Concert for Gandhi, also at the Albert Hall, Yehudi had dressed in a white shirt and sort of white jodhpurs, and sat on the floor with Indians performing a piece which was only brought to a finish by the audience finally taking the initiative and bursting into applause.[2]

---

[2] At a concert held in memory of Cynthia in St John's Smith Square in February 1991, Yehudi Menuhin played the adagio and fugue from Bach's solo violin concerto in G minor, preceding it with a spoken tribute to Cynthia.

Hôtel Prince de Galles, Paris, 4 June

We came here at the weekend and I went to see Nancy, who is in better form than when I last saw her but continually in pain.[3] This shows in her face. Her garden looks too pretty for words at this time of the year. Rather than have a commonplace lawn she has a hayfield profusely sown with marguerites and poppies and here and there peonies, and the effect is enchanting, like a Renoir.

On Tuesday night I dined with Aymone de Brantes and we went to a concert at old Princesse de Polignac's house. It was nice, on a lovely Paris June night, to be going there to hear music as I had done over forty years ago. Blanchie first took me there; and I remember going once with Poulenc after the opera and arriving late in the Sert room, which now I did not find so beautiful, and I remember being rather alarmed by the very musical but masculine Princesse de P, whose reputation was that of a sadistic lesbian.

Whitehall Court, London, 18 June

At the *Daily Telegraph* election party at the Savoy it was almost at once evident that, contrary to expectations, the Tories were going to do well.[4] Wilson had over-reached himself, and his supporters either thought that victory was in the bag, or else they began to take seriously Ted's warnings about the country's economy. It was a melancholy day for the Liberals. Eric Lubbock defeated at Orpington; Laura Grimond defeated by that nit-wit Mad Mitch whose only reason for standing is to save the Argyll and Sutherland Highlanders; so altogether the Liberal seats were reduced to six. Yet it must always be remembered that we got two and a quarter million votes, and if we had proportional representation we would have got forty-five seats. At about midnight we moved on to the *Daily Mirror* party and then to the BBC and then back again to the Savoy.

[3] Nancy Mitford had by now moved from Paris to Versailles, and was to die in 1973. During her last three years of illness Cynthia visited her several times and exchanged frequent letters; and she wrote a major obituary of Nancy in the *Sunday Times*.
[4] The Conservatives obtained an overall majority of 31 seats.

Bramfield, Suffolk, 28 June

We stayed with the Edwards Fords in their pretty house near Rugby, where we had gone for the Birkenhead wedding.[5] Staying also for the first night of the weekend were Rab and Mollie. Rab has to be seen to be believed: huge, shapeless, *mal soigné*, brooding on whether, had he refused to serve under Alec, he might not now be Prime Minister. The Harrods came for a drink, Billa as cosy and warm-hearted as ever, Roy much aged. I asked him what he now felt about the population, since a few years ago he told me that we needed more people in England. He now admits that this island is too full and is all for sending lots of babies to Canada! I said he was like Herod, and G said, 'Yes, Roy Herod'.

Grand Spa Hotel, Bristol, 4 July

How I wish Mother had been alive to join us all in a wonderful expedition to see the *Great Britain* towed up the Avon.[6] Alas, a high wind prevented this tonight, but it was even better this way because, after the Lord Mayor's cocktail party, we went in buses to the dock where she lay and could see her far better and even go on board. A high ladder, roped at a slight angle, was the only method of doing this. After much persuasion on my part, I was allowed to climb it, for which purpose I donned G's mackintosh. It was quite a perilous climb in the drizzling rain with water being pumped from the side of the ship just near the ladder, distracting one's concentration, and quite a gap between the quay and the ship, and G's mac was too long on me and the ship was high above me. But I did it. It was well worth the climb. Being inside the great hulk, with its huge ribs surrounding us, was rather like what one imagines Jonah saw inside the whale. Coming down that wobbly ladder was even more alarming than going up it.

---

[5] Sir Edward Ford (1910–), married to Virginia Brand: formerly Assistant Private Secretary to the Queen.
[6] Brunel's steamship, the *Great Britain*, having been recovered from a beach in the Falkland Islands, and towed up the Atlantic on a pontoon, was to be reinserted into its original dry-dock at Bristol.

Whitehall Court, London, 7 July

I dined quietly with Gay and Martin Charteris at St James's Palace in the rooms Princess Mary [Princess Royal] used to have.[7] They are not allowed to use the garden when the Queen Mother is at Clarence House: apparently she gives luncheon parties in the warm weather under the trees. The object of my visit was to ask Lettie Benson questions about the Embassy, but she couldn't tell me much. However she was a mine of information on other subjects. She is very deaf and speaks non-stop like deaf people often do, in case they lose the thread of the conversation. She said it was perfectly true that Diana was ugly as a child. She also had a little excrescence on her nose, which was later removed; and a curious bump on her forehead, now disappeared, which made her believe she was a unicorn. Their mother the Duchess was so heartbroken when her eldest son died suddenly, that she couldn't face life. Her reason and health were only saved by sculpting a reclining figure of the boy.

Whitehall Court, London, 7 October

We went to France again last Friday to go to Jacqueline de Caraman-Chimay's shoot.[8] The guest of honour was the Prince of Wales. At dinner we were at three tables and Mary Soames was at mine. She makes a tremendous din. Very jolly and kind-hearted, but with all the brashness which, so I have always heard, was characteristic of the home life of the Churchills. Words like bloody and bugger-off were bandied about loudly, and so excited did she get that at one moment her son Nicholas (who promises to have the same dimensions as his father, and is an equerry to the Prince) came over from his table to tick her off and beg her to be quiet.

Next morning we sat down to an enormous breakfast – the French custom, and rather a good one, for it gives an uninterrupted day of shoot-

[7] Sir Martin Charteris, later Lord Charteris of Amisfield (1913–   ), married to Gay Margesson: Assistant Private Secretary (and later Private Secretary) to the Queen, and subsequently Provost of Eton College.
[8] Jacqueline Hennessy, widow of Prince Jean de Caraman-Chimay.

ing. I so seldom go to shoots that I did not want to embark on an expensive outfit; but I had found olive-green boots at Peter Jones, and wore green trousers, my loden coat, and a wonderful green waterproof cap with a peak and earpieces, known as a Devonshire because invented by Debo.

The Prince is charming. Eager to do the right thing, intelligent, artistic and musical by nature. Altogether he has a truly benevolent and sensitive personality; and, anyway, one would not wish him to be too clever or opinionated or original. He has most considerate manners and is easy to talk to. In fact, his whole behaviour is modest and impeccable. Also he has quite a sense of humour and treated me to one or two imitations, done without malice, including one of Annenberg which was very funny. This was apropos of Jeremy Thorpe's imitations of Rab, which the Prince longs to hear.

Whitehall Court, London, 13 October

With Angus Menzies to *Trovatore*, which I would have enjoyed more had I more fully recovered from my cold. Angus is so nice, and certainly has a tremendous knowledge of music, though he lacks animation, which did not help my condition. We went for supper to Peter Coats where also was David Carritt. These are two giggly gossipy homosexuals, full of little jokes and *double entendres* and bright remarks. I am not sure how much I like Carritt, a man of exquisite taste and great knowledge, but extremely conceited.

Whitehall Court, London, 14 October

After lunching at Diana Spearman's I could not resist looking into the house almost next door at the corner of Queen Anne's Gate, which used to be the Glenconners' London house and is now a Conservative club. It was there that Ava used to live, having told Lady Glenconner that her eldest son, Bim, who had been killed in the War, had been an intimate friend of hers – this is believed to be a great exaggeration on Ava's part. The bereaved mother warmly welcomed her, and from this house Ava was able to lay the foundations of her remarkable career, and get her foot into a world she had hitherto not entered.

Whitehall Court, London, 28 October

This evening I read my paper on the Brunels and, thank goodness, it went down very well indeed to great applause.[9] About two hundred and fifty people there, among them members of all the families concerned: descendants of IKB, of Marc Isambard Brunel, of the Horsleys, of the Jameses. Also Lord Spencer, whose ancestor had been a patron to Marc Isambard; Alan Boyd, a Brunel admirer; and the head of the British Rail Western Region. Mar came and was most amiable, and Nessa brought Inigo and Isambard.[10] Everybody seemed to like the lecture, and it is to be printed. How I wish Mother could have heard it!

Hôtel d'Iena, Paris, 16 November

Last night we went to Stella's where there was a charming party for us. Joel, with his brilliant mind for bio-chemistry, is very stimulating to meet at a time when the world we live in seems full of depressing news. He holds out such exciting promise of all that could be done to circumvent much of the trouble. It is so nice to meet people like him and his friends who are interested in ideas and not in money. I was greatly impressed by them all.

British Embassy, Rome, 26 November

We arrived here in time for lunch. Pat Hancock is now Ambassador, and he and his wife give an excellent impression as a tall distinguished-looking English pair who represent their country admirably.[11] We dined the first night with the Minister, and I sat next to Barzini, who wrote that excellent book on the Italians. He told me that if the government refused the right to divorce, there would be a revolution. The Quaronis were there, he looking old. I said to Barzini how changed I found him,

---

[9] Cynthia's paper, *The Isambard Brunels*, was delivered to a joint meeting of the Institute of Civil Engineers and the British section of the Société des Ingénieurs Civils de France.

[10] Vanessa's children are Inigo (b. 1962), Isambard (b. 1964), and Isabella (b. 1966).

[11] Sir Patrick Hancock (1914–80), married to Beatrice Mangeot.

and then there followed a conversation typical of Roman society. Barzini shouted across the table to the lady opposite me, who was actually sitting next to Quaroni, he engaged in conversation with our hostess at the head of the table. Did she not agree with me?, he asked; and added that Quaroni had new false teeth which altered his face. To which she said 'He always puts his tongue out' (a curious habit of Quaroni's); and Barzini retorted that this was to keep his false teeth up! I was terrified lest the object of these flippant remarks should overhear. Roman malice is unequalled.

British Embassy, Rome, 28 November

We lunched with the Schwarzenbergs in their charming apartment with its delightful view of domes from the terrace. We had, as always with them, an intelligent and interesting conversation, and talked much of old days when we were all here together in the early 1930s. They questioned me about Martine de Courcel, having obviously been a little hurt by the way she and Geoffroy had behaved to them. When the Courcels first arrived in London the Schwarzenbergs had given them introductions, but had then been dropped by them.

I am certainly puzzled by Martine, who is sometimes so affectionate and friendly, and then suddenly does this sort of thing. She was very off-hand with Gladwyn the other day at Joel's lecture in London, for no apparent reason. And recently in Luxembourg, when Gladwyn asked a perfectly inoffensive question, which nobody regarded as egregious, as to whether the French Government would divulge the recent talks that had taken place in Russia, Geoffroy went up to him in a state of fury, as red as a turkey cock, and said he had understood that G had not approved of de Gaulle's policy, but now he was criticizing Pompidou. G wrote explaining that the question was perfectly in order, to which Geoffroy replied implying that it was Gladwyn who had got angry and emotional.

British Embassy, Rome, 29 November

At dinner at the Caccia [Club] we saw a number of old friends. Everybody wants my diet, for they find me looking so well. Aubrey Casardi said I must have sold my soul to the devil, and Paolo Miscientelli said that my face had not changed since he knew me in the 1920s and 30s. I wish I could believe this, but it was fun to have such a success at my age, only a week after my horrible birthday.

Whitehall Court, London, 8 December

I took Ben Nicolson to *The Knot Garden*, the new Tippett opera. Try as I would, I did not enjoy it, and I have to admit that I only really like romantic music. Ben is extraordinarily vague but charming. He talked, as he often does, about his parents. He adored his father but was never very close to his mother. She was an avowed lesbian long before she married. She used to walk about London dressed as a man, which she discovered early in life is what she should have been. Ben kept on repeating that Harold was the kindest man in the world, but agreed with me that he had an imp in him, and that he enjoyed apologizing to an absurd degree, saying 'If I go down on my knees, will you forgive me?', and other such expressions of contrition.

1971

Deloraine, Kenya, 22 January[1]

This is the amazing house of a most remarkable woman, Pam Scott, whose father, Lord Francis Scott, had been a tremendous figure in Kenya. Pam lives alone here with her retainers, and runs the farm and school and leads an active life. The house is large, with huge rooms and a wide covered balcony running the full length on both floors. It overlooks the beautifully kept garden, with masses of brilliant bougainvillaea on green lawns, sloping down to a wonderful view of the plain and the distant hills.

After baths we went down to a magnificent drawing-room with a Broadwood piano completely out of order, comfortable furniture, and log fire burning. Everything was on a generous scale, including our hostess's figure, which was now clothed in an Algerian linen garment. Above her enormously fat body, the hefty arms of which were sunburnt the colour and texture of old leather, was her very handsome face, its skin preserved with face creams. She has a tremendous personality, splendidly direct and with a great sense of humour. We sat down at a table in front of the fire, with everything done in great style – shining silver, candles, all very smart – when suddenly she shouted 'Chikoula!', which means food, and the retainer rushed in with it. Thus would hosts in ancient times have shouted, for food or wine or music or dancing-girls.

[1] On a visit to Kenya with Miles and Stella.

Bramfield, Suffolk, 13 February

Last weekend I was most horribly ill. On the Friday I had my second cholera injection, on returning from Kenya, and came down here with Gladwyn. A blood test proved that it was gastro-enteritis, but I think it was probably made worse by the injection. It was altogether a horrible attack and left me quite collapsed. Gradually I began to feel normal again, my sense and muscles returning. At my worst (while we were waiting for the doctor to come) Gladwyn went and fetched the *Encyclopedia Britannica* and read out the symptoms for cholera over my prone form, and I seemed to recognize them all, even to the vomiting of green bile; and I thought of the soldiers at Scutari, and poor Madame Recamier dying of it when she was blind, which must have been a turn of the screw. The doctor didn't want me to go to London on Wednesday, but I insisted on doing so as I had asked my opera gala party all to supper. So I persuaded G to motor down on the Tuesday night and drive me to London the next morning. I had to get up at 7.30 and didn't get properly to bed till 1.30 a.m. I can't think how it did it.

Eugene Onegin was beautiful and romantic. I remarked to Diana what a perfect picture the first act gives of peaceful life in the country, and the timelessness of long summer evenings; and she said, 'It's just what I always remember life to be like when I was a child: two people singing in the drawing-room!'

Whitehall Court, London, 9 March

Tonight I dined with the Andersons. I sat next to Colin and on my right was Sir Hugh Casson, who is architect to the Queen and talked about her nonstop. He said he was 'quite gooey' about her every time she came into the room, which I found quite nauseating.

Whitehall Court, London, 27 March

I have just returned from Newcastle to see the launch of the giant tanker, *Texaco Great Britain*, as being the descendant of the engineer of the original *Great Britain*. The American owners were very critical of the

English ship-builders, who had exceeded the estimate and failed to complete the tanker on time owing to endless strikes and go-slows. Sir John Hunter seemed to me a particularly stupid man. On Friday morning I was given a car to visit the haunts of my childhood. I went first to St George's, where I had been christened for the second time, and at the font I pictured the scene. I then got the car to take me to Jesmond Dene House. Getting no answer from the bell at the front door I got in by the conservatory and introduced myself to a class (for it is a girls' school) being held in the billiard room. I wandered all over the house. Grandpapa's portrait by J. E. Blanche was hanging in the Great Hall.

Whitehall Court, London, 5 April

Virginia Surtees came to lunch today, our annual meeting which we both enjoy immensely and then part, she with something like relief, for another year. Delightful, intelligent, always acting a part, she is one of the strangest people I know. She told me a terrifying story. She arrived, with her quick step, at the counter of the London Library the other day to collect a book, and a woman just in front of her turned round, hearing her coming. They stared at each other and made no sign of recognition, but Virginia is certain it was her mother whom she hasn't seen for something like thirty years. She looked hard and full of hatred as she told me of this strange meeting.

Whitehall Court, London, 20 April

Such a lovely Easter at Bramfield with the whole family together as in the old days: Miles, Nessa and her three children, Stella and her three children. It was all delightful and a great success from every point of view, the staff here and the au pair girls fraternizing, everybody happy. Stella's little boy is enchanting. He gazed for a long time at a coloured picture of Napoleon, and then looked up with his little face and said to me, 'I love him. When can I see him?' I told him about the Duc d'Enghien and the danger Napoleon was to Europe and Wellington defeating him: but this does not deflect this charming little boy of four from his admiration.

Whitehall Court, London, 12 May

Dined with Hugh and Nessa at the Reform Club. A marvellous building, surely the biggest and finest of the clubs. Everything planned for the comfort of men: great leather armchairs and sofas; writing tables beautifully appointed, even with candles for sealing; women at the furthest end of the dining-room, which runs the whole length of the south side. This sort of place could only exist in England, and Englishwomen who are forced to accept such a situation tend to be less attractive than they otherwise might have been. Hugh says the young married male of today does not go to his club so much, being expected to remain at home and help his wife.

Whitehall Court, London, 23 May

Just returned from Bramfield where our weekend guest was Helen Dashwood. She has been clamouring to come for months, and I failed to find a man for her so had her on my hands the whole time. At heart she is a good kind homely woman, but with all the wrong values of life, the worst of which is her snobbery, and an incorrigible boss. She and G are as good as a play together, exaggerating their statements, laying down the law, emphasizing points in falsetto. I tried to hold my own for a bit but in the end just gave in.

Whitehall Court, London, 24 May

Dined at the French Embassy, where we now are much welcomed. Geoffroy told me at dinner (we were speaking about Spears' account of getting de Gaulle away from Bordeaux when Pétain had taken over in June 1940) that there was not a word of truth in Spears' story of de G hiding behind a pillar to avoid detection, and in Spears pulling him on to the plane at the last moment. I believe Geoffroy more than Spears who, to my thinking, put in a lot of all this to show his own importance in order to disguise the fact that he himself was terrified lest he should be left behind. De Gaulle in his memoirs deals with Spears' evidence succinctly: 'The departure took place without drama or difficulty'.

Whitehall Court, London, 26 May

We went to a cocktail party in Whitehall Court given by the Ian McCorquodales, in an immense flat about three times the size of ours. The sensation of the party was the host's mother, the famous Barbara Cartland.[2] She was unutterably vulgar, larger than life and her jewels proportionately so, bursting out of a pink dress (for despite her celebrated diet she is extremely plump), with a lovely skin and the most extraordinary make-up. She is a true example of how awful an extrovert can be. She rushed around, introducing everybody to each other over and over again, and one felt quite exhausted in the presence of such exaggerated energy such as she derives from all the vitamins she takes. Obviously she is good-hearted.

Whitehall Court, London, 9 June

Nessa arranged such a nice thing today. She came for me first and then fetched dear old Mrs Dowsing, aged eighty-nine, and took her to lunch at Ladbroke Grove, where she gave us salmon cutlets, done in tinfoil, and strawberries and cream. It was a real treat for Mrs Dowsing, and she loved it, and told us all about her early days in a cottage at Ardleigh, and how she ran away from a wicked stepmother and became first a nursery maid and then a maid – 'the best maid in the world', Mrs Granville Barker used to say, and she was right.

Whitehall Court, London, 30 June

A wonderful evening to remember. I and Raymond went to *Tristan*, with the great soprano Birgit Nilsson singing Isolde. It was a marvellous performance. Solti conducted, for nearly the last time. Jess Thomas, who sings Tristan, has improved beyond all recognition from the conceited young man who swaggered about the stage as Walther in *Die Meistersinger* three years ago. I hadn't heard *Tristan* since before the War,

[2] Barbara Cartland, later Dame Barbara (1901–   ): author of over 500 novels, including one in which scenes are derived from Cynthia's *The Paris Embassy*.

and it was so beautiful that I feel I do not want to see it again for some time lest it fall short of this performance.

Whitehall Court, London, 6 July

Tonight Gerry and I went to *Hair*. It was ghastly. To begin with, the noise was deafening, as Gerry would sit in the front row, thinking he would not hear otherwise and wanting to see all the nudity. Then it was altogether so squalid and filthy, everybody in the cast looking unwashed and drugged, wearing grubby trendy clothes. The very first thing that happened was when one of the men on the stage made a bee-line for me, removed his dirty blue jeans and said, 'Lady, hold these for me'. I refused to put out my hand, so he dropped them on my feet, later returning for them, when again I did not move, so Gerry had to pick them up. But the worst was when tiny white paper pellets, supposed to be snow, were showered down on to the stage and the first row of the stalls, so that we were covered with confetti which stuck in our hair and went down our necks. We arrived at the Savoy, to the acute embarrassment of Gerry, looking as though we had just been married.

INDEX OF PERSONS

Names and titles are those applying at last mention in the text. Subsequent name-changes and further details are given in footnotes. Where surnames differ from titles, they are given (in brackets). Spouses are listed separately only if treated distinctively in the text.